Lecture Notes in Computer Science

Edited by G. Goos, J. Hartmanis, and J. van Le

T0250846

Springer

Berlin
Heidelberg
New York
Barcelona
Hong Kong
London
Milan
Paris
Tokyo

Ralf-Detlef Kutsche   Herbert Weber (Eds.)

Fundamental Approaches to Software Engineering

5th International Conference, FASE 2002
Held as Part of the Joint European Conferences
on Theory and Practice of Software, ETAPS 2002
Grenoble, France, April 8-12, 2002
Proceedings

 Springer

Series Editors

Gerhard Goos, Karlsruhe University, Germany
Juris Hartmanis, Cornell University, NY, USA
Jan van Leeuwen, Utrecht University, The Netherlands

Volume Editors

Ralf-Detlef Kutsche
Herbert Weber
Technische Universität Berlin
FAK.IV Elektrotechnik und Informatik
Computergestützte Informationssysteme
Einsteinufer 17, 10587 Berlin, Germany
E-mail: {rkutsche,hweber}@cs.tu-berlin.de

Cataloging-in-Publication Data applied for

Die Deutsche Bibliothek - CIP-Einheitsaufnahme

Fundamental approaches to software engineering : 5th international
conference ; proceedings / FASE 2002, held as part of the Joint European
Conferences on Theory and Practice of Software, ETAPS 2002, Grenoble,
France, April 8 - 12, 2002. Ralf-Detlef Kutsche ; Herbert Weber (ed.). -
Berlin ; Heidelberg ; New York ; Barcelona ; Hong Kong ; London ; Milan ;
Paris ; Tokyo : Springer, 2002
    (Lecture notes in computer science ; Vol. 2306)
    ISBN 3-540-43353-8

CR Subject Classification (1998): D.2, D.3, F.3

ISSN 0302-9743
ISBN 3-540-43353-8 Springer-Verlag Berlin Heidelberg New York

Springer-Verlag Berlin Heidelberg New York
a member of BertelsmannSpringer Science+Business Media GmbH

http://www.springer.de

© Springer-Verlag Berlin Heidelberg 2002

Typesetting: Camera-ready by author, data conversion by Christian Grosche, Hamburg
Printed on acid-free paper   SPIN 10846521   06/3142   5 4 3 2 1 0

Foreword

ETAPS 2002 was the fifth instance of the European Joint Conferences on Theory and Practice of Software. ETAPS is an annual federated conference that was established in 1998 by combining a number of existing and new conferences. This year it comprised 5 conferences (FOSSACS, FASE, ESOP, CC, TACAS), 13 satellite workshops (ACL2, AGT, CMCS, COCV, DCC, INT, LDTA, SC, SFEDL, SLAP, SPIN, TPTS, and VISS), 8 invited lectures (not including those specific to the satellite events), and several tutorials.

The events that comprise ETAPS address various aspects of the system development process, including specification, design, implementation, analysis, and improvement. The languages, methodologies, and tools which support these activities are all well within its scope. Different blends of theory and practice are represented, with an inclination towards theory with a practical motivation on one hand and soundly-based practice on the other. Many of the issues involved in software design apply to systems in general, including hardware systems, and the emphasis on software is not intended to be exclusive.

ETAPS is a loose confederation in which each event retains its own identity, with a separate program committee and independent proceedings. Its format is open-ended, allowing it to grow and evolve as time goes by. Contributed talks and system demonstrations are in synchronized parallel sessions, with invited lectures in plenary sessions. Two of the invited lectures are reserved for "unifying" talks on topics of interest to the whole range of ETAPS attendees. The aim of cramming all this activity into a single one-week meeting is to create a strong magnet for academic and industrial researchers working on topics within its scope, giving them the opportunity to learn about research in related areas, and thereby to foster new and existing links between work in areas that were formerly addressed in separate meetings.

ETAPS 2002 was organized by the Laboratoire Verimag in cooperation with

Centre National de la Recherche Scientifique (CNRS)
Institut de Mathématiques Appliquées de Grenoble (IMAG)
Institut National Polytechnique de Grenoble (INPG)
Université Joseph Fourier (UJF)
European Association for Theoretical Computer Science (EATCS)
European Association for Programming Languages and Systems (EAPLS)
European Association of Software Science and Technology (EASST)
ACM SIGACT, SIGSOFT, and SIGPLAN

The organizing team comprised

Susanne Graf - General Chair
Saddek Bensalem - Tutorials
Rachid Echahed - Workshop Chair
Jean-Claude Fernandez - Organization

Alain Girault - Publicity
Yassine Lakhnech - Industrial Relations
Florence Maraninchi - Budget
Laurent Mounier - Organization

Overall planning for ETAPS conferences is the responsibility of its Steering Committee, whose current membership is:

Egidio Astesiano (Genova), Ed Brinksma (Twente), Pierpaolo Degano (Pisa), Hartmut Ehrig (Berlin), José Fiadeiro (Lisbon), Marie-Claude Gaudel (Paris), Andy Gordon (Microsoft Research, Cambridge), Roberto Gorrieri (Bologna), Susanne Graf (Grenoble), John Hatcliff (Kansas), Görel Hedin (Lund), Furio Honsell (Udine), Nigel Horspool (Victoria), Heinrich Hußmann (Dresden), Joost-Pieter Katoen (Twente), Paul Klint (Amsterdam), Daniel Le Métayer (Trusted Logic, Versailles), Ugo Montanari (Pisa), Mogens Nielsen (Aarhus), Hanne Riis Nielson (Copenhagen), Mauro Pezzè (Milan), Andreas Podelski (Saarbrücken), Don Sannella (Edinburgh), Andrzej Tarlecki (Warsaw), Herbert Weber (Berlin), Reinhard Wilhelm (Saarbrücken)

I would like to express my sincere gratitude to all of these people and organizations, the program committee chairs and PC members of the ETAPS conferences, the organizers of the satellite events, the speakers themselves, and finally Springer-Verlag for agreeing to publish the ETAPS proceedings. As organizer of ETAPS'98, I know that there is one person that deserves a special applause: Susanne Graf. Her energy and organizational skills have more than compensated for my slow start in stepping into Don Sannella's enormous shoes as ETAPS Steering Committee chairman. Yes, it is now a year since I took over the role, and I would like my final words to transmit to Don all the gratitude and admiration that is felt by all of us who enjoy coming to ETAPS year after year knowing that we will meet old friends, make new ones, plan new projects and be challenged by a new culture! Thank you Don!

January 2002   José Luiz Fiadeiro

Preface

The conference on Fundamental Approaches to Software Engineering (FASE) as one part of the European Joint Conferences on Theory and Practice of Software (ETAPS) focused on both aspects of 'engineering': rigor and applicability.

FASE 2002 now in its fifth year promoted the paradigm of 'continuous software engineering', including component-based software architecture, model and meta-model-based software engineering, and the understanding of the software process as an evolutionary process for the following reasons, as stated in the call for papers:

Large-scale information and communication infrastructures are of growing concern to industry and public organizations. They are expected to exist for an indefinite length of time, are supposed to be flexibly adjustable to new requirements, and are hence demanded to encompass evolvable software systems. This poses new challenges to software engineering research and practice: new software structuring and scaling concepts are needed for heterogeneous software federations that consist of numerous autonomously developed, communicating, and inter-operating systems; new software development processes are needed to enable the continuous improvement and extension of heterogeneous software federations.

Different component paradigms are under discussion now, a large number of specification and modeling languages have been proposed, and an increasing number of software development tools and environments have been made available to cope with the problems. At the same time research on new theories, concepts, and techniques is under way that aims at the development of their precise and (mathematically) formal foundation. In the call for papers, the following topics were emphasized:

- Component concepts and component-based software architectures, including practical concepts like EJB, DCOM, or CORBA
- Integration platforms and middleware systems for large-scale heterogeneous software federations
- Model-based software engineering
- Semi-formal and formal modeling and specification techniques for component-based software
- Meta-models of modeling and specification concepts
- Experience reports on best practices with component models and specifications, development tools, modeling environments, and software development kits
- Integration of formal concepts and current best-practice concepts in industrial software development

The program committee consisted of:

Egidio Astesiano (Genova, Italy)
Christine Choppy (Paris, France)
José Fiadeiro (Lisbon, Portugal)
Anthony Finkelstein (London, UK)
Marie-Claude Gaudel (Orsay, France)
Heinrich Hußmann (Dresden, Germany)
Ralf-Detlef Kutsche, co-chair (Berlin, Germany)
Michael Löwe (Hannover, Germany)
Tiziana Margaria (Dortmund, Germany)
Narciso Martí Oliet (Madrid, Spain)
Michaël Périn (UJF/Verimag, France)
Herbert Weber, co-chair (Berlin, Germany)

The program committee received almost 60 papers, that were evaluated in an electronic submission and reviewing procedure. The members of the PC worked hard, as did also a number of co-reviewers, who are listed below. The PC cooperated closely with the responsible coordinator of the tool demonstration track, Peter D. Mosses. We would like to cordially express our thanks to all members of the PC and to all co-reviewers for their work.

Finally, the program committee decided to select 21 papers, and, additionally, in a different selection procedure, 4 short papers for the tool demonstrations associated with FASE. The result of the efforts of the reviewers and the PC are the proceedings in front of you, containing valuable new ideas and input to interesting and controversial discussions and further joint work in the challenging area of theory and practice of software engineering.

The invited lecture, with the aim of helping to bridge the gap between theory and practice, was delivered by Hellmuth Broda, the CTO of SUN Microsystems Inc. for Europe, Middle East, and Africa. He has agreed to give a talk on new visions and experiences concerning software architectures and software development in global infrastructures.

Finally, we would like to express our thanks to all contributors to the success of the conference, particularly to José Luiz Fiadeiro, the chairman of the ETAPS steering committee, and to Susanne Graf and her team in Grenoble for their great efforts in the ETAPS global coordination. Last but not least, a special thanks to the team at CIS/TU Berlin, helping with several aspects of the conference and, especially to Lutz Friedel, Claudia Gantzer, and Andreas Leicher for their great support in putting together the proceedings.

January 2002   Ralf-Detlef Kutsche
                                                        Herbert Weber

Referees

Anahita Akhavan
Egidio Astesiano
Didier Bert
Marius Bozga
Volker Braun
Felix Bübl
Christine Choppy
Juliane Dehnert
Giorgio Delzanno
Birgit Demuth
Mireille Ducass
Amal El-Fallah
José Fiadeiro
Anthony Finkelstein
Mike Fischer
Robert France
David de Frutos-Escrig
Falk Fuenfstueck
Marie-Claude Gaudel
Susanne Graf
Martin Grosse-Rhode
Claudia Gsottberger
Armando Haeberer
Heinrich Hußmann
Valérie Issarny
Jean-Claude Fernandez
Peter R. King
Yves Kodratoff
Ralf-Detlef Kutsche
Yassine Lakhnech
Ulrike Lechner
Y. Ledru
Andreas Leicher
Nicole Levy

Ben Lindner
Luis F. Llana-Díaz
Michael Löwe
Antonia Lopes
Tiziana Margaria
Bruno Marre
Ana Moreira
Laurent Mounier
Peter D. Mosses
Markus Nagelmann
Oliver Niese
Thomas Noll
Manuel Núñez
Narciso Martí Oliet
Aomar Osmani
Ricardo Peña
Michaël Périn
Pascal Poizat
Gianna Reggio
Simone Roettger
Michel de Rougemont
Oliver Rüthing
Sylviane R. Schwer
Jörn Guy Süß
Gabriele Taentzer
Anne Thomas
Alberto Verdejo
Frederic Voisin
Herbert Weber
Michel Wermelinger
Haiseung Yoo
Elena Zucca

Table of Contents

Meta-Models

Formal Approaches towards UML

Requirements Engineering

Tool Demonstrations

An Approach to Composition Motivated by *wp*

Michel Charpentier

Department of Computer Science
University of New Hampshire, Durham, NH
`charpov@cs.unh.edu`

Abstract. We consider the question of composition in system design, a fundamental issue in engineering. More precisely, we are interested in deducing system properties from components properties and vice-versa. This requires system and component specifications to be *"compositional"* in some sense. Depending on what systems are and how they are composed, this problem is satisfactorily solved (e.g., sequential composition of terminating programs) or remains a hot research topic (e.g., concurrent composition of reactive systems). In this paper, we aim at providing a logical framework in which composition issues can be reasoned about independently from the kind of systems and the laws of composition under consideration. We show that many composition related statements can be expressed in terms of predicate transformers in a way that presents interesting similarities with program semantics descriptions based on weakest precondition calculus.

1 Motivation

System designers, whether those systems are software, hardware, planes or buildings, are all faced with a common issue: How to compose systems from components and how to partition systems into components. Compositional design offers the hope of managing complexity by avoiding unnecessary details: Systems designers prove properties of systems given properties, but not detailed implementations, of components.

As fundamental as it is, the question of composition is far from being solved in a fully satisfactory way. What does it mean for a formal framework to be *"compositional"*? Are there *"good"* and *"bad"* compositional frameworks? What characterizes *"good"* compositional specifications? Should system designers and components providers use the same kind of specifications? Are there fundamental laws of composition that are common to most areas of engineering? How are composition and reuse issues related? We believe these to be important questions one must (at least partially) answer before suitable solutions to the composition problem are found.

In this paper, we aim at providing a basis that can be used to reason about composition. We seek a logical framework in which many of the questions mentioned above can be formulated and reasoned about. We try to keep the context of our approach as general as possible. Especially, we don't want to decide from

R.-D. Kutsche and H. Weber (Eds.): FASE 2002, LNCS 2306, pp. 1–14, 2002.

the start what systems are, how they can be composed and what specification languages are used to describe them. Instead, we assume generic binary laws of composition and we later introduce specific properties, such as for instance associativity, symmetry or idempotency. In other words, the basis of our framework can be applied to almost any form of composition and any type of system, but more relevant and useful properties can be deduced when additional hypotheses are introduced.

We restrict ourselves to logical properties on systems. More precisely, system properties are predicates on these systems. We use the terms *property* and *specification* interchangeably, the only slight nuance being that specifications are usually provided while properties may have to be deduced.

Since in this context components and systems are seen only through their logical properties, it is convenient to identify systems and system properties and to describe composition at a purely logical level, where everything is expressed in terms of specifications without mentioning components and systems. These specifications behave in different ways when they are composed (compositional versus non compositional specifications). In other words, specifications are *transformed* through composition. They may also be transformed beforehand to give "better" compositional specifications. As a consequence, our approach relies heavily on *predicate transformers* (functions from predicates to predicates). Our transformers present interesting similarities with Dijkstra's *weakest precondition* and *strongest postcondition*, from which we can inherit useful intuition.

The remainder of the paper is organized as follows. Section 2 introduces the basic elements of our framework, namely components, composition, systems and system properties. What it means for specifications to be compositional is precisely stated in section 3. In section 4, we define a family of *"strongest transformers"* which can be used to describe how specifications are transformed when systems are composed. At this point, it is explained how systems and their specifications can be identified. Section 5 introduces another family of predicate transformers (*"weakest transformers"*) which are used to transform non compositional specifications into compositional ones. In section 6, we compare our transformers with *strongest postcondition* and *weakest precondition* transformers. We show in section 7 how to switch between the bottom-up and top-down aspects of the composition problem by using conjugates of predicate transformers. Section 8 instantiates previously defined notions with a more specific context (a single law of composition over a monoid structure). Finally, section 9 shows how this approach to composition can be applied in the context of concurrent and reactive systems.

2   Components, Composition, Systems, and System Properties

We assume the existence of atomic[1] components as well as laws of composition. When applied to components, these laws lead to systems. Systems, in turn, can be composed to provide us with new systems. We only consider systems that involve a finite number of applications of the laws of composition. However, that number may be zero and, by extension, single components are also considered to be systems.

We denote components and systems with capital letters F, G, H, etc. Composition laws are represented by infix binary operators such as $\circ$ or $\star$. We do not assume any property on these operators, such as (mutual) associativity, symmetry, idempotency or distributivity. For example, if F, G and H are systems, so are $F \circ G$, $G \star H$ and $(F \circ G) \star H$.

Some compositions may not be possible (i.e., the resulting system may not exist). For a given law of composition, different definitions of "possible" may be used. For instance, we can allow parallel composition of processes that share variables, or forbid it and request that processes send and receive messages instead. In both cases, the nature of composition is similar (say, fair interleaving of atomic transitions) and it would be awkward to rely on two different laws of composition. Our approach to this situation is to use a compatibility operator to denote that a given composition is possible. The same law of composition, such as concurrent composition of processes, can be coupled to different compatibility operators to allow shared variables or not, for instance. In order not to clutter up our notations, we do not use compatibility operators explicitly here (but we do in [14,13]). Instead, it is implicitly understood that systems that are referred to exist. For instance, in a formula of the form $\langle \forall F, G : \cdots : \cdots F \circ G \cdots \rangle$, the range of the universal quantification is implicitly reduced to those systems F and G for which $F \circ G$ exists.

System properties are point-wise predicates on systems (i.e., functions from systems to booleans) or, equivalently, sets of systems (although, in this paper, we stick to predicate notations). We denote them with capital letters X, Y, Z, S, T, etc. Function application is denoted with a dot (.) which has higher precedence than boolean operators but lower precedence than composition operators and which associates to the left (i.e., $a.b.c = (a.b).c$). For example, if F and G are systems and X is a property, $X.F \circ G$ is the boolean: "property X holds for system $F \circ G$". A system that satisfies property X is called an "X-system".

3   Compositional Specifications

A core issue in compositional design is to relate systems properties and subsystems properties. Designers should be able to deduce a system property from

---

[1] *Atomic* doesn't mean that a component cannot be decomposed. It simply means that its internal structure is not considered here.

subsystems properties (i.e., use components) and subsystems properties from a system property (i.e., develop/find components). The ability to deduce subsystems properties from a system specification is an aspect of the problem that is sometimes ignored. However, we believe it to be as important an issue as the other aspect, since system designers have to identify suitable components in order to build their system. In other words they have to deduce relevant component properties from the given system specification.

In this paper, we focus our attention on the problem of deducing systems properties from subsystems properties, except in section 7 where we show how the other hand of the question can be reached through conjugates of predicate transformers. This way, we avoid presenting symmetric but similar arguments all along the paper but instead we explain how top-down arguments can be deduced in a systematic way from corresponding bottom-up arguments.

With the bottom-up view in mind, we say that a list of properties is *compositional* (with respect to a specific pattern of composition such as $\_\circ(\_\star\_)$) if the last property of the list holds in any system built (by applying the given pattern) from components that satisfy the other properties of the list. For instance, if we consider systems of the form $(F\circ G)\star H^2$, the list of properties (X, Y, Z, T) is compositional if and only if:

$$\langle \forall F, G, H :: X.F \wedge Y.G \wedge Z.H \Rightarrow T.(F\circ G)\star H \rangle \ . \tag{1}$$

Compositional lists of properties allow us to deduce system properties from subsystem properties. In some sense, they are a schematic representation of the composition problem.

We do not introduce a specific syntax to represent compositional lists of properties. Instead, we show in the next section how formula (1) can be expressed without making reference to systems and a property-only syntax is introduced.

4   Components and Systems as Predicates

We consider the following equation in predicates, where S is the unknown:

$$S \ : \ \langle \forall F, G, H :: X.F \wedge Y.G \wedge Z.H \Rightarrow S.(F\circ G)\star H \rangle \ . \tag{2}$$

It is clear that any (finite or infinite) conjunction of solutions of (2) is itself a solution of (2). Therefore, given properties X, Y and Z, equation (2) has a strongest solution [19]. We denote this solution by $(X\circ Y)\star Z$. This notation generalists to other forms of composition and $X\circ Y$ or $(X\star Y)\circ(Z\star T)$, for instance, are also properties.

These properties, defined in terms of the strongest solution of some compositional equation, all enjoy a similar property, expressed by the following proposition:

---

[2] We use systems such as $(F\circ G)\star H$ throughout the paper to illustrate our predicates and predicate transformers definitions. However, definitions are general and can be applied to any other form of composition, such as $(F \diamond (G \uparrow H)) \downarrow K$, whatever $\diamond$, $\uparrow$ and $\downarrow$ are.

Proposition 1. *For any system K:*

$$(X \circ Y) \star Z \ . \ K \ \equiv \ \langle \exists F, G, H : X.F \wedge Y.G \wedge Z.H : (F \circ G) \star H = K \rangle \ .$$

In other words, $(X \circ Y) \star Z$ characterizes those systems that can be obtained by composing an X-system, a Y-system and a Z-system through $\circ$ and $\star$ (in the right order). Any system composed this way satisfies $(X \circ Y) \star Z$ and any system that satisfies $(X \circ Y) \star Z$ can be decomposed this way.

Using proposition 1, we can rewrite the formula that was used to define compositional lists of properties. Formula (1) is equivalent to:

$$\langle \forall K :: (X \circ Y) \star Z.K \Rightarrow T.K \rangle \ ,$$

which, by making use of the "everywhere operator" $[\cdots]$ [19], can be written:

$$[(X \circ Y) \star Z \ \Rightarrow \ T] \ .$$

From this point on, we do not have to refer to systems explicitly and we express all what we need in term of properties. Note that we can always reintroduce systems by using specific properties that are characteristic of one system exactly (singletons). For a system F, we define the property $F_=$ by:

$$\langle \forall G :: F_= \ . \ G \ \equiv \ (F = G) \rangle \ .$$

In other words, $F_=$ is the property *"to be the system F"*. Thanks to the notation we have introduced, the mapping from F to $F_=$ is an isomorphism that preserves the structure of the composition, i.e.,

$$[((F \circ G) \star H)_= \ \equiv \ (F_= \circ G_=) \star H_=] \ .$$

Y and Z being fixed, $(X \circ Y) \star Z$ describes what becomes of property X when an X-system is composed (with two other systems that satisfy Y and Z). If, for instance, $(X \circ Y) \star Z$ is equivalent to X (for some Y and Z), it means that X has a "good" compositional behavior (it is entirely preserved when composed with Y and Z systems). $(X \circ Y) \star Z$ can also be stronger than X, in which case property X is "enriched" through composition with Y and Z. Sometimes, however, $(X \circ Y) \star Z$ will be weaker than X, meaning that only a part of property X survives composition. In the worst case, $(X \circ Y) \star Z$ reduces to *true*: all of X is lost. In other words, the predicate transformer $(\lambda X \cdot (X \circ Y) \star Z)$ tells us what happens to property X when composed in a specific context.

5 "*Weakest Property*" Transformers

In this section, we define "*weakest property*" transformers that allow us to characterize adequate subsystems in a composition.

Given properties Y, Z and T, the equation (in predicate):

$$S \ : \ [(S \circ Y) \star Z \ \Rightarrow \ T] \tag{3}$$

has a weakest solution (the disjunction of all solutions is itself a solution). By the axiom of choice, there is a function that maps T to this weakest solution (Y and Z being fixed). We denote that function by $(?\circ Y)\star Z$. Therefore, the weakest solution of (3) is $((?\circ Y)\star Z).T$. Other functions (such as $(X\circ?)\star Z$ and $(X\circ Y)\star?)$ are defined similarly.

Our notation may seem ambiguous at first sight. Is $(?\circ(Y\star Z)).T$ the weakest solution of:

$$S \; : \; \langle \forall F, G, H :: S.F \wedge Y.G \wedge Z.H \Rightarrow T.F\circ(G\star H)\rangle \; ,$$

or the weakest solution of:

$$S \; : \; \langle \forall F, G :: S.F \wedge (Y\star Z).G \Rightarrow T.F\circ G\rangle \; ?$$

Fortunately, thanks to proposition 1, both equations are equivalent.

It should be emphasized that $(?\circ Y)\star Z$ is a function from properties to properties (i.e., a predicate transformer) while $(X\circ Y)\star Z$ is a property. Furthermore, $(?\circ Y)\star Z$ is *not* the transformer $(\lambda X \cdot (X\circ Y)\star Z)$ described above.

An interesting property of $((?\circ Y)\star Z).T$ is that it characterizes the systems that lead to a T-system when they are extended by a Y-system and a Z-system using $\circ$ and $\star$ (in the right order). This is expressed by the following proposition:

Proposition 2. *For any system K:*

$$((?\circ Y)\star Z).T \; . \; K \; \equiv \; \langle \forall F, G : Y.F \wedge Z.G : T.(K\circ F)\star G\rangle \; .$$

$((?\circ Y)\star Z).T$ is the answer to the question: "What do I have to prove on my component to ensure that, when it is composed with Y and Z components, the resulting system always satisfies T?" If T is a property which already enjoys a nice compositional behavior (for instance, it is such that $[(T\circ Y)\star Z \Rightarrow T]$), it may be enough to verify that the component satisfies T. If, however, T is not one of those properties that compose well, we may have to prove a property stronger than T itself to ensure that at least T will be preserved when the component is composed with Y and Z systems. In the worst case, there may be no way to guarantee that the component will provide the property T when composed with Y and Z systems, in which case $((?\circ Y)\star Z).T$ reduces to *false*.

6   Relationship with *wlp* and *sp*

The approach used in previous sections is very similar to Dijkstra's *wlp* and *sp* [19]. We can define a correspondence between a *"program semantics"* world and a *"composition"* world:

$$\begin{aligned}
\text{state (predicate)} &\leftrightarrow \text{system (property)} \; , \\
\text{run a program} &\leftrightarrow \text{build a system} \; , \\
\text{assign a variable} &\leftrightarrow \text{add a subsystem} \; .
\end{aligned}$$

Then, the "?" transformers we have just defined correspond to *wlp*, the weakest liberal precondition:

wlp.s.q : weakest state predicate such that, if statement *s* is executed from such a state (and *s* terminates), the resulting state satisfies *q*.

$(? \circ F_=).T$: weakest system property such that, if system *F* is added (on the right, through ∘) to such a system, the resulting system satisfies *T*.

Because in our approach everything is property and systems are just a special case, the formulation can be generalized:

$(? \circ Y).T$: weakest system property such that, if a *Y*-system is added (on the right, through ∘) to such a system, the resulting system satisfies *T*.

It can also be shown that, like *wlp*, $(? \circ Y) \star Z$ (and other similar transformers) is universally conjunctive, hence monotonic.

On the other hand, the function $(\lambda X \cdot X \circ Y)$ corresponds to *sp*, the strongest postcondition:

sp.s.p : strongest state predicate that holds after statement *s* is executed from a state that satisfies *p*.

$X \circ Y$: strongest property that holds after a *Y*-system is added (on the right, through ∘) to a system that satisfies *X*.

As the (partial) correctness of a Hoare triple can be expressed equivalently in terms of *wlp* or in terms of *sp*:

$$[p \Rightarrow wlp.s.q] \equiv [sp.s.p \Rightarrow q] ,$$

"composition correctness" can be expressed equivalently in terms of $? \circ Y$ or in terms of $(\lambda X \cdot X \circ Y)$:

$$[X \Rightarrow (? \circ Y).Z] \equiv [X \circ Y \Rightarrow Z] .$$

In the same way, the well known rule of *wlp* for sequential composition of programs:

$$[wlp.(s; s').q \equiv wlp.s.(wlp.s'.q)]$$

also holds for property transformers:

$$[((? \circ Y) \star Z).T \equiv (? \circ Y).((? \star Z).T)] .$$

7   Using Conjugates of Predicate Transformers

So far, we have considered the question of deducing system properties from subsystems properties. As we mentioned earlier, we believe that the converse problem, to deduce subsystems properties from system properties, is equally important.

Every predicate transformer T has a unique conjugate T^* defined by $[T^*.X \equiv \neg T.(\neg X)]$. Therefore, the transformer $(?{\circ}Y){\star}Z$ has a conjugate $((?{\circ}Y){\star}Z)^*$ such that $((?{\circ}Y){\star}Z)^*.T$ characterizes the remainder of a T-system partially built from a Y-system and a Z-system. In other words, it is the answer to the question: "I am building a T-system; I already know that I am going to use a Y-system and a Z-system and I am looking for a component to complete my design; what do I know about this missing component?" So, $((?{\circ}Y){\star}Z)^*.T$ guides us into finding a suitable component to complete the design of a T-system when there exist a constraint that a Y-system and a Z-system must be used. Note that this is only a necessary condition: such a component does not guarantee that the resulting system will satisfy property T. For that, we need that the chosen component also satisfies $((?{\circ}Y){\star}Z).T$.

In the same way, we can consider the conjugate of $(\lambda X \cdot (X{\circ}Y){\star}Z)$. The property $(\lambda X \cdot (X{\circ}Y){\star}Z)^*.T$ represents what has to be proved on a system partially built with Y and Z components in order to ensure that the remaining part satisfies T.

8 Special Case: One Law of Composition

Properties such as $(X{\circ}Y){\star}Z$ or $((?{\circ}Y){\star}Z).T$ make the structure of composition explicit: what operators are used, how many of them and where, all this appear in the writing of the formula.

The next step in our approach is then to "quantify over the structure", i.e., make the structure implicit. This involves introducing generic forms of composition from which, hopefully, the general case can still be reached.

We have started to explore this path in a limited context where a single composition operator $\circ$ is involved. Furthermore, we assume that this operator is associative and has an identity element (monoid). We do not assume other properties such as symmetry or idempotency. Note that these hypotheses make it possible for the composition operator to be either parallel composition ($\|$) or sequential composition (;) of programs, but does not allow us to describe systems where both operators are interleaved. Several predicate transformers have been defined and studied in [14,13]. Here, we show how they can be seen as special cases of our weakest and strongest transformers.

In this context, we focus on two generic forms of composition called *existential* and *universal*. Existential and universal are compositional characteristics of properties. A property X is existential (denoted by *exist.X*) if and only if X holds for any system in which one component at least satisfies X. A property X is universal (denoted by *univ.X*) if and only if X holds in any system in which all components satisfy X [8]. Formally:

$$exist.X \triangleq \langle \forall F, G :: X.F \vee X.G \Rightarrow X.F{\circ}G \rangle ,$$
$$univ.X \triangleq \langle \forall F, G :: X.F \wedge X.G \Rightarrow X.F{\circ}G \rangle .$$

As before, we can choose not to use explicit quantification over components and express *exist* and *univ* in terms of predicates only:

$$
\begin{aligned}
exist.X &= [X \circ true \Rightarrow X] \land [true \circ X \Rightarrow X] \\
&= [(X \circ true) \lor (true \circ X) \Rightarrow X] \\
&= [true \circ X \circ true \Rightarrow X] \ , \\
univ.X &= [X \circ X \Rightarrow X] \ .
\end{aligned}
$$

Some properties are "naturally" existential or universal (which is one reason why we decided to focus on these types of composition). For instance, some fundamental properties in the UNITY logic [24,23] are existential or universal (see section 9). However, in the same context, some useful properties (such as *leads-to*) are neither existential nor universal.

One way to deal with properties that do not enjoy existential or universal characteristics is to *transform* them into existential and universal properties, by strengthening or weakening them. We can for instance define a predicate transformer WE such that WE.X is the weakest existential property stronger than X (such a property always exists because disjunctions of existential properties are existential) [14]. Then, systems can be specified in terms of WE.X instead of X so that, when they are composed with other systems, the property X is preserved. In other words, a stronger component (a WE.X-component instead of an X-component) is developed to make later compositions easier (property X holds in any system that uses such a component). The idea is to keep the property as weak as possible and to compensate for the extra amount of effort required when designing a component by reusing it in several systems, where we benefit from the fact that composition with an existential property leads to simpler proofs.

Formally, WE can be related to "?" transformers:

$$
[\text{WE} \equiv true \circ ? \circ true] \ .
$$

Proposition 3. *For any property X, there exists a weakest existential property stronger than X and it is $(true \circ ? \circ true).X$.*

In other words, using a formulation with an explicit quantification over systems, the weakest existential property stronger than X characterizes those systems that bring the property X to any system that contains them:

"F satisfies the weakest existential property stronger than X"

$$
\equiv
$$

$$
\langle \forall G, H :: X \ . \ G \circ F \circ H \rangle \ .
$$

In a similar way, a property X can be weakened into an existential property SE.X such that SE.X is the strongest existential property weaker than X [13]. SE.X holds in any system that contains a subsystem that satisfies X. It is, in some sense, the "existential part" of X, the part of the property that is preserved when an X-system is composed. SE can also be expressed in terms of our general transformers:

$$[SE.X \; \equiv \; true \circ X \circ true] \; .$$

Proposition 4. *For any property X, there exists a strongest existential property weaker than X and it is $true \circ X \circ true$.*

Things are different with the universal form of composition because it can be shown that, for some properties, there does not exist a weakest universal property that strengthen them [14]. Therefore, we cannot define a transformer WU in the same way as we defined WE. Still, any property X has a strongest universal property weaker than itself, denoted by $SU.X$. $SU.X$ characterizes those systems built from X-components only.

Finally, each one of the transformers WE, SE and SU has a unique conjugate. As WE, SE and SU allow us to deduce system properties from subsystems properties, their conjugates are used to deduce subsystems properties from system properties. For instance, if a system satisfies a property X, all its subsystems must satisfy $WE^*.X$. Components that do not satisfy $WE^*.X$ need not be considered at all when the goal is to build an X-system, since in no case can they lead to such a system. WE^* is an indication of what components can possibly be used to obtain a given system. Similarly, to ensure that at least one subsystem of a system satisfies X, the necessary and sufficient condition is to prove that the system satisfies $SU^*.X$.

9   Special Special Case: Concurrent Composition of Reactive Systems

We can further instantiate the previous framework by choosing what the single law of composition is, what components are, and how they are specified. Because of our interest in formal specification and verification of reactive systems, we have started to investigate the application of our work on composition to reactive systems composed concurrently and specified with temporal logics. Below is a short presentation of what can be done using a UNITY-like logic. The use of other logics, such as CTL, has been investigated as well [25].

In UNITY[3], processes are represented as a form of fair transition systems. Basically, a system consists of a state predicate (the set of possible initial states), a set of atomic transitions, and fairness assumptions. Properties of such systems are described using a fragment of linear temporal logic.

The fundamental safety operator of the logic is *next*: p *next* q is a property that asserts that if the state predicate p is true and an atomic transition is executed, then q is true in the resulting state. The fundamental liveness operator is *transient*: *transient* p means that there is at least one fair transition in the

---

[3] What we refer to as "UNITY" in this paper does not coincide exactly with the framework as it is defined in [7] or in [24,23]. Some liberties are taken with UNITY syntax and semantics, but the general philosophy is retained.

system that falsifies predicate p. These operators usually come in two flavors: a weak form where only reachable states are considered, and a strong form where reachability is not taken into account. In their strong form, UNITY properties can be composed: *transient p* is existential and *p next q* is universal. In their weak form[4] however, they correspond to closed systems properties and that compositionality is lost.

The strong form of the logic can be used as a tool in proofs, but is not suitable for component specifications (it is much too strong). However, transformers such as WE can be applied to the weak form of the logic to obtain useful, compositional specifications. In particular, specifications of the form $WE.(X \Rightarrow Y)$ have proved to be powerful assumption-commitment specifications [12]. The fact that those properties are existential even when X is a progress property (such as *leads-to*) allows us to write component specifications that embed substantial parts of a correctness proof inside a component (see discussion in [10]). This is an important feature because it makes it possible to reuse proof efforts when components are reused. Such a potential reuse of proofs is what makes composition worthwhile in spite of the natural overhead it generates [21].

The absence of a transformer WU and the fact that some properties do not have a weakest universal strengthening give raise to an interesting question: How can the non universal property p *weak-next q* be strengthened into a universal property? We would like to find a universal property X that is stronger than p *weak-next q* but weaker than p *strong-next q* and $WE.(p$ *weak-next q*$)$ (which are universal). Ideally, we would like X to be the weakest universal property stronger than p *weak-next q*, provided it exists. The problem looks deceptively simple but, so far, we have been unable to answer it. We were able to define a universal property that is stronger than p *weak-next q* and weaker than p *strong-next q* and $WE.(p$ *weak-next q*$)$ [9], but we do not know if that property is the weakest solution to our problem or not. We do not even know if such a weakest element exists at all. Such a question deserves to be investigated because a universal *next*-like operator can be useful to specify invariance properties in a compositional way. It is also a first step into finding a suitable definition for a transformer WU. (A more precise statement of these questions can be found at http://www.cs.unh.edu/~charpov/Composition/challenge.html.)

10 Summary

We started this study because of our conviction of the importance of composition is system design. We believe that systems, and especially software systems, should increasingly be constructed from generic "off the shelf" components. This means that *reuse* of systems and components is going to be a central issue.

In order to obtain reusable components, we must be able to describe requirements in a rather abstract way, focusing on the functionality we expect from the

---

[4] The weak form of *transient* is not used directly. A property *leads-to* is used instead, that can be defined in terms of *transient*. *Leads-to* properties are notoriously difficult to compose.

component and without refering to implementation details. However, there is a tradeoff between hiding details and being composable: more abstract specifications lead to more difficult composition, and specifications that are too abstract may even totally prevent composition. Our "?" transformers are a way of describing what is the minimum one has to say about a component to ensure the applicability of specific forms of composition (such as existential or universal or with an explicit system pattern).

This need for abstract specifications made us depart from the process calculus approach and focus our interest on logical specifications. Especially, we are interested in applying our ideas to concurrent systems specified with temporal logics. A great amount of work has been done regarding composition of reactive systems specified with temporal logics. Among the logics that were considered, we can cite the linear temporal logic [20,22], TLA [2], ATL [5] or UNITY [15,16,17,18,26]. All these works, and others [1,3,4], rely on the same hypothesis that systems are described in terms of *open computations*, i.e., infinite traces that are shared with the environment.

One originality of our work is to drop this view on composition and to attempt to reason about composition in the abstract: we do not assume that systems have computations or even states. This way, we hope to better understand what the fundamental issues of composition-based designs are. Nevertheless, we do not forget our interest in temporal logics and concurrent systems. We have used existential and universal properties to derive examples of specifications and correctness proofs of distributed and concurrent systems [11,12,6,25]. Several of these examples make use of an operator called *guarantees* [8] which has been proved to be a special case of the transformer WE [14].

Most of our previous work is based on a single law of composition that is assumed to be associative and to have an identity element. In some cases, we have additional hypotheses regarding the existence of inverses of components. In our work on temporal logic and concurrent composition, we use a law of composition that is symmetric and idempotent in addition to being associative. In this paper, we attempt an exploration of the common basis to all previously defined transformers. We show that our use of predicate transformers can be systematic and that, for each composition related question, there is a predicate or a predicate transformer that relates to it precisely.

Our long term goal is the construction of a calculus for composition. Such a calculus requires us to have access to a large number of generic theorems and proof rules. We have started to state some of these rules. In the context of a single law of composition over a monoid, we were able in some cases to *calculate* WE.X for some properties X, in other words, to answer a question about composition with a systematic calculation [14]. This was only achieved on toy examples and our current work is to find other generic rules as well as rules specific to temporal logic and concurrent composition.

Acknowledgments

This work is based on many discussions with K. Mani Chandy. The author is grateful to him for these helpful exchanges of ideas and the valuable comments he made on an earlier draft of this paper.

References

1. Martín Abadi and Leslie Lamport. Composing specifications. *ACM Transactions on Programming Languages and Systems*, 15(1):73–132, January 1993.
2. Martín Abadi and Leslie Lamport. Conjoining specifications. *ACM Transactions on Programming Languages and Systems*, 17(3):507–534, May 1995.
3. Martín Abadi and Stephan Merz. An abstract account of composition. In Jivrí Wiedermann and Petr Hajek, editors, *Mathematical Foundations of Computer Science*, volume 969 of *Lecture Notes in Computer Science*, pages 499–508. Springer-Verlag, September 1995.
4. Martín Abadi and Gordon Plotkin. A logical view of composition. *Theoretical Computer Science*, 114(1):3–30, June 1993.
5. R. Alur, T.A. Henzinger, and O. Kupferman. Alternating-time temporal logic. In *38th Annual Symposium on Foundations of Computer Science*, pages 100–109. IEEE Computer Society Press, 1997.
6. K. Mani Chandy and Michel Charpentier. An experiment in program composition and proof. *Formal Methods in System Design*, 20(1):7–21, January 2002.
7. K. Mani Chandy and Jayadev Misra. *Parallel Program Design: A Foundation*. Addison-Wesley, 1988.
8. K. Mani Chandy and Beverly Sanders. Reasoning about program composition. http://www.cise.ufl.edu/~sanders/pubs/composition.ps.
9. Michel Charpentier. Making UNITY properties compositional: the transformer $\mathcal{E}$, the predicate *SIC* and the property type *next$_U$*. Unpublished research report, September 1999.
10. Michel Charpentier. Reasoning about composition: A predicate transformer approach. In *Specification and Verification of Component-Based Systems (SAVCBS 2001)*, pages 42–49. Workshop at OOPSLA 2001, October 2001.
11. Michel Charpentier and K. Mani Chandy. Examples of program composition illustrating the use of universal properties. In J. Rolim, editor, *International workshop on Formal Methods for Parallel Programming: Theory and Applications (FMPPTA'99)*, volume 1586 of *Lecture Notes in Computer Science*, pages 1215–1227. Springer-Verlag, April 1999.
12. Michel Charpentier and K. Mani Chandy. Towards a compositional approach to the design and verification of distributed systems. In J. Wing, J. Woodcock, and J. Davies, editors, *World Congress on Formal Methods in the Development of Computing Systems (FM'99), (Vol. I)*, volume 1708 of *Lecture Notes in Computer Science*, pages 570–589. Springer-Verlag, September 1999.
13. Michel Charpentier and K. Mani Chandy. Reasoning about composition using property transformers and their conjugates. In J. van Leeuwen, O. Watanabe, M. Hagiya, P.D. Mosses, and T. Ito, editors, *Theoretical Computer Science: Exploring New Frontiers of Theoretical Informatics (IFIP-TCS 2000)*, volume 1872 of *Lecture Notes in Computer Science*, pages 580–595. Springer-Verlag, August 2000.

14. Michel Charpentier and K. Mani Chandy. Theorems about composition. In R. Backhouse and J. Nuno Oliveira, editors, *International Conference on Mathematics of Program Construction (MPC 2000)*, volume 1837 of *Lecture Notes in Computer Science*, pages 167–186. Springer-Verlag, July 2000.
15. Pierre Collette. *Design of Compositional Proof Systems Based on Assumption-Commitment Specifications. Application to* UNITY. Doctoral thesis, Faculté des Sciences Appliquées, Université Catholique de Louvain, June 1994.
16. Pierre Collette. An explanatory presentation of composition rules for assumption-commitment specifications. *Information Processing Letters*, 50:31–35, 1994.
17. Pierre Collette and Edgar Knapp. Logical foundations for compositional verification and development of concurrent programs in UNITY. In *International Conference on Algebraic Methodology and Software Technology*, volume 936 of *Lecture Notes in Computer Science*, pages 353–367. Springer-Verlag, 1995.
18. Pierre Collette and Edgar Knapp. A foundation for modular reasoning about safety and progress properties of state-based concurrent programs. *Theoretical Computer Science*, 183:253–279, 1997.
19. Edsger W. Dijkstra and Carel S. Scholten. *Predicate calculus and program semantics*. Texts and monographs in computer science. Springer-Verlag, 1990.
20. J.L. Fiadeiro and T. Maibaum. Verifying for reuse: foundations of object-oriented system verification. In I. Makie C. Hankin and R. Nagarajan, editors, *Theory and Formal Methods*, pages 235–257. World Scientific Publishing Company, 1995.
21. Leslie Lamport. Composition: A way to make proofs harder. In W.-P. de Roever, H. Langmaack, and A. Pnueli, editors, *Compositionality: The Significant Difference (COMPOS'97)*, volume 1536 of *Lecture Notes in Computer Science*, pages 402–423. Springer-Verlag, September 1997.
22. Zohar Manna and Amir Pnueli. *The Temporal Logic of Reactive and Concurrent Systems: Specification*. Springer-Verlag, 1992.
23. Jayadev Misra. A logic for concurrent programming: Progress. *Journal of Computer and Software Engineering*, 3(2):273–300, 1995.
24. Jayadev Misra. A logic for concurrent programming: Safety. *Journal of Computer and Software Engineering*, 3(2):239–272, 1995.
25. Beverly A. Sanders and Hector Andrade. Model checking for open systems. Submitted for publication, 2000.
26. Rob T. Udink. *Program Refinement in* UNITY-*like Environments*. PhD thesis, Utrecht University, September 1995.

Compositional Verification of Secure Applet Interactions

Gilles Barthe[1], Dilian Gurov[2], and Marieke Huisman[1]

[1] INRIA Sophia-Antipolis, France
{Gilles.Barthe,Marieke.Huisman}@sophia.inria.fr
[2] Swedish Institute of Computer Science
dilian@sics.se

Abstract. Recent developments in mobile code and embedded systems have led to an increased interest in open platforms, *i.e.* platforms which enable different applications to interact in a dynamic environment. However, the flexibility of open platforms presents major difficulties for the (formal) verification of secure interaction between the different applications. To overcome these difficulties, compositional verification techniques are required.

This paper presents a compositional approach to the specification and verification of secure applet interactions. This approach involves a compositional model of the interface behavior of applet interactions, a temporal logic property specification language, and a proof system for proving correctness of property decompositions. The usability of the approach is demonstrated on a realistic smartcard case study.

1 Introduction

Verification Techniques for Open Platforms. Open platforms allow different software components, possibly originating from different issuers, to interact easily in a single environment. Thanks to their flexibility, such open platforms are becoming pervasive in modern software for mobile code, but also for embedded devices such as smartcards.

Quite unsurprisingly, the flexibility of open platforms raises major difficulties when it comes to establishing global properties of their applications. Such properties, which capture the interface behavior of the platform's components, include many common security properties such as "Component B can only access resource R after being authorized by Component A", or "Component A cannot perform action α between Component B performing action β and Component C performing action γ".

Two problems arise with the verification of such global properties:

- the complexity of the platform. In order to reason about the system, one needs to specify the communication mechanisms supported by the platform. These can be intrinsic (*e.g.* in Java[1] with privileged instructions and visibil-

---

[1] See http://java.sun.com/java2.

R.-D. Kutsche and H. Weber (Eds.): FASE 2002, LNCS 2306, pp. 15–32, 2002.

ity modifiers; in JavaCard[2], with firewalls and secure object sharing mechanisms) and can complicate reasoning substantially;
- the availability of the software. In the case of platforms supporting dynamic loading of software, one often would like to establish properties that are preserved when new software is loaded. In particular, this is true for security properties such as confidentiality and integrity.

These problems can be tackled by enforcing the desired properties through strict local security checks, as is done *e.g.* in bytecode verification, see *e.g.* [13], or in type systems for information flow, see *e.g.* [17]. However, this requires focusing on a very restricted set of properties, that excludes many useful global properties.

Open Platforms for Smartcards. New generation smartcards such as JavaCards are open platforms that support multiple applications on a single card and post-issuance loading of applets (*i.e.* applications can be loaded on the card after being issued to users). As smartcards are typically used as identity documents and money devices, security issues are particularly at stake, and the need for formal verification is widely recognized, as testified *e.g.* by Common Criteria[3].

Despite the advent of on-card bytecode verification [14], current technology prevents complex verifications to be performed on-card, thus applet verification needs to be performed off-card, presumably prior to loading the applet on the card. In this setting, one needs to analyze the possible interactions between the applet being loaded and the applets already on the card without having access to the code of the latter.

Compositional Verification. One possible verification strategy for programs operating on open platforms consists of:

1. reducing global properties of programs to local properties about their components, using compositional verification techniques;
2. verifying local properties of components by standard means, such as model-checking.

Such a strategy can be used to control state-space explosion and has been employed to good effect to establish the correctness of realistic, industrial-size open distributed telecom systems [9]. The main goal of this paper is to show that such a strategy is also applicable to open platforms such as smartcards. To this end, we develop a framework which allows to reduce global properties to local properties about components. The problem of verifying the local properties is not addressed here, since there are standard algorithmic techniques for this (see *e.g.* [4]). Our framework for compositional verification consists of:

- a model of applet interactions that captures, in a language-independent setting, control flow within applets and procedure calls between applets. This model is inspired by [11], and was motivated and presented informally by the present authors in [2].

---

[2] See http://java.sun.com/javacard.
[3] See http://www.commoncriteria.org.

- a specification language based on the modal μ-calculus [12,8], together with a set of specification patterns, inspired from Bandera [1], that allows higher-level specifications and reasoning;
- a compositional proof system in the style of [16,7,9] that is used for proving correctness of property decompositions. This proof system has been proved sound *w.r.t.* the underlying model in PVS [15].

To illustrate the benefits of our method, we also detail an example of property decomposition in the setting of an industrial smartcard case study [3].

Contents. The remainder of the paper is organized as follows. The model, specification language and proof system are introduced in Sections 2, 3 and 5 respectively, whereas Section 4 provides a brief overview of the language of patterns. The case study is detailed in Section 6. Finally, Section 7 concludes with related and future work.

2   Program Model

We focus on the control flow in platforms in which procedure or method calls are the primary means for interaction between components. For proving validity of property decompositions we need a model of program behavior which captures the interaction behavior of programs and program components, and over which the formulae of property specification languages can be interpreted. Standard models of this kind are provided by labeled transition systems (LTS), where the transition labels denote method invocations and returns. Interaction behavior can then be defined in an abstract and language independent fashion, following the approach by Jensen *et al.* [11], as being induced by a transfer/call graph through a set of transition rules. Composition of behaviors is obtained in process algebraic style by using imperfect actions which handshake to produce perfect communications. The program model and its operational semantics have been motivated and described in greater detail (but less formally) in [2].

Model. We formalize the program model we presented in [2].

Definition 1 (Program Model). *A* program model *is a tuple*

$$\mathcal{M} \triangleq (A, V; \mathbf{app}, \mathbf{ret}; \rightarrow^{T}, \rightarrow^{C})$$

where A is a set of applet names*; V is a set of* vertices *called* program points*;* $\mathbf{app} : V \rightharpoonup A$ *is a partial function mapping program points to applet names;* $\mathbf{ret} : V \rightarrow \mathrm{bool}$ *is a program point predicate identifying the program's return points;* $\rightarrow^{T} \subseteq V \times V$ *is a transfer relation respecting applet boundaries, i.e.* $\mathbf{app}(v) = a$ *and $v \rightarrow^{T} v'$ implies $\mathbf{app}(v') = a$; $\rightarrow^{C} \subseteq V \times V$ is a call relation between program points, of which the elements $\langle v, v' \rangle$ are referred to as* calls*.*

We shall use the notation $\mathbf{loc}_{a} v$ for $\mathbf{app}(v) = a$. We next define the notions of applet state and program state.

Definition 2 (State). *Let $\mathcal{M} = (A, V; \mathbf{app}, \mathbf{ret}; \to^T, \to^C)$ be a program model.*

(i) *An* applet state *of $\mathcal{M}$ is a pair $a.\pi$, where $a \in A$ is an applet name, and $\pi \in (V \times V)^*$ is a sequence of program point pairs called the* applet call stack. *An applet state $a.\pi$ is* active *iff the second program point of the last pair in the call stack π is local to applet a; in this case this program point is referred to as the* active program point.

(ii) *A* program state *s of $\mathcal{M}$ is a collection $a_1.\pi_1 \mid a_2.\pi_2 \mid \ldots \mid a_n.\pi_n$ of applet states. A program state is* active *iff it contains an active applet state, and* wellformed *iff it mentions applet names at most once and contains at most one active state. Two program states* intersect *iff they mention the same applet name.*

Intuitively, an applet state represents the unfinished calls that have been made from and to an applet. As method calls can cross applet boundaries, both the source and the destination of a call are remembered, to ensure "proper" returning (*i.e.* to the appropriate callee) from a method call. If intra-procedural execution takes place within an applet, *i.e.* by following the transfer relation, the changing of the active program point is reflected by changing the last element in the call stack. This is described by the operational semantics below.

Operational Semantics. The behavior of programs is given in terms of labeled transition systems.

Definition 3 (Induced LTS). *A program model $\mathcal{M}$ induces a LTS $\mathcal{T}_{\mathcal{M}} \triangleq (\mathcal{S}_{\mathcal{M}}, \mathcal{L}_{\mathcal{M}}; \to_{\mathcal{M}})$ in a straightforward fashion: $\mathcal{S}_{\mathcal{M}}$ is the set of wellformed program states of $\mathcal{M}$; $\mathcal{L}_{\mathcal{M}}$ is the set of transition labels consisting of τ and the triples of the shape $v\,l\,v'$, $v\,l?\,v'$, and $v\,l!\,v'$, where $v, v' \in V$ and $l \in \{\mathsf{call}, \mathsf{ret}\}$; and $\to_{\mathcal{M}} \subseteq \mathcal{S}_{\mathcal{M}} \times \mathcal{L}_{\mathcal{M}} \times \mathcal{S}_{\mathcal{M}}$ is the least transition relation on $\mathcal{S}_{\mathcal{M}}$ closed under the transition rules of [2] (see Appendix A).*

We write $s \xrightarrow{\alpha}_{\mathcal{M}} s'$ for $(s, \alpha, s') \in \to_{\mathcal{M}}$, and by convention omit τ from such transition edges, writing $s \longrightarrow_{\mathcal{M}} s'$ for $s \xrightarrow{\tau}_{\mathcal{M}} s'$.

Two kinds of transition rules are used: (1) applet transition rules, describing state changes in a single applet, and (2) transition rules for composite states, describing the behavior of composed applet sets. An example of a transition rule in the first category is the rule

$$[\text{send call}] \; \frac{v_1 \to^C v_2 \quad \mathbf{loc}_a\, v_1 \quad \neg\mathbf{loc}_a\, v_2}{a.\pi \cdot \langle v, v_1 \rangle \xrightarrow{v_1 \,\mathsf{call}!\, v_2} a.\pi \cdot \langle v, v_1 \rangle \cdot \langle v_1, v_2 \rangle}$$

which describes under which conditions an applet can invoke a method in another applet. This rule specifies that if applet a is in a state where v_1 is the active program point, and if there is an outgoing call edge $v_1 \to^C v_2$ to an external program point v_2, then sending a call over applet boundaries is enabled. The local state of the applet will be extended with a pair $\langle v_1, v_2 \rangle$, to reflect this call.

Notice that this implicitly makes a inactive, because the last program point in the applet state is now no longer local to a.

An example of a transition rule for composite states is the rule

$$[\text{synchro}] \frac{\mathcal{A}_1 \xrightarrow{v_1\, l?\, v_2} \mathcal{A}_1' \qquad \mathcal{A}_2 \xrightarrow{v_1\, l!\, v_2} \mathcal{A}_2'}{\mathcal{A}_1 \mid \mathcal{A}_2 \xrightarrow{v_1\, l\, v_2} \mathcal{A}_1' \mid \mathcal{A}_2'}\, l \in \text{call}, \text{ret}$$

which describes how two applets synchronize if one sends out a message call or return, which is received by the other applet. It is said that the imperfectly labeled transitions $v_1\, l?\, v_2$ and $v_1\, l!\, v_2$ synchronize into one perfectly labeled transition $v_1\, l\, v_2$.

3   Property Specification Language

Properties of component interaction can be conveniently expressed in a modal logic with recursion, such as Kozen's modal μ-calculus [12], extended with model-specific atomic formulae, where the modalities are indexed by transition labels. In addition, such a logic is suitable for compositional reasoning (*cf.* [16,8,9]).

Let a range over applet name variables[4], v over program point variables, π over applet call stack variables, Π over applet call stack terms generated by $\Pi ::= \epsilon \mid \pi \mid \Pi \cdot \langle v, v' \rangle$, $\mathcal{X}$ and $\mathcal{Y}$ over program state variables, $\mathcal{A}$ over program state terms generated by $\mathcal{A} ::= a.\Pi \mid \mathcal{A} \mid \mathcal{A}$, and α over transition labels, all of these possibly indexed or primed.

Definition 4 (Syntax). *Atomic formulae σ and formulae ϕ are generated by the following grammar, where x ranges over program point variables and applet call stack variables, t over program point variables and applet call stack terms, α over transition labels, and X over propositional variables:*

$$\sigma ::= t = t \mid \text{return } v \mid \text{local}_\mathcal{A}\, v$$
$$\phi ::= \sigma \mid \text{active} \mid \neg\phi \mid \phi \wedge \phi \mid \forall x.\phi \mid [\alpha]\phi \mid X \mid \nu X.\phi$$

We write $\text{local}_a\, v$ for $\text{local}_{a.\pi}\, v$.

An occurrence of a subformula ψ in ϕ is *positive*, if ψ appears in the scope of an even number of negation symbols; otherwise the occurrence is negative. The formation of fixed point formulae is subject to the usual formal monotonicity condition that occurrences of X in ϕ are positive. A formula ϕ is *propositionally closed* if ϕ does not have free occurrences of propositional variables. Standard abbreviations apply, like for instance $\exists x.\phi \stackrel{\Delta}{=} \neg\forall x.\neg\phi$, $\langle \alpha \rangle \phi \stackrel{\Delta}{=} \neg[\alpha]\neg\phi$, and $\mu X.\phi \stackrel{\Delta}{=} \neg\nu X.\neg(\phi[\neg X/X])$.

The semantics of formulae is given relative to a program model $\mathcal{M}$, its induced LTS $\mathcal{T}_\mathcal{M}$, and an environment ρ mapping variables to members of their

---

[4] By abuse of notation we use the same letters for the variables of the logic and for arbitrary constants of the respective domain in the model.

respective domains, lifted to expressions Π and $\mathcal{A}$ in the natural way. The semantic interpretation $[\![\sigma]\!]_\rho^{\mathcal{M}}$ of an atomic formula σ maps σ to a boolean, while the semantics $\|\phi\|_\rho^{\mathcal{M}}$ of a formula ϕ is described as the set of program states satisfying formula ϕ.

Definition 5 (Semantics). *Let $\mathcal{M}$ be a program model, $\mathcal{T}_\mathcal{M}$ be its induced LTS, and let ρ be an environment. The semantics of atomic formulae is defined by:*

$$[\![t_1 = t_2]\!]_\rho^{\mathcal{M}} \triangleq t_1\rho = t_2\rho$$

$$[\![\text{return } v]\!]_\rho^{\mathcal{M}} \triangleq \textbf{ret}(v\rho)$$

$$[\![\text{local}_\mathcal{A}\, v]\!]_\rho^{\mathcal{M}} \triangleq \textbf{app}(v\rho) \text{ is defined and occurs in } \mathcal{A}\rho$$

The semantics of formulae is standard [12], except for:

$$\|\sigma\|_\rho^{\mathcal{M}} \triangleq if \; [\![\sigma]\!]_\rho^{\mathcal{M}} \; then \; \mathcal{S}_\mathcal{M} \; else \; \emptyset$$

$$\|\text{active}\|_\rho^{\mathcal{M}} \triangleq \{s \in \mathcal{S}_\mathcal{M} \mid s \text{ is active}\}$$

4   Specification Patterns

The property specification language presented above is rather low-level. To facilitate high-level formal reasoning, we introduce a collection of specification patterns, following the approach of the Bandera project [6].

In the context of the present work, the use of specification patterns has an additional purpose: as explained in the introduction, we have two different kind of verification tasks in our framework, namely model-checking the local properties of the individual applets, and proving property decompositions correct. The use of general temporal logic patterns allows us to use different verification techniques (based on different logics) for the different tasks. For example, we can model check the local applet properties by translating, as appropriate, the specifications into CTL (*e.g.* as input for NuSMV [5]) or LTL (*e.g.* as input for SPIN [10]), while we can use the modal μ-calculus to prove the correctness of the property decomposition, as this is more suitable for the task.

A typical specification pattern used to express invariant properties is:

$$\text{ALWAYS } \phi \triangleq \nu X.\ \phi \wedge [\tau]\, X$$
$$\wedge\ \forall v_1.\ \forall v_2.\ [v_1\ \text{call}\ v_2]\, X$$
$$\wedge\ [v_1\ \text{call?}\ v_2]\, X$$
$$\wedge\ [v_1\ \text{call!}\ v_2]\, X$$
$$\wedge\ [v_1\ \text{ret}\ v_2]\, X$$
$$\wedge\ [v_1\ \text{ret?}\ v_2]\, X$$
$$\wedge\ [v_1\ \text{ret!}\ v_2]\, X$$

When components communicate via procedure or method calls one frequently needs to specify that some property ϕ holds within a call, *i.e.* from the point of

invocation to the point of return. For these purposes we propose the following
pattern:

$$\text{WITHIN } v \ \phi \ \stackrel{\Delta}{=} \ \forall v_1. \ [v_1 \text{ call } v] \text{ ALWAYS}_{-\text{ret } v_1} \phi$$
$$\wedge \ [v_1 \text{ call? } v] \text{ ALWAYS}_{-\text{ret! } v_1} \phi$$

where $\text{ALWAYS}_{-\lambda \, v} \ \phi$ is defined as $\text{ALWAYS} \ \phi$, but with the corresponding con-
junct $[v_1 \lambda \ v_2] \, X$ replaced by $[v_1 \lambda \ v_2] \, ((v_2 = v) \vee X)$.

In the example of Section 6 we also use the abbreviations:

$$\text{CALLSEXTONLY } V \ \stackrel{\Delta}{=} \ \forall v_1. \ \forall v_2. \ [v_1 \text{ call! } v_2] \, v_2 \in V$$

$$\text{CANNOTCALL } a \ V \ \stackrel{\Delta}{=} \ \forall v_1. \ \forall v_2. \ [v_1 \text{ call } v_2] \, \neg \, (\text{local}_a \, v_1 \wedge v_2 \in V)$$
$$\wedge \ [v_1 \text{ call! } v_2] \, \neg \, (\text{local}_a \, v_1 \wedge v_2 \in V)$$

where V denotes an explicit enumeration $v_1, \ldots, v_n$ of vertices and $v \in V$ is
syntactic sugar for $v = v_1 \vee \cdots \vee v = v_n$.

5 Proof System

For proving correctness of property decompositions, we develop a Gentzen-style
proof system based on the compositional approach advocated by Simpson [16].
This approach has been successfully used for the compositional verification of
CCS programs [7], and even of complex telecommunications software written in
the Erlang programming language [9].

The proof system uses Gentzen style sequents, *i.e.* proof judgments of the
form $\phi_1, \ldots, \phi_n \vdash \psi_1, \ldots, \psi_n$. The intuitive interpretation of such a sequent
is that the conjunction of the antecedents implies the disjunction of the conse-
quents, *i.e.* $\phi_1 \wedge \ldots \wedge \phi_n \Rightarrow \psi_1 \vee \ldots \vee \psi_n$. Formally, we define the building blocks
of our proof system as follows.

Definition 6 (Assertion, Sequent).

(i) An assertion *γ is either a* satisfaction assertion *$\mathcal{A} : \phi$, where ϕ is a propositionally closed formula, a* transition assertion *$\mathcal{A}_1 \stackrel{\alpha}{\to} \mathcal{A}_2$, an* atomic formula
assertion *σ, a* transfer-edge assertion *$v \to^T v'$, a* call-edge assertion *$v \to^C v'$,
or a* wellformedness assertion *$\text{wf}(\mathcal{A})$.*

(ii) Assertion $\mathcal{A} : \phi$ is valid *for program model $\mathcal{M}$ and environment ρ if $\mathcal{A}\rho \in
\|\phi\|_\rho^{\mathcal{M}}$. $\mathcal{A}_1 \stackrel{\alpha}{\to} \mathcal{A}_2$ is valid for $\mathcal{M}$ and ρ if $\mathcal{A}_1 \rho \stackrel{\alpha\rho}{\longrightarrow}_{\mathcal{M}} \mathcal{A}_2\rho$. σ is valid for $\mathcal{M}$
and ρ if $[\![\sigma]\!]_\rho^{\mathcal{M}}$. $v \to^T v'$ is valid for $\mathcal{M}$ and ρ if $v\rho \to^T v'\rho$ in $\mathcal{M}$. $v \to^C v'$
is valid for $\mathcal{M}$ and ρ if $v\rho \to^C v'\rho$ in $\mathcal{M}$. $\text{wf}(\mathcal{A})$ is valid for $\mathcal{M}$ and ρ if $\mathcal{A}\rho$
is wellformed in $\mathcal{M}$.*

(iii) A sequent *is a proof judgment of the form $\Gamma \vdash \Delta$, where Γ and Δ are sets
of assertions.*

(iv) Sequent $\Gamma \vdash \Delta$ is valid *if, for all program models $\mathcal{M}$ and environments ρ,
whenever all assertions in Γ are valid for $\mathcal{M}$ and ρ then also some assertion
in Δ is valid for $\mathcal{M}$ and ρ.*

Note that wellformedness of program states does not lift to program-state terms in a way which can be captured purely syntactically, and therefore has to be dealt with explicitly in the proof system.

We now present, in groups, the proof rules of our proof system. Since many of these are standard, we only show the most interesting ones here; the remaining rules can be found in Appendix B. The side condition "fresh x" appearing in some of the rules means "x does not appear free in the *conclusion* of the rule".

Structural and Logical Rules. As structural rules, we assume the standard identity, cut and weakening rules of Gentzen-style proof systems. We have rules for the various atomic formula constructs. Equality is handled through standard congruence rules, plus standard rules for freely generated datatypes (for dealing with equality on program stack terms). The rules for $\mathsf{local}_{\mathcal{A}}\, v$ proceed by decomposing the program state terms; in addition we have:

$$(\mathsf{LocInt}) \; \frac{\cdot}{\Gamma,\; \mathsf{local}_{\mathcal{A}_1}\, v,\; \mathsf{local}_{\mathcal{A}_2}\, v \vdash \mathsf{intersect}(\mathcal{A}_1, \mathcal{A}_2),\; \Delta}$$

$$(\mathsf{LocTransf}) \; \frac{\cdot}{\Gamma,\; \mathsf{local}_{\mathcal{A}}\, v,\; v \to^{T} v' \vdash \mathsf{local}_{\mathcal{A}}\, v',\; \Delta}$$

where $\mathsf{intersect}(\mathcal{A}_1, \mathcal{A}_2)$ is an auxiliary assertion used to capture program state intersection.

Most of the logical rules (dealing with satisfaction assertions $\mathcal{A} : \phi$) are standard. Not so are the proof rules for active:

$$(\mathsf{ActComL}) \; \frac{\Gamma,\; \mathcal{A}_1 : \mathsf{active} \vdash \Delta \qquad \Gamma,\; \mathcal{A}_2 : \mathsf{active} \vdash \Delta}{\Gamma,\; \mathcal{A}_1 \,|\, \mathcal{A}_2 : \mathsf{active} \vdash \Delta}$$

$$(\mathsf{ActComR}) \; \frac{\Gamma \vdash \mathcal{A}_1 : \mathsf{active},\; \mathcal{A}_2 : \mathsf{active},\; \Delta}{\Gamma \vdash \mathcal{A}_1 \,|\, \mathcal{A}_2 : \mathsf{active},\; \Delta}$$

$$(\mathsf{ActL}) \; \frac{\Gamma,\; \Pi = \pi \cdot \langle v_1, v_2 \rangle,\; \mathsf{local}_a\, v_2 \vdash \Delta}{\Gamma,\; a.\Pi : \mathsf{active} \vdash \Delta} \; \text{fresh } \pi, v_1, v_2$$

$$(\mathsf{ActR}) \; \frac{\Gamma \vdash \Pi = \Pi' \cdot \langle v_1, v_2 \rangle,\; \Delta \qquad \Gamma \vdash \mathsf{local}_a\, v_2,\; \Delta}{\Gamma \vdash a.\Pi : \mathsf{active},\; \Delta}$$

Fixed–point formulae are handled as in [8] through fixed-point approximation by using explicit ordinal variables κ to represent approximation ordinals:

$$(\mathsf{NuL}) \; \frac{\Gamma,\; \mathcal{A} : \phi[\nu X.\phi/X] \vdash \Delta}{\Gamma,\; \mathcal{A} : \nu X.\phi \vdash \Delta} \qquad (\mathsf{NuR}) \; \frac{\Gamma \vdash \mathcal{A} : (\nu X.\phi)^{\kappa},\; \Delta}{\Gamma \vdash \mathcal{A} : \nu X.\phi,\; \Delta} \; \text{fresh } \kappa$$

$$(\mathsf{ApproxR}) \; \frac{\Gamma,\; \kappa' < \kappa \vdash \mathcal{A} : \phi[(\nu X.\phi)^{\kappa'}/X],\; \Delta}{\Gamma \vdash \mathcal{A} : (\nu X.\phi)^{\kappa},\; \Delta} \; \text{fresh } \kappa'$$

These ordinal variables are examined by a global *discharge rule*, which checks whether the proof tree constitutes a valid well-founded induction scheme. Informally, the discharge rule applies if (1) every non-axiom leaf of the proof tree is an instance (up to a substitution) of some ancestor sequent in the proof tree, (2) for each such sequent, this substitution maps some ordinal variable approximating a fixed-point formula to an ordinal variable which is assumed to be smaller, and (3) these separate induction schemes are *consistent* with each other. For the technical details the interested reader is referred to [8,7,9].

Transition Rules. These rules deal with transition assertions $\mathcal{A}_1 \xrightarrow{\alpha} \mathcal{A}_2$.

We first consider the case where $\mathcal{A}$ is a composite state. The r.h.s. rules follow directly from the transition rules for program states (see Appendix A), after making the wellformedness conditions explicit.

$$\text{(ComTauR)} \quad \frac{\Gamma \vdash \mathcal{A}_1 \to \mathcal{A}_1', \Delta \qquad \Gamma \vdash \mathsf{wf}(\mathcal{A}_1 \,|\, \mathcal{A}_2), \Delta \qquad \Gamma \vdash \mathsf{wf}(\mathcal{A}_1' \,|\, \mathcal{A}_2), \Delta}{\Gamma \vdash \mathcal{A}_1 \,|\, \mathcal{A}_2 \to \mathcal{A}_1' \,|\, \mathcal{A}_2, \Delta}$$

$$\text{(ComSyncR)} \quad \frac{\Gamma \vdash \mathcal{A}_1 \xrightarrow{v_1\,l!\,v_2} \mathcal{A}_1', \Delta \qquad \Gamma \vdash \mathsf{wf}(\mathcal{A}_1 \,|\, \mathcal{A}_2), \Delta}{\begin{array}{c}\Gamma \vdash \mathcal{A}_2 \xrightarrow{v_1\,l?\,v_2} \mathcal{A}_2', \Delta \qquad \Gamma \vdash \mathsf{wf}(\mathcal{A}_1' \,|\, \mathcal{A}_2'), \Delta \\ \hline \Gamma \vdash \mathcal{A}_1 \,|\, \mathcal{A}_2 \xrightarrow{v_1\,l\,v_2} \mathcal{A}_1' \,|\, \mathcal{A}_2', \Delta\end{array}}$$

$$\text{(ComPropR)} \quad \frac{\Gamma \vdash \mathcal{A}_1 \xrightarrow{v_1\,\lambda\,v_2} \mathcal{A}_1', \Delta \qquad \Gamma, \mathsf{local}_{\mathcal{A}_2}\,v_1 \vdash \Delta \qquad \Gamma \vdash \mathsf{wf}(\mathcal{A}_1 \,|\, \mathcal{A}_2), \Delta}{\begin{array}{c}\Gamma, \mathsf{local}_{\mathcal{A}_2}\,v_2 \vdash \Delta \qquad \Gamma \vdash \mathsf{wf}(\mathcal{A}_1' \,|\, \mathcal{A}_2), \Delta \\ \hline \Gamma \vdash \mathcal{A}_1 \,|\, \mathcal{A}_2 \xrightarrow{v_1\,\lambda\,v_2} \mathcal{A}_1' \,|\, \mathcal{A}_2, \Delta\end{array}}$$

where l is call or ret and λ is l, $l?$ or $l!$. All three rules have symmetric counterparts which we omit.

Notice that in each rule two proof obligations arise on the wellformedness of the state. This may seem a heavy proof burden, but almost all these proof obligations can be discharged immediately. It is future work to derive optimized proof rules which result in less proof obligations.

The l.h.s. rules apply when we assume that a certain transition is possible. By the closure condition of the transition semantics, the possible transitions are exactly those inferable by the transition rules, thus these proof rules have to capture the conditions under which we can assume that this transition is possible.

For example, a transition $\mathcal{A}_1 \,|\, \mathcal{A}_2 \xrightarrow{v_1\,\mathsf{call}\,v_2} \mathcal{X}$ only is possible if the transition rules [synchro] or [propagation] apply. The transition rule [synchro] applies if: (1) $\mathcal{A}_1$ can do a transition to $\mathcal{A}_1'$ labeled v_1 call! v_2, (2) $\mathcal{A}_2$ can do a transition to $\mathcal{A}_2'$, labeled v_1 call? v_2, and (3) $\mathcal{X}$ is of the form $\mathcal{A}_1' \,|\, \mathcal{A}_2'$, or the symmetric counterpart of this applies. Similarly, it can be decided under which conditions the transition rule [propagation] applies. If we assume that such a transition $\mathcal{A}_1 \,|\, \mathcal{A}_2 \xrightarrow{v_1\,\mathsf{call}\,v_2} \mathcal{X}$ is possible, one of these rules must have been applied, and thus for one of these rules all conditions must have been satisfied. This is exactly captured by the proof rule (ComPerfL), with explicit wellformedness conditions added.

$$\text{(ComTauL)}\ \frac{\begin{array}{l}\Gamma[(\mathcal{Y}\,|\,\mathcal{A}_2)/\mathcal{X}],\ \mathcal{A}_1 \to \mathcal{Y},\ \mathsf{wf}(\mathcal{A}_1\,|\,\mathcal{A}_2),\ \mathsf{wf}(\mathcal{Y}\,|\,\mathcal{A}_2) \vdash \Delta[(\mathcal{Y}\,|\,\mathcal{A}_2)/\mathcal{X}]\\ \Gamma[(\mathcal{A}_1\,|\,\mathcal{Y})/\mathcal{X}],\ \mathcal{A}_2 \to \mathcal{Y},\ \mathsf{wf}(\mathcal{A}_1\,|\,\mathcal{A}_2),\ \mathsf{wf}(\mathcal{A}_1\,|\,\mathcal{Y}) \vdash \Delta[(\mathcal{A}_1\,|\,\mathcal{Y})/\mathcal{X}]\end{array}}{\Gamma,\ \mathcal{A}_1\,|\,\mathcal{A}_2 \to \mathcal{X} \vdash \Delta}\ \text{fresh } \mathcal{Y}$$

$$\text{(ComImpL)}\ \frac{\begin{array}{l}\Gamma[(\mathcal{Y}\,|\,\mathcal{A}_2)/\mathcal{X}],\ \mathcal{A}_1 \xrightarrow{v_1\,l?!v_2} \mathcal{Y},\ \mathsf{wf}(\mathcal{A}_1\,|\,\mathcal{A}_2),\ \mathsf{wf}(\mathcal{Y}\,|\,\mathcal{A}_2) \vdash \mathsf{local}_{\mathcal{A}_2}\,v_1,\ \mathsf{local}_{\mathcal{A}_2}\,v_2,\ \Delta[(\mathcal{Y}\,|\,\mathcal{A}_2)/\mathcal{X}]\\ \Gamma[(\mathcal{A}_1\,|\,\mathcal{Y})/\mathcal{X}],\ \mathcal{A}_2 \xrightarrow{v_1\,l?!v_2} \mathcal{Y},\ \mathsf{wf}(\mathcal{A}_1\,|\,\mathcal{A}_2),\ \mathsf{wf}(\mathcal{A}_1\,|\,\mathcal{Y}) \vdash \mathsf{local}_{\mathcal{A}_1}\,v_1,\ \mathsf{local}_{\mathcal{A}_1}\,v_2,\ \Delta[(\mathcal{A}_1\,|\,\mathcal{Y})/\mathcal{X}]\end{array}}{\Gamma,\ \mathcal{A}_1\,|\,\mathcal{A}_2 \xrightarrow{v_1\,l?!v_2} \mathcal{X} \vdash \Delta}$$

fresh $\mathcal{Y}$

$$\text{(ComPerfL)}\ \frac{\begin{array}{l}\Gamma[(\mathcal{Y}\,|\,\mathcal{A}_2)/\mathcal{X}],\ \mathcal{A}_1 \xrightarrow{v_1\,l v_2} \mathcal{Y},\ \mathsf{wf}(\mathcal{A}_1\,|\,\mathcal{A}_2),\ \mathsf{wf}(\mathcal{Y}\,|\,\mathcal{A}_2) \vdash \mathsf{local}_{\mathcal{A}_2}\,v_1,\ \mathsf{local}_{\mathcal{A}_2}\,v_2,\ \Delta[(\mathcal{Y}\,|\,\mathcal{A}_2)/\mathcal{X}]\\ \Gamma[(\mathcal{A}_1\,|\,\mathcal{Y})/\mathcal{X}],\ \mathcal{A}_2 \xrightarrow{v_1\,l v_2} \mathcal{Y},\ \mathsf{wf}(\mathcal{A}_1\,|\,\mathcal{A}_2),\ \mathsf{wf}(\mathcal{A}_1\,|\,\mathcal{Y}) \vdash \mathsf{local}_{\mathcal{A}_1}\,v_1,\ \mathsf{local}_{\mathcal{A}_1}\,v_2,\ \Delta[(\mathcal{A}_1\,|\,\mathcal{Y})/\mathcal{X}]\\ \Gamma[(\mathcal{X}_1\,|\,\mathcal{X}_2)/\mathcal{X}],\ \mathcal{A}_1 \xrightarrow{v_1\,l!v_2} \mathcal{X}_1,\ \mathcal{A}_2 \xrightarrow{v_1\,l?v_2} \mathcal{X}_2,\ \mathsf{wf}(\mathcal{A}_1\,|\,\mathcal{A}_2),\ \mathsf{wf}(\mathcal{X}_1\,|\,\mathcal{X}_2) \vdash \Delta[(\mathcal{X}_1\,|\,\mathcal{X}_2)/\mathcal{X}]\\ \Gamma[(\mathcal{X}_1\,|\,\mathcal{X}_2)/\mathcal{X}],\ \mathcal{A}_1 \xrightarrow{v_1\,l?v_2} \mathcal{X}_1,\ \mathcal{A}_2 \xrightarrow{v_1\,l!v_2} \mathcal{X}_2,\ \mathsf{wf}(\mathcal{A}_1\,|\,\mathcal{A}_2),\ \mathsf{wf}(\mathcal{X}_1\,|\,\mathcal{X}_2) \vdash \Delta[(\mathcal{X}_1\,|\,\mathcal{X}_2)/\mathcal{X}]\end{array}}{\Gamma,\ \mathcal{A}_1\,|\,\mathcal{A}_2 \xrightarrow{v_1\,l v_2} \mathcal{X} \vdash \Delta}$$

fresh $\mathcal{X}_1, \mathcal{X}_2, \mathcal{Y}$

In rule (ComImpL), $l?!$ stands for either $l?$ or $l!$.

We now turn to the case when $\mathcal{A}$ is a singleton set, *i.e.* an applet state. Again, the r.h.s. rules follow immediately from the transition rules. However, in many transition rules there is an implicit condition on the form of the applet state, *e.g.* to be able to apply the rule [send call], the call stack has to be of the form $\Pi \cdot \langle v_1, v_2 \rangle$. These conditions are made explicit in the proof rules.

$$\text{(LocCallR)}\ \frac{\Gamma \vdash v_1 \to^C v_2,\ \Delta \qquad \Gamma \vdash \Pi = \Pi' \cdot \langle v, v_1 \rangle,\ \Delta \qquad \Gamma \vdash \mathsf{local}_a\,v_1,\ \Delta \qquad \Gamma \vdash \mathsf{local}_a\,v_2,\ \Delta}{\Gamma \vdash a.\Pi \xrightarrow{v_1\ \mathsf{call}\ v_2} a.(\Pi \cdot \langle v_1, v_2 \rangle),\ \Delta}$$

$$\text{(LocRetR)}\ \frac{\Gamma \vdash v_1 \to^T v_2,\ \Delta \quad \Gamma \vdash \Pi = \Pi' \cdot \langle v, v_1 \rangle \cdot \langle v_1, v_3 \rangle,\ \Delta \quad \Gamma \vdash \mathsf{local}_a\,v_1,\ \Delta \quad \Gamma \vdash \mathsf{local}_a\,v_3,\ \Delta \quad \Gamma \vdash \mathsf{return}\,v_3,\ \Delta}{\Gamma \vdash a.\Pi \xrightarrow{v_3\ \mathsf{ret}\ v_1} a.(\Pi' \cdot \langle v, v_2 \rangle),\ \Delta}$$

$$\text{(LocTransfR)}\ \frac{\Gamma \vdash v_1 \to^T v_2,\ \Delta \qquad \Gamma \vdash \mathsf{local}_a\,v_1,\ \Delta \qquad \qquad}{\Gamma \vdash a.\Pi \to a.(\Pi' \cdot \langle v, v_2 \rangle),\ \Delta}\ \frac{\Gamma, v_1 \to^C v_3 \vdash \Delta \qquad \Gamma \vdash \Pi = \Pi' \cdot \langle v, v_1 \rangle,\ \Delta}{}\ \text{fresh } v_3$$

$$\text{(SendCallR)}\ \frac{\Gamma \vdash v_1 \to^C v_2,\ \Delta \qquad \Gamma \vdash \Pi = \Pi' \cdot \langle v, v_1 \rangle,\ \Delta \qquad \Gamma \vdash \mathsf{local}_a\,v_1,\ \Delta \qquad \Gamma, \mathsf{local}_a\,v_2 \vdash \Delta}{\Gamma \vdash a.\Pi \xrightarrow{v_1\ \mathsf{call!}\ v_2} a.(\Pi \cdot \langle v_1, v_2 \rangle),\ \Delta}$$

$$\text{(RecCallR)}\ \frac{\Gamma \vdash v_1 \to^C v_2,\ \Delta \qquad \Gamma, a.\Pi : \mathsf{active} \vdash \Delta \qquad \Gamma, \mathsf{local}_a\,v_1 \vdash \Delta \qquad \Gamma \vdash \mathsf{local}_a\,v_2,\ \Delta}{\Gamma \vdash a.\Pi \xrightarrow{v_1\ \mathsf{call?}\ v_2} a.(\Pi \cdot \langle v_1, v_2 \rangle),\ \Delta}$$

$$\text{(SendRetR)}\ \frac{\Gamma, \mathsf{local}_a\,v_1 \vdash \Delta \qquad \Gamma \vdash \Pi = \Pi' \cdot \langle v_1, v_2 \rangle,\ \Delta \qquad \Gamma \vdash \mathsf{local}_a\,v_2,\ \Delta \qquad \Gamma \vdash \mathsf{return}\,v_2,\ \Delta}{\Gamma \vdash a.\Pi \xrightarrow{v_2\ \mathsf{ret!}\ v_1} a.\Pi',\ \Delta}$$

$$\text{(RecRetR)}\ \frac{\Gamma \vdash v_1 \to^T v_2,\ \Delta \quad \Gamma \vdash \Pi = \Pi' \cdot \langle v, v_1 \rangle \cdot \langle v_1, v_3 \rangle,\ \Delta \quad \Gamma, \mathsf{local}_a\,v_3 \vdash \Delta \quad \Gamma, \mathsf{local}_a\,v_4 \vdash \Delta \quad \Gamma \vdash \mathsf{local}_a\,v_1,\ \Delta}{\Gamma \vdash a.\Pi \xrightarrow{v_4\ \mathsf{ret?}\ v_1} a.(\Pi' \cdot \langle v, v_2 \rangle),\ \Delta}$$

The l.h.s. rules are constructed from the transition rules in the same way as the l.h.s. rules for composite states above.

$$\text{(LocCallL)}\ \frac{\Gamma[a.(\Pi \cdot \langle v_1, v_2\rangle))/\mathcal{X}],\ \Pi = \pi \cdot \langle v, v_1\rangle,\ v_1 \to^C v_2,\ \text{local}_a\ v_1,\ \text{local}_a\ v_2\ \vdash}{\Gamma,\ a.\Pi \xrightarrow{v_1\ \text{call}\ v_2} \mathcal{X} \vdash \Delta}\ \Delta[a.(\Pi \cdot \langle v_1, v_2\rangle))/\mathcal{X}]\ \text{fresh } v, \pi$$

$$\text{(LocRetL)}\ \frac{\Gamma[a.(\pi \cdot \langle v, v_2\rangle))/\mathcal{X}],\ \Pi = \pi \cdot \langle v, v_1\rangle \cdot \langle v_1, v_3\rangle,\ v_1 \to^T v_2,\ \text{local}_a\ v_1,\ \text{local}_a\ v_3,\ \text{return}\ v_3\ \vdash}{\Gamma,\ a.\Pi \xrightarrow{v_3\ \text{ret}\ v_1} \mathcal{X} \vdash \Delta}\ \Delta[a.(\pi \cdot \langle v, v_2\rangle))/\mathcal{X}]$$

$$\text{fresh } v, v_2, \pi$$

$$\text{(LocTransfL)}\ \frac{\Gamma[a.(\pi \cdot \langle v, v_2\rangle))/\mathcal{X}],\ \Pi = \pi \cdot \langle v, v_1\rangle,\ v_1 \to^T v_2,\ \text{local}_a\ v_1\ \vdash}{\Gamma,\ a.\Pi \to \mathcal{X} \vdash \Delta}\ v_1 \to^C v_3,\ \Delta[a.(\pi \cdot \langle v, v_2\rangle))/\mathcal{X}]\ \text{fresh } v, v_1, v_2, \pi$$

$$\text{(SendCallL)}\ \frac{\Gamma[a.(\Pi \cdot \langle v_1, v_2\rangle))/\mathcal{X}],\ \Pi = \pi \cdot \langle v, v_1\rangle,\ v_1 \to^C v_2,\ \text{local}_a\ v_1\ \vdash}{\Gamma,\ a.\Pi \xrightarrow{v_1\ \text{call!}\ v_2} \mathcal{X} \vdash \Delta}\ \text{local}_a\ v_2,\ \Delta[a.(\Pi \cdot \langle v_1, v_2\rangle))/\mathcal{X}]$$

$$\text{fresh } v, \pi$$

$$\text{(RecCallL)}\ \frac{\Gamma[a.(\Pi \cdot \langle v_1, v_2\rangle))/\mathcal{X}],\ v_1 \to^C v_2,\ \text{local}_a\ v_2\ \vdash}{\Gamma,\ a.\Pi \xrightarrow{v_1\ \text{call?}\ v_2} \mathcal{X} \vdash \Delta}\ \text{local}_a\ v_1,\ a.\Pi : \text{active},\ \Delta[a.(\Pi \cdot \langle v_1, v_2\rangle))/\mathcal{X}]$$

$$\text{(SendRetL)}\ \frac{\Gamma[a.\pi/\mathcal{X}],\ \Pi = \pi \cdot \langle v_1, v_2\rangle,\ \text{local}_a\ v_2,\ \text{return}\ v_2\ \vdash}{\Gamma,\ a.\Pi \xrightarrow{v_2\ \text{ret!}\ v_1} \mathcal{X} \vdash \Delta}\ \text{local}_a\ v_1,\ \Delta[a.\pi/\mathcal{X}]\ \text{fresh } \pi$$

$$\text{(RecRetL)}\ \frac{\Gamma[a.(\pi \cdot \langle v, v_2\rangle))/\mathcal{X}],\ \Pi = \pi \cdot \langle v, v_1\rangle \cdot \langle v_1, v_3\rangle,\ v_1 \to^T v_2,\ \text{local}_a\ v_1\ \vdash}{\Gamma,\ a.\Pi \xrightarrow{v_4\ \text{ret?}\ v_1} \mathcal{X} \vdash \Delta}\ \text{local}_a\ v_3,\ \text{local}_a\ v_4,\ \Delta[a.(\pi \cdot \langle v, v_2\rangle))/\mathcal{X}]$$

$$\text{fresh } v, v_2, v_3, \pi$$

Wellformedness Rules. These rules reflect Definition 2, which states that a composed state $\mathcal{A}_1 \mid \mathcal{A}_2$ is wellformed *iff* its components are wellformed, at most one of the components is active, and the applet names in the components do not intersect.

$$\text{(WfAppletR)}\ \frac{}{\Gamma \vdash \text{wf}(a.\Pi),\ \Delta}$$

$$\text{(WfComR)}\ \frac{\Gamma \vdash \text{wf}(\mathcal{A}_1),\ \Delta \qquad \Gamma,\ \text{intersect}(\mathcal{A}_1, \mathcal{A}_2) \vdash \Delta}{\Gamma \vdash \text{wf}(\mathcal{A}_1 \mid \mathcal{A}_2),\ \Delta}$$

$$\text{(WfComL)}\ \frac{\Gamma,\ \text{wf}(\mathcal{A}_1),\ \text{wf}(\mathcal{A}_2),\ \mathcal{A}_1 : \text{active} \vdash \text{intersect}(\mathcal{A}_1, \mathcal{A}_2),\ \mathcal{A}_2 : \text{active},\ \Delta}{\Gamma,\ \text{wf}(\mathcal{A}_1 \mid \mathcal{A}_2) \vdash \Delta}$$

(with additional premises)

$$\Gamma,\ \text{wf}(\mathcal{A}_1),\ \text{wf}(\mathcal{A}_2),\ \mathcal{A}_2 : \text{active} \vdash \text{intersect}(\mathcal{A}_1, \mathcal{A}_2),\ \mathcal{A}_1 : \text{active},\ \Delta$$
$$\Gamma,\ \text{wf}(\mathcal{A}_1),\ \text{wf}(\mathcal{A}_2) \vdash \text{intersect}(\mathcal{A}_1, \mathcal{A}_2),\ \mathcal{A}_1 : \text{active},\ \mathcal{A}_2 : \text{active},\ \Delta$$

Soundness. The program model has been formalized and the proof rules have been proven sound *w.r.t.* the underlying model in PVS [15].

6   Example: Electronic Purse

To illustrate the working of the proof system, we take the electronic purse smart-card example of [3], which we discussed in greater detail (by providing the program model) in [2], and we outline the correctness proof of the decomposition of its specification. In this example an electronic purse is presented, which contains three applets: a `Purse` applet, and two loyalty applets: `AirFrance` and `RentACar`, with the standard functionalities. Besides, the `Purse` keeps a log table of bounded size of all transactions. Loyalties can subscribe to a (paying) `logFull` service, which signals that the log table is full and entries will be overridden. In the example, `AirFrance` is subscribed to this service. If it gets a `logFull` message, it will update its local balance, by asking the entries of the log table of the `Purse`, and by asking the balances of loyalty partners (`RentACar` in this example). In this way, `RentACar` can implicitly deduce that the log table is full, because it receives a `getBalance` message from `AirFrance`. A malicious implementation of `RentACar` can therefore request the information stored in the log table, before returning the value of its local balance. This is unwanted, because `RentACar` has not paid for the `logFull` service.

Thus, an invocation of `logFull` in the `AirFrance` applet by the `Purse` should not trigger a call from `RentACar` to `getTrs` (to ask the transactions) in the `Purse`. Using the macro definitions from Section 4 we can formally specify this as:

$$\text{SPEC} \overset{\Delta}{=} \text{WITHIN AirFrance.logFull SPEC}'$$
$$\text{SPEC}' \overset{\Delta}{=} \text{CANNOTCALL RentACar Purse.getTrs}$$

The individual applets are specified as follows:

$$\text{SPEC}_\text{P} \overset{\Delta}{=} \text{local}_\text{Purse} \text{ Purse.getTrs} \wedge \text{SPEC}'_\text{P}$$
$$\text{SPEC}'_\text{P} \overset{\Delta}{=} \text{ALWAYS (WITHIN Purse.getTrs (CALLSEXTONLY } \emptyset))$$

$$\text{SPEC}_\text{AF} \overset{\Delta}{=} \text{local}_\text{AirFrance} \text{ AirFrance.logFull} \wedge \text{SPEC}'_\text{AF}$$
$$\text{SPEC}'_\text{AF} \overset{\Delta}{=} \text{ALWAYS (WITHIN AirFrance.logFull SPEC}''_\text{AF})$$
$$\text{SPEC}''_\text{AF} \overset{\Delta}{=} \text{CALLSEXTONLY Purse.getTrs, RentACar.getBalance}$$

$$\text{SPEC}_\text{RaC} \overset{\Delta}{=} \text{local}_\text{RentACar} \text{ RentACar.getBalance} \wedge \text{SPEC}'_\text{RaC}$$
$$\text{SPEC}'_\text{RaC} \overset{\Delta}{=} \text{ALWAYS (WITHIN RentACar.getBalance(CALLSEXTONLY } \emptyset))$$

To show that this property decomposition is correct, we have to parameterize these specifications by replacing the concrete applet names `Purse`, `AirFrance` and `RentACar` by the applet variables a_P, a_{AF} and a_{RaC}, and the concrete method names `Purse.getTrs`, `AirFrance.logFull` and `RentACar.getBalance` by the program point variables v_{GT}, v_{LF} and v_{GB}, respectively. We employ the proof system presented above to prove validity of the following sequent:

$a_P.\pi_P$: SPEC$_P$, $a_{AF}.\pi_{AF}$: SPEC$_{AF}$, $a_{RaC}.\pi_{RaC}$: SPEC$_{RaC}$
$\vdash$ $a_P.\pi_P | a_{AF}.\pi_{AF} | a_{RaC}.\pi_{RaC}$: SPEC

There is a systematic method of proving validity of such sequents based on stepwise symbolic execution and loop detection. *Symbolic execution* refers to the process of computing the symbolic next-states of a program-state term (here $a_P.\pi_P | a_{AF}.\pi_{AF} | a_{RaC}.\pi_{RaC}$) guided by the modalities of the formula (here SPEC). In this process some parameter terms of the program-state term might change. This requires the assumptions on these parameter terms to be updated. Some of the resulting symbolic next-states might be impossible, for example due to the accumulation of contradicting assumptions about the locality of program points, or because they violate the wellformedness restrictions on program states. *Loop detection* refers to detecting when a sequent is an instance of some ancestor sequent in the proof tree. This is necessary for checking the discharge condition.

We exemplify the method on the sequent above. First, we unfold the pattern and apply logical rules based on the outermost logical connectives of SPEC until reaching a box-formula. In this way two subgoals are obtained; we focus on the first (the correctness proof of the second subgoal will follow the same structure):

local$_{a_P}$ v_{GT}, local$_{a_{AF}}$ v_{LF}, local$_{a_{RaC}}$ v_{GB},
$a_P.\pi_P$: SPEC$'_P$, $a_{AF}.\pi_{AF}$: SPEC$'_{AF}$, $a_{RaC}.\pi_{RaC}$: SPEC$'_{RaC}$
$\vdash$ $a_P.\pi_P | a_{AF}.\pi_{AF} | a_{RaC}.\pi_{RaC}$: $[v_1$ call $v_{LF}]$ ALWAYS$_{-ret\ v_1}$ SPEC$'$

Second, we apply rule BoxR followed by left transition rules for composite states until possible; this yields nine sequents corresponding to the nine different ways in which a perfect call action can come about in a system composed of three applets. Of these, four subgoals consider the cases where a_{AF} is not involved in the communication, and these can immediately be discarded (by applying the Id rule) due to contradicting assumptions about locality of v_{LF}. Two other sequents contain an assumption $a_{AF}.\pi_{AF} \xrightarrow{v_1 \text{ call! } v_{LF}} \mathcal{X}$, *i.e.* a_{AF} sends a call to an external v_{LF}, and these can be discarded immediately by applying SendCallL and Id. The remaining three subgoals consider the three possible ways of producing a perfect call to vertex v_{LF} which is local to a_{AF}: by making a local call from within a_{AF}, or by calling from a_P or a_{RaC}.

Here, we focus on the case that v_{LF} is invoked by a local call from within a_{AF}. Verification of the other two cases continues along the same lines.

local$_{a_P}$ v_{GT}, local$_{a_{AF}}$ v_{LF}, local$_{a_{RaC}}$ v_{GB},
$a_P.\pi_P$: SPEC$'_P$, $a_{AF}.\pi_{AF}$: SPEC$'_{AF}$, $a_{RaC}.\pi_{RaC}$: SPEC$'_{RaC}$,
wf$(a_P.\pi_P | a_{AF}.\pi_{AF} | a_{RaC}.\pi_{RaC})$, wf$(a_P.\pi_P | \mathcal{X} | a_{RaC}.\pi_{RaC})$,
$a_{AF}.\pi_{AF} \xrightarrow{v_1 \text{ call } v_{LF}} \mathcal{X}$
$\vdash$ $a_P.\pi_P | \mathcal{X} | a_{RaC}.\pi_{RaC}$: ALWAYS$_{-ret\ v_1}$ SPEC$'$

Next, we derive from the assumption(s) about $a_{AF}.\pi_{AF}$ assumptions about $\mathcal{X}$. We do this by applying l.h.s. logical rules (including NuL), until we obtain a box-formula with label v_1 call v_{LF}. To this formula we apply BoxL (taking $\mathcal{X}$ for $\mathcal{A}'$), which results in two subgoals. The first subgoals requires to show the transition assertion $a_{AF}.\pi_{AF} \xrightarrow{v_1 \text{ call } v_{LF}} \mathcal{X}$, and can immediately be discarded (by Id). The other sequent looks as follows (after weakening):

$$\begin{aligned}
&\mathsf{local}_{a_P}\, v_{GT},\ \mathsf{local}_{a_{AF}}\, v_{LF},\ \mathsf{local}_{a_{RaC}}\, v_{GB},\\
&a_P.\pi_P : \mathrm{SPEC}'_{\mathsf{P}},\ \mathcal{X} : \mathrm{ALWAYS}_{-\mathsf{ret}\, v_1} \mathrm{SPEC}''_{\mathsf{AF}},\ a_{RaC}.\pi_{RaC} : \mathrm{SPEC}'_{\mathsf{RaC}},\\
&a_{AF}.\pi_{AF} \xrightarrow{v_1 \text{ call } v_{LF}} \mathcal{X},\\
&\mathsf{wf}(a_P.\pi_P\,|\,a_{AF}.\pi_{AF}\,|\,a_{RaC}.\pi_{RaC}),\ \mathsf{wf}(a_P.\pi_P\,|\,\mathcal{X}\,|\,a_{RaC}.\pi_{RaC})\\
&\vdash\ a_P.\pi_P\,|\,\mathcal{X}\,|\,a_{RaC}.\pi_{RaC} : \mathrm{ALWAYS}_{-\mathsf{ret}\, v_1} \mathrm{SPEC}'
\end{aligned}$$

And fourth, the transition assertion on the left is eliminated by applying the appropriate l.h.s. local transition rule, here LocCallL:

$$\begin{aligned}
&\mathsf{local}_{a_P}\, v_{GT},\ \mathsf{local}_{a_{AF}}\, v_{LF},\ \mathsf{local}_{a_{AF}}\, v_1,\ \mathsf{local}_{a_{RaC}}\, v_{GB},\\
&a_P.\pi_P : \mathrm{SPEC}'_{\mathsf{P}},\ a_{AF}.\pi_{AF} \cdot \langle v_1, v_{LF}\rangle : \mathrm{ALWAYS}_{-\mathsf{ret}\, v_1} \mathrm{SPEC}''_{\mathsf{AF}},\\
&a_{RaC}.\pi_{RaC} : \mathrm{SPEC}'_{\mathsf{RaC}},\ \pi_{AF} = \pi \cdot \langle v, v_1 \rangle,\ v_1 \to^C v_{LF},\\
&\mathsf{wf}(a_P.\pi_P\,|\,a_{AF}.\pi_{AF}\,|\,a_{RaC}.\pi_{RaC}),\ \mathsf{wf}(a_P.\pi_P\,|\,a_{AF}.\pi_{AF}\cdot\langle v_1, v_{LF}\rangle\,|\,a_{RaC}.\pi_{RaC})\\
&\vdash\ a_P.\pi_P\,|\,a_{AF}.\pi_{AF} \cdot \langle v_1, v_{LF}\rangle\,|\,a_{RaC}.\pi_{RaC} : \mathrm{ALWAYS}_{-\mathsf{ret}\, v_1} \mathrm{SPEC}'
\end{aligned}$$

As a result of the above steps we computed a symbolic next-state $a_P.\pi_P\,|\,a_{AF}.\pi_{AF}\cdot\langle v_1, v_{LF}\rangle\,|\,a_{RaC}.\pi_{RaC}$ from the original symbolic state $a_P.\pi_P\,|\,a_{AF}.\pi_{AF}\,|\,a_{RaC}.\pi_{RaC}$ and updated the assumptions on its parameters.

Proof search continues by showing that in this symbolic next-state the formula $\mathrm{ALWAYS}_{-\mathsf{ret}\, v_1} \mathrm{SPEC}'$ is true. This amounts to showing that (by applying NuR, ApproxR, and AndR) in this state SPEC' is true, and in all possible next states within the call (*i.e.* those that are reached through transitions which are not labeled v ret v_1), again $\mathrm{ALWAYS}_{-\mathsf{ret}\, v_1} \mathrm{SPEC}'$ holds. SPEC' says that a_{RaC} does not call v_{GT}, thus it follows immediately that $a_P.\pi_P\,|\,a_{AF}.\pi_{AF}\cdot\langle v_1, v_{LF}\rangle\,|\,a_{RaC}.\pi_{RaC} : \mathrm{SPEC}'$ is satisfied from the wellformedness of the current state: a_{AF} is the active applet, thus a_{RaC} cannot issue calls.

We consider all possible next states of $a_P.\pi_P\,|\,a_{AF}.\pi_{AF}\cdot\langle v_1, v_{LF}\rangle\,|\,a_{RaC}.\pi_{RaC}$ within the call. In most cases, we detect a loop and immediately can apply the discharge condition, but in the case that the next state is reached because a_{AF} has sent out an external call, we cannot do this. Here we have to use the assumption on a_{AF}, which says that such a call can only be to v_{GT} or v_{GB}. Thus there are two possible symbolic next states and for both these states we have to show that $\mathrm{ALWAYS}_{-\mathsf{ret}\, v_1} \mathrm{SPEC}'$ holds. This is done by showing that in this state SPEC' holds (either because a_P is active, thus a_{RaC} cannot send a message, or because of the specification on a_{RaC}, which says that it does not make outgoing calls from within v_{GB}), and that in all possible next states again $\mathrm{ALWAYS}_{-\mathsf{ret}\, v_1} \mathrm{SPEC}'$ holds. Thus, proof search continues in the same way from these states, considering all possible computations, until all branches of the proof tree can be discharged, therewith concluding our proof.

Notice that the construction of the proof is exactly prescribed by the structure of the formula. Therefore we believe that having a tailored proof tool and well-developed proof strategies will help us to achieve a sufficiently high degree of automation in constructing the decomposition correctness proofs.

7   Conclusion and Future Work

This paper introduces a language-independent framework for the specification and verification of secure applet interactions in open platforms. It is shown that the framework can be instantiated to JavaCard and that it allows the decomposition of global properties about applet interactions into local properties of applets, as shown on a realistic case study.

Related Work. Our program models can alternatively be cast in terms of context-free processes; for these there exist algorithmic verification techniques *w.r.t.* modal μ-calculus specifications [4]. The development of our program model follows earlier work by Jensen *et al.* [11] which addresses security properties expressible as stack invariants. These form a strict subset of the properties which can be expressed in our framework, but allow for more efficient model checking procedures.

Future Work. Our primary objective is to complete our work on the proof system by studying completeness and decidability issues for suitable fragments of the logic. This is crucial for providing adequate automated tools for property decomposition. Further, we intend to combine such tools with off-the-shelf model checkers, so that local properties of applets can be checked automatically. We believe that such a combination will provide an effective environment to address further, more challenging, case studies.

In a different line of work, it would be of interest to enhance our model with data – so as to capture properties such as "Action Credit increases the balance of the Purse Component" – and with multi-threading, but the theoretical underpinnings of such extensions remain to be unveiled.

Acknowledgment

The authors would like to thank Christoph Sprenger at SICS and the anonymous referees for many useful remarks on the manuscript.

References

1. Bandera project. http://www.cis.ksu.edu/santos/bandera
2. G. Barthe, D. Gurov, and M. Huisman. Compositional specification and verification of control flow based security properties of multi-application programs. In *Proceedings of Workshop on Formal Techniques for Java Programs (FTfJP)*, 2001.

3. P. Bieber, J. Cazin, V. Wiels, G. Zanon, P. Girard, and J.-L. Lanet. Electronic purse applet certification: extended abstract. In S. Schneider and P. Ryan, editors, *Proceedings of the workshop on secure architectures and information flow*, volume 32 of *Elect. Notes in Theor. Comp. Sci.* Elsevier Publishing, 2000.
4. O. Burkart and B. Steffen. Model checking the full modal mu-calculus for infinite sequential processes. In *Proceedings of ICALP'97*, number 1256 in LNCS, pages 419–429, 1997.
5. A. Cimatti, E. Clarke, F. Giunchiglia, and M. Roveri. NuSMV: a new symbolic model checker. *Software Tools for Technology Transfer (STTT)*, 2/4:410–425, 2000.
6. J. Corbett, M. Dwyer, J. Hatcliff, and Robby. A language framework for expressing checkable properties of dynamic software. In K. Havelund, J. Penix, and W. Visser, editors, *SPIN Model Checking and Software Verification*, number 1885 in LNCS. Springer, 2000.
7. M. Dam and D. Gurov. Compositional verification of CCS processes. In D. Bjørner, M. Broy, and A.V. Zamulin, editors, *Proceedings of PSI'99*, number 1755 in LNCS, pages 247–256, 1999.
8. M. Dam and D. Gurov. μ-calculus with explicit points and approximations. *Journal of Logic and Computation*, 2001. To appear.
9. L.-å. Fredlund, D. Gurov, T. Noll, M. Dam, T. Arts, and G. Chugunov. A verification tool for Erlang. *Software Tools for Technology Transfer (STTT)*, 2002. To appear.
10. G. Holzmann. The model checker SPIN. *Transactions on Software Engineering*, 23(5):279–295, 1997.
11. T. Jensen, D. Le Métayer, and T. Thorn. Verification of control flow based security policies. In *Proceedings of the IEEE Symposium on Research in Security and Privacy*, pages 89–103. IEEE Computer Society Press, 1999.
12. D. Kozen. Results on the propositional μ-calculus. *Theoretical Computer Science*, 27:333–354, 1983.
13. X. Leroy. Java bytecode verification: an overview. In G. Berry, H. Comon, and A. Finkel, editors, *Proceedings of CAV'01*, number 2102 in LNCS, pages 265–285. Springer, 2001.
14. X. Leroy. On-card bytecode verification for JavaCard. In I. Attali and T. Jensen, editors, *Smart Card Programming and Security (E-Smart 2001)*, number 2140 in LNCS, pages 150–164. Springer, 2001.
15. S. Owre, J. Rushby, N. Shankar, and F von Henke. Formal verification for fault-tolerant architectures: Prolegomena to the design of PVS. *IEEE Transactions on Software Engineering*, 21(2):107–125, 1995.
16. A. Simpson. Compositionality via cut-elimination: Hennesy-Milner logic for an arbitrary GSOS. In *Proceedings of the Tenth Annual IEEE Symposium on Logic in Computer Science (LICS)*, pages 420–430, 1995.
17. G. Smith and D. Volpano. Secure information flow in a multi-threaded imperative language. In *Proceedings of POPL'98*, pages 355–364. ACM Press, 1998.

A Transition Rules

We use $\mathbf{loc}_a\, v$ as abbreviation for $\mathbf{app}\, v = a$.

Transition Rules for Composite States (With Symmetric Counterparts).

$$[\text{tau}] \quad \frac{\mathcal{A}_1 \xrightarrow{\tau} \mathcal{A}_1'}{\mathcal{A}_1 \mid \mathcal{A}_2 \xrightarrow{\tau} \mathcal{A}_1' \mid \mathcal{A}_2}$$

$$[\text{synchro}] \quad \frac{\mathcal{A}_1 \xrightarrow{v_1\, l?\, v_2} \mathcal{A}_1' \qquad \mathcal{A}_2 \xrightarrow{v_1\, l!\, v_2} \mathcal{A}_2'}{\mathcal{A}_1 \mid \mathcal{A}_2 \xrightarrow{v_1\, l\, v_2} \mathcal{A}_1' \mid \mathcal{A}_2'} \quad l \in \text{call}, \text{ret}$$

$$[\text{propagation}] \quad \frac{\mathcal{A}_1 \xrightarrow{v_1\, l?!\, v_2} \mathcal{A}_1' \qquad \neg \mathbf{loc}_{\mathcal{A}_2}\, v_1 \qquad \neg \mathbf{loc}_{\mathcal{A}_2}\, v_2}{\mathcal{A}_1 \mid \mathcal{A}_2 \xrightarrow{v_1\, l?!\, v_2} \mathcal{A}_1' \mid \mathcal{A}_2} \quad l \in \text{call}, \text{ret}$$

Applet Transition Rules.

$$[\text{local call}] \quad \frac{v_1 \xrightarrow{C} v_2 \qquad \mathbf{loc}_a\, v_1 \qquad \mathbf{loc}_a\, v_2}{a.\pi \cdot \langle v, v_1 \rangle \xrightarrow{v_1\, \text{call}\, v_2} a.\pi \cdot \langle v, v_1 \rangle \cdot \langle v_1, v_2 \rangle}$$

$$[\text{local return}] \quad \frac{v_1 \xrightarrow{T} v_2 \qquad \mathbf{loc}_a\, v_1 \qquad \mathbf{loc}_a\, v_3 \qquad \text{ret}\, v_3}{a.\pi \cdot \langle v, v_1 \rangle \cdot \langle v_1, v_3 \rangle \xrightarrow{v_3\, \text{ret}\, v_1} a.\pi \cdot \langle v, v_2 \rangle}$$

$$[\text{local transfer}] \quad \frac{v_1 \xrightarrow{T} v_2 \qquad \mathbf{loc}_a\, v_1 \qquad v_1 \not\xrightarrow{C}}{a.\pi \cdot \langle v, v_1 \rangle \longrightarrow a.\pi \cdot \langle v, v_2 \rangle}$$

$$[\text{send call}] \quad \frac{v_1 \xrightarrow{C} v_2 \qquad \mathbf{loc}_a\, v_1 \qquad \neg \mathbf{loc}_a\, v_2}{a.\pi \cdot \langle v, v_1 \rangle \xrightarrow{v_1\, \text{call!}\, v_2} a.\pi \cdot \langle v, v_1 \rangle \cdot \langle v_1, v_2 \rangle}$$

$$[\text{receive call}] \quad \frac{v_1 \xrightarrow{C} v_2 \qquad \neg \mathbf{loc}_a\, v_1 \qquad \mathbf{loc}_a\, v_2 \qquad \neg \text{active}\, a}{a.\pi \xrightarrow{v_1\, \text{call?}\, v_2} a.\pi \cdot \langle v_1, v_2 \rangle}$$

$$[\text{send return}] \quad \frac{\neg \mathbf{loc}_a\, v_1 \qquad \mathbf{loc}_a\, v_2 \qquad \text{ret}\, v_2}{a.\pi \cdot \langle v_1, v_2 \rangle \xrightarrow{v_2\, \text{ret!}\, v_1} a.\pi}$$

$$[\text{receive return}] \quad \frac{v_1 \xrightarrow{T} v_2 \qquad \mathbf{loc}_a\, v_1 \qquad \neg \mathbf{loc}_a\, v_3 \qquad \neg \mathbf{loc}_a\, v_4}{a.\pi \cdot \langle v, v_1 \rangle \cdot \langle v_1, v_3 \rangle \xrightarrow{v_4\, \text{ret?}\, v_1} a.\pi \cdot \langle v, v_2 \rangle}$$

B Remaining Proof Rules of the Proof System

Structural Rules.

$$(\text{Id}) \quad \frac{}{\Gamma, \gamma \vdash \gamma, \Delta}$$

$$(\text{Cut}) \quad \frac{\Gamma, \gamma \vdash \Delta \qquad \Gamma \vdash \gamma, \Delta}{\Gamma \vdash \Delta}$$

$$(\text{WeakL}) \quad \frac{\Gamma \vdash \Delta}{\Gamma, \gamma \vdash \Delta} \qquad\qquad (\text{WeakR}) \quad \frac{\Gamma \vdash \Delta}{\Gamma \vdash \gamma, \Delta}$$

Atomic Formula Rules.

$$(\text{EqSymL}) \; \frac{\Gamma, \, t_2 = t_1 \vdash \Delta}{\Gamma, \, t_1 = t_2 \vdash \Delta} \qquad (\text{EqReflR}) \; \frac{\cdot}{\Gamma \vdash t = t, \, \Delta}$$

$$(\text{EqSubstL}) \; \frac{\Gamma[t/x] \vdash \Delta[t/x]}{\Gamma, \, x = t \vdash \Delta}$$

$$(\text{EqNilL}) \; \frac{\cdot}{\Gamma, \, \epsilon = \Pi \cdot \langle v_1, v_2 \rangle \vdash \Delta}$$

$$(\text{EqConsL}) \; \frac{\Gamma, \, \Pi = \Pi', \, v_1 = v_1', \, v_2 = v_2' \vdash \Delta}{\Gamma, \, \Pi \cdot \langle v_1, v_2 \rangle = \Pi' \cdot \langle v_1', v_2' \rangle \vdash \Delta}$$

$$(\text{EqConsR}) \; \frac{\Gamma \vdash \Pi = \Pi', \, \Delta \qquad \Gamma \vdash v_1 = v_1', \, \Delta \qquad \Gamma \vdash v_2 = v_2', \, \Delta}{\Gamma \vdash \Pi \cdot \langle v_1, v_2 \rangle = \Pi' \cdot \langle v_1', v_2' \rangle, \, \Delta}$$

$$(\text{LocComL}) \; \frac{\Gamma, \, \text{local}_{\mathcal{A}_1} v \vdash \Delta \qquad \Gamma, \, \text{local}_{\mathcal{A}_2} v \vdash \Delta}{\Gamma, \, \text{local}_{\mathcal{A}_1 | \mathcal{A}_2} v \vdash \Delta}$$

$$(\text{LocComR}) \; \frac{\Gamma \vdash \text{local}_{\mathcal{A}_1} v, \, \text{local}_{\mathcal{A}_2} v, \, \Delta}{\Gamma \vdash \text{local}_{\mathcal{A}_1 | \mathcal{A}_2} v, \, \Delta}$$

Logical Rules.

$$(\text{PredL}) \; \frac{\Gamma, \, \sigma \vdash \Delta}{\Gamma, \, \mathcal{A} : \sigma \vdash \Delta} \qquad\qquad (\text{PredR}) \; \frac{\Gamma \vdash \sigma, \, \Delta}{\Gamma \vdash \mathcal{A} : \sigma, \, \Delta}$$

$$(\text{NotL}) \; \frac{\Gamma \vdash \mathcal{A} : \phi, \, \Delta}{\Gamma, \, \mathcal{A} : \neg \phi \vdash \Delta} \qquad\qquad (\text{NotR}) \; \frac{\Gamma, \, \mathcal{A} : \phi \vdash \Delta}{\Gamma \vdash \mathcal{A} : \neg \phi, \, \Delta}$$

$$(\text{AndL}) \; \frac{\Gamma, \, \mathcal{A} : \phi, \, \mathcal{A} : \psi \vdash \Delta}{\Gamma, \, \mathcal{A} : \phi \wedge \psi \vdash \Delta} \qquad (\text{AndR}) \; \frac{\Gamma \vdash \mathcal{A} : \phi, \, \Delta \qquad \Gamma \vdash \mathcal{A} : \psi, \, \Delta}{\Gamma \vdash \mathcal{A} : \phi \wedge \psi, \, \Delta}$$

$$(\text{AllL}) \; \frac{\Gamma, \, \mathcal{A} : \phi[t/x] \vdash \Delta}{\Gamma, \, \mathcal{A} : \forall x. \phi \vdash \Delta} \qquad (\text{AllR}) \; \frac{\Gamma \vdash \mathcal{A} : \phi, \, \Delta}{\Gamma \vdash \mathcal{A} : \forall x. \phi, \, \Delta} \; \text{fresh } x$$

$$(\text{BoxL}) \; \frac{\Gamma \vdash \mathcal{A} \xrightarrow{\alpha} \mathcal{A}', \, \Delta \qquad \Gamma, \, \mathcal{A}' : \phi \vdash \Delta}{\Gamma, \, \mathcal{A} : [\alpha] \phi \vdash \Delta} \qquad (\text{BoxR}) \; \frac{\Gamma, \, \mathcal{A} \xrightarrow{\alpha} \mathcal{X} \vdash \mathcal{X} : \phi, \, \Delta}{\Gamma \vdash \mathcal{A} : [\alpha] \phi, \, \Delta} \; \text{fresh } \mathcal{X}$$

Auxiliary Rules for Intersection.

$$(\text{IntR}) \; \frac{\cdot}{\Gamma \vdash \text{intersect}(a.\Pi_1, a.\Pi_2), \, \Delta} \qquad (\text{IntReflR}) \; \frac{\cdot}{\Gamma \vdash \text{intersect}(\mathcal{A}, \mathcal{A}), \, \Delta}$$

$$(\text{IntComL}) \; \frac{\Gamma, \, \text{intersect}(\mathcal{A}_1, \mathcal{A}_3) \vdash \Delta \qquad \Gamma, \, \text{intersect}(\mathcal{A}_2, \mathcal{A}_3) \vdash \Delta}{\Gamma, \, \text{intersect}(\mathcal{A}_1 \,|\, \mathcal{A}_2, \mathcal{A}_3) \vdash \Delta}$$

$$(\text{IntComR}) \; \frac{\Gamma \vdash \text{intersect}(\mathcal{A}_1, \mathcal{A}_3), \, \text{intersect}(\mathcal{A}_2, \mathcal{A}_3), \, \Delta}{\Gamma \vdash \text{intersect}(\mathcal{A}_1 \,|\, \mathcal{A}_2, \mathcal{A}_3), \, \Delta}$$

(with symmetric counterparts).

A Generic Component Framework
for System Modeling

Hartmut Ehrig[1], Fernando Orejas[2],
Benjamin Braatz[1], Markus Klein[1], and Martti Piirainen[1]

[1] Technische Universität Berlin
Franklinstrasse 28/29, 10587 Berlin, Germany
{ehrig,bbraatz,klein,martti}@cs.tu-berlin.de
[2] Universidad Politècnica de Catalunya
Campus Nord, Mòdul C6, Jordi Girona 1-3, 08034 Barcelona, Spain
orejas@lsi.upc.es

Abstract. The aim of this paper is to present a generic component framework for system modeling which is especially useful for a large class of graph- and net-based modeling techniques. Moreover, the framework is also flexible with respect to a hierarchical connection of components, providing a compositional semantics of components. This means more precisely that the semantics and internal correctness of a system can be inferred from the semantics of its components. In contrast to constructor-based component concepts for data type specification techniques, our component framework is based on a generic notion of transformations. Refinements and transformations are used to express intradependencies, between the export interface and the body of a component, and inter-dependencies, between the import and the export interfaces of different components. This is shown by a small case study on modeling Java threads by high-level Petri nets in this paper.

1 Introduction

It is becoming a standard practice in software development to base the design and implementation of component-based systems on architectures such as CORBA or COM+. In these architectures, components are generic in the sense that they are, to some extent, independent of specific programming languages. Unfortunately, components in these frameworks lack a precise semantics, making difficult to reason about this kind of systems. This is probably due to the fact that these approaches are mainly addressed to system implementation, but do not include the modeling phase.

1.1 Main Concepts and Results of this Paper

The aim of this paper is to present a generic component framework for system modeling that can be used for a large class of graph- and net-based modeling

R.-D. Kutsche and H. Weber (Eds.): FASE 2002, LNCS 2306, pp. 33–48, 2002.

techniques, but in principle also for other kinds of semi-formal and formal techniques. More precisely, we present in Sect. 2 a component concept based on a very general notion of specification. According to this concept, a component consists of a body and of an import and an export interface, connected in a suitable way, such that the import connection defines an inclusion from the import interface to the body, and the export connection defines a suitable transformation from the export interface to the body. These import and export connections represent the intradependencies between different parts of a single component. The interdependencies between import and export of different components are represented by connectors. Again, we only require connectors to define a suitable transformation. Consequently, our framework is also generic concerning the connection of components. The key concept of our framework is a generic notion of transformations of specifications, especially motivated by - but not limited to - rule based transformations in the sense of graph transformation and high-level replacement systems [8,5,19].

According to the general requirement that components are self contained units not only on the syntactical but also on the semantical level, we are able to define the semantics of each component independently of other components in the system. This semantics is also given in terms of transformations. It must be pointed out that this semantics can be used to give meaning to components based not only on a formal, but also on a semi-formal modeling technique. In this paper, however, we mainly consider graph- and net-based techniques. Moreover, our transformation semantics is shown to be compositional. More precisely, we are able to show that the semantics of a system can be inferred from that of its components.

In order to illustrate our concepts, we present in Sect. 3 a small case study where Java threads ([11]) are modeled by high-level Petri nets. A larger case study concerning a component-based telephone service center modeled by low-level Petri nets is given in [18], where the corresponding component concept is an instantiation of our generic framework. This and other kinds of instantiation are discussed in Sect. 4. A short summary and open problems are presented in Sect. 5.

1.2   Related Work

The generic component concept, presented in this paper, has been mainly motivated by the ideas in [15] for a component concept in the German BMBF project "Continuous Software Engineering" and by the module concepts for graph transformation systems in [20] and for Petri nets in [18]. In contrast to these concepts and that for UML [3] an important new aspect in our framework is the fact that we are able to give a self-contained, compositional semantics for each component. The syntactical level of the approaches in [20,18] is partly motivated by algebraic module specifications in [6]. The semantics of algebraic module specifications is based on free constructions between import and body part. This constructor-based semantics has been dropped in [18,20] for graph- and net-based modules, where the key concepts are now refinements between export and body parts.

This leads directly to our transformation-based component framework, where transformations include refinements and abstractions.

Although we mainly focus on our new component framework in this paper, we think that the concepts introduced here are a good basis for other interesting architectural issues. In this sense, we think that the papers [9,23,24,1] could be considered complementary to ours. In particular, the use of graph transformation techniques proposed by Fiadeiro in [23] and also by Löwe in [13] for architecture reconfiguration seems to be most promising, in view of a component concept for continuous software engineering, including software reconfiguration and evolutionary software development in the sense of [15].

2   Main Concepts for a Generic Component Framework

In this section, we present the main concepts for our generic component framework. We start with some general assumptions concerning our modeling technique, which is one of the key generic concepts in our framework.

2.1   Generic Modeling Techniques

We propose that a generic modeling technique is a general framework for describing systems. These descriptions have a syntactical part, consisting of specifications $SPEC$, and a semantical part, consisting of behavior or models of the corresponding specification. Moreover, it should be possible to deal with specific formal or semi-formal modeling approaches as concrete instances of the generic technique. A modeling technique is called formal, if the syntactical and semantical parts are mathematically well-defined. For a semi-formal technique we only require that the syntactical part is formalized, but the semantical part may only be given by informal documents, like natural language.

In order to express properties of behaviors or of models, we assume that we have a constraint language, which allows us to formulate constraints in an informal way, using diagrams or natural language, or in a formal way, based on some logical formalism. For simplicity we do not consider constraints explicitly in this paper.

From the software engineering point of view, we also require to have suitable horizontal and vertical structuring techniques. Especially in this paper we require a suitable notion of transformation including abstraction and refinement of specifications as special cases.

2.2   A Generic Component Concept

Components are self-contained modeling units, where some details are hidden to the external user. This is usually achieved by providing a clear separation between the interface of the component (what the external user, or other components, can "see") and the body (the detailed definition or implementation of the functionality provided by the component). Moreover, the interface can be divided into two parts: the import interface, describing what the component assumes about the environment (e.g. a description of the services provided by other components) and the export interface, describing the services provided by the component itself. Obviously, the import and export interfaces are connected to the body in some well-defined way.

In this sense, given a generic modeling technique with model specifications in the sense of 2.1, we are now able to define our *generic component concept*. A *component specification*, in short *component*,

$$COMP = (IMP, EXP, BOD, imp, exp)$$

consists of model specifications and connections:

- IMP, called *import interface*,
- EXP, called *export interface*,
- BOD, called *body*,
- $imp: IMP \to BOD$, called *import connection*,
- $exp: EXP \to BOD$, called *export connection*.

In order to be generic, we do not require any specific type of connections between interfaces and body. We only require that each export connection, $exp: EXP \to BOD$, uniquely defines a transformation of model specifications (see 2.3), $exp: EXP \Rightarrow BOD$, called export transformation. We assume that this transformation is a *refinement* describing how the elements presented in the export interface are implemented by the body. In other words the export is an *abstraction* of the body.

With respect to the import connection, we may assume that the body of a component is an extension of the import interface, in the sense that the functionality defined in the body is built upon the elements of the import interface. As a consequence, for the sake of simplicity, we assume that each import connection, $imp: IMP \to BOD$, defines an inclusion $imp: IMP \subseteq BOD$, of the corresponding specifications.

2.3   A Generic Transformation Concept

We need a generic transformation concept in order to formulate properties of export connections (see 2.2) and of connectors between import and export interfaces of different components (see 2.5, below). Again, we will try to be as general as possible.

We assume that a transformation framework $\mathcal{T}$ consists of a class of transformations, which includes identical transformations, is closed under composition and satisfies the following *extension property*: For each transformation $trafo: SPEC_1 \Rightarrow SPEC_2$, and each inclusion $i_1: SPEC_1 \subseteq SPEC_1'$ there is a selected transformation $trafo': SPEC_1' \Rightarrow SPEC_2'$, with inclusion $i_2: SPEC_2 \subseteq SPEC_2'$, called the *extension* of $trafo$ with respect to i_1, leading to the extension diagram in Fig. 1.

$$SPEC_1 \xoverset{trafo}{\Longrightarrow} SPEC_2$$

$$\Bigg\uparrow i_1 \qquad\qquad \Bigg\uparrow i_2$$

$$SPEC_1' \xoverset{trafo'}{\Longrightarrow} SPEC_2'$$

Fig. 1. Extension diagram for the extension property

It must be pointed out that, in a given framework, given $trafo$ and i_1 as above, there may be several $trafo'$ and i_2, that could satisfy this extension property. However, our assumption means that, in the given framework $\mathcal{T}$ only one such $trafo'$ and one inclusion i_2 are chosen, in some well-defined way, as the extension of $trafo$ with respect to i_1.

The idea underlying this extension property is to ask a transformation framework to satisfy, what we may call, a locality assumption: if one can apply a transformation on a certain specification, then it should be possible to apply the "same" transformation on a larger specification. This assumption has been formulated, in a more precise way in [16]. In this paper, for the sake of simplicity, we have avoided the technical details.

We could have also required that these extensions would only exist when the given $trafo$ is consistent with i_1 in a specific sense. For instance, in the case of graph transformations, the extension property corresponds to the embedding of a transformation into a larger context. The corresponding embedding theorem in [8] requires that the "boundary" of i_1 has to be preserved by $trafo$. Again, for the sake of simplicity, in this paper we drop this consistency condition.

If transformations and inclusions of specifications can be considered as suitable morphisms in a category of specifications, then the extension diagram may be a pushout in this category. In general, however, the extension diagram is not required to be a pushout. Especially the embedding of graph transformations discussed above does not lead to a pushout in general.

2.4   Transformation Semantics of Components

According to general requirements, components should be self-contained units, with respect to syntax and semantics. Hence, it is necessary to have a semantics for each single component. Moreover, the semantics of composite components (and, eventually, the entire system) must be inferred from that of single components. In this subsection, we propose a semantics of components satisfying these requirements.

The most standard way of defining the semantics of a given component concept consists in considering that the meaning of a component is some kind of function mapping models of the import to models of the export interface like in the case of algebraic module specifications ([6]). Unfortunately, this kind of semantics is not adequate for our purposes in this paper. There are two main problems. On one hand, this kind of semantics assumes that the specifications involved in a component have a well-defined model semantics. This is true in the case of a formal modeling technique, but not in the case of a semi-formal one. On the other hand, this kind of semantics implicitly assumes that the import interface of a component is a loose specification having more than one model (otherwise, if the import has just one model the function associated to a component becomes trivial). However, this is not the case for components used in connection with most graph- and net-based modeling techniques. For instance, as can be seen in our small case study, the import interface of a Petri net component is a Petri net, which one would typically consider to define a single model.

The solution provided for these problems is a semantics that takes into account the environment of a component, in a similar way as the continuation semantics of a programming language assigns the meaning of a program statement in terms of the environment of the statement. Here, the idea is to think that, what characterizes the import interface of a component is not its class of models, but the possible refinements or transformations of this interface that we can find in the environment of the component. In this sense, it is natural to consider that the semantical effect of a component is the combination of each possible import transformation, $trafo\colon IMP \Rightarrow SPEC$, with the export transformation $exp\colon EXP \Rightarrow BOD$ of the component. Since IMP is included in BOD, we have to extend the import transformation from IMP to BOD in order to be able to compose both transformations. Due to the extension property for transformations, we obtain $trafo'\colon BOD \Rightarrow SPEC'$, as shown in Fig. 2.

$$
\begin{array}{ccccc}
EXP & \overset{exp}{\Longrightarrow} & BOD & \overset{trafo'}{\Longrightarrow} & SPEC' \\
 & & \uparrow{\scriptstyle imp} & & \uparrow{\scriptstyle imp'} \\
 & & IMP & \overset{trafo}{\Longrightarrow} & SPEC
\end{array}
$$

Fig. 2. Transformation semantics

Let us call the class of all transformations $trafo\colon IMP \Rightarrow SPEC$ from IMP to some specification $SPEC$ the *transformation semantics* of IMP, denoted by $Trafo(IMP)$, and similar for EXP. According to Fig. 2 the *transformation semantics* of the component $COMP$ can be considered as a function

$$TrafoSem(COMP)\colon Trafo(IMP) \to Trafo(EXP)$$

defined for all $trafo \in Trafo(IMP)$, by $TrafoSem(COMP)(trafo) = trafo' \circ exp \in Trafo(EXP)$.

It may be pointed out that the two problems mentioned above are now solved. On one hand, semiformal modeling techniques may include precise notions of transformation or refinements (the case of visual modeling techniques is briefly discussed in Sect. 4.4). Similarly, a Petri net may have just one model, but it may be refined in many different ways. Therefore, in both cases, there would not be a problem to define a transformation semantics for these kinds of components.

2.5   Composition of Components

Several different operations on components can be considered in our generic framework. Depending on the underlying architecture intended for a given system, some specific operations may be needed. For instance, in a hierarchical system one could need an operation to compose components by matching the import of one (or more) components with the export of other component(s). On the contrary, on a non-hierarchical system one may need an operation of circular composition, where the components of a system are connected in a non-hierarchical way. Especially connectors in the sense of [1] and the architectural description language WRIGHT should be considered in this context.

In the following, for the sake of simplicity, we only consider one basic operation, which allows one to compose components $COMP_1$ and $COMP_2$ by providing a *connector, connect*: $IMP_1 \to EXP_2$, from the import interface IMP_1 of $COMP_1$ to the export interface EXP_2 of $COMP_2$. Similar to an export connection, we only require that the connector uniquely defines a transformation *connect*: $IMP_1 \Rightarrow EXP_2$.

Different generalizations and variations of this operation, for instance by allowing to compose (simultaneously) several components, would not pose too many difficulties, only some additional technical complication. Circular composition may be more difficult to handle, however previous experience in dealing with module operations (see e.g. [6]) would provide good guidelines.

Now, we are able to define the composition

$$COMP_3 = COMP_1 \circ_{connect} COMP_2$$

as follows. Let $xconnect = exp_2 \circ connect$. The extension property implies a unique extension $xconnect'$: $BOD_1 \Rightarrow BOD_3$, with inclusion imp'_1: $BOD_2 \subseteq BOD3$ in Fig. 3. The composition $COMP_3$ is now defined by

$$COMP_3 = (IMP_3, EXP_3, BOD_3, imp_3, exp_3)$$

with $imp_3 = imp'_1 \circ imp_2$ and $exp_3 = xconnect' \circ exp_1$. Since we have $IMP_3 = IMP_2$ and $EXP_3 = EXP_1$, this means especially that the result of the composition concerning the interfaces is independent of the body parts.

Note, that each connector *connect*: $IMP_1 \to EXP_2$ can also be considered as a separate component $COMP_{12}$ with $exp_{12} = connect$ and $imp_{12} = id_{EXP_2}$. This allows to consider $COMP_3$ in Fig. 3 as the composition of three components $COMP_1$, $COMP_{12}$ and $COMP_2$, where all connectors are identities.

2.6   Compositionality of Transformation Semantics

Given a connector, *connect*: $IMP_1 \to EXP_2$, between IMP_1 of $COMP_1$ and EXP_2 of $COMP_2$, the composition $COMP_3$ of these components via *connect* is well-defined, and we have the following compositionality result:

$$TrafoSem(COMP_3) =$$
$$TrafoSem(COMP_1) \circ Trafo(connect) \circ TrafoSem(COMP_2)$$

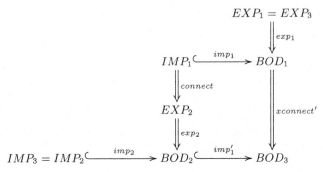

Fig. 3. Composition of Components

where $Trafo(connect)(trafo) = trafo \circ connect$. This means that the transformation semantics of the composition $COMP_3$ can be obtained by functional composition of the transformation semantics of $COMP_1$ and $COMP_2$ with a most simple intermediate function

$$Trafo(connect): Trafo(EXP_2) \to Trafo(IMP_1)$$

defined above.

In order to prove this important compositionality result, we only need to require that the extension property for transformations is closed under horizontal and vertical composition. This essentially means that the horizontal and vertical composition of extension diagrams, as given in Fig. 2, is again an extension diagram. This is very similar – and in some instantiations equal – to the well-known horizontal and vertical composition of pushouts in Category Theory.

3   Modeling Java Threads with Components in the Framework of High-Level Nets

As a small case study we will model a few aspects of the behavior of threads in the programming language Java with algebraic high-level Petri nets. For a larger case study we refer to [18]. An overview reference for Java threads is given in [11].

We use a notation where an algebraic high-level net N consists of an algebraic signature $\Sigma_N = (S, OP, X)$ with sorts S, operation symbols OP and variables X, a Σ_N-algebra A_N and a Petri net, where each place pl has a type $type(pl) \in S$, the in- and outgoing arcs of a transition tr are inscribed with multisets of terms over Σ_N and a transition tr itself is inscribed with a set of equations over Σ_N. In our example, however, we only use single terms as arc inscriptions and do not use equations for transitions.

We use a transformation concept similar to [17] based on rules and double pushouts in a suitable category of high-level nets. In our example we directly present the corresponding high-level net transformations. The extension property is satisfied because the redex of a rule applied to a net is preserved by the inclusion into another net. The application of the rule to the larger net yields the extended transformation.

Our small case study consists of two components $COMP_1$ and $COMP_2$ leading to a composition $COMP_3$ as shown in Fig. 3.

3.1   Implementation of the Run-Method

In the first component $COMP_1$, we define a rough model of the lifecycle of a thread in the export, and refine it in the body by adding a *run*-transition that represents the execution of the thread. This step corresponds to the extension of the **Thread**-class by a class implementing a **run**-method.

The export signature Σ_{EXP_1} consists of one sort *Thread* and two constant symbols $thread_1: \to Thread$ and $thread_2: \to Thread$ representing two different threads of control. The net structure of the export interface is shown in Fig. 4. The type of all places is *Thread* and all arcs are inscribed with the variable t of sort *Thread*.

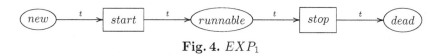

Fig. 4. EXP_1

The export interface corresponds to the fact that the class **Thread** has a **start**-method which makes a newly created thread runnable and a **stop**-method which kills a runnable thread:

```
public class Thread {
    public void start() { ... }
    public void stop() { ... }
    ...
}
```

The export transformation $exp_1: EXP_1 \Rightarrow BOD_1$ refines the signature by adding a sort *RunState* representing the states that can occur during the execution of **run**, a sort *Object* representing the states an arbitrary object can be in, operations $st: Thread\,Object \to RunState$ and $con: \to Object$ and an operation $do: Object \to Object$ representing the run-time changes to the object. The net structure is refined by removing the *stop*-transition and adding places *started* and *finished* of type *RunState* and transitions *run* and *exit*. The details can be found in Fig. 5. We have replaced the *stop*-transition by an *exit*-transition because now the thread can exit normally by completing its task. This is modeled by the *run*-transition that transfers the *RunState* from *started* to *finished*.

The addition of the *run*-transition corresponds to the implementation of the **run**-method and the *Object* in the constructor st of *RunState* to the existence of an attribute object that is changed by the **run**-method:

```
class MyThread extends Thread {
```

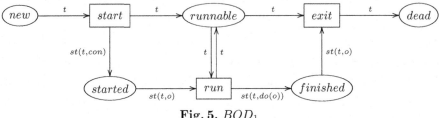

Fig. 5. BOD_1

```
    Object anObject;
    public void run() { ... }
}
```

In the import interface (Fig. 6) only the *run*-transition and the adjacent places are kept, because this transition is useful to be further refined.

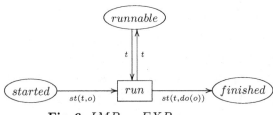

Fig. 6. $IMP_1 = EXP_2$

3.2   Further Refinement of the Method

In the second component $COMP_2$ the *run*-transition is refined by a model with two phases. The export interface EXP_2 is the same net as the import interface IMP_1 of $COMP_1$. The export transformation $exp_2: EXP_2 \Rightarrow BOD_2$ adds two new operations $do1, do2: Object \rightarrow Object$ to the signature. The *run*-transition is removed and replaced by two new transitions *act1* and *act2* with an intermediate place *working* (see Fig. 7). We assume that the algebra A_{BOD_2} satisfies the equation $do2(do1(o)) = do(o)$ because sequential firing of *act1* and *act2* should still produce the same result as before.

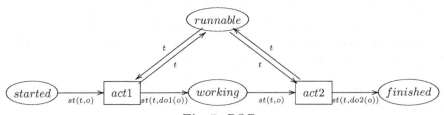

Fig. 7. BOD_2

This replacement corresponds to a further extension of `MyThread`, where the `run`-method is overwritten with a method that does the same by calling two sequential actions:

```
class MyThread2 extends MyThread {
    public void run() {
        act1();
        act2();
    }
    private void act1() { ... }
    private void act2() { ... }
}
```

The import interface IMP_2 could consist of the whole body, if both transitions should be refined further, but to make it more interesting, we assume that $act1$ is already an atomic action and only $act2$ shall be refined. This leads to an import (Fig. 8) with only the transition $act2$ and the adjacent places.

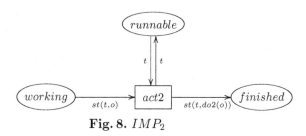

Fig. 8. IMP_2

3.3   Composition of the Components

The composition of the two components $COMP_1$ and $COMP_2$ presented above with identical connection from IMP_1 to EXP_2 yields a component $COMP_3$ with $EXP_3 = EXP_1$, $IMP_3 = IMP_2$ and a body BOD_3 (Fig. 9) resulting from application of the rule underlying exp_2 to the net BOD_1, replacing the transition run by $act1$ and $act2$.

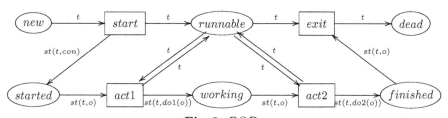

Fig. 9. BOD_3

4   Instantiations of the Generic Component Framework

We have pointed out, already, that our component framework is generic with respect to several aspects. First of all, it is generic with respect to the technique used for system modeling. Secondly, it is generic with respect to the semantics of components and with respect to the composition operation, using a generic notion of connector, where the semantics and the connectors are based on a generic notion of transformation.

In this section, we discuss instantiations of the generic component framework leading to existing and new component concepts for different kinds of Petri nets and graph transformations, as well as some ideas for other visual modeling techniques, like UML.

4.1   Instantiations of Transformations

Transformation and refinement concepts have been developed for a great variety of data type and process modeling techniques in the literature. In the following, we will focus on algebraic graph transformation concepts and transformation of high-level structures [8,5]. The extension property for transformations formulated in Sect. 2 is well-known, as an embedding theorem, in the case of algebraic graph transformations based on the double pushout approach. This approach has been generalized to the categorical framework of high-level structures, including low- and high-level Petri nets. Several concepts and results for algebraic graph transformations have been generalized to the categorical framework of high-level structures and replacement systems, including a basic version of the embedding theorem. The horizontal and vertical composition property, required in 2.6, can be shown under suitable assumptions for high-level replacement systems and instantiated for Petri nets and other modeling techniques. Explicit examples of transformations in the case of algebraic high-level nets are given in our small case study in Sect. 3.

4.2   Component Concepts for Low- and High-Level Petri Nets

Various kinds of Petri nets are suitable for our framework. Rule-based transformations of Petri nets, in the sense of graph transformations and high-level replacement systems, can be used as instantiation of transformations in the generic component concept of Sect. 2. In fact, two different kinds of Petri nets have been considered for the formal instantiation: place/transition nets and algebraic high-level nets. But, also, other kinds of low-level and high-level nets are suitable. A specific example of components, in the case of algebraic high-level nets, has been given in Sect. 3, including composition of components. This component concept for high-level Petri nets is closely related to the component concepts for low-level Petri nets presented in [18]. In fact, refinements of transitions, in the sense of [18], are closely related to rule-based transformations of Petri nets, where the left-hand side of the rule consists of a single transition only. This means that the larger case study in [18], in the application domain of telephone services, is another example of our component concept.

4.3   Component Concepts for Graph Transformation Systems

Similar to the case of Petri nets discussed above, also different kinds of graph transformation systems are suitable for our framework. M. Simeoni ([20]) has considered a notion of refinement for graph transformation systems, which is used as export connection between the graph transformation systems in the export and in the body part. It should be pointed out that a refinement of graph transformation systems is conceptually different from a refinement or transformation of graphs. Actually, the structures to be refined or transformed in the first case are graph transformation systems, i.e., a set of graph productions, while the structures are graphs in the second case. In fact the refinements of graph transformation systems, in the sense of [20], can be considered as transformations in the sense of 2.3, because they are shown to satisfy the extension property. More precisely, it is shown in [20] that the corresponding category of refinements has pushouts, if at least one morphism is an inclusion. This property is shown for typed algebraic graph transformation systems ([10]) and local action systems in the sense of [12]. In both cases this means that the extension diagram is a special kind of pushout considered in [20]. This means that these two module concepts for graph transformation systems with interesting examples in [20] can be considered as different instantiations and examples of our generic component concept. In [7] we discussed already an extension towards attributed graph transformations ([14]) which leads now to a new component concept for this case. It has to be checked how far other module concepts for different kinds of graph transformation systems fit into our framework.

4.4   Towards a Component Concept for Visual Modeling Techniques

As shown by R. Bardohl [2], a large number of visual modeling techniques can be formulated in the framework of GENGED, based on attributed graph transformations ([14]). It is shown how attributed graph transformations can be used to define transformations of visual sentences for different visual modeling techniques. This seems to be a good basis to define a component concept for visual modeling techniques as instantiations of the general framework presented in this paper. This applies especially to the different diagram formalisms of the UML ([22]), where already suitable simplified versions of class diagrams and statecharts have been considered in the framework of GENGED.

More directly, there are already suitable refinement and transformation concepts for different kinds of UML techniques, which might be used as transformations in the sense of our generic component concept. However, it remains open which of these transformation concepts satisfy our extension property in order to obtain other interesting instantiations of our component concept. In particular, in [4], a transformation concept for statecharts has been introduced, which can be considered as an instantiation of transformations for high-level replacement systems, as discussed in 4.1. This seems to be a good basis for a component concept for statecharts.

5   Conclusion

We have presented a generic component framework for system modeling. This framework is generic in the sense that it can be instantiated by different system modeling techniques, especially by graph- and net-based integrated data type and process techniques. Moreover, it is based on a generic transformation concept, which is used to express intra- and interdependencies of interfaces and bodies of components.

Our proposed framework meets to a large extent the requirements stated in [15] for a component concept for continuous software engineering. Due to lack of space, in this paper we just study a simple operation of (hierarchical) composition of components. However, we have already studied a union operation for components and our experience on algebraic specification modules provides good guidelines to define other more complex operations like, for instance, circular composition. Moreover, it remains open to extend our framework to architectural issues in the sense of [9,23,13,24,1] discussed in the introduction and Sect. 2.5.

We have defined components not only as syntactical, but also as self contained semantical units. This allows to obtain the important result that our semantics based on transformations is compositional.

In our paper [7] we have given a conceptual and formal framework for the integration of data type and process modeling techniques. In a forthcoming paper we will show how this framework can be combined with our component approach in this paper leading to a component framework for a generic integrated modeling technique with special focus on different kinds of constraints.

Finally let us point out again that our generic framework is suitable not only for formal graph- and net-based modeling techniques mainly discussed in this paper, but also for other formal and semi-formal techniques. However, it remains open to tailor our framework to specific requirements for visual modeling techniques including UML and to relate it to existing capsulation, package and component concepts for some of these techniques ([3]).

Acknowledgments

This work is partially supported by the German DFG project IOSIP within the DFG priority program "Integration of Software Specification Techniques for Applications in Engineering", the German BMBF project on "Continuous Software Engineering" and by the Spanish project HEMOSS (TIC 98-0949-C02-01). We would like to thank the FASE 2002 referees for several valuable comments leading to a much more comprehensive paper.

References

1. R. Allen, D. Garlan. A Formal Basis for Architectural Connection. In *ACM TOSEM'97*, pp. 213–249.
2. R. Bardohl. GENGED – *Visual Definition of Visual Languages Based on Algebraic Graph Transformation*. PhD Thesis, TU Berlin, Verlag Dr. Kovac, Germany (1999).
3. J. Cheesman, J. Daniels. *UML Components*. Addison-Wesley (2001).
4. H. Ehrig, R. Geisler, M. Klar, J. Padberg. Horizontal and Vertical Structuring for Statecharts. In *Proc. CONCUR'97*, Springer LNCS 1301 (1997), pp. 327–343.
5. H. Ehrig, A. Habel, H.-J. Kreowski, F. Parisi-Presicce. Prallelism and Concurrency in High-Level Replacement Systems. In *Math. Struct. in Comp. Science 1*. Cambridge Univ. Press (1991), pp. 361–404.
6. H. Ehrig, B. Mahr. *Fundamentals of Algebraic Specification 2: Module Specifications and Constraints*, vol. 21 of *EATCS Monographs on Theor. Comp. Science*. Springer Verlag, Berlin (1990).
7. H. Ehrig and F. Orejas. A Conceptual and Formal Framework for the Integration of Data Type and Process Modeling Techniques. In *Proc. GT-VMT 2001, ICALP 2001 Satellite Workshop*. Heraclion, Greece (2001), pp. 201–228. Also in *Electronic Notes in Theor. Comp. Science 50,3* (2001).
8. H. Ehrig, M. Pfender, H. Schneider. Graph Grammars: An Algebraic Approach. In *Proc. SWAT'73*, pp.167 - 180.
9. J.L. Fiadero, A. Lopes. Semantics of Architectural Connectors. In *Proc. TAPSOFT'97, Springer LNCS 1214* (1997), pp. 505–519.
10. R. Heckel, A. Corradini, H. Ehrig, M. Löwe. Horizontal and Vertical Structuring of Typed Graph Transformation Systems. In *MSCS, vol. 6* (1996), pp. 613–648.
11. Cay S. Horstmann, Gary Cornell. *Core Java 2. Volume II – Advanced Features*. Sun Microsystems Press, Prentice Hall PTR (2000).
12. D. Janssens, N. Verlinden. A Framework for ESM and NLC: Local Action Systems. In *Springer LNCS 1764* (2000), pp. 194–214.
13. M. Löwe. Evolution Patterns. In *Proc. Conf. on Systemics, Cybernetics and Informatics 1999, vol. II*, pp. 110–117.
14. M. Löwe, M. Korff, A. Wagner. An Algebraic Framework for the Transformation of Attributed Graphs. In *Term Graph Rewriting: Theory and Practice* (1993), chapter 14, pp. 185–199.
15. S. Mann, B. Borusan, H. Ehrig, M. Große-Rhode, R. Mackenthun, A. Sünbül, H. Weber. Towards a Component Concept for Continuous Software Engineering. FhG-ISST Report 55/00 (2000).
16. F. Orejas, H. Ehrig, E. Pino. Tight and Loose Semantics for Transformation Systems. To appear in *Proc. Workshop on Algebraic Development Techniques 2001, Springer LNCS*. Genova, Italy (2001).
17. J. Padberg, H. Ehrig, L. Ribeiro. Algebraic High-Level Net Transformation Systems. In *Math. Struct. in Comp. Science 5*. Cambridge Univ. Press (1995), pp. 217–256.
18. J. Padberg, K. Hoffmann, M. Buder, A. Sünbül. Petri Net Modules for Component-Based Software Engineering. Technical Report, TU Berlin, 2001.
19. G. Rozenberg, editor. *Handbook of Graph Grammars and Computing by Graph Transformations, Volume 1: Foundations*. World Scientific, Singapore (1997).
20. M. Simeoni. *A Categorical Approach to Modularization of Graph Transformation Systems using Refinements*. PhD thesis, Dip. di Scienze dell'Informazione, Università di Roma La Sapienza (2000). Condensed version to appear in JCSS.

21. C. Szyperski. *Component Software – Beyond Object-Oriented Programming.* Addison-Wesley (1997).
22. *Unified Modeling Language – version 1.3* (2000). Available at http://www.omg.org/uml.
23. M. Wermelinger, A. Lopes, J.L. Fiadero. A Graph Based Architectural Reconfiguration Language. In *Proc. ESEC/FSE 2001.* ACM Press (2001).
24. A.M. Zaremski, J.M. Wing. Specification Matching of Software Components. In *ACM TOSEM'97*, pp. 333–369.

Implementing Condition/Event Nets in the Circal Process Algebra

Antonio Cerone

Software Verification Research Centre
The University of Queensland, QLD 4072, Australia
Phone +61-7-3365-1651, Fax +61-7-3365-1533
antonio@svrc.uq.edu.au
http://www.itee.uq.edu.au/~antonio/

Abstract. We define a translation from Condition/Event nets to the Circal process algebra. Such a translation exploits the Circal feature of allowing the simultaneous occurrence of distinct actions. This permits us to give Condition/Event nets a semantics based on true concurrency, in addition to the interleaving-based semantics. In this way the true concurrency aspects of Condition/Event nets are preserved in the process algebra representation and can be analysed using the verification facilities provided by the Circal System. Systems modelled partly using Condition/Event nets partly using the Circal process algebra can also be analysed within the same verification environment.

1 Introduction

Petri nets and process algebras are very popular formalisms used for modelling and verifying concurrent systems. However, they express different modelling styles, have different underlying semantics and different mathematical and graphical representations, and are associated with different analysis techniques.

In this paper, we define a translation from Condition/Events nets (C/E nets) [20,19], a subclass of Petri nets where every place contains at most one token, to the Circal process algebra [13]. Among the many process algebras available we have chosen Circal because of its distinctive feature of having processes guarded by sets of actions, rather than by single actions, as in all other process algebras [2,12,14]. Having events consisting of simultaneously occurring actions allows the representation of true concurrency and causality, which is explicit in Petri net based formalisms such as C/E nets.

The paper is structured as follows. In Section 2 we motivate our approach. Section 3 is a brief introduction to C/E nets. In Section 4 we present the Circal process algebra and its implementation, the XCircal language. Our framework for modelling Petri nets is presented in Section 5. Techniques for analysing properties of C/E nets modelled in the Circal process algebra are presented in Section 6. Finally, Section 7 highlights the novelty of this work and discusses the extension of our approach to Place/Transition nets.

R.-D. Kutsche and H. Weber (Eds.): FASE 2002, LNCS 2306, pp. 49–63, 2002.
© Springer-Verlag Berlin Heidelberg 2002

2   Background and Motivation

Condition/Events nets (C/E nets) [20,19], allow the modelling of finite state systems and are, therefore, as expressive as Finite State Machines (FSMs). However, FSMs have a global control, which describes a sequential behaviour, whereas C/E nets have a distributed control, which is defined by distinct tokens being in distinct places at the same time, so allowing an explicit representation of causality.

FSMs have been extended with higher level constructs, which allow the association of complex conditions or statements to states and transitions and the representation of structured data types, and with compositional mechanisms.

Process algebras [2,12,13,14] can be seen as mathematical formalisms for describing systems of concurrent, interacting FSMs. That is a way of giving compositionality to FSMs. The behaviour of the composite system is, however, still defined by a global FSM, where the concurrency among different components is expressed as non-deterministic interleaving. Therefore, the distributed aspects of the system specification do not appear in the behaviour of the composite system.

Petri nets, instead, do not support compositionality. Every attempt to introduce compositionality into Petri nets has resulted in a very restricted form of composition, which is not very useful in system design.

Both FSMs and Petri nets have visual representations, which make them attractive modelling tools also for those system designers who are not familiar with formal specification languages and techniques. Moreover, due to their different characteristics, FSMs and Petri nets are useful in modelling different aspects of the same system.

Let us consider, for example, a process control application. Petri nets are the appropriate formalism for specifying the distributed control of the whole system or the protocol that governs the communication among the system components. On the other hand system modes and system components might be easily specified by FSMs. A similar situation occurs in modelling asynchronous hardware [6,8]. Gate-level or CMOS-level components are easily specified by finite state machines, whereas the asynchronous handshaking control protocol is usually modelled by Signal Transition Graphs (STGs) [10], a subclass of Petri nets. In both examples the Petri net-based part of the specification is usually finite state, and may be modelled by C/E nets.

Among the many existing formal methods automatic tools [11], none is able to manage system specifications consisting of a combination of Petri nets and FSMs. Properties of the system which involve both aspects of the sub-systems modelled by Petri nets and aspects of the sub-systems modelled by FSMs cannot be analysed using such tools. This is the case for fundamental correctness properties, such as the correctness of the circuitry implementation, modelled by an FSM, of an asynchronous handshaking control protocol with respect to its specification, modelled by an STG. This property has been automatically verified by defining a translation from STGs to the Circal process algebra [13], the FSM-based formalism used to model the circuit implementation, and then feeding the specification and implementation models to the Circal System, an automatic verification tool based on the Circal process algebra [6,8].

3   Condition/Event Nets

Petri nets are an abstract formal model of information flow. They were introduced by Carl Adam Petri in 1962 [18]. The basic notion in *Petri net theory* is the notion of a *net*, which is usually described as a triple $\langle S, T, F \rangle$ [19]. Sets S and T are disjoint and are called the set of *places* and the set of *transitions*, respectively. $F \subseteq (S \times T) \cup (T \times S)$ is a binary relation called the *flow relation*.

The basic notion of net is given a state, which is called a *marking* and is an assignment of *tokens* to places. Depending on the number of tokens that can be assigned to the same place and on the possible information carried by a token we can have different classes of Petri nets [19,20]. The dynamic behaviour of a Petri net is given by transition *firings*, which consume and produce tokens.

Condition/Event nets (C/E nets) are Petri nets where tokens are just markers for places and every place contains at most one token [20]. In a C/E net, places are called *conditions*, transitions are called *events* and markings, which are defined as the sets of places that are marked by one token, are called *cases*.

A C/E net is defined as a quadruple $N = \langle B, E, F, C \rangle$ such that $\langle B, E, F \rangle$ is a net and $C \subseteq B$ is a case.

A condition $b \in B$ is a *precondition* of an event $e \in E$ if and only if $(b, e) \in F$. A condition $b \in B$ is a *postcondition* of an event $e \in E$ if and only if $(e, b) \in F$.

An example of C/E net $N_1 = \langle B_1, E_1, F_1, C_1 \rangle$ is given in Figure 1(a). In the

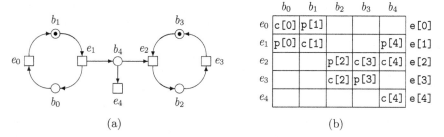

	b_0	b_1	b_2	b_3	b_4	
e_0	c[0]	p[1]				e[0]
e_1	p[0]	c[1]		p[4]		e[1]
e_2			p[2]	c[3]	c[4]	e[2]
e_3			c[2]	p[3]		e[3]
e_4					c[4]	e[4]

(a)   (b)

Fig. 1. (a): A C/E net N_1 defining a producer-consumer system; (b): Correspondence between conditions and events of N_1 and Circal actions

pictorial representation, conditions are represented as circles, events are represented as boxes, with arrows from circles to boxes and from boxes to circles defining the flow relation. Tokens are represented by solid circles, each inside the place to which it is assigned.

C/E net N_1 defines an *unreliable producer-consumer system*. The producer consists of conditions b_0 and b_1 and events e_0 and e_1. When b_0 is marked by a token the producer is ready to produce, and event e_0 models the production of a message; when b_1 is marked the producer is ready to send, and event e_1 models the sending of a message. The consumer consists of conditions b_2 and b_3 and events e_2 and e_3. When b_3 is marked the consumer is ready to receive, and event e_2 models the receiving of a message; when b_2 is marked the consumer is ready to consume, and event e_3 models the consumption of a message. Condition b_4

models a 1-cell buffer between the producer and the receiver. Event e_4 models the loss of the message from the buffer.

4   The Circal Process Algebra

In this section we give a brief description of the the Circal process algebra and the Circal System [13,15].

Each Circal *process* has associated with it a *sort*, which specifies the set of actions through which it may interact with other processes. Every sort will be a non-empty subset of $\mathcal{A}$, the collection of all available actions.

The *behaviour* of a process is defined in terms of the $/\backslash$ constant and the operators of *guarding*, *external choice*, and *internal choice* (*behavioural operators*).

The $/\backslash$ constant represents a process which can participate in no communication. This is a process that has terminated or deadlocked.

In guarded process Γ P the P process may be guarded by a set Γ of simultaneously occurring actions. This is a key feature of Circal which greatly enriches the modelling potential of the algebra in contrast to process algebras such as CSP [12], CCS [14] and LOTOS [2], which only permit a single action to occur at one computation instant.

A name can be given to a Circal process with the *definition* operator (<-). Recursive process definitions, such as P <- Γ P, are permitted.

The + operator defines an *external choice*, which is decided by the environment where the process is executed, whereas the & operator defines an *internal choice*, which is decided autonomously by the process itself without any influence from its environment. Internal choices appear to an external observer as *non-determinism*.

The *structure* of a process is defined in terms of the operators of *composition* and *hiding* (*structural operators*).

Given processes P and Q, the term P * Q represents the process which can perform the actions of the subterms P and Q together (*composition*). Any synchronisation which can be made between two terms, due to some action being common to the sorts of both subterms, must be made, otherwise the actions of the subterms may occur asynchronously.

Term P - a b defines the *hiding* of actions a and b from process P.

The Circal process algebra has been extended with additional features and resulted in the XCircal language, which is implemented by the Circal System [13]. In XCircal the application of the structural operators (composition and hiding) needs to be explicitly enforced using the ˜ operator. XCircal has the usual primitive data types, such as int for the integers and bool for the booleans. There are also two datatypes which define *events* and *processes*.

The Event data-type implements sets of actions. Atomic events, which are events consisting of a single action, must be declared before the use.

Event a, b, c[2]

The line above is the declaration of two events a, b and an array c of two events, c[0] and c[1]. An event consisting of the set of actions a, b is represented in

Circal as (a b). Singletons may be shortened by removing the parentheses. Thus a is the same as (a).

In the following an object of type **Event** will be called a *set of actions* (or an *action*, if it is a singleton) rather than an *event*, and the word *event* will be reserved to the C/E net concept to avoid ambiguity.

The **Process** data-type implements *processes*. A process must be declared before use. An array of processes may be declared. The composition of all the elements of an array P of processes is denoted by *P. The same operator * is used, with a different semantics, to denote the set of all elements of an array of actions. Therefore, given the declaration of c above, *c is a short form for (c[0] c[1]).

Other features of XCircal that are used in this paper are the following:

Control Structures. These have a syntax immediately derived from the programming language C.

Output. Values are sent to the standard output by the **print** function and process behaviours are formatted and sent to the standard output by the **display** function.

Testing Equivalence. The Circal System implements the testing equivalence defined by Moller [15] giving to the expression P == Q the result **true** if P and Q are equivalent, and **false** otherwise. The equivalence checking automatically enforces the application of structural operators without requiring the use of the ~ operator.

The composition operator of Circal provides synchronisation among an arbitrary number of processes as in CSP and LOTOS. This particular nature of the composition operator is exploited by the *constraint-based* modelling methodology [21], which has been used in several application domains such as communication protocols [5], safety-critical systems and asynchronous hardware [6,8].

When a process P is composed with a process Q, we say that Q *constrains* P if and only if there is a part of the behaviour of P whose restriction to the intersections of the sorts of P and Q is not consistent with the behaviour of Q.

The notion of constraining is used in synthesising complex behaviours by composing simple general behaviours with specific constraints. In Section 6 we will also see how the notion of constraining can characterise behavioural inclusion between processes.

5   Modelling Framework

5.1   Conditions and Cases

In C/E nets conditions can be seen as 1-cell buffers of tokens. A condition can be modelled in Circal by two processes representing the two states, *empty* and *full*, of the 1-cell buffer. We set the **CONDS** XCircal variable to be equal to the maximum number of conditions and we define two arrays **Empty** and **Full**, each consisting of **CONDS** processes. Then, for each i, processes **Empty**[i] and **Full**[i] model respectively the empty and full states of the $(i + 1)$-th condition.

The transition from Empty[i] to Full[i] is triggered by the production of a token in the $(i+1)$-th condition, which is modelled by produce action p[i]. Analogously, the transition from Full[i] to Empty[i] is triggered by the consumption of a token from the $(i+1)$-th condition, which is modelled by consume action c[i]. Figure 1(b) shows how actions p[i] and c[i] are associated with conditions and events of the C/E net N_1 given in Figure 1(a). For example, action c[0] is in position $\langle e_0, b_0 \rangle$ of the table because an occurrence of e_0 consumes the token in b_0; action p[1] is in position $\langle e_0, b_1 \rangle$ of the table because an occurrence of e_0 produces one token in b_1.

The Circal code is given as follows.

```
Event p[CONDS], c[CONDS]
Process Empty[CONDS], Full[CONDS]
for(i=0;i<CONDS;i++) Empty[i] <- p[i] Full[i]
for(i=0;i<CONDS;i++) Full[i] <- c[i] Empty[i]
```

The first line of the Circal code above is the declaration of two arrays of sets of action, p and c; the second line is the declaration of two arrays of processes, Empty and Full; the other lines are the definitions of the processes that are elements of arrays Empty and Full.

Let us consider C/E net N_1 in Figure 1(a). The initial case of N_1 associates tokens only with b_0 and b_3. Thus the producer is ready to send, the buffer is empty and the consumer is ready to receive. Such an initial case is represented in Circal as follows.

```
InitCase1 = Empty[0] * Full[1] * Empty[2] * Full[3] * Empty[4]
```

Process InitCase1 is the parallel composition of all the processes that define the states of the buffers that implement the conditions of the net. Processes Full[1] and Full[3] model the two fulfilled conditions, b_1 and b_3, respectively. Processes Empty[0], Empty[2] and Empty[4] model the three unfulfilled conditions, b_0, b_2 and b_4, respectively.

5.2   Events and Sequential Semantics

In the first two decades of Petri nets' life, their semantics was based on the philosophy that a transition firing is considered to be instantaneous, that is to take zero time. Since time is usually considered as a continuous variable, the probability of any two or more firings happening simultaneously is zero [16]. This is the main argument to support an operational semantics, where transitions cannot fire simultaneously and a single execution of a net can be seen as an interleaving of markings or an interleaving of transitions or an interleaving of alternating markings and transitions [17]. The behaviour of a C/E net can thus be represented as a state graph, called a *reachability graph*, whose nodes are cases and whose arcs are labelled by single events [17].

Given a C/E net $N = \langle B, E, F, C \rangle$ and a case $\bar{C} \subseteq B$, an event e is *enabled* in $\bar{C}$ if and only if each of its preconditions is fulfilled and none of its postconditions is fulfilled. That is $\forall b \in B.((b, e) \in F \rightarrow b \in \bar{C}) \wedge ((e, b) \in F \rightarrow b \notin \bar{C})$.

If an event e is enabled in $\bar{C}$, then e may occur in $\bar{C}$. The occurrence of e generates a new case C' by consuming tokens from all preconditions of e and producing tokens in all postconditions of e. This is written as $\bar{C}[e\rangle C'$.

We set the EVENTS XCircal variable equal to the maximum number of events and we define an array e consisting of EVENTS actions. The declaration of the e array of actions is as follows.

```
Event e[EVENTS]
```

Since only one event may occur at any time, the behaviour of the net is given by a process consisting of a choice among all enabled events. For C/E net N_1 this is modelled by the EvSeq1 Circal process given as follows.

```
Process EvSeq1
EvSeq1 <- (c[0] p[1] e[0])        EvSeq1 +
          (p[0] c[1] p[4] e[1]) EvSeq1 +
          (p[2] c[3] c[4] e[2]) EvSeq1 +
          (c[2] p[3] e[3])        EvSeq1 +
          (c[4] e[4])             EvSeq1
```

Every possible choice in the definition of EvSeq1 corresponds to a row in Figure 1(b). For instance, the first choice corresponds to the first row, which is associated with event e_0, whose occurrence is modelled by action e[0]. Since the occurrence of e_0 consumes the token from b_0 and produces a token in b_1, then c[0], p[1] and e[0] are forced to occur simultaneously. Their simultaneous occurrence is expressed in Circal by (c[0] p[1] e[0]).

The state graph that defines the behaviour of N_1 can thus be modelled by process EvSeq1Sem, which consists of the parallel composition of InitCase1 and EvSeq1, followed by the hiding of the actions that represent the consumption and production of tokens.

```
EvSeq1Sem = ~(InitCase1 * EvSeq1 - (*c) (*p))
```

Process InitCase1 provides process EvSeq1 with the production and consumption actions that are feasible in the initial case. In this way InitCase1 constrains EvSeq1 to perform the second choice, which is the only one to be feasible in the initial case and corresponds to the occurrence of e_1.

We use the Circal command

```
display EvSeq1Sem
```

to print the behaviour of process EvSeq1Sem, which appears as follows.

```
S0 == e[1] S1
S1 == ((e[0] S2 + e[2] S3) + e[4] S4)
S2 == (e[2] S5 + e[4] S0)
S3 == (e[0] S5 + e[3] S4)
S4 == e[0] S0
S5 == (e[1] S6 + e[3] S0)
S6 == ((e[0] S7 + e[3] S1) + e[4] S3)
S7 == (e[3] S2 + e[4] S5)
```

Such a behaviour is a representation of the reachability graph of N_1.

Every state in the generated behaviour defines a case of N_1. Thus S0 defines the initial case $C_1 = \{b_1, b_3\}$, S1 defines $C_{1,1} = \{b_0, b_3, b_4\}$, S2 defines $C_{1,2} = \{b_1, b_3, b_4\}$. One possible interleaving of alternating cases and events is then: $C_1[e_1\rangle C_{1,1}[e_0\rangle C_{1,2}[e_4\rangle C_1$.

5.3   Parallel Semantics

The sequential semantics of Petri nets resolves the concurrency and the causality expressed by the definition of the Petri net in terms of a non-deterministic interleaving of single event occurrences. However, the underlying assumption that the probability of any two or more events happening simultaneously is zero is too restrictive. A more modern view of Petri net semantics [19] is based on *true concurrency* and emphasises the causality and independence of events, important aspects of any net which are concealed by a sequential semantics. In our paper such a true concurrency semantics is called *parallel semantics*.

Given a C/E net $N = \langle B, E, F, C \rangle$ and a case $\bar{C} \subseteq B$, a set of events $T \subseteq E$ is *enabled* in $\bar{C}$ if and only if the three following properties hold:

- for every event $e \in T$, preconditions of e are fulfilled and no postcondition of e is fulfilled;
- the sets of the preconditions of the events in T are pairwise disjoint;
- the sets of the postconditions of the events in T are pairwise disjoint.

If a set of events T is enabled in $\bar{C}$, then all events in T may simultaneously occur in $\bar{C}$ generating a new case C'. This is written as $\bar{C}[T\rangle C'$.

In order to allow events to occur simultaneously in our Circal model of C/E nets, we need to represent the occurrence of different events as a parallel composition rather than a choice. We set CONDS1 to the number of conditions in N_1 and we define an array Cctrl of processes, one process for every condition. Then we define process EvPar1 as the parallel composition of the processes that are elements of Cctrl.

```
CONDS1 = 5
Process Cctrl[CONDS1]
Cctrl[0] <- (e[1] p[0]) Cctrl[0] + (c[0] e[0]) Cctrl[0]
Cctrl[1] <- (e[0] p[1]) Cctrl[1] + (c[1] e[1]) Cctrl[1]
Cctrl[2] <- (e[2] p[2]) Cctrl[2] + (c[2] e[3]) Cctrl[2]
Cctrl[3] <- (e[3] p[3]) Cctrl[3] + (c[3] e[2]) Cctrl[3]
Cctrl[4] <- (e[1] p[4]) Cctrl[4] + (c[4] e[2]) Cctrl[4] +
                                   (c[4] e[4]) Cctrl[4]
EvPar1 = ~(*Cctrl)
```

The Cctrl[i] process, which corresponds to condition b_i, consists of all possible choices of consumption of a token from b_i or production of a token in b_i. For instance, let us discuss the definition of process Cctrl[4]. A token can be produced in b_4 only by an occurrence of event e_1. This corresponds to the choice (e[1] p[4]) Cctrl[4]. A token can be consumed from b_4 either by an occurrence of event e_2 or by an occurrence of event e_4. This corresponds to the other two possible choices (c[4] e[2]) Cctrl[4] and (c[4] e[4]) Cctrl[4].

The behaviour of N_1 can thus be represented by a graph whose nodes are cases and whose arcs are labelled by set of events occurring simultaneously. Such a graph is modelled by process EvPar1Sem, which consists of the parallel composition of InitEvent1 and EvPar1, followed by the hiding of the actions that represent the consumption and production of tokens.

```
EvPar1Sem = ~(InitCase1 * EvPar1 - (*c) (*p))
display EvPar1Sem
```

The display command outputs the behaviour of process EvPar1Sem as follows.

```
S0 == e[1] S1
S1 == ((((e[0] S2 + (e[0] e[4]) S0) + (e[0] e[2]) S3) +
       e[2] S4) + e[4] S5)
S2 == (e[2] S3 + e[4] S0)
S3 == ((e[1] S6 + (e[3] e[1]) S1) + e[3] S0)
S4 == ((e[0] S3 + (e[0] e[3]) S0) + e[3] S5)
S5 == e[0] S0
S6 == ((((((e[0] S7 + (e[0] e[4]) S3) + (e[0] e[3]) S2) +
       (e[0] e[3] e[4]) S0) + e[3] S1) + (e[3] e[4]) S5) + e[4] S4)
S7 == ((e[3] S2 + (e[3] e[4]) S0) + e[4] S3)
```

Again, every state in the generated behaviour defines a case of N_1. Now S0 defines the initial case $C_1 = \{b_1, b_3\}$, S1 defines $C_{1,1} = \{b_0, b_3, b_4\}$, and S2 defines $C_{1,2} = \{b_1, b_3, b_4\}$. One possible interleaving of alternating states and sets of events is then: $C_1[\{e_1\}\rangle C_{1,1}[\{e_0, e_4\}\rangle C_1$.

5.4   Read-Only and Overwrite Arcs

The semantics of C/E nets given in the previous section does not allow an event to occur when one of its postconditions is fulfilled. This causes the following implicit restrictions on C/E nets:

1. an event whose set of preconditions and set of postconditions have a non-empty intersection can never occur (*self-loop*);
2. an event with all preconditions fulfilled might be prevented from occurring by one of its postconditions being fulfilled (*contact*).

A semantics which does not associate an active behaviour to a self-loop is very limiting. It is often useful to model a system where the content of a condition can be read without consuming the token. In the C/E net N_2 in Figure 2(a), event e_5 models a test on condition b_4: we would like e_5 to occur when there is a token in b_4, but without consuming the token. This is impossible using the Circal implementation of C/E nets given above. However, we can modify the Empty and Full arrays of processes defined in Section 5.1 by allowing a simultaneous occurrence of c[i] and p[i] in Full[i]. Therefore, we replace arrays Full and Empty respectively with arrays ReadFull and ReadEmpty defined as follows.

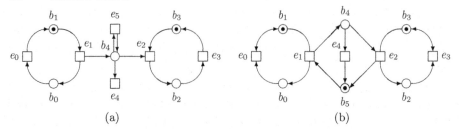

Fig. 2. (a): A C/E net N_2 defining a producer-consumer system with test on the buffer; (b): A C/E net N_3 defining a contact-free producer-consumer system

```
Process ReadEmpty[CONDS], ReadFull[CONDS]
for(i=0;i<CONDS;i++) ReadEmpty[i] <- p[i] ReadFull[i]
for(i=0;i<CONDS;i++) ReadFull[i] <- c[i] ReadEmpty[i] +
                                    (c[i] p[i]) ReadFull[i]
```

Term (c[i] p[i]) ReadFull[i] now allows an event to simultaneously consume and produce a token in the same condition, which is equivalent to a read-only operation on that condition. The initial case of N_2 allowing active self-loops is then given as follows.

```
InitCase2R = ReadEmpty[0] * ReadFull[1] *
             ReadEmpty[2] * ReadFull[3] * ReadEmpty[4]
```

The choice among all enabled events is modelled by the EvSeq1R Circal process given as follows.

```
Process EvSeq1R
EvSeq1R <- (c[0] p[1] e[0]) EvSeq1R +
   (p[0] c[1] p[4] e[1]) EvSeq1R +
   (p[2] c[3] c[4] e[2]) EvSeq1R + (c[2] p[3] e[3]) EvSeq1R +
   (c[4] e[4]) EvSeq1R + (c[4] p[4] e[5]) EvSeq1R
EvSeq1RSem = ~(InitCase2R * EvSeq1R - (*c) (*p))
```

The last term of the definition of EvSeq1R models that event e_5 (implemented by e[5]) simultaneously consumes a token (action c[4]) from and produces a token (action p[4]) to b_4.

In order to allow an event to occur even though at least one of its postconditions is fulfilled, we define arrays OWFull and OWEmpty as follows.

```
Process OWEmpty[CONDS], OWFull[CONDS]
for(i=0;i<CONDS;i++) OWEmpty[i] <- p[i] OWFull[i]
for(i=0;i<CONDS;i++) OWFull[i] <- c[i] OWEmpty[i] + p[i] OWFull[i]
```

Term p[i] OWFull[i] in the definition of process OWFull[i] now allows an event to produce a token in a fulfilled condition. When defining the initial case of a given C/E net, we will then use the Full[k] and Empty[k] processes for each non-overwritable condition b_k and the OWFull[j] and OWEmpty[j] processes for each overwritable condition b_j. For instance, if we want buffer overwriting in the C/E net N_1 in Figure 1(a), we need to make condition b_4 overwritable. The initial case is then represented in Circal as follows.

```
InitCase1OW = Full[0] * Empty[1] * Full[2] * Empty[3] * OWEmpty[4]
```

We will see an application of overwritable conditions in Section 6.1.

We can also have both read-only arcs and overwrite conditions by using the following processes.

```
Process ROWEmpty[CONDS], ROWFull[CONDS]
for(i=0;i<CONDS;i++) ROWEmpty[i] <- p[i] ROWFull[i]
for(i=0;i<CONDS;i++) ROWFull[i] <- c[i] ROWEmpty[i] +
                     p[i] ROWFull[i] + (c[i] p[i]) ROWFull[i]
```

The initial case is for C/E net N_2 in Figure 2(a), with read-only in self loops and condition b_4 overwritable is implemented in Circal as follows.

```
InitCase2RW4 = ReadEmpty[0] * ReadFull[1] *
               ReadEmpty[2] * ReadFull[3] * ROWEmpty[4]
```

6   Analysis of Properties

A correctness concept that can be readily characterised in Circal is the behavioural equivalence P == Q between two given processes P and Q, which is implemented by the Circal System.

However, in performing formal verification equivalence is often too strong a property. Analysing systems often consists of determining that certain properties hold, where these properties do not constitute a complete specification. Concurrent systems frequently require us to determine if the behaviour of a given process Q is included in the behaviour of another process P.

The constraint-based modelling technique supports a clear characterisation of such a behavioural inclusion. The behaviour of Q is strictly included in the behaviour of P if and only if the following three properties hold:

1. P and Q have the same sort;
2. Q constrains P;
3. P does not constrain Q

We want to prove that if P and Q are not equivalent and Condition 1 holds, then Conditions 2 and 3 hold if and only if the equivalence check Q * P == Q gives true as a result. If P and Q are not equivalent, then the equivalence above gives true as a result if and only if the part of the behaviour of P that is not consistent with the behaviour of Q disappears after the composition (that is Condition 2 holds) and the behaviour of Q is preserved after the composition (it is fully consistent with the behaviour of P, that is Condition 3 holds).

As an example of behavioural inclusion we would like to verify for the C/E net N_1 given in Figure 1(a) that the behaviour defined by the parallel semantics introduced in Section 5.3 strictly includes the behaviour defined by the sequential semantics introduced in Section 5.2. We first verify that the two semantics are not equivalent. The equivalence check

```
EvSeq1 == EvPar()
```

gives **false** as a result.

The two semantics have the same sort. Thus we check that the following equivalence is true.

```
EvSeq1 * EvPar() == EvSeq1
```

Notice that this result is independent of the initial case of N_1.

The behavioural inclusion checking allows the analysis of interesting properties of concurrent systems. Together with the equivalence checking and with other techniques for safety [5] and performance [6,8] analysis introduced in previous papers it may be used for the verification of systems in part modelled as C/E nets and in part directly modelled as Circal processes. In the next section, we present an example of verification of a simple property of C/E nets.

6.1   Contacts and Complementation

We have said in Section 5.4 that an event with all preconditions fulfilled might be prevented from occurring by one of its postconditions being fulfilled. This situation is called a *contact*. More precisely, in a C/E net there is a contact if and only if all preconditions and at least one postcondition of an event are fulfilled. A C/E net is *contact-free* if and only if a contact can never occur.

It might be considered not very elegant that the occurrence or non-occurrence of an event depends on both preconditions and postconditions [20, p.16]. This is an argument for avoiding contact situations in design. It is indeed possible to remove a situation of contact by adding additional conditions to the C/E net. In order to remove contacts, we introduce the concept of a *complement* to a condition.

In a C/E net a condition b' is a *complement* to a condition b if and only if for every event e the following properties hold:

- b is a precondition of e if b' is a postcondition of e;
- b is a postcondition of e if b' is a precondition of e;
- b' is unfulfilled in the initial case if and only if b is fulfilled in the initial case.

It is easy to show that if b' is a complement of a condition b, exactly one of the two conditions is fulfilled in each case. Therefore, adding a complement to a condition does not change the behaviour of the net.

A C/E net can be made contact-free by adding a complement to every postcondition that causes a contact.

In the C/E net N_1 in Figure 1(a) the occurrence of e_1 followed by the occurrence of e_0 results in a case with tokens both in b_1 and b_4. Event e_1 has its only precondition b_1 fulfilled, but it cannot occur because its postcondition b_4 is also fulfilled. This is a contact situation.

In order to detect the contacts in N_1 using the Circal System, we define the **OverWrite1** array of processes such that, for each i, process **OverWrite1**[i] is obtained by replacing in the initial case the **Empty**[i] and **Full**[i] processes respectively with the **OWEmpty**[i] and **OWFull**[i] processes defined in Section 5.4. For example process **OverWrite1**[1] is defined as follows.

```
OverWrite1[1] = Empty[0] * OWFull[1] * Empty[2] * Full[3] *
                Empty[4] * EvSeq1 - (*c) (*p)
```

We can now detect all contacts in N_1 through the following equivalence checks

```
for(i=0;i<CONDS1;i++){print(EvSeq1Sem == OverWrite1[i]); print" "}
```

which give as result: **true true true true false**. For each i, `OverWrite1`[i] is equivalent to `EvSeq1Sem` if and only if the `p`[i] action may not occur in `OWFull`[i]. Action `p`[i] may occur in `OWFull`[i] if and only if the token in b_i is overwritten by the occurrence of an event having b_i as a postcondition, that is when b_i being fulfilled causes a contact. Thus the equivalence of `OverWrite1`[i] and `EvSeq1Sem` holds if and only if there is no contact caused by b_i. Therefore, the equivalence checks above show that in N_1 contacts are only caused by b_4. This contact can be removed by adding a complement to condition b_4 as in C/E net N_3 given in Figure 2(b). Since b_4 was the only cause of contact, N_3 is contact-free. The Circal sequential model of N_3 is given as follows.

```
InitCase3 = Empty[0] * Full[1] * Empty[2] *
            Full[3] * Empty[4] * Full[5]
Process EvSeq3
EvSeq3 <- (c[0] p[1] e[0]) EvSeq3 +
          (c[1] c[5] p[0] p[4] e[1]) EvSeq3 +
          (c[3] c[4] p[2] p[5] e[2]) EvSeq3 +
          (c[2] p[3] e[3]) EvSeq3 +
          (c[4] p[5] e[4]) EvSeq3
EvSeq3Sem = ~(InitCase3 * EvSeq3 - (*c) (*p))
```

Now, if we build the `OverWrite3` process for N_3 in the same way as we have built the `OverWrite1` process for N_1 and we set `CONS3` equal to 6, then the following equivalence checks

```
for(i=0;i<CONDS3;i++){print(EvSeq3Sem == OverWrite3[i]); print" "}
```

give as result: **true true true true true true**. This proves that N_3 is contact-free. We can also check that N_3 has the same behaviour as N_1 through the following equivalence.

```
EvSeq1Sem == EvSeq3Sem
```

7   Conclusion and Future Work

We have presented a technique for implementing Condition/Event nets in a process algebra. We have chosen the Circal process algebra, which has the distinctive feature of allowing simultaneity of actions. We have exploited such a feature to implement a true concurrency semantics as an alternative to the implementation based on non-deterministic interleaving.

We have also seen that our implementation allows the design of systems modelled by C/E nets and the verification of general properties of C/E nets, such as equivalence and behavioural inclusion, or more specific properties, such as contact-freedom. Moreover, having an implementation of C/E nets within a process algebra allows the use of a unique verification engine in the analysis of systems which are modelled using different specification formalisms such as Petri nets and Finite State Machines.

All the Circal code used in this paper can be downloaded from the World Wide Web [3]. In order to run it it is necessary to install the Circal System [1]. Our implementation of C/E nets is exploited by the *Petrinette* graphical design and verififcation tool [9,3].

A natural continuation of this work is its extension to Place/Transition nets (P/T nets) and higher-level Petri nets. Circal allows the modelling of finite state systems, whereas P/T nets may have infinite states. Thus P/T nets cannot be translated into a finite state process algebra without an abstraction step which reduces the behaviour to a finite state system. Therefore, in order to have a complete translation, we must restrict our work to bounded P/T nets. However, the technique presented in this paper cannot be directly applied to bounded P/T nets. The main change to the modelling framework involves the implementation of places. Conditions in C/E nets have been implemented using 1-cell buffers, but the implementation of a place in a P/T net would require a buffer consisting of at least as many cells as the capacity of the buffer. Moreover we have to implement a test on the number of tokens in the buffer to check the enabling of transitions. The main problem is how to exploit the result of the test taking into account possible conflicts among transitions. The problem becomes even more complex if we allow the simultaneous firing of distinct transitions or even multiple concurrent firings of the same transition. Investigating all these problems is part of our current research.

Finally, we would like to point out that the Circal feature of allowing the simultaneous occurrence of distinct actions has eased the definition of the modelling framework presented in Section 5 and made possible the definition of the parallel semantics presented in Section 5.3. This is further evidence that the simultaneity of actions enriches the ability to model aspects of concurrent system which are believed hard to characterise in process algebra frameworks. Among these aspects we have already investigated priorities among actions [4,5], the modelling of dense time [7] and the verification of performance properties [6,8]. All such works exploit simultaneous actions in modelling systems and verifying properties. In our future work we plan to investigate the use of such a feature in further application domains, such as multitasking, security and mobility.

Acknowledgements

I would like to thank Colin Fidge and Nathan Spargo for helpful comments.

References

1. Circal System. Web Page, 2001.
   http://www.acrc.unisa.edu.au/doc/circal/circal_distribution.html.
2. T. Bolognesi and E. Brinksma. Intoduction to the ISO specification language LOTOS. *Computer Systems and ISDN Systems*, 14(1):25–59, 1987.
3. A. Cerone. Modelling Petri nets in Circal. Web Page, 2001.
   http://www.itee.uq.edu.au/~antonio/Research/Misc/pntocir.html.
4. A. Cerone, A. J. Cowie, G. J. Milne, and P. A. Moseley. Description and verification of a time-sensitive protocol. Technical Report CIS-96-009, University of South Australia, Adelaide, 1996.
5. A. Cerone, A. J. Cowie, G. J. Milne, and P. A. Moseley. Modelling a time-dependent protocol using the Circal process algebra. In *Proc. of HART97*, volume 1201 of *Lecture Notes in Computer Science*, pages 124–138. Springer, 1997.
6. A. Cerone, D. A. Kearney, and G. J. Milne. Integrating the verification of timing, performance and correctness properties of concurrent systems. In *Proc. of the Int. Conf. on Application of Concurrency to System Design (CSD'98)*, pages 109–119. IEEE Comp. Soc. Press, 1998.
7. A. Cerone and G. J. Milne. Specification of timing constraints within the Circal process algebra. In *Proc. of AMAST97*, volume 1349 of *Lecture Notes in Computer Science*, pages 108–122. Springer, 1997.
8. A. Cerone and G. J. Milne. A methodology for the formal analysis of asynchronous micropipelines. In *Proc. of FMCAD00*, volume 1954 of *Lecture Notes in Computer Science*, pages 246–262. Springer, 2000.
9. A. Cerone and N. Spargo. Petrinette: A tool for the integrated analysis of Petri nets and finite state machines. Technical Report 01-39, Software Verification Research Centre, The University of Queensland, Brisbane, 2001.
10. T. Chu, C. Leung, and T. Wanuga. A design methodology for concurrent VLSI systems. In *Proc. of ICDD*, pages 407–410, 1985.
11. Formal methods. Web Page, 2001. http://www.afm.sbu.ac.uk/fm/.
12. C. Hoare. *Communicating Sequential Processes*. Prentice Hall, 1985.
13. G. J. Milne. *Formal Specification and Verification of Digital Systems*. McGraw Hill, 1994.
14. R. Milner. *Communication and Concurrency*. Prentice Hall, 1989.
15. F. Moller. The semantics of Circal. Technical Report HDV-3-89, University of Strathclyde, Glasgow, UK, 1989.
16. J. Peterson. Petri nets. *Computing Surveys*, 9(3):223–252, 1977.
17. J. Peterson. *Petri Net Theory and the Modeling of Systems*. Prentice-Hall, 1981.
18. C. A. Petri. Kommunication mit automaten. Schrift der IIM Nr. 2, Institut für Instrumentelle Mathematik, University of Bonn, 1962. *English translation*: Technical Report RADC-TR-65-337, Griffiths Air Force Base, New York, 1966.
19. W. Reisig. *Petri Nets — An introduction*. Springer, 1985.
20. W. Reisig. *A Primer in Petri Nets Design*. Springer, 1992.
21. C. Vissers, G. Scollo, M. van Sinderen, and E. Brinksma. Specification styles in distributed systems design and verification. *Theoretical Computer Science*, 89:179–206, 1991.

Integrated State Space Reduction for Model Checking Executable Object-Oriented Software System Designs

Fei Xie and James C. Browne

Dept. of Computer Sciences
Univ. of Texas at Austin, Austin, TX 78712, USA
{feixie,browne}@cs.utexas.edu Fax: +1 (512) 471-8885

Abstract. This paper presents a general framework for integrated state space reduction in model checking executable object-oriented software system designs. The framework structures the application of state space reduction algorithms into three phases with different algorithms applied in each phase. The interactions between these algorithms are explored to maximize the aggregate effect of state space reduction. Automation support for the framework has been proposed and partially implemented. The framework is presented for system designs modeled in xUML [1][2], an executable dialect of UML, but can also be used to structure integrated state space reduction for other representations. To further improve the applicability of the framework, domain-specific design patterns can be explored to instantiate the framework for different application domains. An instantiation of the framework for distributed transaction systems is defined and its partial implementation has been applied to the design model of an online ticket sale system. The dimension of software system designs that are model checkable is found to be greatly extended.

1 Introduction

Executable object-oriented modeling languages such as xUML [1][2], an executable dialect of UML, are widely applied in industry to model software system designs. Model checking [3][4] can potentially enhance the reliability and robustness of executable object-oriented software system designs. However, model checking software system designs of arbitrary size is intractable due to the well-known state space explosion problem. Therefore, state space reduction algorithms have to be applied to reduce the model checking complexity.

Executable object-oriented software system designs are ideal candidates for model checking due to their complete execution semantics and natural incorporation of state models. Furthermore, their major features potentially enable effective state space reductions, for instance, compositional structures may lead to effective decompositions, inheritance relationships may facilitate abstractions, and multiple instances of a class may simplify the identification of symmetries.

This paper defines and describes a general framework for integrated state space reduction in model checking executable object-oriented software system

R.-D. Kutsche and H. Weber (Eds.): FASE 2002, LNCS 2306, pp. 64–79, 2002.

designs. The framework assumes that the executable system designs can be translated into model checkable languages and is discussed using system designs modeled in xUML. An earlier paper [5] has been focused on model checking an xUML model by translating the model into the S/R [6] automaton language. Under the framework, state space reduction algorithms are applied in an integrated way to xUML models before and during the translation and to the resulting S/R models. Interactions between these algorithms are explored to maximize the aggregate effect of state space reduction.

Many software system designs are constructed following domain-specific design patterns that provide information about structures and behaviors of these systems. Reduction algorithms such as decomposition, abstraction, and symmetry reduction, whose effectiveness depends on structures and behaviors of software systems, can be readily formulated on design models due to the fact that execution behaviors of different components are more observable at the design level and due to the existence of domain-specific design patterns. State space reduction algorithms are often applied in combinations. These facts taken together suggest instantiating the general state space reduction framework for different application domains based on domain specific design patterns.

Distributed transaction systems, which are commonly constructed in a design pattern of dispatchers, agents, and servers with customer initiated transactions as observable units of work, are examples of a family of systems for which a structured process for applying state space reduction algorithms at the design model level can be formulated. This paper illustrates the general framework with its instantiation for distributed transaction systems, a systematic process for reducing model checking a property on the design model of a transaction system to discharging a well-defined set of less complex model checking problems. The process represents a transaction as message sequences, associates the property to be checked with a transaction, partitions the model into sub-models, and decomposes the property into sub-properties and assumptions defined over these sub-models. The process is evaluated by its application in model checking an online ticket sale system. The dimension of transaction systems that can be model checked is materially extended by the systematic process.

There has been extensive research on state space reduction algorithms for either hardware systems or software systems, which is surveyed in [4]. Our work, instead of focusing on particular state space reduction algorithms, explores the integrated application of reduction algorithms in the context of the general framework and investigates how domain specific design patterns can help adapt the general framework to different application domains to achieve more automatic and effective state space reduction. Our work is distinguished from the integrated state space reduction for hardware systems [7][8] by focusing on software systems and incorporating both reduction algorithms effective for asynchronous semantics and those effective for synchronous semantics.

Section 2 defines the general framework, informally describes the state space reduction algorithms currently applied in the context of the framework, and gives some guidelines for when to apply each state space reduction algorithm and for the application order of these algorithms. Section 3 sketches the partially implemented automation support for the general framework. Section 4 defines, describes, and illustrates the instantiation of the general framework on distributed transaction systems. Section 5 evaluates the instantiation with results from model checking an online ticket sale system. Section 6 gives the conclusion.

2   Integrated State Space Reduction

In this section, a structured framework for integrated application of state space reduction algorithms to executable object-oriented software system designs is defined. The framework is presented for system designs modeled in xUML, but can be used to structure integrated state space reduction for other representations. The state space reduction algorithms being applied in the context of this framework are described and interactions between these algorithms are discussed.

2.1   General Framework

The model checking process for an xUML model, previously reported in [5], is a sequential application of the following two procedures on the xUML model:

- xUML-to-S/R translation that translates the xUML model and an xUML level query to be checked on the model to an S/R model and an S/R query;
- S/R level model checking that checks the S/R query on the S/R model by invoking the COSPAN model checker.

The process, referred to as the basic model checking process in Figure 1, works effectively on xUML models with small numbers of class instances, but cannot scale due to the state space explosion problem. On the other hand, for well-structured xUML models, there are system structure and property specific reduction algorithms at the xUML model level, which cannot be recognized by the xUML-to-S/R translator and the COSPAN model checker, but which can effect major state space reduction on the resulting S/R model that is to be model checked. Therefore, the general framework prefaces the basic model checking process with a user-driven state reduction procedure.

The general framework establishes a three-level hierarchy for integrated state space reduction, as shown in Figure 1. Different reduction algorithms are invoked on different levels of the hierarchy and applied to models of different forms:

- In the user-driven state space reduction procedure, user-driven reduction algorithms such as decomposition, abstraction, and symmetry reduction are applied to reduce a complex model checking task T, a complex query on a complex xUML model, into a set of subtasks. Each subtask checks a sub-query of the original query on a sub-model of the original model. A sub-model is either a component or an abstraction of the original model. Each subtask is either discharged by invoking the basic model checking process or further reduced. The reductions applied are validated by invoking the basic model checking process or conducting a simple theorem proving.
- In the xUML-to-S/R translation procedure, automatic reduction algorithms, such as static partial order reduction, are applied, which transform an xUML model prior to its translation into S/R with respect to a given xUML query and construct an equivalent model that has a smaller state space.

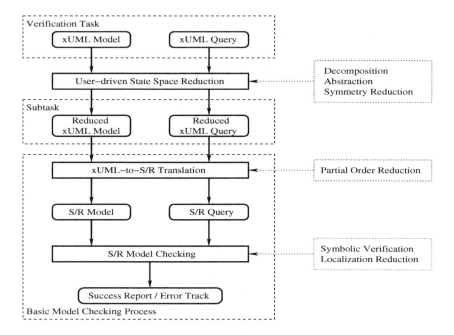

Fig. 1. Reduction Hierarchy of General Framework

- In the S/R level model checking procedure, automatic reduction algorithms implemented by COSPAN, such as symbolic model checking and localization reduction, are applied. These algorithms make use of the semantic information of an S/R model to reduce the state space to be explored by COSPAN.

Under the general framework, the extended model checking process for xUML models operates recursively and interactively as shown in Figure 2. A model checking task, T_0, is recursively reduced into subtasks. A reduction conjecture from users is always validated before its resulting model checking subtasks are discharged. The basic model checking process becomes a model checking engine for discharging subtasks. When a reduction conjecture or a subtask is verified to be false, user interaction is requested. Upon user inputs, either a new reduction conjecture is introduced, or the model checking process is aborted.

2.2 Major State Space Reduction Algorithms

There are many possible state space reduction algorithms that can be applied to xUML models under the general framework. Some of them are summarized as they are applied to xUML models.

Decomposition. The compositional hierarchy, the asynchronous message communication semantics, and the interleaving execution semantics of xUML make decomposition a natural state space reduction algorithm for xUML models.

```
Enqueue(ToDo, T_0); Done ={ }; /* ToDo is a queue and Done is a set. */
Do
  T = Dequeue(ToDo);
  If (T is Directly Model Checkable) Then
    If (Basic-model-checking-process(T)) Then
      Done = Done + {T}; Continue;
    Else
      Error-report-generation(T); Invoke-user-interface ( );
    End;
  < T_1, ..., T_n > = User-driven-state-space-reduction(T);
  If (Valid(T, < T_1, ..., T_n >) Then Enqueue(ToDo, T_1, ..., T_n);
  Else
    Error-report-generation(T, < T_1, ..., T_n >); Invoke-user-interface( );
  End;
Until (Empty(ToDo));
```

Fig. 2. Recursive and Interactive Model Checking Process Under General Framework

- **Query Decomposition.** A query on an xUML model can often be broken into a set of sub-queries on the model, its components, or its abstractions so that checking the sub-queries is simpler than checking the original query and verification of the sub-queries guarantees verification of the original query.
- **Component-Based Decomposition.** To facilitate the query decomposition, the hierarchical structure of an xUML model may be explored to decompose the model into components that have simple and clear interfaces between each other. Dependencies between components are formulated as assumptions of every component on other components. Therefore, a sub-query can be checked on a component under its assumptions, which consumes less memory and time than checking the sub-query on the original model.
- **Case Splitting.** In many xUML models, concurrent operations may be grouped into units of work, for example, transactions in an e-business system. Commonly there is little interaction between these units of work. If a query on the whole system can be decomposed into sub-queries on units of work and the units of work can be decoupled when these sub-queries are checked, significant state space reduction can often be achieved.

Abstraction. Three abstraction algorithms can be applied:

- **State Model Abstraction.** If a query is over one or several components of a system, state models in the components not directly involved in the query may be abstracted to reduce the state space to be explored for checking the query. If the abstraction is sound (Executions of the abstract system contain all behaviors of the original system.), then if the query is verified to be true on the abstract system, it will also be true on the original system. The most common form of state model abstraction is the non-deterministic abstraction. For instance, a decision point in a state model may be made non-deterministic and a set of state models that are only differentiated by their unique identifiers may be simulated by a state model with a non-deterministic identity. A major advantage of non-deterministic abstraction over other kinds of state model abstraction is that its correctness is automatically guaranteed.

- **Data Abstraction.** If a mapping can be found between data values of an xUML model and a small set of abstract data values, then an abstract xUML model that simulates the original model can be constructed by extending the mapping to states and transitions. Since the state space of the abstract model is usually smaller, it is often easier to check properties on the abstract model.
- **Localization Reduction.** Given a model and a property, localization reduction [9], also known as cone of influence reduction [4], eliminates variables in the model that do not influence the variables in the property. The checked property is preserved, but the size of the model to be checked is smaller.

Symmetry Reduction. Symmetry reduction can often reduce the number of queries to be checked on an xUML model or the state space size of the model.

- **Symmetric Query Reduction.** Given two queries on an xUML model, if a nontrivial mapping can be defined between variables in the model or between values of variables, which maps the model to itself and the two queries to each other, then only one of the two queries need to be checked on the model.
- **Quotient Model Reduction.** Having symmetry in a model implies the existence of nontrivial permutation groups that preserve both the state labeling and the transition relation. The quotient model induced by this relation is often smaller than the original model. Moreover it is bisimulation equivalent to the original model. Therefore, all queries on the original model can be instead checked on the quotient model.

Partial Order Reduction. Partial order reduction takes advantages of the fact that, in many cases, when components of a system are not tightly coupled, different execution orders of actions or transitions of different components may result in the same global state. Then, under some conditions [10] [11] [12], in particular, when the interim global states are not relevant to the query being checked, model checkers only need to explore one of the possible execution orders. This may radically reduce model checking complexity.

Asynchronous interleaving semantics of xUML suggest application of static partial order reduction [13] to an xUML model prior to its translation into S/R, which transforms the xUML model by restricting its transition structure with respect to a query to be checked. This enables integrated application of partial order reduction while applying symbolic model checking to the S/R model.

Symbolic Model Checking. Symbolic model checking represents the state transition structure of an xUML model with binary decision diagrams, which enables manipulation of entire sets of states and transitions instead of individual states and transitions. This heuristic is fully automatic and has shown encouraging reduction promise on some xUML models. (to be elaborated in Section 5).

2.3   Interactions between Reduction Algorithms

Under the general framework, state space reduction algorithms are applied to xUML models in an integrated way. To maximize the aggregate effect of state space reduction, the selection of reduction algorithms and the application order of the selected reduction algorithms need to be carefully considered.

Selection of Reduction Algorithms. The structure of an xUML model and the knowledge of its execution behavior can help select the reduction algorithms to be applied to the model:

a. Symmetry reduction is often selected if there exist many instances of the same class;
b. Partial order reduction is often selected if there is intensive execution inter-leaving;
c. Symbolic model checking is often selected if there is much randomness.
d. Localization reduction is always applied to S/R models.

xUML models from different application domains, different xUML models from the same application domain, or different queries on the same xUML model may lead to different selections of reduction algorithms. Therefore, domain, model, and query specific knowledge also need to be involved in the algorithm selection process besides the selection guidelines provided.

Application Order of Reduction Algorithms. To maximize the state space reduction effect, it is always attempted to apply each reduction algorithm to the minimum models with which the algorithm has to deal. Therefore, the framework hard-codes some application ordering relations between reduction algorithms:

– Algorithms in the user-driven reduction procedure are always applied prior to algorithms in the xUML-to-S/R translation procedure.
– Algorithms in the xUML-to-S/R translation procedure are always applied prior to algorithms in the S/R level model checking procedure.
– In the S/R level model checking procedure, localization reduction is always applied prior to symbolic model checking.

There is no ordering relation defined between reduction algorithms applied in the user-driven reduction procedure because the ordering relations between these algorithms are also domain, model, and query specific.

2.4   Instantiations of General Framework for Application Domains

The framework defines a general process for structuring integrated state space reductions, but requires certain amount of user interaction. System designs from the same application domains commonly follow a set of domain-specific design patterns and require satisfaction of queries in similar formats. Therefore, domain-specific design patterns and query patterns can often be explored to establish an instantiation of the general framework for a given domain. The instantiation should provide additional guidelines for selecting reduction algorithms and additional relations for ordering these reduction algorithms. With these extra efforts, the instantiation may significantly reduce the user interaction required and make the integrated state space reduction for the given domain more automatic and effective. In Section 4, we demonstrate how the general framework is instantiated by instantiating it for distributed transaction systems.

3 Automation of Integrated State Space Reduction

Automation support, which is crucial to the wide application of the general framework, is provided through selecting an appropriate model checker, extending the xUML-to-S/R translator, and introducing a reduction manager.

3.1 Selection of Model Checker

COSPAN, which has synchronous and parallel semantics, is selected as the model checking engine for xUML models because it supports both symbolic model checking, which is not readily supported by effective model checkers with asynchronous interleaving semantics, and localization reduction. Localization reduction is always applied to any S/R model while symbolic model checking can be switched on or off by setting an option of COSPAN.

3.2 Extension to xUML-to-S/R Translator

The xUML-to-S/R translator was extended by incorporating the optimization module of SDLCheck [14] that implements static partial order reduction and other software-specific model checking optimizations. These optimizations transforms the xUML model with respect to the xUML query before the translation into S/R and can be switched on or off without affecting the translation.

3.3 Reduction Manager

A reduction manager has been designed and is under development, which coordinates the recursive model checking process in Figure 2. If the current subtask is not directly model checkable, the manager invokes a user interface to input:

- Selected reduction algorithms and their application order;
- Sub-queries of a complex xUML query;
- Boundaries and environment assumptions of a system component;
- Correspondence between sub-queries and components (or units of work);
- Class instances involved in a unit of work;
- Abstract state models and their corresponding concrete state models;
- Abstract data types and their mapping relations to concrete data types;
- Symmetries between class instances (or queries).

The inputs form a reduction conjecture. The manager applies the selected user-driven reduction algorithms in the user-defined order and generates subtasks. The manager then validates the reduction conjecture by invoking either the basic model checking process or a theorem prover. If the reduction conjecture is not valid, an error handling user interface is invoked to report the error and request a new reduction conjecture or termination of the model checking process.

If the current subtask is model checkable, the manager invokes the basic model checking process to discharge the task. Several tasks can be discharged simultaneously if there is no dependency between them. If a subtask is checked to be false, the manager rolls the whole model checking process back to the reduction that generates the false task

4   Framework Instantiation on Transaction Systems

Transaction systems such as banking systems and online sale systems play more and more important roles in the electronic infrastructure of our society. These systems are complex and require high reliability. Their designs follow similar patterns. Therefore, it is worthwhile to instantiate the integrated state space reduction framework for model checking xUML models of transaction systems.

4.1   Common Patterns of Transaction Systems

A transaction system executes transactions concurrently. A transaction consists of sequences of interactions between system components. Transactions may be of different types and transactions of the same type are often symmetric. The correctness of the system can be established by determining the correctness of each transaction it performs and the correctness of interactions between transactions.

Definition 1. *The model, M, of a transaction system, S, is the xUML model of S, which consists of a set of interacting class instances. A model, M', is a sub-model of M if M' consists of a subset of class instances of M.*

Definition 2. *A transaction type, T, of M is a message sequence template, which consists of sequences of message types defined in M. An instance of T is a transaction executed by M, whose message sequences follow T. A type, T', is a sub-type of T if each sequence in T' is a sub-sequence of a sequence in T.*

Definition 3. *A transaction property, P, is a temporal logic predicate over all instances of a transaction type, T, or over an instance of T.*

Definition 4. *A model checking task is a tuple, $< M, T, P, A >$, where M is a model, T is a transaction type defined on M, P is a transaction property defined on T, and A is the set of assumed temporal properties defined on the environment of M. The environment of M is the aggregation of all inputs to M. A model checking task, $< M', T', P', A' >$, is a subtask of $< M, T, P, A >$ if M' is a sub-model of M, T' is a sub-type of T, and P' is a temporal predicate that* is defined on M' and derived from P through reductions such as decompositions, and A' is the union of A and a set of assumed properties on $M - M'$. Each assumed property in A or A' is a tuple of a temporal predicate and a model (or the environment) on which the predicate is defined.

Definition 5. A model checking task, $< M, T, P, A >$, is directly model checkable if it can be discharged by the basic model checking process using a reasonable amount of time and memory.

4.2   Domain Specific Reduction Algorithm

The domain specific reduction algorithm for checking a task, $< \hat{M}, \hat{T}, \hat{P}, \hat{A} >$, on a transaction system is given in Figure 3. For simplicity, only the reduction aspect of the algorithm is covered in Figure 3. The algorithm constructs the reduction tree for $< \hat{M}, \hat{T}, \hat{P}, \hat{A} >$ on-the-fly. The root of the tree is $< \hat{M}, \hat{T}, \hat{P}, \hat{A} >$. Each non-root node in the tree is a subtask of its parent. The tree is expanded in a breadth first fashion. Every execution of the do loop either discharges a task at a leaf of the tree or expands the tree by reducing the task into its subtasks through symmetry reduction, decomposition, or case splitting. The expansion stops when all subtasks at the leaves of the tree are directly model checkable.

4.3   Case Study: An Online Ticket Sale System

The xUML model of an online ticket sale system [15], M_0, is employed to illustrate the domain specific reduction algorithm for transaction systems. There are four classes in the system: Customer, Dispatcher, Agent, and Ticket Server. Both the Dispatcher class and the Ticket Server class have only one instance. The Agent class and the Customer class may have an arbitrary number of instances. The system processes ticketing transactions of the type, T_0, concurrently for many customers. The message sequence diagram of T_0 is shown in Figure 4. T_0 has four branching points where the decisions made affect the message sequences:

1. Upon processing a *request* message from a customer, the dispatcher assigns an idle agent to the customer if there is an idle agent; Otherwise, the dispatcher replies to the customer with a *TryLater* message;
2. Upon processing a *Hold* message from an agent, the ticket server replies to the agent with: A *Held* message if the number of tickets available is greater than the requested number; A *Later* message if the sum of tickets available or being held is greater than the requested number; An *Out* message otherwise;
3. Upon receiving a *TicketHeld* message from an agent, the customer may or may not reply to the agent with its payment;
4. If the valid payment from the customer is received before the agent times out, the agent sends a *Ticket* message to the customer and a *Buy* message to the ticket server; Otherwise, it sends a *Release* message to the ticket server.

A property which should hold on each transaction of the type, T_0, is that after a *request* message from a customer is processed by the dispatcher, eventually the

---

Enqueue($ToDo$, $< \hat{M}, \hat{T}, \hat{P}, \hat{A} >$); $Done =\{ \ \}$;
Do
  $< T, M, P, A > = $ Dequeue($ToDo$);
  If ($< T, M, P, A >$ is Directly Model Checkable) Then
   Model check $< T, M, P, A >$; $Done = Done + \{< T, M, P, A >\}$; Continue;
  End;
  If (P is a query over all instances of T) Then
   Reduce P with Symmetry Reduction to P_1 where P_1 is on Instance 1 of T;
   Enqueue($ToDo$, $< T, M, P_1, A >$); Continue;
  End;
  If (M consists of instances from different classes) Then
   $Current = $ The first class that appears in T;
   Decompose M into $M_1=\{$All instances of $Current\}$ and $M_2=M - M_1$;
   Decompose T into T_1 performed by M_1 and T_2 performed by M_2;
   Decompose P into $P_1, \ldots, P_i$ on M_1 and $P_{i+1}, \ldots, P_m$ on M_2;
   $U_1 = \{P_1, \ldots, P_i\}$; $U_2 = \{P_{i+1}, \ldots, P_m\}$; $D_1 = \{ \ \}$; $D_2 = \{ \ \}$;
   While(!Empty(U_1) or !Empty(U_2))
    If (!Empty(U_1)) THEN
     $P' = $ Remove-an-element(U_1); $A' = \{$Assumptions of P' on $M_2\}$
     Enqueue($ToDo$, $< T_1, M_1, P', A' >$); $D_1 = D_1 + \{P'\}$; $U_2 = U_2 + A' - D_2$;
    End;
    If (!Empty(U_2)) THEN
     $P'' = $ Remove-an-element(U_2); $A'' = \{$Assumptions of P'' on $M_1\}$
     Enqueue($ToDo$, $< T_2, M_2, P'', A'' >$); $D_2 = D_2 + \{P''\}$; $U_1 = U_1 + A'' - D_1$;
    End;
   End;
  End;
  If (M consists only of all instances of a class, C) Then
   Reduce M with Case Splitting to M_1 where $M_1 = \{$Instance 1 of $C\}$;
   Enqueue($ToDo$, $< T, M_1, P, A >$); Continue;
  End;
Until (Empty($ToDo$));

Fig. 3. Domain Specific Reduction Algorithm for Transaction Systems

system will send a *TicketHeld* message, or a *TryLater* message, or a *SoldOut* message back to the customer. The property is formulated as P_0 in Figure 5 using an xUML level query logic derived from a query logic defined in [7]. For simplicity, in Figure 5 some details are left out and i (or j) is used to index a general instance of the Customer class (or the Agent class, respectively).

Although the structure of the system is simple, the arbitrary number of customers and agents make directly model checking P_0 infeasible even for the most powerful model checkers. Therefore, the domain specific reduction algorithm is applied to reduce the model checking task, $< M_0, T_0, P_0, \Phi >$. The assumption set is empty since customers are also modeled as class instances in M_0. The sub-queries involved in the reduction process are defined in Figure 5. The sub transactions and the sub-models involved in the process are shown in Figure 6. The reduction tree generated by the process is shown in Figure 7. Assumptions

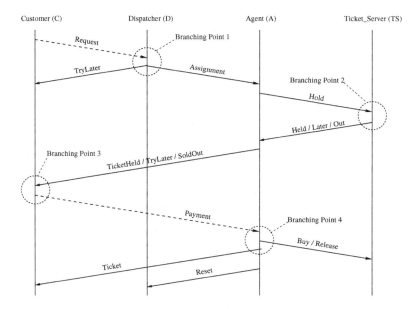

Customer (C)   Dispatcher (D)   Agent (A)   Ticket_Server (TS)

Fig. 4. Message Sequence Diagram of Ticketing Transaction

of a subtask are represented in Figure 7 by dashed arrows which lead to the subtasks that check the assumed properties on the corresponding sub-models. Reductions applied in the process are grouped into six general steps as follows:

Step 1: Symmetry Reduction. P_0 is a temporal predicate over all transactions of the type T_0. Since customers are symmetric to each other, checking P_0 on M_0 is reduced to checking P_1 on M_0 where P_1 is a predicate only over the transaction that involves Customer 1.

Step 2: Decomposition. T_0 is decomposed into three sub transaction types, T_{11}, T_{12} and T_{13}. Accordingly, M_0 is decomposed into three sub-models, M_{11}, M_{12}, and M_{13}. Transactions of the types, T_{11}, T_{12} or T_{13}, are conducted by M_{11}, M_{12}, or M_{13} respectively. P_1 is decomposed into three sub-queries: P_{21}, P_{22}, and P_{23}. P_{21} is directly model checkable on M_{12} without any assumption on M_{11} or M_{13}. P_{22} is directly model checkable on M_{12} by assuming that P_{31}, P_{32}, and P_{33} hold on M_{13}.

Step 3: Symmetry Reduction. In M_{13}, agents are symmetric. P_{31}, P_{32}, P_{33}, and P_{23} have no assumption on M_{11} and M_{12}. Therefore, checking P_{31}, P_{32}, P_{33}, and P_{23} on M_{13} is reduced to checking P_{41}, P_{42}, P_{43}, and P_{44} on M_{13}.

Step 4: Decomposition. T_{13} is further decomposed into two sub-types: T_{21} and T_{22}. Accordingly, M_{13} is decomposed into two sub-models: M_{21} and M_{22}. Transactions of the types T_{21} or T_{22} are conducted by M_{21} or M_{22} respectively. Checking P_{41}, P_{42}, P_{43}, and P_{44} on M_{13} is reduced to checking P_{41}, P_{42}, P_{43}, and P_{44} on M_{22} by assuming P_5 holds on M_{22}.

P_0 : **After** Request(i) **Eventually** TicketHeld(i) or TryLater(i) or SoldOut(i)

P_1 : **After** Request(1) **Eventually** TicketHeld(1) or TryLater(1) or SoldOut(1)

P_{21}: **After** Request(1) and **Forall** k { D.Agent_Free[k] = FALSE }
    Eventually TryLater(1)
P_{22}: **After** Request(1) and **Exists** k { D.Agent_Free[k] = TRUE }
    Eventually Assignment(j, 1) and A(j).$ = Idle
    /* A(j).$ represents the current state of the class instance, A(j). */
P_{23}: **After** Assignment(j, 1) and A(j).$ = Idle
    Eventually TicketHeld(1) or TryLater(1) or SoldOut(1)

P_{31}: **After** A(j).$ = Idle **Always** A(j).$ = Idle **UntilAfter** Assignment(j)
P_{32}: **After** Assignment(j) and A(j).$ = Idle **Eventually** Reset(j)
P_{33}: **After** Reset(j) **Eventually** A(j).$ = Idle

P_{41}: **After** A(1).$ = Idle **Always** A(1).$ = Idle **UntilAfter** Assignment(1)
P_{42}: **After** Assignment(1) and A(1).$ = Idle **Eventually** Reset(1)
P_{43}: **After** Reset(1) **Eventually** A(1).$ = Idle
P_{44}: **After** Assignment(1) and A(1).$ = Idle
    Eventually TicketHeld(1) or TryLater(1) or SoldOut(1)

P_5 : **After** Hold(j) **Eventually** Held(j) or Later(j) or Out(j)

P_6 : **After** Hold(1) **Eventually** Held(1) or Later(1) or Out(1)

Fig. 5. Original Query and All Intermediate Sub-queries

Step 5: Case Splitting. In M_{21}, under the assumption P_5 on M_{22}, transactions of the type T_{21} and performed by agents are independent of each other. Therefore P_{41}, P_{42}, P_{43}, and P_{44} is instead checked over M_3 by assuming P_5 on M_{22}.

Step 6: Symmetry Reduction. In M_{22}, transactions of the type, T_{22}, are symmetric. Therefore, checking P_5 on M_{22} is reduced to checking P_6 on M_{22}.

5   Evaluation of Integrated State Space Reduction

Under the general framework, reduction algorithms applied in the user-driven reduction procedure recursively break a complex model checking task into subtasks that are directly model checkable while reduction algorithms applied in the other two procedures facilitate directly model checking larger tasks. In this section, experiment results from the model checking study of the online ticket sale system are employed to evaluate the integrated application of these algorithms.

5.1   Evaluation of User-Driven Reduction Algorithms

Statistics from model checking Property P_0 in Figure 5 on the xUML model of the online ticket sale system are employed to demonstrate the effectiveness of

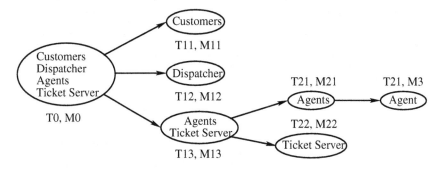

Fig. 6. Decomposition Relations between Sub-models Involved in Reduction

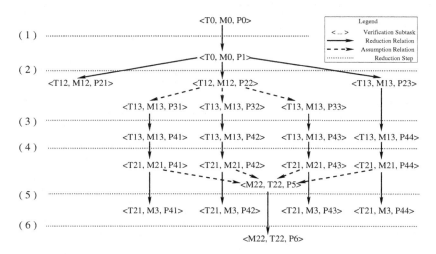

Fig. 7. Reduction Tree for Verifying P_0 on Online Ticket Sale System

the user-driven reduction algorithms. The memory and time usage for directly model checking P_0 is compared with the memory and time usage for checking the subtasks generated by applying these reduction algorithms.

Directly model checking P_0 on the xUML model with two customer instances and two agent instances requires two separate model checking runs, one for each customer instance. With state partial order reduction (SPOR) and symbolic model checking (SMC) applied, each run takes 152.79 megabytes and 16273.7 seconds. The complexity of the xUML model increases rapidly as the number of customers increases. Directly model checking P_0 on the xUML model with 6 customer instances cannot be fulfilled. Therefore, directly model checking the xUML model with arbitrary number of customers is not feasible.

The memory and time usage for model checking each subtask from the reduction tree in Figure 7 is shown in Table 1. It can be observed that the memory and time usage for each subtask is substantially lower than that for directly model

Table 1. Time and Memory Usage of Subtasks in Verifying P_0

Criteria	P_{21}	P_{22}	P_{41}	P_{42}	P_{43}	P_{44}	P_6
Memory	0.30M	0.95M	0.28M	0.29M	0.28M	0.29M	0.35M
Time	0.02S	1.81S	0.01S	0.04S	0.01S	0.04S	0.63S

checking P_0 on the xUML model with two customers. The model checking result from the reduction process can be scaled up to xUML models with arbitrary number of customer and agent instances by further applying non-deterministic abstraction and symmetry reduction. The complexity of symmetric query reduction is not shown due to an unfinished feature of our reduction system. However, the complexity is theoretically bounded by the complexity of the static structure of an xUML model because the reduction only checks the static structure of the model instead of exploring the full state space of the model.

5.2   Evaluation of SPOR, SMC, and their Combined Application

Being able to directly discharge larger model checking tasks reduces user interaction and makes the integrated state space reduction more automatic. Currently, to scale up directly model checkable tasks, SPOR is applied in the xUML-to-S/R translation and SMC is applied in the S/R level model checking. To demonstrate

Table 2. Model Checking Memory and Time Usage Comparison

SPOR	SMC	Memory Usage	Time Usage
Off	Off	167.072M	193748S
On	Off	16.0604M	10476.5S
Off	On	142.746M	471.32S
On	On	102.527M	280.1S

the reduction ability of SPOR and SMC, Property P_{21} in Figure 5 is directly checked on the whole model under the four possible on/off combinations of SPOR and SMC. The model checking complexities under the four combinations are compared in Table 2. It can be observed that both SPOR and SMC lead to significant reduction on the model checking complexity. SPOR offers a better memory usage while SMC offers a better time usage. Their combined application achieves the best time usage with a medium memory usage.

6   Conclusion

This paper defines and describes a general framework for integrated state space reduction in model checking executable object-oriented software system designs.

The framework is presented for system designs modeled in xUML, but is readily applicable to other representations. Partially implemented automaton support for the framework is discussed. The framework is illustrated by its instantiation for distributed transaction systems and is evaluated by applying the instantiation in model checking an online ticket sale system. The dimension of the software system designs that are model checkable is found to be substantially extended.

Acknowledgment

We gratefully acknowledge Robert P. Kurshan, Vladimir Levin, Huaiyu Liu, Nancy Macmahon, and Kedar Namjoshi for their generous help.

References

1. Kennedy Carter: http://www.kc.com/html/xuml.html. Kennedy Carter (2001)
2. Project Tech.: http://www.projtech.com/pubs/xuml.html. Project Tech. (2001)
3. Clarke, E.M., Emerson, E.A.: Design and Synthesis of Synchronization Skeletons Using Branching Time Temporal Logic. Logic of Programs Workshop (1981)
4. Clarke, E.M., Grumberg, O., Peled, D.: Model Checking. The MIT Press (1999)
5. Xie, F., Levin, V., Browne, J.C.: Model Checking for an Executable Subset of UML. Proc. of 16th IEEE International Conf. on Automated Software Engineering (2001)
6. Hardin, R.H., Har'El, Z., Kurshan, R.P.: COSPAN. Proc. of 8th International Conf. on Computer Aided Verification (1996)
7. Cadence: FormalCheck User Guide. Cadence (2001)
8. McMillan, K.L.: A Methodology for Hardware Verification Using Compositional Model Checking. Cadence Technical Report (1999)
9. Kurshan, R.P.: Computer-Aided Verification of Coordinating Processes: The Automata-Theoretic Approach. Princeton University Press (1994)
10. Godefroid, P., Pirottin, D.: Refining Dependencies Improves Partial-Order Verification Methods. 5th International Conf. on Computer Aided Verification (1993)
11. Peled, D.: Combining Partial Order Reductions with On-the-fly Model-Checking. Formal Methods in System Design (1996)
12. Valmari, A.: A Stubborn Attack on State Explosion. Proc. of 2th International Conf. on Computer Aided Verification (1990)
13. Kurshan, R.P., Levin, V., Minea, M., Peled, D., Yenigün, H.: Static Partial Order Reduction. Proc. of 4th International Conf. on Tools and Algorithms for the Construction and Analysis of Systems (1998)
14. Levin, V., Yenigün, H.: SDLCheck: A Model Checking Tool. Proc. of 13th International Conf. on Computer Aided Verification (2001)
15. Wang, W., Hidvegi, Z., Bailey, A.D., Whinston, A.B.: E-Processes Design and Assurance Using Model Checking. IEEE Computer Vol. 33 (2000)

Model Generation by Moderated Regular Extrapolation

Andreas Hagerer[1], Hardi Hungar[1], Oliver Niese[2], and Bernhard Steffen[2]

[1] METAFrame Technologies GmbH, Dortmund, Germany
{AHagerer,HHungar}@METAFrame.de
[2] Chair of Programming Systems, University of Dortmund, Germany
{Oliver.Niese,Steffen}@cs.uni-dortmund.de

Abstract. This paper introduces **regular extrapolation**, a technique that provides descriptions of systems or system aspects a posteriori in a largely automatic way. The descriptions come in the form of models which offer the possibility of mechanically producing system tests, grading test suites and monitoring running systems. Regular extrapolation builds models from observations via techniques from machine learning and finite automata theory. Also expert knowledge about the system enters the model construction in a systematic way. The power of this approach is illustrated in the context of a test environment for telecommunication systems.

1 Motivation

The aim of our work is improving quality control for reactive systems as can be found e.g. in complex telecommunication solutions. A key factor for effective quality control is the availability of a specification of the intended behavior of a system or system component. In current practice, however, only rarely precise and reliable documentation of a system's behavior is produced during its development. Revisions and last minute changes invalidate design sketches, and while systems are updated in the maintenance cycle, often their implementation documentation is not. It is our experience that in the telecommunication area, revision cycle times are extremely short, making the maintenance of specifications unrealistic, and at the same time the short revision cycles necessitates extensive testing effort. All this could be dramatically improved if it were possible to generate and then maintain appropriate reference models steering the testing effort and helping to evaluate the test results.

We propose a new method for model generation, called (moderated) *regular extrapolation*, which is tailored for a posteriori model construction and model updating during the system's lifecycle. The method, which comprises many different theories and techniques, makes formal methods applicable even in situations where no formal specification is available: based on knowledge accumulated from many sources, i.e. observations, test protocols, available specifications and last not least knowledge of experts, an operational model in terms of a state

R.-D. Kutsche and H. Weber (Eds.): FASE 2002, LNCS 2306, pp. 80–95, 2002.

and edge-labeled finite automaton is constructed that uniformly and concisely resembles the input knowledge in a way that allows for further investigation.

Though it is particularly well suited to be applied in regression testing (cf. section 2.2), where a previous version of the system is available as an approximate reference, regular extrapolation is not limited to this situation. Indeed, our experience so far has been encouraging. We were able to extrapolate an expressive model for some part of a nontrivial telephone switch as a basis for a monitor application (cf. section 5.3), and we could demonstrate its power for test-suite enhancement. Both applications are illustrated in a companion demo paper [8].

The paper is structured as follows: In section 2 we give a short overview about the considered scenario and discuss the design decisions. Section 3 briefly describes the ingredients of our approach for the model generation. The following section provides more details on some of the less standard techniques and the use we make of them regarding the considered scenario: the test of complex telecommunication systems. The usage of the generated models is described on the basis of examples in Section 5. Finally Section 6 draws some conclusions.

2   Regular Extrapolation

2.1   Sketch of the Approach

A key feature of our approach is the largely automatic nature of the extrapolation process. The main source of information is observation of the system, i.e. a set of system traces. These traces may be obtained passively by profiling a running system, or they may be gathered as reactions of the system to external stimulation (like in testing). These traces are abstracted and, after the introduction of a concept of state based on observable system attributes, they are combined into an automaton. This automaton extrapolates from the finite traces which have been observed to infinite behavior following regular patterns. Its language contains all abstract images of the traces observed so far. The general picture is as follows:

(Subset of) Concrete Traces   Abstract Traces $\subseteq$ Model Traces

Extrapolation from passively obtained observations and protocols of test runs may yield a too rough model of the system, leaving out many of its features and generalizing too freely. So these models have to be refined. We adapt machine learning algorithms and also incorporate expert's knowledge. Learning consists in running specific tests with the aim of distinguishing superficially similar states and finding additional system traces. Experts can either be implementors or people concerned with the environment of the system, for instance people knowing the protocols to be observed. Their knowledge enters the model in the form of declarative specifications, either to rule out certain patterns or to guide state distinguishing searches. Technically this is done by employing the bridge from temporal logic to automata, model-checking techniques and partial-order methods.

Conflicts arising during the extrapolation process between the different sources of information have to be examined and resolved manually (moderation).

2.2   The Regression Testing Scenario

Regression testing provides a particularly fruitful application scenario for regular extrapolation. Here, previous versions of a system are taken as the reference for the validation of future releases: changes typically concern new features, enhanced speed or capacities, some bugs or other often customer-driven change requests. However, by and large, the new version should provide everything the previous version did. I.e., if we compare the new with the old, there should not be too many essential differences. Thus if it were possible to (semi-) automatically maintain models comprising the knowledge obtained during previous development, testing, use and updating phases, regression testing could be largely improved. Besides providing a structure for managing the test suites, these models would be capable of providing flexible means for test run evaluation: note that it is inadequate to simply compare protocols of test runs with stored reference protocols, as besides the few essential differences there are many inessential ones, and it is very hard to distinguish between those two types. However there are formal means to construct models that factor out many of the minor differences between successive versions and thus reduce the manual effort of grading a test run.

2.3   The Design Decisions

Starting point of our investigation was the regression testing problem in the so-called black box scenario: a technique was needed to deal with a large legacy telephony system in which most of the involved applications (the so-called "plus products") running on and with the platform are third party. There was no hope to obtain formal specifications. The only source of information were intuitive user manuals, interaction with experienced test engineers and observations, observations, observations. As none of these sources could be fully trusted (and since what is true today may not be true tomorrow), the only approach was to faithfully and uniformly model all the information and to manually investigate arising inconsistencies. This lead to a change management process with continuous moderated updates:

- initially automata theoretic techniques are used to construct a consistent operational model along the lines of [19] (already here, expert knowledge may be required to guarantee consistency (cf. section 3 and 4)),
- this initial model is immediately used for test evaluation and monitoring (section 5.3).
- whenever unexpected observations arise, these are taken care of by either modifying the model or correcting the running system. Whereas debugging the system is standard, model modification is again done using involved automata-theoretic means (cf. section 3 and 4).

It is impossible in practice to find a precise model of the system under consideration, even on an abstract level. Such a model would usually be far too large and, as results from learning theory indicate, too time-consuming to obtain and to manage. Instead we are aiming at concise, problem-specific models, expressive enough to provide powerful guidance and to enhance the system understanding. In fact, many quite different models of this kind may be required to cover different goals, like monitoring, test generation, test grading or even simulation.

Also, in contrast to "classical" modeling scenarios, we cannot expect our models to *safely* approximate the intended system behaviors, as there is no safe information we can base on. On the one hand, this complicates the moderation in case of discrepancies between the modeled and the observed behaviors. On the other hand, it allows us to use with no loss powerful automata theoretic methods which do not preserve safe approximation. This accelerates the gain of expressiveness of our models, making them a strong aid already very early on.

It is of course very important that the models are reasonably close to the system. Exploiting all the information at hand, independently of their source, to obtain a comprising "hypothesis" model is the best we can do. In fact, our experience with a nontrivial real-life system[1] indicates that "brave" guesses are much better than too conservative ones, as the interaction with the "hypothesis" model enhances the expert's system understanding, and the closer the interaction the faster proceeds the extrapolation process.

2.4   Related Work

Central to our work is the theory of finite automata and regular languages as described for instance in [10]. A less known and more recent part of that theory concerns the problem of determining a model in terms of a deterministic finite automaton from observations. This is intensively discussed in the domain of *machine learning* [13]. There exists in general no efficient method that can compute such a model in polynomial steps. So several methods try through weakening of the requirements or through additional information to achieve the aims. The two most prominent learning models are the *Probably approximately correct learning model (PAC learning)* [24] and the *Query learning model* [1]. Whereas in PAC learning the algorithms gets random positive examples, is it possible in the Query learn model to inquire information about the investigated system actively. To some extent our approach is orthogonal to both of these learning models. The reason for this is basically that we do not aim at determining an exact model for an unknown system, which is unrealistic in practice. Rather we express all the available heterogeneous information about a system (observations, expert knowledge, . . .) in a consistent and uniform way. This is similar to the approach of *unifying models* [19] where a heterogeneous specification, consisting of several aspects specified in different formalisms, is combined into a single consistent model.

---

[1] Gained with a prototype implementation built on top of our already existing *Integrated Test Environment* [16].

3   Ingredients of a Posteriori Model Generation

This section describes the ingredients of a posteriori model generation. The considered class of systems are complex, reactive systems, as can be found e.g. in telecommunication systems. These systems normally consist of several subcomponents which communicate with and affect each other, typically via standardized protocols. As a prerequisite to our approach the system has to provide *points-of-observation (PO)* and *points-of-control-and-observation (PCO)*, i.e. we must be able to make observations of the system and, additionally, to influence it in order to test its reactions to certain (critical) stimuli sequences.

Fig. 1 sketches briefly our iterative approach. It starts with a model (initially empty) and a set of observations. The observations are gathered from a reference system in the form of traces. They can be obtained either *passively*, i.e. a running reference system is observed, or *actively*, i.e. a reference system is stimulated through test cases. The set of traces (i.e. the observations) is then be preprocessed, extrapolated and used to extend the current model. After extension the model is completed through several techniques, including adjusting to expert specifications. The last step validates the current hypothesis for the model, which can lead to new observations.

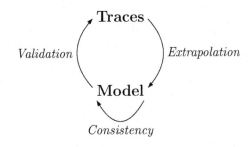

Fig. 1. Generation of models

The realization of this approach uses heavily automata operations and related techniques. The basis is given by standard automata operations like homomorphisms and boolean operations like meet, join and complement [10]. These are complemented by some specific operations for extrapolation. In particular, these are abstraction mappings more general than language homomorphisms, and a particular folding operation, which by identifying similar states introduces cycles in the finite traces. This borrows from automata learning techniques as discussed in [1] but is quite different in several aspects.

The adequate incorporation of expert knowledge requires further techniques. On the one hand, temporal logic [5] serves to formulate specifications which limit the model from above. I.e., experts formulate properties which they believe to be true of the system, and extrapolation results should be limited by them. Temporal-logic model checking is employed to check adherence of the model to these constraints. Counter examples generated by the model checker in case of a violation are to be studied to pinpoint the source of the discrepancy.

On the other hand, experts can identify events in sequences which lead to distinguishing similar states which would otherwise be identified in the extrapolation step. A third way in which expert knowledge enters is in specifying independence relations between events. This, by employing ideas of partial order approaches [15,25], leads to generalizing from (randomly) sequential observations to parallel patterns.

Finally, the validation of models draws on testing theory (cf. e.g. [14] for a survey) to generate stimuli sequences helping to discover wrongly identified states and missed behavior.

In the following, the steps of the model construction process will be explained one by one. Further details on some of them are given in Section 4.

3.1   Extrapolation

The model will be extended through a set of observations in form of traces. However before the traces are added to the model they have to be generalized. This comprises two steps:

1. abstraction from unnecessary detail, and
2. folding the tree of traces to a finite automaton with joins and cycles.

Abstraction. Abstraction has two aspects: *focus* and (true) *abstraction*. Focus means that if we are not interested in certain events or parameters we can eliminate them from the observation traces. An example are concrete time stamps. (True) abstraction takes care of first-order aspects we cannot simply ignore like participant identities. These have to be represented by propositional means to fit into the world of finite automata. Generally, we restrict the models to represent only instances of behavior with a certain bound on the number of active participants (or other first-order valued sets).

Folding. Before the traces are added to the model we combine them into a single *trace automaton*. If all traces start in the initial state of the system, they are merged using an unique start state into a tree. After that, all states which are seemingly equivalent will be identified. In our telephony system application, states are identified only if all external observations are the same. In particular, each telephone must have the same display and LED state. Further distinguishing criteria formalized as expert knowledge may refer to the history of traces.

3.2   Consistency

Each extrapolation step is followed by a consistency check. It checks whether the extension performed is consistent with the expert specification bounding the permitted behavior. The specifications are given as linear-time temporal-logic (LTL, [5]) constraints. Each constraint defines a formal language, i.e. a set of traces. These constraints are interpreted as loose upper bounds of the system language. The system, and therefore the model, should not contain any trace violating any of the constraints. As the models are finite automata, the LTL constraints can be checked one by one using a model checker. The model checker either ascertains that a constraint is satisfied or it produces a counter example, consisting of a trace of the model which violates the constraint. The discovery of such errors leads to an investigation whether the specification is wrong, or the extrapolation was too loose, or there is in error in the trace set which lead to the exploration.

This is essentially a manual step to be performed in collaboration with system or application experts. If a constraint is found to be too restrictive, its correction is rather straightforward. Or if it can be attributed to an erroneous observation, i.e. an error in the reference system, its correction is easy: we leave out the observation for the construction of our model and as a side benefit of model construction we have discovered an error. More difficult for our construction procedure is an error introduced by the abstraction step. The simplest, not always appropriate remedy is to remove all paths which violate the constraint. This works for safety constraints, for liveness constraints a deeper analysis is required which removes incorrect cycles.

Besides constraint checking, the consistency check uses the independency relation to complete the model (in the sense of partial-order methods). This is described in more detail in Section 4.4.

3.3   Validation

To ensure the validity of the obtained model a validation step completes the cycle. Here, tests are generated to further check for the correctness of state identifications and to look for additional model traces. I.e., like in learning an automaton from its external behavior, it is tried to verify the current hypothesis against the reference system. Besides state splits necessary to remedy too optimistic distinctions, these tests may lead to new observations which reenter the cycle.

The main point of validation is to make sure that the model is rather precise on short sequences. As most errors will already show up in short sequences,[2] this is not only the easiest but also the most useful thing to do. Remember that we are not aiming at a precise model, but only at an approximation comprising all the information currently available. Thus we do not suffer from the problem of deep "combination locks" [13] which make the learning problem inherently difficult (in the worst case).

Summarizing, tests covering all the essential short sequences are produced in order to validate the models state identifications. I.e. stimuli are generated to observe system reactions on input events which have not been seen so far. This in order to check whether after following different paths in the model which lead to the same state of the model there is indeed no (easily) discernable difference in system behavior. In particular, this is applicable to cycles (cycle validation).

---

[2] A fact explaining why the current practice does in fact find the most severe errors. Of course, the more complex the overall scenario, the longer are the required "short" sequences. This explains today's urgent need for new test technology.

4   Handling a Posteriori Model Generation

In this section we present the structure of the generated models, the considered application scenario and afterwards details of the key aspects of the extrapolation step and the consistency check.

4.1   Model Structure

Fig. 2 shows a part of a model. The filled states are called *stable system states*, i.e. states in which the system cannot continue without a stimulus from its environment. The other states are called *internal states*. In this example the system is in state S_1 and it can receive e.g. the event (or action) $?a$[3]. The system produces two events ($!x$ and $!y$), which are sent to the environment and afterwards it reaches the stable state S_2. In general there are additional observations attached to both states and actions of the model. Exam-

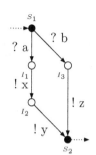

Fig. 2. Model structure

ples for state observations are e.g. the display status of a specific device. Action observations can be e.g. concrete parameter values of a protocol event.

4.2   Application Scenario: System-Level Testing of CTI Systems

Fig. 3 shows the considered scenario, a complex *Computer telephony integrated (CTI) system*, concretely a *Call Center solution*. A midrange telephone switch is connected to the ISDN telephone network or, more generally, to the public switched telephone network (PSTN), and acts as a 'normal' telephone switch to the phones. Additionally, it communicates directly via a LAN or indirectly via an application server with CTI applications that are executed on PCs. Like the phones, CTI applications are active components: they may stimulate the switch (e.g. initiate calls), and they also react to stimuli sent by the switch (e.g. notify incoming calls). Moreover the applications can be seen as logical devices, which can not only be used as a phone, but form a compound with physical devices.

In our point of view the switch has one *PCO* (via the *Corporate Network Protocol* (CorNet)) and one *PO* (via the *Computer Supported Telecommunications Applications Protocol* (CSTA) [4]). The technical realization of these test interfaces is provided by the *Integrated Test Environment* (ITE) [16,18], in particular the *Test Coordinator*. The ITE is an environment for the management of the overall test process for complex systems, i.e. specification of tests, execution of tests and analysis of test runs. The ITE is able to steer different test tools (dedicated to the subcomponents of a complex system) and to coordinate and evaluate the test runs. In the considered scenario two different kind of test tools are used by the test coordinator:

---

[3] We mutate the $?a$ and $!a$ notation of process algebra to denote inputs and output actions respectively.

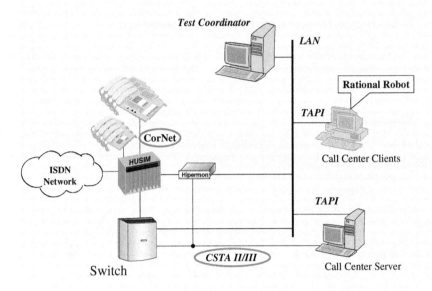

Fig. 3. Overview of the considered CTI scenario

1. A proprietary protocol analyzer (*Hipermon* [9]) which is connected to a telephone simulator (*Husim*) and to the connection between the switch and the application server.
2. A GUI test tool (*Rational Robot* [11]), which is used in several instances, i.e. for every considered call center client.

The heart of the environment is the Test Coordinator tool (cf. fig. 3), built on top of METAFrame's *Agent Building Center* [21], which is a generic and flexible workflow management system. So far the ITE has been successfully applied to the system level testing of complex system solutions like *Web-based applications* [17] or *CTI-Solutions* [16].

Based on this environment we are able to build a model for the telephone switch on CSTA-level [4].

4.3   Performing Regular Extrapolation

Abstraction. Abstraction is concerned with single traces of the system to be modeled. In a first step we filter and generalize the observations attached to states and transitions. In the considered scenario we concretely:

- restrict of the set of devices to be considered
- restrict of the set of physical attributes of system devices which enter the model, e.g.:
  (*ignore: (obs-id, obs-attribute, attribute-value) = (LED, LED-id, 27)*),
- generalize nongeneric information, e.g. date and time in displays are substituted by generic place holders
  (*replace: (obs-id, obs-attribute, attribute-value, attribute-pattern, replacement) = (DISPLAY, DISPLAY-no, 1, "LETTER (2:3) DIGIT (1:2) '.' LETTER (3) DIGIT (2)", "DATE")*)

In a second step concrete identifications of devices and system components are substituted by symbolic names that reflects the "roles" in a telecommunication scenario. Using symbolic names allows identifying information that is partially already included in a model when newly observed system behavior is to be added to the model. This results in smaller models. E.g. different tests that are related to specific switch features may differ only in the activities after establishment of a connection between two devices and in the identifications of the devices concretely used in the tests. Then, determining a common prefix of traces is facilitated if symbolic names are used. Furthermore, models generalized in this way are independent of the environment used to collect the traces. The generalization resembles that we determine symbolic names of actors. An actor encompasses a group of devices and components that have any interrelated association with the control and observation of calls, e.g. displays, buttons and lamps of a telephone set. For each possible actor able to act in the system a specification is prepared which consists of a set of replace-criterion-value pairs and which is used to determine actors associated with observations.

The trace automaton is then further generalized through the *folding step*.

Folding. Behaviorally equivalent stable states are identified through a comparison of their observations and can then be merged. More precisely, two states are (locally) behaviorally equivalent if their attached observations are identical, i.e. concretely all observed devices have the same status regarding display messages and LED's. It is in this step that the behavior of the system is extrapolated: with folding we can obtain an automaton with infinite behavior when cycles are introduced, cf. Fig. 4. However this step provides only an optimistic hypothesis and not a "real" (global) behavioral equivalence, as we cannot ensure that no "hidden" causalities exists. Thus sometimes it is necessary to refine this approach by distinguishing locally similar states, which can elegantly and systematically be done following the property-oriented expansion approach proposed in [20].

4.4   Adding Expert Knowledge

Generalization through Partial Order Methods. Another formalism to specify expert knowledge is inspired from the *partial order reduction* methods for communicating processes [15,25]. Normally these methods help avoiding having

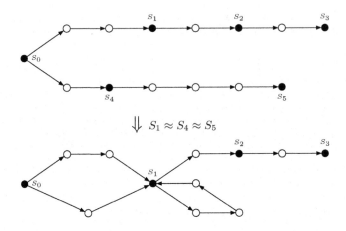

Fig. 4. Folding of equivalent states

to examine all possible interleavings among processes. However these methods can also be used as a specification formalism for generalization in the following way:

1. An expert specifies explicitly an **independence relation**, e.g. *Two independent calls can be shuffled in any order.*
2. A trace is inspected if it contains independent subparts.
3. Instead of the explicit observed trace, a whole equivalence class of traces (of which the observed trace is a representative) can be added to the model.

Partial order methods can be used both for a generalization and for a reduction of the generated models, where the independence relations can be found on a coarse granular level and on a fine granular level.

Coarse Granular Level. Fig. 5 shows how a coarse granular independence relation between stable states can be used for a further generalization of the model. When actions are independent from each other, then it is possible to change the order. The example fig. 5(a) shows two independent *offHook/onHook* sequences: the permutations fig. 5(b) and fig. 5(c) are equivalent to fig. 5(a) from the behavioral point of view.

Fine Granular Level. Under certain circumstances it is however sensible if not necessary to distinguish reorderings between internal states, e.g.: after sending an *?offHook* to the phone the switch responds with at least two messages. One message ensures that the text on the display is updated and the other one sets the actual LED status. If the switch works under normal conditions there exist priorities that schedule the order of the messages. However if the test is done

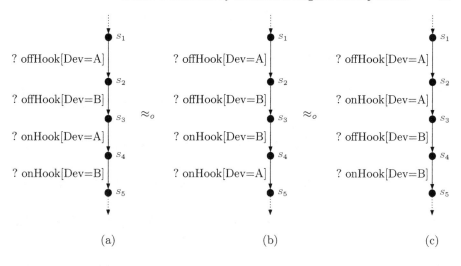

Fig. 5. Examples for reordering

e.g. under performance pressures it is allowed that the messages be reordered, so that other orderings of the events are acceptable and should not be marked as erroneous.

5   Examples for the Usage of Models

Within this section we will demonstrate several applications of the generated models, that enhance the overall test process.

5.1   Enhanced Test Result Evaluation

Current test practice shows that test case evaluation is mostly done via only few observation criteria and is therefore grossly incomplete. The example in Fig. 6(left) shows a typical test case where two devices get connected. The evaluation of the test case is done by observation of the display of the participating devices, which is sufficient for a correct system. However an incorrect system might produce non-conforming display messages or other erroneous signals on one of the other external interfaces, e.g. it is possible that one or more LED's are enabled which should be disabled. Additionally it is also possible that wrong devices were addressed. For our regression test application we therefore gather *all* the visible information of the reference system in response to the test inputs, which provides us with valuable information during the test run/evaluation. Fig. 6(right) shows a fraction of a model with a set of observations. One can see that for *all considered devices* (not only the stimulated ones) the whole set of observations is stored. In particular, this approach allows test engineers to design test cases concisely without bothering about completeness issues.

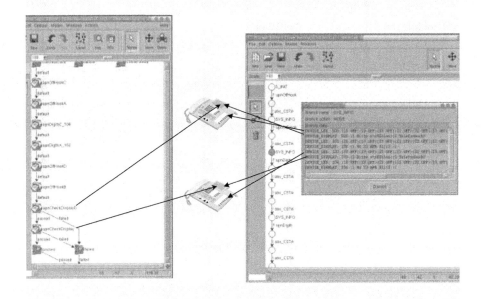

Fig. 6. Enhanced test evaluation

5.2 Improved Error Diagnosis

Automatically refined models in the regression test scenario enable an improved error diagnosis. When a test run evaluates to *failed* the detailed error diagnosis is sometimes a hard task. This is because some causalities between stimuli and events are not straightforward so that stimuli may result in errors not directly observable as erroneous user feedback (e.g. as a display message on a device) but in internal errors that become visible only in later contexts. The error diagnosis for this kind of errors can be quite tricky for a test engineer as he must know about these causalities in order to understand the real reason for errors, which lie (far away) in the past. However in the automatically refined models these causalities are stored and can be used for a more precise error diagnosis. Consider the example of fig. 7, where a trace is shown on the left and the corresponding fraction of the (correct) model on the right. When a test run is evaluated to *passed*, because e.g. $S_2 \approx S_2'$, the missing event must be marked as suspicious and presented to the user as it is possible that it is responsible for later errors. Otherwise, when the test run is evaluated to *failed*, the missing event is probably responsible for the failure and must be object of further investigation by an expert. However it is very useful for an expert to obtain exact hints where (remarkable) differences between the trace and the model lie instead of having to analyze the whole log file.

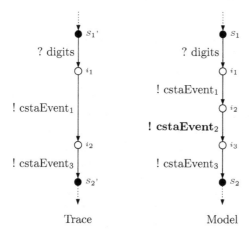

Fig. 7. Examples for Improved Error Diagnosis

5.3 Further Applications

Out of the manifold usages of the generated model, we mention here the most immediately test related ones.

Test suite evaluation and test generation. As soon as a model is generated, all the standard methods for test generation and test evaluation become applicable (e.g. [3,7] for finite state machines or [2,23,6,22] for labeled transition systems resp. input/output transition systems): it can be investigated how much of the model is actually covered by a given test suite, and it is also possible to automatically generate test suites guaranteeing certain coverage criteria. However, in contrast to the classical approach, where the model (specification) is typically considered correct, we do not have such a point of reference: neither the system nor the model can be trusted. Thus it is not clear how well the coverage measured on the model applies to the structure of the real system.

We do not consider this situation as disadvantageous, as in reality, up-to-date models or specifications are very rare, and therefore methods dealing with a symmetric situation are required, where the truth lies "between" the system and specification (model). Moreover, even if up-to-date models exist, our approach is adequate for keeping system and specification aligned.

Monitor. A *monitor* application observes a running system and is able to notify when an error occurs or an unexpected situation arises. In the latter case it is e.g. possible to start automatically a detailed trace. This is particularly useful to catch sporadic errors in systems already delivered to customers. Otherwise, they are hard to detect because it is not feasible to trace over long periods of time. The monitor enables selective tracing, and even a preliminary (and therefore incomplete) model could very well prove to be useful.

6   Conclusion

We have presented an approach, which we called *regular extrapolation*, that solves the specification problem for reactive systems a posteriori. Regular extrapolation comprises many different theories and techniques that make formal methods applicable even in situations where no formal specification is available. Though it is particularly well suited to be applied in regression testing, where a previous version of the system is available as an approximate reference, regular extrapolation is not limited to that situation. Indeed, our experience so far has been encouraging. We were able to extrapolate an expressive model for some part of a nontrivial telephone switch as a basis for a monitor application (cf. section 5.3), and we were able to demonstrate its usefulness for test-suite enhancement, as presented in a companion demo paper [8].

The approximative models resulting from our process are typically no safe approximations of the real systems. In learning complex systems, safety comes at the price of rather inaccurate models. Striving for a best match of all available information accelerates the convergence of the process. However our models can only be used in cases where safety is not a vital requirement. This is true for the majority of scenarios where no formal models exists. There gaining understanding of the system is the major goal. In these cases a thermometer with a precision of 1 percent is preferred to a thermometer with a precision of 5 percent which additional preserves *underapproximation*.

Currently, we investigate various directions to enhance our approach. Particularly important are new methods for diagnosis in case a discrepancy between a system and its model is found. These methods must be more advanced than in the usual safe approximation settings, because no direction of approximation is known. Thus decision support in form of additional diagnostic information is required, in order to decide for adequate updating steps on the model or corrections of the system. Although we are only at the beginning here, we are convinced that our regular extrapolation approach will significantly enhance the impact of formal methods in the industrial practice.

References

1. D. Angluin. Learning regular sets from queries and counterexamples. *Information and Computation*, 2(75):87–106, 1987.
2. E. Brinksma. A theory for the derivation of tests. *Proc. of PSTV VIII*, pages 63–74, 1988.
3. T.S. Chow. Testing software design modeled by finite-state machines. *IEEE Transactions on Software Engineering*, 4(3):178–187, 1978.
4. European Computer Manufactures Association (ECMA). Services for computer supported telecommunications applications (CSTA) phase II/III, 1994/1998.
5. E.A. Emerson. Temporal and modal logic. In J. van Leeuwen, editor, *Handbook of theoretical computer science*. Elsevier, 1990.
6. J.C. Fernandez, C. Jard, T. Jéron, L. Nedelka, C. Viho. Using on-the-fly verification techniques for the generation of test suites. In *Proc. CAV 1996*, LNCS 1102. Springer Verlag, 1996

7. S. Fujiwara, G. von Bochmann, F. Khendek, M. Amalou, and A. Ghedamsi. Test selection based on finite state models. *IEEE Trans. on Software Engineering*, 17(6):591–603, 1991.
8. A. Hagerer, H. Hungar, T. Margaria, O. Niese, B. Steffen, and H.-D. Ide. Demonstration of an operational procedure for the model-based testing of CTI systems. In *Proc. of the 5th Int. Conf. on Fundamental Approaches to Software Engineering (FASE 2002)*, this Volume.
9. Herakom GmbH. `http://www.herakom.de`.
10. J.E. Hopcroft and J.D. Ullman. *Introduction to Automata Theory, Languages, and Computation*. Addison-Wesley, 1979.
11. Rational Inc. The rational robot.
12. B. Jonsson, T. Margaria, G. Naeser, J. Nyström, and B. Steffen. Incremental requirement specification for evolving systems. Nordic Journal of Computing, vol. 8(1):65, Also in *Proc. of Feature Interactions in Telecommunications and Software Systems 2000*, 2001.
13. M.J. Kearns and U.V. Vazirani. *An Introduction to Computational Learning Theory*. MIT Press, 1994.
14. D. Lee and M. Yannakakis. Principles and methods of testing finite state machines - A survey. In *Proc. of the IEEE*, volume 84, pages 1090–1123, 1996.
15. A. Mazurkiewicz. Trace theory. *Petri Nets, Applications and Relationship to other Models of Concurrency*, LNCS 255, pages 279–324. Springer Verlag, 1987.
16. O. Niese, T. Margaria, A. Hagerer, M. Nagelmann, B. Steffen, G. Brune, and H. Ide. An automated testing environment for CTI systems using concepts for specification and verification of workflows. *Annual Review of Communication*, 54, 2000.
17. O. Niese, T. Margaria, and B. Steffen. Automated functional testing of web-based applications. In *Proc. QWE 2001*, 2001.
18. O. Niese, B. Steffen, T. Margaria, A. Hagerer, G. Brune, and H. Ide. Library-based design and consistency checks of system-level industrial test cases. In H. Hußmann, editor, *Proc. FASE 2001*, LNCS 2029, pages 233–248. Springer Verlag, 2001.
19. B. Steffen. Unifying models. In R. Reischuk and M. Morvan, editors, *Proc. STACS'97*, LNCS 1200, pages 1–20. Springer Verlag, 1997.
20. B. Steffen. Property oriented expansion. In *Proc. Int. Static Analysis Symposium (SAS'96)*, LNCS 1145, pages 22–41. Springer Verlag, 996.
21. B. Steffen and T. Margaria. *METAFrame in Practice: Design of Intelligent Network Services*, LNCS 1710, pages 390–415. Springer Verlag, 1999.
22. Q.M. Tan and A. Petrenko. Test generation for specifications modeled by input/output automata. In *In Proc. Of 11th IFIP Workshop on Testing of Communicating Systems (IWTCS'98)*, pages 83–99, 1998.
23. J. Tretmans. Test generation with inputs, outputs, and quiescence. In *Proc. TACAS'96*, LNCS 1055, pages 127–146. Springer Verlag, 1996.
24. L.G. Valiant. A theory of the learnable. *Communications of the ACM*, 27(11):1134–1142, 1984.
25. A. Valmari. On-the-fly verification with stubborn sets. In *Proc. CAV 1993*, LNCS 697, pages 397–408. Springer Verlag, 1993.

Better Slicing of Programs
with Jumps and Switches

Sumit Kumar[1] and Susan Horwitz[1,2]

[1] University of Wisconsin
{sumit,horwitz}@cs.wisc.edu
[2] GrammaTech, Inc.

Abstract. Program slicing is an important operation that can be used as the basis for programming tools that help programmers understand, debug, maintain, and test their code. This paper extends previous work on program slicing by providing a new definition of "correct" slices, by introducing a representation for C-style switch statements, and by defining a new way to compute control dependences and to slice a program-dependence graph so as to compute more precise slices of programs that include jumps and switches. Experimental results show that the new approach to slicing can sometimes lead to a significant improvement in slice precision.

1 Introduction

Program slicing, first introduced by Mark Weiser in [13], is a topic of on-going interest. For example, Jens Krinke maintains a website [7] with over 100 references to published work on slicing. This paper makes the following four contributions in the area of program slicing:

Defining Correct Slices: Weiser defined a *correct* slice of a program P to be a projection of P with certain properties (see Section 3). Podgurski and Clarke [10] defined a notion of *semantic dependence* that can also be used as the basis for a definition of a correct slice; however, their definition did not take jump statements (`goto`, `break`, etc.) into account. We give an example to illustrate a shortcoming of Weiser's definition, and offer a new definition, similar to the one for semantic dependence, that overcomes the problem with Weiser's definition, and also makes sense for programs with jump statements.

Language Extension: We discuss how to represent C-style switch statements in a program's control-flow and program-dependence graphs. To our knowledge, this is the first time switch statements have been discussed as such, rather than assuming that they have been implemented at a low level using gotos. Handling switch statements is important because many slicing applications involve displaying the result of a slice to the programmer, or using the results to create new source code. Thus, for those applications, if a slice includes code from a switch, it needs to be displayed/represented in the new code as a switch rather than in some low-level form. Representing and slicing a switch in a low-level form

R.-D. Kutsche and H. Weber (Eds.): FASE 2002, LNCS 2306, pp. 96–112, 2002.

and then mapping the results back to the source level may lead to a final result that is less precise than the one produced by working on the switch directly.

Improved Precision: Finding correct, minimal slices is an undecidable problem, whether correctness is defined according to Weiser, Podgurski/Clarke, or using the new definition proposed here. However, it is still a reasonable goal to design a slicing algorithm that is more precise than previous ones; i.e., to define a new algorithm that is correct, and also produces smaller slices than previous algorithms. In this spirit, we introduce some example programs with jumps and switches for which previous slicing algorithms produce slices that include too many components. While the examples with jumps are somewhat artificial, the examples with switches are motivated by code from real programs. We show that the reason extra components are included in the slices has to do both with how control dependences are defined, and how slices are computed. We then give a new definition of control dependence and a new slicing algorithm that is more precise than previous algorithms in the presence of jumps and/or switches. Due to space constraints, we discuss only intraprocedural slicing; extending the algorithm to be interprocedural is straightforward [8].

Experimental Results: While it is possible to produce artificial examples in which our new approach to slicing provides arbitrarily smaller slices than previous approaches, it is important to know how well it will work in practice. We provide some experimental results that show that while in most cases slice sizes are reduced by no more than 5%, there are examples of reductions of up to 35%.

2   Background

2.1   Assumptions

We assume that we are dealing with *well formed* programs; in particular, that there is neither unreachable code (i.e., there is a path in the program's control-flow graph from the enter node to every other node) nor explicit infinite loops (i.e., there is a path from every node in the control-flow graph to the exit node).

2.2   Slicing Using the PDG

Informally, the slice of a program from statement S is the set of program components that might affect S, either by affecting the value of some variable used at S, or by affecting whether and how often S executes. More precise definitions have been proposed, and are discussed below in Section 3.

Slicing was originally defined by Weiser [13] as the solution to a dataflow problem specified using the program's control-flow graph (CFG). Ottenstein and Ottenstein [9] provided a more efficient algorithm that uses the program-dependence graph (PDG) [4]:

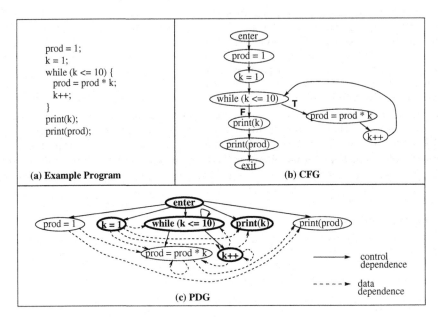

Fig. 1. Example program, its CFG, and its PDG. The PDG nodes in the slice from "`print(k)`" are shown in bold

Algorithm 1 *(Ottensteins' Algorithm for Building and Slicing the PDG)*

Step 1: *Build the program's CFG, and use it to compute data and control dependences: Node N is **data dependent** on node M iff M defines a variable x, N uses x, and there is an x-definition-free path in the CFG from M to N. Node N is **control dependent** on node M iff N postdominates one but not all of M's CFG successors.*

Step 2: *Build the PDG. The nodes of the PDG are almost the same as the nodes of the CFG: a special enter node, and a node for each predicate and each statement in the program; however, the PDG does not include the CFG's exit node. The edges of the PDG represent the data and control dependences computed using the CFG.*

Step 3: *To compute the slice from statement (or predicate) S, start from the PDG node that represents S and follow the data- and control-dependence edges backwards in the PDG. The components of the slice are all of the nodes reached in this manner.*

Example: Figure 1 shows a program that computes the product of the numbers from 1 to 10, its CFG, and its PDG. The nodes in the slice of the PDG from "`print(k)`" are shown using bold font. (For the purposes of control-dependence computation, an edge is added to the CFG from the *enter* node to the *exit* node; to avoid clutter, those edges are not shown in the CFGs given in this paper).

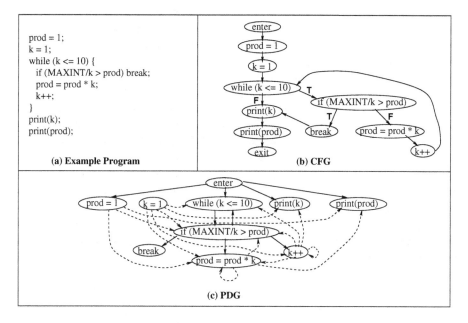

Fig. 2. Example program with a **break** statement, its CFG, and its PDG

2.3 Handling Jumps

Early slicing algorithms (including Weiser's and the Ottensteins') assumed a
structured language with conditional statements and loops, but no jump statements (such as **goto**, **break**, **continue**, and **return**). Both [2] and [3] pointed out
that if a CFG is used in which a jump statement is represented as a node with
just a single outgoing edge (to the target of the jump), then no other node will
be control dependent on the jump, and thus it will not be in the slice from any
ot her node. For example, Figure 2(a) shows a modified version of the program
from Figure 1, now including a **break** statement. Figures 2(b) and 2(c) show the
program's CFG and the corresponding PDG. Note that in this PDG, there is
no path from the **break** to "**print(k)**" or to "**print(prod)**", and therefore the
break is (erroneously) not included in the slices from those two print statements
even though the presence of the **break** can affect the values that are printed.

The solution proposed by [2] and [3] involves using an augmented CFG,
called the ACFG, to build a dependence graph whose control-dependence edges
are different from those in the PDG used by Algorithm 1. We will refer to the
new dependence graph as the *APDG*, to distinguish it from the PDG.

Algorithm 2 *(Building and Slicing the APDG)*

Step 1: *Build the program's ACFG. In the ACFG, jump statements are treated
as pseudo-predicates. Each jump statement is represented by a node with
two outgoing edges: the edge labeled true goes to the target of the jump, and
the (non-executable) edge labeled false goes to the node that would follow the*

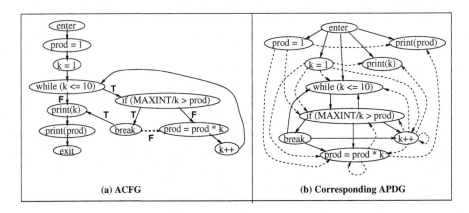

Fig. 3. ACFG and the corresponding APDG for the example program from Figure 2

> jump if it were replaced by a no-op. Labels are treated as separate statements; i.e., each label is represented in the ACFG by a node with one outgoing edge to the statement that it labels.
>
> **Step 2:** *Build the program's APDG. Ignore the non-executable ACFG edges when computing data-dependence edges; do not ignore them when computing control-dependence edges. (This way, the nodes that are executed only because a jump is present, as well as those that are not executed but would be if the jump were removed, are control dependent on the jump node, and therefore the jump will be included in their slices.)*
>
> **Step 3:** *To compute the slice from node S, follow data- and control-dependence edges backwards from S as in Algorithm 1. A label L is included in a slice iff a statement "goto L" is in the slice.*

Example: Figure 3 shows the ACFG for the program in Figure 2(a), and the corresponding APDG. (The non-executable *false* edge out of the **break** in Figure 3(a) is shown using a dotted arrow.) Note that in Figure 3(b), there are control-dependence edges from the **break** to "prod = prod * k" and to "k++"; therefore, the **break** is (correctly) included in every slice that includes one of those two nodes.

3   Semantic Foundations for Slicing

In his seminal paper on program slicing [13], Weiser defined a slice of a program P from point S with respect to a set of variables V to be any program P' such that:

Program	Intuitive Slice	Also Correct by Weiser's Definition
[1] x = 2;		[1] x = 2;
[2] y = 2;		[2] y = 2;
[3] w = x * y;		
[4] x = 1;	[4] x = 1;	
[5] y = 3;	[5] y = 3;	
[6] z = x + y;	[6] z = x + y;	[6] z = x + y;

Fig. 4. Example illustrating a shortcoming of Weiser's definition of a correct slice

- P' can be obtained from P by deleting zero or more statements.
- Whenever P halts on input I, P' also halts on input I, and the two programs produce the same sequences of values for all variables in set V at point S if it is in the slice, and otherwise at the nearest successor to S that is in the slice.

One problem with this definition is that it can be inconsistent with the intuitive idea that the slice of a program from point S is the set of program components that might *affect* S. For example, Figure 4 shows a program, the slice that a programmer would probably produce if asked to slice the program from statement [6] with respect to variable z, and another slice that is correct according to Weiser's definition, but that does not match our intuition about slicing. Furthermore, the requirement that a slice be an executable program may be too restrictive in some contexts (e.g., when using slicing to understand how a program works, or to understand the effects of a proposed change). In those cases, it might be more appropriate to define the slice of a program simply to be a subset of the program's components, rather than an executable projection of the program.

Given these observations, we propose to define the slice of program P from component S to be the components of P that might have a semantic effect on S. But what does it mean for a statement or predicate X to have a semantic effect on another statement/predicate S? To make that notion more precise, we consider what happens when a new program P' is created by modifying X or removing it from program P as follows:

X **is a normal predicate:** P' is created by replacing X with a different predicate that uses the same set of variables as X. (For example, in the program whose ACFG is shown in Figure 3, the predicate "MAXINT/k > prod" could be replaced by any other predicate that uses only variables k and prod, such as: "k < prod", or "k != 0 && prod > 22".)

X **is a pseudo-predicate (a jump statement):** P' is created by removing statement X from P.

X **is a non-jump statement:** P' is created by replacing X with a different statement that uses and defines the same sets of variables as X. (For example, in the program whose ACFG is shown in Figure 3, the statement "prod = prod*k" could be replaced by any other statement that uses only variables

prod and k, and that defines variable prod, such as: "prod = k + prod", or
"prod = prod-k-4".)

Definition 0. *(Semantic Effect): X has a **semantic effect** on S iff there is
some program P' created by modifying or removing X from P as defined above,
and some input I such that:*

- *Both P and P' halt on I.*
- *The two programs produce a different sequence of values for some variable
  used at S.*

Note that the sequence of values produced for a variable used at S can differ
either because the two sequences are of different lengths, or because their k^{th}
values differ (for some k).

Definition 0 is similar to the definition of *finitely demonstrable semantic dependence* given by Podgurski and Clarke in [10]. However, that definition did
not take jump statements into account: according to their definition, no program component is ever semantically dependent on a jump; therefore, if a correct slice from S is defined to include all components on which S is semantically
dependent, jump statements will never be included in a slice. This is clearly contrary to one's intuition, and therefore is a shortcoming of the Podgurski/Clarke
definition.

As usual with any interesting property of a program, determining which
components have a semantic effect on a given component S, according to Definition 0, is an undecidable problem. Therefore, we must say that a (correct) slice
of program P from component S is any superset of the components of P that
have a semantic effect on S.

Note that using Definition 0, statements [4] and [5] in the example program
in Figure 4 (but not statements [1] and [2]) have a semantic effect on statement
[6]. Therefore, a correct slice from statement [6] must include statements [4]
and [5] (but not statements [1] and [2]), which is consistent with our intuition
about that slice.

4   Representing Switch Statements

Consider a C switch statement of the form:

```
switch (E) {
    case e1: S1; break;
    ...
    case en: Sn; break;
    default: S;
}
```

Clearly, "switch(E)" should be represented in the CFG (and the ACFG)
using a (normal) predicate node with $n + 1$ outgoing edges: one to each case
including the default. If there were no default, the $n + 1^{st}$ edge should go
to the first statement following the switch (because in C, if the value of the

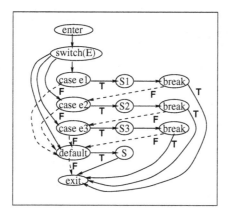

Fig. 5. ACFG for a switch statement

switch expression does not match any case label, and there is no `default` then execution continues immediately after the switch).

Now consider how to represent the case labels. One's initial intuition might be that they are similar to other labels in a program (the targets of `goto` statements). However, there is an important difference: if a program includes "`goto L1`", then label `L1` must be in the program, or it is not syntactically correct. If there is *no* "`goto L1`", then it doesn't matter whether label `L1` is in the program: its presence or absence has no semantic effect. However, these observations are not true of a case label. Removing a case label from a program never causes a syntax error, but *can* have a semantic effect. For example, if expression `E` in the code given above evaluates to `e1`, then statement `S1` will execute. However, if "`case e1`" is removed, then statement `S1` will not execute; instead, statement `S` will execute. Therefore, it makes sense for "`case e1`" to be in the slice from `S1` as well as in the slice from `S`.

This suggests that, like jumps, case labels should be represented using pseudo-predicates in the ACFG. The target of the outgoing *true* edge from a case-label node should be the first statement inside the `case`, and the target of the outgoing *false* edge should be the node that represents the default label if there is one, and otherwise the first statement that follows the switch (because if the case label is removed, and the switch expression matches that value, then execution proceeds with the first statement after the switch). The target of the outgoing *false* edge from the default case should always be the first statement that follows the switch.

Example: Figure 5 shows the ACFG for the switch statement given above (for $n = 3$).

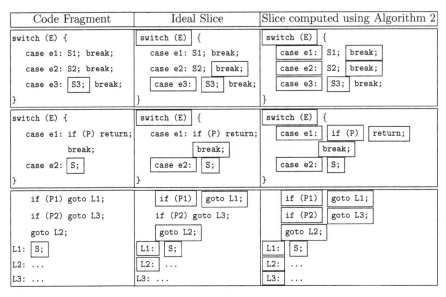

Fig. 6. Examples for which Algorithm 2 produces slices with extra components. The first column gives a code fragment, with one statement enclosed in a box. The second column shows the ideal slice from the boxed statement (according to Definition 0 given above in Section 3). The third column shows the slice computed using Algorithm 2

5   Motivation for a New Slicing Algorithm

Figure 6 gives three examples where Algorithm 2 (see Section 2.3) produces slices that include unwanted components. (In these examples, we assume that switch statements are represented in the ACFG as discussed above in Section 4.) The first column in Figure 6 gives a code fragment, with one statement enclosed in a box. The second column shows the ideal slice from the boxed statement (according to Definition 0 given above in Section 3). The third column shows the slice computed using Algorithm 2. The first two examples involve switches, while the third example involves only gotos.

Note that in the first example the slice from S3 should include the **break** from the previous case, because the presence/absence of that **break** affects whether or not S3 executes. In particular, consider what happens when expression E evaluates to e2. If the **break** is *not* in the program, S3 executes, while if the **break** *is* in the program, S3 does not execute.

In the second example, the slice from S should include neither "if (P)" nor "**return**". Whatever the value of predicate P, statement S will not execute (because either the **return** or the **break** prevents execution from "falling through" from "case e1" to "case e2"). Similarly, whether or not the **return** is in the program makes no difference since it is followed by the **break** (and thus S is always prevented from executing).

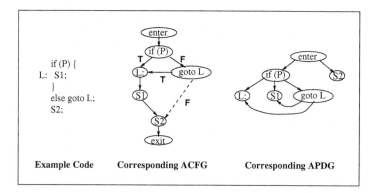

Example Code   **Corresponding ACFG**   **Corresponding APDG**

Fig. 7. Example in which a control dependence does not reflect a semantic effect. The APDG includes a control-dependence edge from "if (P)" to S1. However, "if (P)" cannot in fact affect the execution of S1; it always executes, regardless of whether P evaluates to *true* or to *false*

In all three examples, extra components are included in the slices computed using Algorithm 2 because of a chain of control-dependence edges. For instance, the APDG for the second example includes the following chain: case e1 → if (P) → return → break → case e2 → S. Thus, since Algorithm 2 follows all control-dependence edges backwards, all of those components are included in the slice from S[1]. In this example, each individual control-dependence edge represents a possible semantic effect: "case e1" has a semantic effect on "if (P)", which has a semantic effect on "return", which has a semantic effect on "break", which has a semantic effect on "case e2", which has a semantic effect on S. However, the backwards closure of the control-dependence relation starting from S yields a superset of the components that have a semantic effect on S; i.e., the "semantic-effect" relation is not transitive.

It is also possible to have an example in which even an individual control dependence (computed using the ACFG) does not reflect a semantic effect, as illustrated in Figure 7. In this example, the APDG includes a control-dependence edge from "if (P)" to S1 because S1 postdominates the *true* successor of the if in the ACFG, but does not postdominate its *false* successor (because the goto's non-executable *false* edge bypasses S1). However, "if (P)" cannot in fact affect the execution of S1; it always executes, regardless of whether P evaluates to *true* or to *false*.

These examples motivate the need for a new definition of control dependence to avoid control-dependence edges like the one in Figure 7 that do not reflect a semantic effect. They also motivate the need for a new way to compute slices

---

[1] Furthermore, the entire backward closure from predicate P of the control- and data-dependence relations will be included in the slice computed by Algorithm 2, making it arbitrarily larger than the ideal slice.

that does not involve taking the transitive closure of the control-dependence edges, since, as discussed above, the semantic-effect relation is not transitive.

6   New Definition of Control Dependence and New Slicing Algorithm

Recall that the definition of control dependence used in Algorithm 1 is as follows:

Definition 1. *(Original Control Dependence): Node N is **control dependent** on node M iff N postdominates, in the CFG, one but not all of M's CFG successors.*

To permit control dependence on jumps, Algorithm 2 replaces "CFG" with "ACFG" in the definition of control dependence:

Definition 2. *(Augmented Control Dependence): Node N is **control dependent** on node M iff N postdominates, in the ACFG, one but not all of M's ACFG successors.*

Unfortunately, as illustrated in Figure 7, Definition 2 is too liberal; it can cause a spurious control dependence of N on M due to the presence of an intervening pseudo-predicate. For example, in the ACFG in Figure 7, node S1 fails to postdominate the *false* successor of the if only because of the non-executable edge from "goto L1" to S2. Since the execution of S1 *is* affected by the presence/absence of the goto it *should* be considered to be control dependent on the goto; however, (as noted previously), S1 will execute regardless of the value of predicate P, and therefore it should *not* be considered to be control dependent on the if. So in this case, the actual influence of "goto L1" on statement S1 causes an apparent (but spurious) influence of "if (P)" on S1.

The solution to this dilemma is to replace only the *second* instance of "CFG" with "ACFG" in Definition 1:

Definition 3. *(Control Dependence in the Presence of Pseudopredicates): Node N is **control-dependent** on node M iff N postdominates, in the CFG, one but not all of M's ACFG successors.*

We will refer to a dependence graph that includes control-dependence edges computed using Definition 3 as a PPDG (pseudo-predicate PDG) to distinguish them from the PDGs whose control-dependence edges are computed using Definition 1, and the APDGs whose control-dependence edges are computed using Definition 2.

Example: The program and ACFG from Figure 7 are given again in Figure 8, with the corresponding PPDG. Note that neither label L nor statement S1 is control dependent on "if (P)".

Definition 3 addresses the problem of control-dependence edges that do not reflect semantic effects. The next problem that needs to be addressed is the fact that even when every control-dependence edge does represent a semantic effect, the backward closure of control-dependence edges from a node S may include

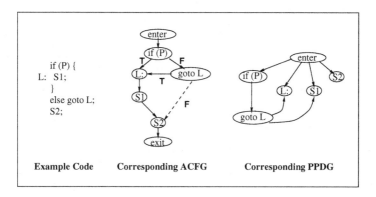

Fig. 8. Example code and ACFG from Figure 7 with the corresponding PPDG

nodes that have no semantic effect on S. For example, consider again the PPDG in Figure 8. If the slice from node S1 includes all nodes reached by following control-dependence edges backwards, then "if (P)" will (erroneously) be in the slice because of the chain of control-dependence edges: if (P) → goto L → S1.

To address this problem, we need the following definition:

Definition 4. *(IPD)*: *The **immediate post dominator (IPD)** of a set of ACFG nodes is the node that is the least-common ancestor of that set of nodes in the CFG's postdominator tree.*

Consider a (normal or pseudo) predicate P, with ACFG successors $n_1...n_k$, and let $D = \text{IPD}(n_1...n_k)$. Intuitively, P may affect the execution of a program component S only if there is a path in the CFG from one of P's ACFG successors to S that does not include node D. (If there is such a path, we say that S **is controlled by** P.) The value of P (for a normal predicate), or its presence/absence (for a pseudo-predicate) determines which of its ACFG successors is executed. The execution of the nodes along the paths from those ACFG successors to D are also affected by the value (or presence/absence) of P. However, since whenever P is executed, execution will always reach D (barring an infinite loop or other abnormal termination), the execution of nodes "beyond" D are not affected by P.

As discussed above, following control-dependence edges backwards from S in the PPDG can cause extra nodes to be included in the slice from S. In terms of the "is controlled by" relation, this is because there may be a chain of control-dependence edges in the PPDG from a predicate P to S, yet S is not controlled by P. However, we have proved the following Theorem [8]:

Theorem: Node S is controlled by (normal or pseudo) predicate P iff there is a chain of control-dependence edges in the PPDG: $P \to M_1 \to M_2 \to ... \to M_k \to S$, such that every M_i in the chain is a normal predicate node. (Note that there may also be no M_i's at all; i.e., there may be a single control-dependence edge $P \to S$.)

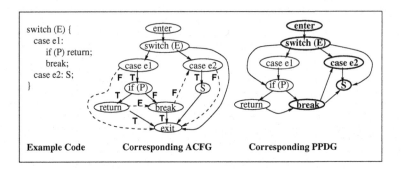

Fig. 9. The code, ACFG, and PPDG for the second example in Figure 6. The PPDG nodes in the slice from S, computed using Algorithm 3, are shown in bold

This Theorem tells us that it is not necessary to follow control-dependence edges back from a pseudo-predicate; for any predicate P such that there is a node S in the slice that is controlled by P, P will be picked up by following chains backwards only from normal predicates.

The new algorithm for building and slicing the PPDG is given below.

Algorithm 3 *(Building and Slicing the PPDG)*

Step 1: *Build the ACFG as described above for Algorithm 2.*

Step 2: *Build the PPDG: Ignore the non-executable ACFG edges when computing data-dependence edges; compute control-dependence edges according to Definition 3.*

Step 3: *To compute the slice from node S, include S itself and all of its data- and control-dependence predecessors in the slice. Then follow backwards all data-dependence edges, and all control-dependence edges whose targets are not pseudo-predicates; add each node reached during this traversal to the slice. Include label L in the slice iff a statement "goto L" is in the slice.*

Examples: (1) Using Algorithm 3, the slice from S1 of the program in Figure 8 would include the nodes for S1, "goto L", L, and the *enter* node. It would not include the node for "if (P)" because, since "goto L" is a pseudo-predicate, its incoming control-dependence edge would not be followed back to the if node.

(2) Figure 9 shows the code, ACFG, and PPDG for the second example in Figure 6. Bold font is used to indicate the nodes that would be in the slice from statement S computed using Algorithm 3. Note that "case e1", "if (P)", and "return" are correctly omitted from the slice.

6.1   Complexity

The time required for Algorithm 3 includes the time to build the PPDG and the time to compute a slice. Like previous slicing algorithms that use a dependence

	lines of source code	number of APDG/PPDG nodes	number of slices	Av. slice size (# of nodes)	
				Alg 2	Alg 3
gcc.cpp	4,079	16,784	1,932	11,693	11,670
byacc	6,626	21,239	468	2,119	2,110
CADP	12,930	35,965	499	7,921	7,905
flex	16,236	31,354	1,716	8,150	8,082

Fig. 10. Information about the C programs used in the experiments

graph, the time for slicing itself is extremely efficient, requiring only time proportional to the size of the slice (the number of nodes and edges in the sub-PPDG that represents the slice). The only difference in the time required to build the PPDG as compared to the time required to build the APDG is for the computation of control dependences. Computing control dependences can be done for both the APDG and the PPDG in time $O(E + C)$, where E is the number of edges in the ACFG and C is the number of control-dependence edges. However, C may be different for the APDG and PPDG. For example, in Figure 9, the PPDG includes edges from "switch (E)" to "if (P)" and to S that would not be in the corresponding APDG. Figures 7 and 8 illustrate control-dependence edges that are in the APDG but not in the PPDG.

7   Experimental Results

To evaluate our work, we implemented Algorithms 2 and 3, and used each of them to compute slices in four C programs (information about the programs, the number of slices taken in each, and the average sizes of those slices is given in the table in Figure 10). Slices were taken from all of the nodes that could be reached by following one control-dependence edge forward from a node representing a switch case, and then following five data-dependence edges forward. This ensured that every slice would include a switch, but (by starting further along the chain of data dependences) avoided, for example, slices that would include *only* switch cases and breaks.

More details about the experimental results are given in the tables in Figures 11 and 12. Figure 11 presents information about the differences in the sizes of the individual slices taken using the two algorithms. The first column gives the number of cases where the two algorithms produced slices of exactly the same size. The other columns give the number of cases where the slice produced by Algorithm 2 was larger than the slice produced by Algorithm 3; the second column gives the number of cases where the size difference was between 1 and 10, the third column gives the number of cases where the size difference was between 11 and 20, etc.

Figure 12 presents information about how much the use of Algorithm 3 reduced the sizes of the slices. The first column gives the number of cases where there was no reduction in slice size (a 0% reduction). The other columns give the number of cases where the reduction in size falls within the range specified

	0	1-10	11-20	21-30	31-40	41-50	51-60	61-70	71-80	81-90
gcc.cpp	2	0	48	1881	0	1	0	0	0	0
byacc	0	229	239	0	0	0	0	0	0	0
CADP	18	152	160	169	0	0	0	0	0	0
flex	0	0	5	127	48	41	8	79	1405	3

Fig. 11. Differences in slice sizes using the two algorithms. Each entry gives the number of cases where the size difference in the slices produced by Algorithms 2 and 3 falls into the range given at the top of the column

	0%	5%	10%	15%	20%	25%	30%	35%
gcc.cpp	2	1918	3	1	8	0	0	0
byacc	0	438	18	7	5	0	0	0
CADP	18	481	0	0	0	0	0	0
flex	0	1572	0	5	13	52	66	8

Fig. 12. Percent reduction in slice sizes achieved using Algorithm 3. Each entry gives the number of cases where the reduction in slice size falls into the range specified by the previous and current column headings

by the previous and current column headers. For example, the second column gives the number of cases where there was a size reduction greater than 0% and less than or equal to 5%; the third column gives the number of cases where there was a size reduction greater than 5% and less than or equal to 10%.

Note that in almost all cases Algorithm 3 did produce smaller slices than Algorithm 2. Although this led to only a small reduction in the total size of the slice in most cases, there were some cases in both gcc.cpp and byacc where Algorithm 3 provided reductions in slice sizes of more than 15%, and some cases in flex where it provided reductions in slice sizes of more than 30%.

8   Related Work

Choi-Ferrante: The paper by Choi and Ferrante [3] that presents Algorithm 2 also includes a second algorithm: Given a node S, it starts with the slice from S computed using Algorithm 1, then adds goto statements to the slice to form a program that will always produce the same sequence of values for the variables used at S as the original program. This technique may produce smaller slices than those produced using Algorithm 2. However, the gotos that are added are not necessarily in the original program; therefore, it satisfies neither Weiser's definition of a correct slice, nor Definition 0 from Section 3.

Agrawal: Agrawal [1] also gives an algorithm that involves adding jump statements to the slice computed using the standard PDG, but the statements that he adds *are* from the original program. He states that this algorithm produces the same results as Algorithm 2; however, no proof is provided.

Harman-Danicic: More recently, Harman and Danicic [5] have defined an extension to Agrawal's algorithm that produces smaller slices by using a refined criterion for adding jump statements (from the original program) to the slice computed using Algorithm 1. When applied to programs without switches, it may or may not produce slices that satisfy Definition 0. This is because their algorithm includes some nondeterminism: when there are cycle-free paths from a predicate to its immediate-postdominator both via its *true* and its *false* branches, then the jump statements along either of the paths can be chosen to be in the slice. Unfortunately, when applied to programs with switch statements, this algorithm can be as imprecise as Algorithm 2. For example, when used to slice the switch statement in the first example in Figure 6, it produces exactly the same slice as Algorithm 2. Another disadvantage of this algorithm as compared to ours is that the worst-case time to compute a slice can be quadratic in the size of the CFG, while our algorithm is linear in the size of the computed slice.

Sinha-Harrold-Rothermel: In [12], Sinha, Harrold, and Rothermel discuss interprocedural slicing in the presence of arbitrary interprocedural control flow; e.g., statements (like `halt`, `setjmp-longjmp`) that prevent procedures from returning to their call sites. That issue is orthogonal to the one addressed here (better slicing of programs with jumps and switches); thus, the two approaches can be combined to handle programs with arbitrary interprocedural control flow as well as jumps and switches.

Schoenig-Ducassé: An algorithm for slicing Prolog programs is given in [11]. It is observed that some arguments of some clauses (referred to as *failure positions*) must be included in a slice because they may cause a relevant goal to fail (so excluding them from the slice might change the control-flow of the program). This idea is related to our notion of the semantic effect of a jump statement (because in that case too, removing the statement might change the control-flow of the program).

9 Summary

We have provided a new definition for a "correct" slice, a new definition for control dependences, and a new slicing algorithm. The algorithm has essentially the same complexity as previous algorithms that compute slices using program dependence graphs, and is more precise than previous algorithms when applied to programs with jumps and switch statements.

The motivation for this work was the observation that slices of code with switch statements computed using the approach to handling jumps proposed by [2,3] (as implemented in the CodeSurfer [6] programming tool) often include many extra components, which is confusing to users of the tool. We expect that the new approach will have an important practical benefit (to users of slicing tools) as well as being an interesting theoretical advance.

Acknowledgments

This work was supported in part by the National Science Foundation under grants CCR-9970707 and CCR-9987435.

References

1. H. Agrawal. On slicing programs with jump statements. In *Proc. ACM Conf. on Programming Language Design and Implementation (PLDI)*, pages 302–312, June 1994.
2. T. Ball and S. Horwitz. Slicing programs with arbitrary control flow. In *Lecture Notes in Computer Science*, volume 749, New York, NY, November 1993. Springer-Verlag.
3. J. Choi and J. Ferrante. Static slicing in the presence of goto statements. *ACM Trans. on Programming Languages and Systems*, 16(4):1097–1113, July 1994.
4. J. Ferrante, K. Ottenstein, and J. Warren. The program dependence graph and its use in optimization. *ACM Trans. on Programming Languages and Systems*, 9(3):319–349, July 1987.
5. M. Harman and S. Danicic. A new algorithm for slicing unstructured programs. *Jrnl. of Software Maintenance*, 10(6):415–441, Nov./Dec. 1998.
6. http://www.codesurfer.com.
7. http://www.infosun.fmi.uni-passau.de/st/staff/krinke/slicing/.
8. S. Kumar and S. Horwitz. Better slicing of programs with jumps and switches. Technical Report TR-1429, Computer Sciences, University of Wisconsin-Madison, 2001.
9. K. Ottenstein and L. Ottenstein. The program dependence graph in a software development environment. In *Proc. ACM SIGSOFT/SIGPLAN Software Engineering Symp. on Practical Software Development Environments*, pages 177–184, 1984.
10. A. Podgurski and L. Clarke. A formal model of program dependences and its implications for software testing, debugging, and maintenance. *IEEE Trans. on Software Engineering*, 16(9):965–979, September 1990.
11. S. Schoenig and M. Ducassé. A backward slicing algorithm for Prolog. In *Lecture Notes in Computer Science*, volume 1145, pages 317–331, New York, NY, 1996. Springer-Verlag.
12. S. Sinha, M. Harrold, and G. Rothermel. System-dependence-graph-based slicing of programs with arbitrary interprocedural control flow. In *Int. Conf. on Software Engineering*, pages 432–441, May 1999.
13. M. Weiser. Program slicing. *IEEE Trans. on Software Engineering*, SE-10(4):352–357, July 1984.

Architectural Types Revisited: Extensible And/Or Connections

Marco Bernardo and Francesco Franzè

Università di Urbino - Italy
Centro per l'Applicazione delle Scienze e Tecnologie dell'Informazione

Abstract. The problem of formalizing architectural styles has been recently tackled with the introduction of the concept of architectural type. The internal behavior of the system components can vary from instance to instance of an architectural type in a controlled way, which preserves the absence of deadlock related architectural mismatches proved via the architectural compatibility and interoperability checks. In this paper we extend the notion of architectural type by permitting a controlled variability of the component topology as well. This is achieved by declaring some component connections to be extensible, in the sense that the number of connected components can vary from instance to instance of an architectural type. We show that such a controlled variability of the topology is still manageable from the analysis viewpoint, as the architectural compatibility and interoperability checks scale with respect to the number of components attached to the extensible connections.

1 Introduction

An important goal of the software architecture discipline [10,11] is the creation of an established and shared understanding of the common forms of software design. Starting from the user requirements, the designer should be able to identify a suitable organizational style, in order to capitalize on codified principles and experience to specify, analyze, plan, and monitor the construction of a software system with high levels of efficiency and confidence. An architectural style defines a family of software systems having a common vocabulary of components as well as a common topology and set of constraints on the interactions among the components. Since an architectural style encompasses an entire family of software systems, it is desirable to formalize the concept of architectural style both to have a precise definition of the system family and to study the architectural properties common to all the systems of the family. This is not a trivial task because there are at least two degrees of freedom: variability of the component topology and variability of the component internal behavior.

Some papers have appeared in the literature that address the formalization of the architectural styles. In [1] a formal framework based on Z has been provided for precisely defining architectural styles and analyzing within and between different architectural styles. This is accomplished by means of a small set of mappings from the syntactic domain of architectural descriptions to the semantic domain of architectural meaning, following the standard denotational

R.-D. Kutsche and H. Weber (Eds.): FASE 2002, LNCS 2306, pp. 113–127, 2002.
© Springer-Verlag Berlin Heidelberg 2002

approach developed for programming languages. In [7] a syntactic theory of software architecture has been presented that is based on set theory, regular expressions, and context free grammars. Architectural styles have been categorized through the typing of the nodes and the connections in the diagrammatic syntax as well as a pattern matching mechanism. In [9] architectural styles have been represented as logical theories and a method has been introduced for the stepwise refinement of an abstract architecture into a relatively correct lower level one. In [4] a process algebraic approach is adopted. In such an approach the description of an architectural style via WRIGHT [3] comprises the definition of component and connector types with a fixed internal behavior as well as topological constraints, whereas the component and connector instances and the related attachments are separately specified in the configurations of the style, so that the set of component and connector instances and the related attachments can vary from configuration to configuration. Also in [5] a process algebraic approach is adopted. An intermediate abstraction called architectural type is introduced, which denotes a set of software architectures with the same topology that differ only for the internal behavior of their architectural elements and satisfy the same architectural compatibility and interoperability properties [6].

The purpose of this paper is to encompass the two complementary, process algebra based approaches of [5] and [3]. This is accomplished by enriching the expressivity of an architectural type by adding the capability of modeling extensible and/or connections, i.e. connections to which a variable number of coordinated/independent architectural elements can be attached. From the analysis viewpoint, the main contribution of the paper is to show that, under certain constraints, the architectural compatibility and interoperability checks of [6] are still effective as they scale w.r.t. the number of software components attached to the extensible and/or connections.

This paper is organized as follows. In Sect. 2 we recall syntax, semantics, and architectural checks for PADL, a process algebra based ADL for the description of architectural types. In Sect. 4 we enrich PADL with extensible and/or connections and we prove the scalability of the architectural checks. Finally, in Sect. 4 we discuss some future work.

2   PADL: A Process Algebra Based ADL

In this section we recall the syntax, the semantics, and the architectural checks for PADL, a process algebra based ADL for the compositional, graphical, and hierarchical modeling of architectural types. For a complete presentation and comparisons with related work, the reader is referred to [5,6].

The set of process terms of the process algebra PA on which PADL is based is generated by the following syntax

$$E ::= \underline{0} \mid a.E \mid E/L \mid E[\varphi] \mid E + E \mid E \parallel_S E \mid A$$

where a belongs to a set Act of actions including a distinguished action τ for unobservable activities, $L, S \subseteq Act - \{\tau\}$, φ belongs to a set $ARFun$ of action relabeling functions preserving observability (i.e., $\varphi^{-1}(\tau) = \{\tau\}$), and A belongs

to a set *Const* of constants each possessing a (possibly recursive) defining equa-
tion of the form $A \stackrel{\Delta}{=} E$. In the syntax above, "$\underline{0}$" is the term that cannot execute
any action. Term $a.E$ can execute action a and then behaves as term E. Term
E/L behaves as term E with each executed action a turned into τ whenever
$a \in L$. Term $E[\varphi]$ behaves as term E with each executed action a turned into
$\varphi(a)$. Term $E_1 + E_2$ behaves as either term E_1 or term E_2 depending on whether
an action of E_1 or an action of E_2 is executed. Term $E_1 \|_S E_2$ asynchronously
executes actions of E_1 or E_2 not belonging to S and synchronously executes
equal actions of E_1 and E_2 belonging to S. The action prefix operator and the
alternative composition operator are called dynamic operators, whereas the hiding operator, the relabeling operator, and the parallel composition operator are
called static operators. A term is called sequential if it is composed of dynamic
operators only. The notion of equivalence that we consider for PA is the weak
bisimulation equivalence [8], denoted $\approx_B$, which captures the ability of two terms
to simulate each other behaviors up to τ actions.

A description in PADL represents an architectural type (AT). Each AT is
defined as a function of its architectural element types (AETs) and its architectural topology. An AET is defined as a function of its behavior, specified either
as a family of PA sequential terms or through an invocation of a previously
defined AT, and its interactions, specified as a set of PA actions. The architectural topology is specified through the declaration of a fixed set of architectural
element instances (AEIs), a fixed set of architectural interactions (AIs) for the
whole AT when viewed as a single component, and a fixed set of directed architectural attachments (DAAs) among the AEIs. We show in Table 1 a PADL
textual description for a client-server system. The same system is depicted in
Fig. 1 through the PADL graphical notation, which is based on flow graphs [8].

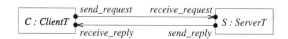

Fig. 1. Flow graph of *ClientServer*

The semantics of a PADL specification is given by translation into PA in two
steps. In the first step, the semantics of all the instances of each AET is defined
to be the behavior of the AET projected onto its interactions.

Definition 1. *Given a PADL specification, let $\mathcal{C}$ be an AET with behavior E
and interaction set $\mathcal{I}$. The semantics of $\mathcal{C}$ and its instances is defined by*
$$[\![\mathcal{C}]\!] = E/(Act - \{\tau\} - \mathcal{I}) \qquad \blacksquare$$

In our client-server example we have $[\![ClientT]\!] = [\![C]\!] = Client$ and $[\![ServerT]\!] =$
$[\![S]\!] = Server/\{process\_request\}$.

In the second step, the semantics of an AT is obtained by composing in
parallel the semantics of its AEIs according to the specified DAAs. In our client-
server example we have $[\![ClientServer]\!] = [\![C]\!][send\_request \mapsto a, receive\_reply \mapsto$

Table 1. Textual description of *ClientServer*

archi_type	*ClientServer*
archi_elem_types	
elem_type	*ClientT*
behavior	$Client \overset{\Delta}{=} send\_request.receive\_reply.Client$
interactions	**output** *send_request*
	input *receive_reply*
elem_type	*ServerT*
behavior	$Server \overset{\Delta}{=} receive\_request.process\_request.send\_reply.Server$
interactions	**input** *receive_request*
	output *send_reply*
archi_topology	
archi_elem_instances	$C : ClientT$
	$S : ServerT$
archi_interactions	
archi_attachments	**from** *C.send_request* **to** *S.receive_request*
	from *S.send_reply* **to** *C.receive_reply*
end	

$b] \parallel_{\{a,b\}} \llbracket S \rrbracket [receive\_request \mapsto a, send\_reply \mapsto b]$, where the use of the relabeling operator is necessary to make the AEIs interact. In general, let $C_1, \dots, C_n$ be AEIs of an AT, with interaction sets $\mathcal{I}_{C_1}, \dots, \mathcal{I}_{C_n}$ containing the AI sets $\mathcal{AI}_{C_1}, \dots, \mathcal{AI}_{C_n}$, respectively. Let i, j, k range over $\{1, \dots, n\}$. We say that $C_i.a_1$ is connected to $C_j.a_2$ iff either there is a DAA between them, or there exists an interaction a_3 of C_k such that $C_i.a_1$ is connected to $C_k.a_3$ and there is a DAA between $C_k.a_3$ and $C_j.a_2$. We say that a subset of interactions of $C_1, \dots, C_n$ is connected iff they are pairwise connected via DAAs involving interactions of $C_1, \dots, C_n$ only and the subset is maximal. Since the actions of a connected subset of interactions must be identically relabeled in order to result in a synchronization at the semantic level, denoted by $\mathcal{I}_{C_i;C_1,\dots,C_n} \subseteq \mathcal{I}_{C_i}$ the subset of interactions of C_i attached to $C_1, \dots, C_n$, let $\mathcal{S}(C_1, \dots, C_n)$ be a set of as many fresh actions as there are connected subsets of interactions among the considered AEIs, let $\varphi_{C_i;C_1,\dots,C_n} : \mathcal{I}_{C_i;C_1,\dots,C_n} \longrightarrow \mathcal{S}(C_1, \dots, C_n)$ be injective relabeling functions such that $\varphi_{C_i;C_1,\dots,C_n}(a_1) = \varphi_{C_j;C_1,\dots,C_n}(a_2)$ iff $C_i.a_1$ is connected to $C_j.a_2$, and let $\mathcal{S}(C_i; C_1, \dots, C_n) = \varphi_{C_i;C_1,\dots,C_n}(\mathcal{I}_{C_i;C_1,\dots,C_n})$ and $\mathcal{S}(C_i, C_j; C_1, \dots, C_n) = \mathcal{S}(C_i; C_1, \dots, C_n) \cap \mathcal{S}(C_j; C_1, \dots, C_n)$.

Definition 2. *Let $C_1, \dots, C_n$ be AEIs of an AT. The closed and the open interacting semantics of C_i restricted to $C_1, \dots, C_n$ are defined by*

$$\llbracket C_i \rrbracket^c_{C_1,\dots,C_n} = \llbracket C_i \rrbracket / (Act - \{\tau\} - \mathcal{I}_{C_i;C_1,\dots,C_n}) \quad [\varphi_{C_i;C_1,\dots,C_n}]$$
$$\llbracket C_i \rrbracket^o_{C_1,\dots,C_n} = \llbracket C_i \rrbracket / (Act - \{\tau\} - (\mathcal{I}_{C_i;C_1,\dots,C_n} \cup \mathcal{AI}_{C_i})) \quad [\varphi_{C_i;C_1,\dots,C_n}] \quad \blacksquare$$

Definition 3. *Let $C_1, \ldots, C_n$ be AEIs of an AT. The closed and the open interacting semantics of the set of AEIs are defined by*

$$[\![C_1, \ldots, C_n]\!]^c = [\![C_1]\!]^c_{C_1, \ldots, C_n} \parallel_{\mathcal{S}(C_1, C_2; C_1, \ldots, C_n)}$$
$$[\![C_2]\!]^c_{C_1, \ldots, C_n} \parallel_{\mathcal{S}(C_1, C_3; C_1, \ldots, C_n) \cup \mathcal{S}(C_2, C_3; C_1, \ldots, C_n)} \cdots$$
$$\cdots \parallel_{\cup_{i=1}^{n-1} \mathcal{S}(C_i, C_n; C_1, \ldots, C_n)} [\![C_n]\!]^c_{C_1, \ldots, C_n}$$

$$[\![C_1, \ldots, C_n]\!]^o = [\![C_1]\!]^o_{C_1, \ldots, C_n} \parallel_{\mathcal{S}(C_1, C_2; C_1, \ldots, C_n)}$$
$$[\![C_2]\!]^o_{C_1, \ldots, C_n} \parallel_{\mathcal{S}(C_1, C_3; C_1, \ldots, C_n) \cup \mathcal{S}(C_2, C_3; C_1, \ldots, C_n)} \cdots$$
$$\cdots \parallel_{\cup_{i=1}^{n-1} \mathcal{S}(C_i, C_n; C_1, \ldots, C_n)} [\![C_n]\!]^o_{C_1, \ldots, C_n} \qquad \blacksquare$$

Definition 4. *The semantics of an AT $\mathcal{A}$ with AEIs $C_1, \ldots, C_n$ is defined by*

$$[\![\mathcal{A}]\!] = [\![C_1, \ldots, C_n]\!]^o \qquad \blacksquare$$

A PADL description represents a family of software architectures called an AT. An instance of an AT can be obtained by invoking the AT and passing actual behavior preserving AETs and actual names for the AIs, whereas it is not possible to pass an actual topology. This restriction allows us to efficiently check whether an AT invocation conforms to an AT definition.

Definition 5. *Let $\mathcal{A}(\mathcal{C}'_1, \ldots, \mathcal{C}'_m; a'_1, \ldots, a'_l)$ be an invocation of the AT $\mathcal{A}$ defined with formal AETs $\mathcal{C}_1, \ldots, \mathcal{C}_m$ and AIs $a_1, \ldots, a_l$. $\mathcal{C}'_i$ is said to conform to $\mathcal{C}_i$ iff there exist an injective relabeling function φ'_i for the interactions of $\mathcal{C}'_i$ and an injective relabeling function φ_i for the interactions of $\mathcal{C}_i$ such that*

$$[\![\mathcal{C}'_i]\!][\varphi'_i] \approx_B [\![\mathcal{C}_i]\!][\varphi_i] \qquad \blacksquare$$

Definition 6. *Let $\mathcal{A}(\mathcal{C}'_1, \ldots, \mathcal{C}'_m; a'_1, \ldots, a'_l)$ be an invocation of the AT $\mathcal{A}$ defined with formal AETs $\mathcal{C}_1, \ldots, \mathcal{C}_m$ and AIs $a_1, \ldots, a_l$. If $\mathcal{C}'_i$ conforms to $\mathcal{C}_i$ for all $i = 1, \ldots, m$, then the semantics of the AT invocation is defined by*

$$[\![\mathcal{A}(\mathcal{C}'_1, \ldots, \mathcal{C}'_m; a'_1, \ldots, a'_l)]\!] = [\![\mathcal{A}]\!][a_1 \mapsto a'_1, \ldots, a_l \mapsto a'_l] \qquad \blacksquare$$

Theorem 1. *Let $\mathcal{A}(\mathcal{C}'_1, \ldots, \mathcal{C}'_m; a'_1, \ldots, a'_l)$ be an invocation of the AT $\mathcal{A}$ defined with formal AETs $\mathcal{C}_1, \ldots, \mathcal{C}_m$ and AIs $a_1, \ldots, a_l$ and let $C'_1, \ldots, C'_n$ be the AEIs of the AT invocation. If $\mathcal{C}'_i$ conforms to $\mathcal{C}_i$ for all $i = 1, \ldots, m$, then there exist an injective relabeling function φ' for the interactions of the AT invocation and an injective relabeling function φ for the interactions of the AT definition such that $[\![C'_1, \ldots, C'_n]\!]^o[\varphi'] \approx_B [\![\mathcal{A}]\!][\varphi]$.*

PADL is equipped with two architectural checks to detect system blocks. The first check (compatibility) is concerned with the well formedness of acyclic ATs, while the second check (interoperability) is concerned with the well formedness of sets of AEIs forming a cycle. Both checks are preserved by conformity.

Definition 7. *Given an acyclic AT, let $C_1, \ldots, C_n$ be the AEIs attached to AEI K. C_i is said to be compatible with K iff*

$$[\![K]\!]^c_{K, C_1, \ldots, C_n} \parallel_{\mathcal{S}(K; K, C_1, \ldots, C_n)} [\![C_i]\!]^c_{K, C_1, \ldots, C_n} \approx_B [\![K]\!]^c_{K, C_1, \ldots, C_n} \qquad \blacksquare$$

Theorem 2. *Given an acyclic AT, let $C_1, \ldots, C_n$ be the AEIs attached to AEI K. If $[\![K]\!]^c_{K,C_1,\ldots,C_n}$ is deadlock free and C_i is compatible with K for all $i = 1, \ldots, n$, then*

$$[\![K; C_1, \ldots, C_n]\!] = [\![K]\!]^c_{K,C_1,\ldots,C_n} \, \|_{\mathcal{S}(K;K,C_1,\ldots,C_n)}$$
$$[\![C_1]\!]^c_{K,C_1,\ldots,C_n} \, \|_{\mathcal{S}(K;K,C_1,\ldots,C_n)} \cdots$$
$$\cdots \, \|_{\mathcal{S}(K;K,C_1,\ldots,C_n)} [\![C_n]\!]^c_{K,C_1,\ldots,C_n}$$

is deadlock free.   ■

Corollary 1. *Given an acyclic AT, if every restricted closed interacting semantics of each AEI is deadlock free and every AEI is compatible with each AEI attached to it, then the AT is deadlock free.*   ■

Definition 8. *Given an AT, let $C_1, \ldots, C_n$ be AEIs forming a cycle. C_i is said to interoperate with $C_1, \ldots, C_{i-1}, C_{i+1}, \ldots, C_n$ iff*

$$[\![C_1, \ldots, C_n]\!]^c / (Act - \{\tau\} - \mathcal{S}(C_i; C_1, \ldots, C_n)) \approx_B [\![C_i]\!]^c_{C_1,\ldots,C_n}$$ ■

Theorem 3. *Given an AT, let $C_1, \ldots, C_n$ be AEIs forming a cycle. If there exists C_i such that $[\![C_i]\!]^c_{C_1,\ldots,C_n}$ is deadlock free and C_i interoperates with $C_1, \ldots, C_{i-1}, C_{i+1}, \ldots, C_n$, then $[\![C_1, \ldots, C_n]\!]^c$ is deadlock free.*   ■

Theorem 4. *Let $\mathcal{A}(\mathcal{C}'_1, \ldots, \mathcal{C}'_m; a'_1, \ldots, a'_l)$ be an invocation of the AT $\mathcal{A}$ defined with formal AETs $\mathcal{C}_1, \ldots, \mathcal{C}_m$ and AIs $a_1, \ldots, a_l$. If $\mathcal{C}'_i$ conforms to $\mathcal{C}_i$ for all $i = 1, \ldots, m$, then the AT invocation and the AT definition have the same compatibility and interoperability properties.*   ■

3   Adding Extensible And/Or Connections to ATs

The instances of an AT can differ for the internal behavior of their AETs. However, it is desirable to have some form of variability in the topology as well. As an example, consider the client-server system of Table 1. Every instance of such an AT can admit a single client and a single server, whereas it would be useful to allow for an arbitrary number of clients (to be instantiated when invoking the AT) that can connect to the server. In this section we enrich the notion of AT by introducing extensible and/or connections and we investigate to which extent they preserve the effectiveness of the architectural checks.

3.1   Syntax and Semantics for Extensible And/Or Connections

From the syntactical viewpoint, the extensible and/or connections are introduced in PADL by further typing the interactions of the AETs. Besides the input/output qualification, the interactions are classified as uniconn, andconn, and orconn, with only the three types of DAA shown in Fig. 2 considered legal. A uniconn interaction is an interaction to which a single AEI can be attached; e.g., all the interactions of *ClientServer* are of this type. An andconn interaction

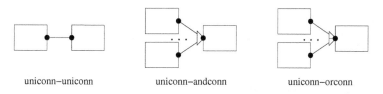

uniconn–uniconn   uniconn–andconn   uniconn–orconn

Fig. 2. Legal DAAs in case of extensible and/or connections

is an interaction to which a variable number of AEIs can be attached, such that all the attached AEIs must synchronize when that interaction takes place; e.g., a broadcast transmission. An orconn interaction is an interaction to which a variable number of AEIs can be attached, such that only one of the attached AEIs must synchronize when that interaction takes place; e.g., a client-server system with several clients. We observe that, whenever an AEI is attached (with a uniconn interaction) to an andconn/orconn interaction of another AEI, then the former AEI cannot be attached (with uniconn/andconn/orconn interactions) to uniconn interactions of the latter AEI. If this were not the case, in case of extension some interactions of the former AEI should be attached to interactions of the latter AEI that are not extensible (see Fig. 3(a)) or should be made extensible even if they are not (see Fig. 3(b)).

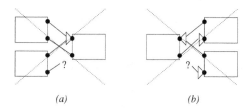

(a)   (b)

Fig. 3. Forbidden DAAs

As an example, let us define an AT *XClientServer* obtained from *ClientServer* by letting the number of clients connected to the server vary. To achieve that, we redefine the interactions of *ServerT* as follows:

         input   orconn *receive_request*

         output orconn *send_reply*   **dep** *receive_request*

and the interactions of *ClientT* as follows:

         output uniconn *send_request*

         input   uniconn *receive_reply*

This means that in an invocation of *XClientServer* arbitrarily many instances of *ClientT* can be declared and attached to the single instance of *ServerT*, with every occurrence of *receive_request* in *Server* replaced by a choice among as many indexed occurrences of *receive_request* as there are instances of *ClientT* attached to the only instance of *ServerT*. In order to make the server send a reply to the client (among the connected ones) that issued the processed request, *send_reply* is declared to depend on *receive_request*. This establishes that every occurrence of *send_reply* must be given the same index as the indexed occurrence of *receive_request* that precedes it.

In order to make the indexing mechanism work in case of dependencies, we impose the following constraints. In every AET, for each output orconn interaction there must be exactly one input orconn interaction on which it depends, with all pairs of related input output orconn interactions attached to the same AEIs. The behavior of each AET possessing orconn interactions must be i/o alternating: along every maximal simple path of the state transition graph starting from the initial state, it must be the case that every occurrence of an output orconn interaction is preceded by an occurrence of the related input orconn interaction, and that no two occurrences of the same input (output) orconn interaction appear without an intervening occurrence of each of the related output orconn interactions (of the related input orconn interaction). We denote by $\mathcal{G}_{\text{seq,i/o}}$ the set of sequential, i/o alternating terms.

If an AET contains only uniconn/andconn interactions, then its semantics and the semantics of its instances are defined exactly as in Def. 1. The reason is that in the case of a uniconn interaction only one AEI is attached to the interaction, while in the case of an andconn interaction all the AEIs attached to the interaction must synchronize when the interaction takes places. As a consequence, if all the AETs of an AT contain only uniconn/andconn interactions, then the semantics of the AT is defined exactly as in Def. 4.

In the case of an AT with orconn interactions, Def. 1 and Def. 4 still apply provided that they are preceded by a suitable modification of the terms representing the behavior of the AETs containing those interactions and a suitable modification of those interactions themselves, respectively. Such modifications, which are completely transparent to the architect, are necessary to reflect the fact that an orconn interaction expresses a choice among different attached AEIs whenever the interaction takes place. For the sake of simplicity, we formalize below the case in which every input orconn interaction has exactly one output orconn interaction depending on it.

The first modification, which is concerned with the applicability of Def. 1, works as follows on the behavior section of the definition of the AETs. From a conceptual viewpoint, we view every term $E \in \mathcal{G}_{\text{seq,i/o}}$ representing the behavior of an AET with orconn interactions as expressing the behavior of an instance of the AET when cooperating with a selection of the AEIs attached to its orconn interactions. Therefore, in order to take into account all the possible selections, in principle term E must be rewritten into

$$\sum_{i_1=1}^{m_1} \cdots \sum_{i_n=1}^{m_n} E_{i_1,\ldots,i_n}$$

where n is the number of pairs of related input output orconn interactions, m_j is the number of AEIs attached to pair $j = 1,\ldots,n$, and $E_{i_1,\ldots,i_n}$ is the term obtained from E by attaching index $i_j = 1,\ldots,m_j$ to all the occurrences of the interactions of pair $j = 1,\ldots,n$. In practice, this is realized in a different way, because the choice of the right summand cannot be made at the beginning of the computation but only during the computation. More precisely, denoted by (a,b) the j-th pair of related input output orconn interactions and by F an arbitrary term in $\mathcal{G}_{\text{seq},\text{i/o}}$, we rewrite each subterm $a.F$ of E into

$$\sum_{i_j=1}^{m_j} a_{i_j}.F$$

and each occurrence of b in E into b_k if k if the index of the last encountered occurrence of a. [1]

The second modification, which is concerned with the applicability of Def. 4, works as follows on the interaction section of the definition of the AETs and on the attachment section of the definition of the architectural topology. For all $j = 1, \ldots, n$, the j-th pair (a, b) of related input output orconn interactions is transformed into $2 \cdot m_j$ indexed, uniconn interactions $a_1, \ldots, a_{m_j}, b_1, \ldots, b_{m_j}$ where a_{i_j} and b_{i_j} are attached to the i_j-th AEI originally attached to a and b. Such a transformation is consistent with the rewriting carried out by the first modification and must be applied before computing the connected subsets of interactions.

In order to make Def. 1 applicable to both the case in which there are no orconn interactions and the case in which there are orconn interactions, we assume that in Def. 1 term E is replaced by term $orbeh(E, \emptyset)$. The second argument of function $orbeh$ represents a set of pairs concerned with occurrences of input orconn interactions encountered along a computation of E, where the first element of a pair is the name of the input orconn interaction, while the second element is the index associated with the encountered occurrence of the first element.

Definition 9. *Function* $orbeh : \mathcal{G}_{\text{seq},\text{i/o}} \times 2^{Act \times \mathbb{N}} \longrightarrow \mathcal{G}_{\text{seq},\text{i/o}}$ *determines the smallest term satisfying the following equalities:*
$$orbeh(\underline{0}, I) = \underline{0}$$

$$orbeh(a.E, I) = \begin{cases} a.orbeh(E, I) \\ \quad \text{if } a \text{ not orconn interaction} \\ \sum_{i=1}^{n} a_i.orbeh(E, I \cup (a, i)) \\ \quad \text{if } a \text{ input orconn interaction with } n \text{ attached AEIs} \\ a_{index(b,I)}.orbeh(E, I - \{(b, index(b, I))\}) \\ \quad \text{if } a \text{ output orconn interaction referring to } b \end{cases}$$

$$orbeh(E_1 + E_2, I) = orbeh(E_1, I) + orbeh(E_2, I)$$
$$orbeh(A, I) = A^I \text{ with } A^I \overset{\triangle}{=} orbeh(E, I) \qquad \text{if } A \overset{\triangle}{=} E$$
where $index(b, I)$ *is the index with which* b *occurs in* I. ∎

Definition 10. *Given a PADL specification, let* C *be an AET with behavior* E *and interaction set* $\mathcal{I}$. *The semantics of* C *and its instances is defined by*
$$[\![C]\!] = orbeh(E, \emptyset)/(Act - \{\tau\} - \mathcal{I})$$ ∎

As an example, consider an instance of *XClientServer* with two instances C_1, C_2 of *ClientT* attached to the only instance S of *ServerT*. Then $[\![C_1]\!] = [\![C_2]\!] = orbeh(Client, \emptyset) = Client$ while $[\![S]\!] = orbeh(Server, \emptyset) = Server^{\emptyset}$ where:

---

[1] This technique is similar in spirit to that of [2] for dealing with dynamic software architectures through a mapping on static descriptions.

$$Server^0 \stackrel{\Delta}{=} receive\_request_1.process\_request.send\_reply_1.Server^0 +$$
$$receive\_request_2.process\_request.send\_reply_2.Server^0$$

After transforming the two orconn interactions $receive\_request$ and $send\_reply$ into the following four interactions

> **input   uniconn** $receive\_request_1$, $receive\_request_2$
> **output uniconn** $send\_reply_1$, $send\_reply_2$

and modifying the related attachments as follows

> **from** $C_1.send\_request$ **to** $S.receive\_request_1$
> **from** $C_2.send\_request$ **to** $S.receive\_request_2$
> **from** $S.send\_reply_1$ **to** $C_1.receive\_reply$
> **from** $S.send\_reply_2$ **to** $C_2.receive\_reply$

we have that the semantics for the whole AT is given by

$$Client[send\_request \mapsto a_1, receive\_reply \mapsto b_1] \parallel_\emptyset$$
$$Client[send\_request \mapsto a_2, receive\_reply \mapsto b_2] \parallel_{\{a_1,a_2,b_1,b_2\}}$$
$$Server^0[receive\_request_1 \mapsto a_1, receive\_request_2 \mapsto a_2,$$
$$send\_reply_1 \mapsto b_1, send\_reply_2 \mapsto b_2]$$

Theorem 5. *Let $E \in \mathcal{G}_{seq,i/o}$. Then there exists a relabeling function φ such that $orbeh(E, \emptyset)[\varphi] \approx_B E$.*

Proof. It suffices to take φ such that every action that is not an orconn interaction is mapped to itself, while every indexed occurrence of an action that is an orconn interaction is mapped to the action. For all constant A occurring in E, the weak bisimulation demonstrating the equivalence of $orbeh(E, \emptyset)[\varphi]$ and E will in particular contain a pair (A, A^I) for every I built during the application of orbeh. ∎

Corollary 2. *Let $E \in \mathcal{G}_{seq,i/o}$. (i) If E has no orconn interactions, then $orbeh(E, \emptyset)$ is isomorphic to E. (ii) If E has no orconn interactions, then $orbeh(E, \emptyset)$ does not depend on the number of AEIs attached to the andconn interactions of the AEI whose behavior is E.* ∎

3.2   AT Invocations: Topology Conformity

When invoking an AT, we can pass actual behavior preserving AETs and actual names for the AIs. Now that we can declare extensible andconn/orconn interactions in the definition of an AT, in case of invocation we can also pass an actual topology. Such an actual topology is expressed in an AT invocation between the two previous arguments by means of four additional arguments that declare the actual AEIs, the actual AIs, the actual DAAs, and the list of interaction extensions, respectively. As an example, we provide below the invocation of the AT *XClientServer* with two instances of *ClientT*:

$XClientServer(ClientT, ServerT;$
$\qquad C_1 : ClientT, S : ServerT;$
$\qquad ;$

$\qquad$ **from** $C_1.send\_request$ **to** $S.receive\_request,$
$\qquad$ **from** $S.send\_reply$ **to** $C_1.receive\_reply;$
$\qquad$ **extend**$(S.receive\_request, S.send\_reply;$
$\qquad\qquad C_2 : ClientT;$
$\qquad\qquad ;$

$\qquad\qquad$ **from** $C_2.send\_request$ **to** $S.receive\_request,$
$\qquad\qquad$ **from** $S.send\_reply$ **to** $C_2.receive\_reply;$
$\qquad\qquad$);

$\quad$)

Every interaction extension starts with the keyword extend and comprises six arguments: the andconn/orconn interactions that are extended, the additional AEIs, the additional AIs, the additional DAAs, and the list of further extensions concerning andconn/orconn interactions of the additional AEIs only.

When invoking an AT, as before we have to check the conformity of the actual AETs to the formal AETs according to Def. 5. Additionally, we now have to check the conformity of the actual topology to the formal topology. Besides verifying that the number and type of actual AEIs, AIs, and DAAs coincide with the number and type of formal AEIs, AIs, and DAAs, respecitvely, the check amounts to investigate whether every interaction extension preserves the formal DAAs and is maximal. This means that the specification of an interaction extension must include not only the additional DAAs between the specified andconn/orconn interactions to be extended and the interactions of additional AEIs according to the formal DAAs, but also the additional DAAs between the interactions of such AEIs and the uniconn interactions of further additional AEIs that preserve the formal DAAs, and so on (additional DAAs between the interactions of such additional AEIs and andconn/orconn interactions cannot be encountered if the set of specified andconn/orconn interactions to be extended is maximal). As an example, if in the definition of *XClientServer* we include a further AET called *BrowserT* an we declare an instance B of *BrowserT* whose only uniconn interaction is attached to a new uniconn interaction of C, then in every invocation of the new version of *XClientServer* there must be as many instances of *BrowserT* as there are instances of *ClientT* in order to conform to the formal topology (see Fig. 4).

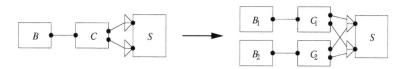

Fig. 4. An extension of the new version of *XClientServer*

3.3   Architectural Check Scalability

In this section we investigate whether the compatibility/interoperability results proved on the instance of an AT with the smallest number of AEIs attached to the andconn/orconn interactions scale to all of its extensions. Here we assume that an AEI attached to an orconn interaction of another AEI cannot be attached to other andconn and unrelated orconn interactions of that AEI.

Definition 11. *Given an andconn/orconn interaction to which instances of certain AETs must be attached, we say that the interaction is minimally (subminimally) attached if one instance (two instances) of each of the AETs above is (are) attached to the interaction. We say that an AT is minimal (subminimal) if each of its andconn/orconn interactions is minimally (subminimally) attached. We say that a (sub)minimal AT is acyclic if so is each of its extensions.* ∎

In the case of the architectural compatibility check, which is concerned with acyclic ATs, we always get the desired scalability from the minimal AT to all of its extensions, i.e. when attaching additional AEIs of certain types to the andconn/orconn interactions without introducing cycles.

Theorem 6. *Given an acyclic minimal AT, let $C_1, \ldots, C_n$ be the AEIs attached to AEI K. If $[\![K]\!]_{K,C_1,\ldots,C_n}^{c}$ is deadlock free and C_i is compatible with K for all $i = 1, \ldots, n$, then $[\![K; C_1, \ldots, C_n]\!]$ and all of its extensions are deadlock free.*

Proof. The first part of the result stems directly from Thm. 2. The second part of the result is trivial if $[\![K; C_1, \ldots, C_n]\!]$ cannot be extended, i.e. K has no andconn/orconn interactions to which additional AEIs of the same type as $C_1, \ldots, C_n$ can be attached, and none among $C_1, \ldots, C_n$ has andconn/orconn interactions. We now examine the nontrivial case concerned with the second part of the result.

Suppose that K has only andconn interactions and that we attach additional AEIs to them. Let us denote by $beh(K)$ the term representing the behavior of K. Since $orbeh(beh(K), \emptyset) = beh(K)$ by virtue of Cor. 2(ii) and each additional AEI has the same type as one among $C_1, \ldots, C_n$, each additional AEI passes the compatibility check. Thus the second part of the result follows.

Suppose now that K has orconn interactions and that we attach additional AEIs to them. In this case $orbeh(beh(K), \emptyset) \neq beh(K)$ because of the choices that function orbeh introduces. Let C be an arbitrary AEI attached to K in the considered extension of $[\![K; C_1, \ldots, C_n]\!]$ and let us investigate the compatibility of C with the extension of K. Since C has the same type as one (say C') among $C_1, \ldots, C_n$, we have that C is compatible with K. Now, if we compute the state transition graph of the parallel composition of the extension of K and C, we observe differences w.r.t. the state transition graph of the parallel composition of K and C' only when we encounter an occurrence of an input orconn interaction of K to which C' is attached (if C' is not attached to it, then from the point of view of C the choice of the summand of the extension of K is irrelevant as the summands differ only for the index given to the occurrence of the input orconn interaction and the occurrences of its related output orconn interactions). At that point, there are two options. The first option is that C synchronizes with the extension of K on the properly indexed occurrence of the input orconn interaction similarly to what C' did with K, so from that point to the next occurrence of an input orconn interaction of K to which C' is attached there is compatibility. The second option is that C does not synchronize with the extension of K, hence the extension of K drives the computation of the parallel composition by performing one of the other indexed occurrences of the input orconn interaction. The computation is driven by the extension of K until we encounter an occurrence of an interaction of K to which C' is attached. Due to the assumption made at the beginning of this section, we know that this must be an occurrence of the same input orconn interaction considered earlier, hence deadlock cannot arise while the computation is driven by the extension of K. Thus the second part of the result follows.

Finally, let us consider the case in which at least one (say D) among $C_1, \ldots, C_n$ has andconn/orconn interactions. This can give rise to a replication of the structure under consideration (if D has an andconn/orconn interaction to which K is attached) or to an extension of a structure interacting with the one under consideration via D (if D has no andconn/orconn interaction to which K is attached). In both cases, by applying to D an argument similar to that applied above to K, we can derive the second part of the result.   ∎

Corollary 3. *Given an acyclic minimal AT, if every restricted closed interacting semantics of each AEI is deadlock free and every AEI is compatible with each AEI attached to it, then the AT and all of its extensions are deadlock free.*   ∎

We observe that verifying whether a minimal AT is cyclic does not require the construction of all the extensions of the AT. It simply requires to build the corresponding subminimal AT and to check that it is acyclic. The reason is that every cycle in an extension of the subminimal AT that is not in the subminimal AT must be a replica of a cycle in the subminimal AT, possibly sharing some AEIs with the original cycle.

In the case of the architectural interoperability check, which is concerned with cyclic ATs, we obtain the desired scalability (for individual cycles) only from the subminimal (instead of minimal) AT to all of its extensions. The reason is that new cycles can be generated when building the subminimal AT corresponding to a minimal AT, whereas every cycle in an extension of the subminimal AT that is not in the subminimal AT must be a replica of a cycle in the subminimal AT.

Theorem 7. *Given a subminimal AT, let $C_1, \ldots, C_n$ be AEIs forming a cycle. If there exists C_i such that $[\![C_i]\!]^c_{C_1, \ldots, C_n}$ is deadlock free and C_i interoperates with $C_1, \ldots, C_{i-1}, C_{i+1}, \ldots, C_n$, then $[\![C_1, \ldots, C_n]\!]^c$ and all of its extensions are deadlock free.*

Proof. The first part of the result stems directly from Thm. 3. The second part of the result is trivial if $[\![C_1, \ldots, C_n]\!]^c$ cannot be replicated, i.e. none among $C_1, \ldots, C_n$ has andconn/orconn interactions to which additional AEIs among which one of the same type as $C_1, \ldots, C_n$ can be attached, and none among $C_1, \ldots, C_n$ has andconn/orconn interactions to which additional AEIs having types different from those of $C_1, \ldots, C_n$ can be attached. We now examine the nontrivial case concerned with the second part of the result.

Suppose that C_j has only andconn interactions and that we attach additional AEIs to them, among which one of the same type as $C_1, \ldots, C_{j-1}, C_{j+1}, \ldots, C_n$. Let us denote by $beh(C_j)$ the term representing the behavior of C_j. Since $orbeh(beh(C_j), \emptyset) = beh(C_j)$ by virtue of Cor. 2(ii) and the AEIs in the replica of the cycle have the same type as the corresponding AEIs in the cycle under examination, the replica of C_i interoperates with each AEI in the replica of the cycle. Thus the second part of the result follows.

Suppose now that C_j has orconn interactions and that we attach additional AEIs to them, among which one of the same type as $C_1, \ldots, C_{j-1}, C_{j+1}, \ldots, C_n$. In this case $orbeh(beh(C_j), \emptyset) \neq beh(C_j)$ because of the choices that function orbeh introduces, and a replica of the cycle is generated with the cycle and its replica sharing the extended version of C_j. Let C be an AEI in the cycle or in the cycle replica having the same type as C_i (the AEI passing the interoperability check by the initial hypothesis) and let us investigate the interoperability of C in the cycle or in the cycle replica. If we compute the state transition graph expressing the semantics of the cycle or its replica (depending on whether C is), we observe differences w.r.t. the state transition graph expressing the semantics of the original version of the cycle (in which C_j is not extended) only when we encounter an occurrence of an input orconn interaction of C_j. If C is not attached to such an interaction, then interoperability is preserved because, from the point of view of C, the choice of the summand of the extension of C_j is irrelevant as the summands differ only for the index given to the occurrence of the input orconn interaction and the occurrences of its related output orconn interactions. If instead C is attached to such an interaction, there are two options. The first option is that C synchronizes with the extension of C_j on the properly indexed occurrence of the input orconn interaction. In this case, from that point to the next occurrence of an input orconn interaction of C_j to which C is attached there is interoperability. The second option is that C does not synchronize with the extension of C_j, hence the extension of C_j drives the computation by performing one of the other indexed occurrences of the input orconn interaction. From the point of view of C, the computation is driven by the extension of C_j until we encounter an occurrence of an interaction of C_j to which C is attached. Due to the assumption made at the beginning of this section, we know that this must be an occurrence of the same input orconn interaction considered earlier, hence deadlock cannot arise while the computation is driven by the extension of C_j. Thus the second part of the result follows.

Finally, let us consider the case in which at least one (say D) among $C_1, \ldots, C_n$ has andconn/orconn interactions to which additional AEIs having types different from those of $C_1, \ldots, C_n$ can be attached. This can give rise to an extension of a structure interacting with the cycle under consideration via D. By applying to D an argument similar to that applied above to C_j, we can derive the second part of the result. ∎

4 Conclusion

In this paper we have enriched the notion of AT of [5] by introducing the capability of expressing extensible and/or connections between software components, in such a way that the architectural checks of [6] scale w.r.t. the number of software components attached to the extensible and/or connections.

As far as future work is concerned, first of all we would like to investigate whether information can be gained about the interoperability of cycles that are generated when building the subminimal AT corresponding to a minimal AT, starting from the compatibility of the involved AEIs of the minimal AT. Second, we would like to investigate the scalability of the architectural checks when relaxing the assumption at the beginning of Sect. 3.3. Finally, we would like to investigate the scalability of the architectural checks when taking a different view in the definition of function *orbeh*. As said in Sect. 3.1, we have taken the view that the term representing the behavior of an AET with orconn interactions expresses the behavior of an instance of the AET when cooperating with a selection of the AEIs attached to its orconn interactions. In the future, we would like to examine the case in which an instance of the AET can simultaneously cooperate with many or all of the AEIs attached to its orconn interactions. An example of this case would be *ServerT* of Table 1 if it had a queue where requests coming from different clients could be buffered.

References

1. G.D. Abowd, R. Allen, D. Garlan, *"Formalizing Style to Understand Descriptions of Software Architecture"*, in ACM Trans. on Software Engineering and Methodology 4:319-364, 1995
2. R. Allen, R. Douence, D. Garlan, *"Specifying and Analyzing Dynamic Software Architectures"*, in Proc. of FASE 1998, 1998
3. R. Allen, D. Garlan, *"A Formal Basis for Architectural Connection"*, in ACM Trans. on Software Engineering and Methodology 6:213-249, 1997
4. R. Allen, D. Garlan, *"A Case Study in Architectural Modelling: The AEGIS System"*, in Proc. of IWSSD-8, 1998
5. M. Bernardo, P. Ciancarini, L. Donatiello, *"On the Formalization of Architectural Types with Process Algebras"*, in Proc. of FSE-8, ACM Press, pp. 140-148, 2000
6. M. Bernardo, P. Ciancarini, L. Donatiello, *"Detecting Architectural Mismatches in Process Algebraic Descriptions of Software Systems"*, in Proc. of WICSA 2001, IEEE-CS Press, pp. 77-86, 2001
7. T.R. Dean, J.R. Cordy, *"A Syntactic Theory of Software Architecture"*, in IEEE Trans. on Software Engineering 21:302-313, 1995
8. R. Milner, *"Communication and Concurrency"*, Prentice Hall, 1989
9. M. Moriconi, X. Qian, R.A. Riemenschneider, *"Correct Architecture Refinement"*, in IEEE Trans. on Software Engineering 21:356-372, 1995
10. D.E. Perry, A.L. Wolf, *"Foundations for the Study of Software Architecture"*, in ACM SIGSOFT Software Engineering Notes 17:40-52, 1992
11. M. Shaw, D. Garlan, *"Software Architecture: Perspectives on an Emerging Discipline"*, Prentice Hall, 1996

Mapping an ADL to a Component-Based Application Development Environment[*]

Virgínia C.C. de Paula and Thais V. Batista

Department of Informatics and Applied Mathematics - DIMAp
Federal University of Rio Grande do Norte - UFRN
{vccpaula,thais}@ufrnet.br

Abstract. In this paper we discuss the mapping of an Architecture Description Language, ZCL, to an environment for configuring distributed application using CORBA components, LuaSpace. We focus on the mapping of the structural properties of ZCL and LuaSpace. In order to deal with compatibility issues, we propose an extension to ZCL. The result of this work is an integrated environment that combines the flexibility and execution platform provided by LuaSpace with a tool for design and for consistency checking - ZCL. The experience in combining an ADL with a configuration based environment can give clues on how integrating the activities of design and implementation during the lifetime of a software system.
Keywords: Software architecture, configuration, component, CORBA, ADL, scripting language, dynamic reconfiguration.

1 Introduction

Component-based development is a current trend in software engineering mainly because it promises to concretize the idea of reusing existing components by pluging-and-playing them in order to compose an application. Frameworks for component interoperability are playing an important role in component based application development because they offer support for working with heterogeneous components despite differences in language and in the execution platform. The CORBA model [22] has drawn special attention as a framework for interoperability because it is independent of language and manufacturer and provides easy access to components with transparent distribution. However, CORBA, like other frameworks for component interoperability, does not have facilities to describe the global organization of an application [25].

Several development environments [25,6,24] have been proposed to support the construction of component-based applications. In general these environments are based in a two level development model, in which not only the *component*

---

[*] Research for this paper was done with valuable support from CNPq (Brazilian Council for Development of Science and Technology) under processes 68.0103/01-5 and 68.0102/01-9.

R.-D. Kutsche and H. Weber (Eds.): FASE 2002, LNCS 2306, pp. 128–142, 2002.

level is considered but also the *configuration level*. In this second level, the structure of the application is composed of components and their interaction. Both level support the implementation phase of a software application.

Another important field that has gain an momentum in component-based development is *Software Architecture* [14]. The concept of software architecture, also said system structure or system configuration, is especially important to design complex software systems, providing a model of the large scale structural properties of systems. These properties include the decomposition and interaction among parts as well as global system issues such as coordination, synchronization and performance [15]. Structural issues include the organization of a system as a composition of components; global control structures; the protocols for communication [14]. Therefore, it addresses the high-level design of a system [21], named *Architecture level*. In this level the correct characterization of component composition and relationship among components are defined using a Software Architecture Description Language (ADL).

Although the terms *architecture* and *configuration* are usually treated as synonymous in software architecture literature, in this work we call *architecture* the abstract level via which we model an application. The term *configuration* we use when talking about a level close to the application implementation.

In [21], it is mentioned that software architecture and configuration based programming are related research areas that evolved separately but the solutions in these areas center around the same system model. Despite some differences, the approaches are complementary and share some features such as a related terminology and the notion of components and configuration.

As mentioned in [16], some ADLs *are taking a more pragmatic approach to the development of distributed systems*. This approach is worried about dealing with middleware infrastructures, such as CORBA.

In this paper, we describe the mapping of an ADL, named ZCL [1,3] to a component-based application environment - LuaSpace [24]. The motivation that lead us to develop this work arise from both sides involved. From the perspective of ZCL, it is necessary an underlying execution platform to run the application described using ZCL and to avoid *architectural erosion* [21]. From the perspective of LuaSpace, the use of an ADL can document the application design phase, give an overall vision of the application topology and guide the application consistency maintenance. In a more generic way, we want to integrate the flexibility and execution platform provided by LuaSpace with a tool for design and for consistency checking - ZCL.

One of the main features of ZCL is to have an associated formal framework [1], specified in Z [4], to describe and reason about dynamic distributed software architectures. It focuses on the operations necessary for the construction of dynamic software architectures. ZCL deals with execution issues defining states for the components and connections. So, the architect can concentrate on architectural issues or he/she can also analyze execution issues. Although ZCL considers execution issues, a platform is not available do run applications specified using ZCL. Nevertheless, simulations are allowed using Z tools.

The main advantage of LuaSpace is to provide a flexible way to compose application using CORBA components and to support dynamic reconfiguration of applications. LuaSpace uses an interpreted and procedural language - Lua - and a set of tools based on this language as a configuration tool to programming a component-based application. LuaSpace focuses on flexibility for dynamic reconfiguration.

Architecture descriptions and middleware are used in different phases of software development. The decision of modeling an application to be executed using an specific middleware is a typical case in which the implementation has direct influence on architecture decisions. Therefore, we intend to provide an appropriate way to model an architecture to be executed in LuaSpace, because *for a system to be implemented in a straightforward manner on top of a middleware, the corresponding architecture has to be compliant with the architectural constraints imposed by the middleware* [16].

ZCL and LuaSpace were originally thought in a completely independent way. However, they share a common interest in dynamic reconfiguration, supporting dynamism in different abstraction levels. The integration must keep unharmed the advantages of both approaches and it may enhance them with new functionality.

This paper is structured as follows. Section 2 presents the background of this work describing LuaSpace and ZCL. Section 3 discusses their integration. Section 4 presents related works. Finally, section 5 presents our final remarks.

2   Background

2.1   ZCL

The ZCL language is based on the CL language [11,12], which uses most of the principles of other MILs, but it has introduced new concepts, like planned reconfiguration. In this kind of reconfiguration, the designer can predict some modifications as likely to happen.

In ZCL, an architecture has a hierarchical structure in which the architecture is a composition of components that can also be composite. Those components that implement a functionality are simply called *components* or *task components*. *Composite components* can be seen as (sub)architectures and are also called *group components*. *Task components* are the smaller unit of computation we are considering. An architecture in ZCL is constructed by successive use of its operations. The components must exist in the library of components to be used in the description of an architecture. ZCL includes (auxiliary) operations to add components to the library.

Task components, composite components and ports of communication are the basic elements of an architecture in ZCL. Communication ports constitute the interface of a component through which it communicates to other components. A *link* is a connection between two communication ports.

One important feature of ZCL is to have an associated formal framework [1,3], by which the software architect can describe and reason about dynamic distributed software architectures. ZCL was specified using Z[4]. In order to illustrate a Z schema, we present below the *ZCL_Component* schema which represents a task component. It specifies the *interfaces* as a set of *PortNames*. Every port has *Port_Attributes*: direction (*DIR*) to indicate that it receives messages (entryport) or sends messages (exitport); mode (*MODE*) to indicate that it can be *notify* (asynchronous) or *requestreply* (synchronous); and type (*TYPE*) to indicate the type of data that can be transmitted by the port. It is also possible specify application specific attributes of a component (*component_attr*). The given sets *Indices* and *Attributes* are used to classify application specific attributes. *ID_Component*, *Nodes*, *PortNames* and *Location* are given sets representing respectively identifiers of components, of instances, of ports and of machines in which instances are executed. Each element in ZCL is specified by a schema in Z. So, we have schemas specifying components, composite components, instances of components (or composite components), etc.

$$
\begin{array}{|l}
\hline
\_\,ZCL\_Component \,\underline{} \\
\quad component\_attr : Indices \nrightarrow Attributes \\
\quad interfaces : \mathbb{F}_1\, PortNames \\
\quad port\_attr : PortNames \nrightarrow Port\_Attributes \\
\hline
\quad \mathrm{dom}\, port\_attr \subseteq interfaces \\
\hline
\end{array}
$$

ZCL works with the concept of *library of components*. Components existing in the library can be *used* in the context of an architecture description. Instances of components can be *created* and *linked* to other instances. They must have the same interface to be linked. In ZCL, instances are not automatically activated. This allows better control over parallelism. The architect must explicitly say that an instance has to be activated. In summary, we can say that ZCL allows the following commands to create an initial architecture: *use, create, link* and *activate*. The commands to allow reconfiguration are: *remove*, to remove a component from the context; *delete*, to delete an instance; *unlink*, to disconnect ports; and *deactivate*, to stop an instance. Moreover, each link is associated to a *ZCL_Connection*, which stores information about each pair of ports connected. In ZCL, an instance of port is always associated with an instance of component (*Nodes*). Each connection has a buffer in which messages exchanged between the sender (output port) and the receiver (input port) are stored.

Static verifications can be carried automatically by the framework. For example, to verify whether a component being declared by the architecture exists in the library or to verify whether an activate command is referring to an instance already created.

As said above, ZCL focuses on the operations necessary for the construction of dynamic software architectures. Each operation to mount an architecture has a corresponding one to annul its effect. Therefore, an architect can modify an architecture, but ZCL assures that the modification is done just in case it is a valid one (it leaves the architecture in a valid state). To do that, the ZCL framework has also an execution model based on states, which has the responsibility for verifying whether an architecture is in a valid state. So, the architect can concentrate on architectural issues or he/she can also analyze execution issues.

The architecture being described is stored in the *configuration table*, which is dynamically modified to reflect changes suffered by the application architecture. The ZCL operations use this table to ensure that the application is in a state suitable for modifications. All operations contain error cases also specified as schemas in Z. When any constraint of the operation is not obeyed, the error case schema of the operation is used.

As said in [13], if an architectural fact is not explicit in the architecture, or deducible from the architecture, then the fact is not intended to be true of the architecture. Therefore, it is extremely important to have a model in which all relevant features of an architecture can be specified. Observe that the designer can use ZCL to both analyze static architectures and run-time issues, such as dynamic reconfiguration. Observe also that the ZCL framework is highly modular and we have separated the schemas related to structural (static) analysis from those related to dynamic analysis. This means that the execution model based on states can be easily replaced or modified.

2.2 LuaSpace

LuaSpace is an environment for development of component-based applications integrating the CORBA platform with the interpreted and procedural language Lua [19], used to glue components. The application is written in Lua and can be composed by components implemented in any language that has a binding to CORBA.

LuaSpace provides a set of tools based on Lua that offer strategic functions to facilitate the development of component based applications and to promote dynamic application configuration. These tools are: LuaOrb, Generic Connector, Meta-Interface and ALua [18]. Next, Lua, LuaOrb and Generic Connector are briefly presented. The other tools are not presented here because they are not necessary in the context of this work.

- *Lua* [19] is an dynamically typed, interpreted and procedural configuration language that integrates strong data description facilities and reflexivity with a simple sintax. Lua includes conventional aspects, such as syntax and control structures similar to those of Pascal. It also has several non-conventional features: functions are *first-class* values; associative arrays (called *tables* in Lua) are the single data structuring facility; *tag methods* are Lua's most generic mechanism for reflection. Tag methods can be specified to be called in situations in which the Lua interpreter does not know how to proceed. It is the base for the implementation of the tools that compose LuaSpace because in LuaSpace when the Lua interpreter does not know execute a command, it invokes the appropriate tag method that knows to handle the command.
- *LuaOrb* [26] is a binding between Lua and CORBA based on CORBA's Dynamic Invocation Interface (DII) that provides dynamic access to CORBA components available at remote servers exactly like any other Lua object.

This is done transparently and at runtime. Moreover, it uses CORBA Dynamic Skeleton Interface (DSI) to permit dynamic installation of new objects in a running server.

– the *generic connector* [23] is a mechanism to configure an application as a set of services without being aware of the specific components that implements the service. Those components, if available, would be inserted into the application during its execution. At runtime, the generic connector searches for components that can provide the service stated in the application configuration program, activates the service and returns the result to the client. This mechanism introduces a great flexibility in application modeling since the developer can abstract away about specific components. It also addresses dynamic reconfiguration because different invocations of the same service may result in the selection of different components. With the use of the generic connector, it becomes impossible to distinguish the tasks of configuration and of reconfiguration in the configuration program.

To illustrate development using LuaSpace, we present the producer-consumer application. This application consists of *producer* and *consumer* components, whose IDL interfaces are illustrated in Figure 1. The *producer* component periodically adds an item in a buffer and can removes items from buffer. The *consumer* component can retrieve an item from the same buffer when it receives a notification that there is an item to be consumed. It can also ignore the notification. Issues regarding the concurrency control of the producer and consumer application are not in the scope of this work. Figure 2 shows an example of a configuration program developed using LuaSpace to the producer-consumer application. There are three *consumers* that receive a notification (`receive_note` method) when an item is produced (`produce` method) and eventually it is interested in retrieve an item (`retrieve(item = ''OK'')`) from buffer. In this case, `remove` method of the producer is invoked.

```
interface producer{
    string produce(item);
    void remove(item);
}

interface consumer{
    void receive_note();
    string retrieve(item);
}
```

Fig. 1. Producer-Consumer IDL interfaces

The use of an interpreted and procedural configuration language introduces a different style of configuring an application where explicit linking and unlinking commands are not necessary. The procedural model is used to describe an

```
i = 1
p = createproxy{''producer''}
while i<=3 do
    c[i] = createproxy{''consumer''}
    i = i + 1
end
i = 1
while true do
    if (p:produce(item) = ''OK'') then
        while i<=3 do
            c[i].receive_note()
            if (c[i].retrieve(item) = ''OK'') then
                p:remove(item)
            end
            i = i + 1
        end
    end
end
```

Fig. 2. LuaSpace configuration program

application. As a consequence there is no rigid distinction between the configuration and reconfiguration of an application. The simple use of conditional (if) or iteration (while) command in the configuration program implies in dynamic reconfiguration. Through an interactive console is possible to directly build and modify configuration programs. As Lua is a dynamically typed language, it is not necessary previously to declare the component instances that will be used in a program. New components can be selected dynamically according to runtime conditions.

LuaSpace provides support to implement both programmed and ad-hoc reconfiguration. For programmed reconfiguration, the Lua conditional commands can be used to establish the conditions that determine reconfiguration in the application source code. In this way, reconfiguration points are explicitly defined by the programmer. Moreover, the generic connector introduces the possibility of automatic reconfiguration, since for each call, different components can be selected to execute the required service.

Ad-hoc reconfiguration can be programmed interactively through the Lua console. This tool offers the programmer a way to have control over the application by directly interacting with the system. Another way is to use the ALua mechanism in which reconfiguration can be defined by sending the application a message with the reconfiguration code to be executed.

LuaSpace can be used in two scenarios of applications. In one scenario, LuaSpace is used to develop applications that explores the flexibility in lieu of static checking and that are not worried with consistency. This is the original proposal of LuaSpace because these features fit in Lua dynamic style that promotes flexibility. In the other scenario, LuaSpace is used in applications that need to maintain integrity. In this case, a software architecture should guide the evolution of the application. Dynamic reconfiguration is done according the architectural model, following the restrictions imposed. The use of LuaSpace in this kind of application is useful because the application can explore the set of tools to facilitate dynamic reconfiguration, access to CORBA components and object localization regardless programmer intervention and, at same time, it has the guarantee that the architectural model is preserved. This work address the second scenario, integrating an ADL to the LuaSpace environment. In this context, a specific ADL, ZCL, will support the semantics of reconfiguration in order to verify the validity of the changes.

3   Mapping ZCL to LuaSpace

Figure 3 illustrates the two stages of development involved in this work: ZCL at design phase and LuaSpace at implementation phase.

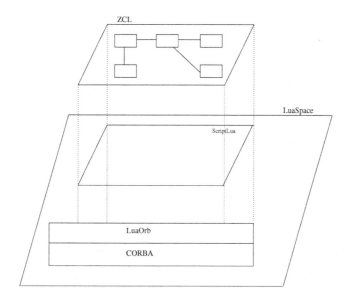

Fig. 3. Overall view of development phases

The mapping from ZCL to LuaSpace consists of defining the conversion of ZCL architectural elements to LuaSpace configuration aspects. There are significant structural differences between ZCL and LuaSpace. While ZCL follows the structure proposed by the configuration paradigm [10], LuaSpace does not obey any specific structural model. With this mapping it is possible to move from the high level specification toward the corresponding implementation.

In LuaSpace, a configuration program of an application consists of components, scripts and glue codes. Components are CORBA entities whose interface is described using the CORBA Interface Description Language (IDL). No information about implementation issues is published in component interface. Interface describes only component provided services. An application is composed of CORBA components that communicate through the CORBA bus that acts as an intermediary between components.

Since LuaSpace uses a procedural and interpreted language as a configuration tool, there is no explicit linking and unlinking command. Interconnection between components are represented by method invocation. In the same way, there is no explicit reconfiguration command. Conditional and interaction structures can determine dynamic reconfiguration. Another way of dynamically reconfiguring an application is interactively via the Lua console. In this way, there is no rigid distinction between configuration and reconfiguration in a program.

$$
\begin{array}{l}
\rule{0pt}{0pt}\text{—} \: ZCL\_ExplicitConnector \text{————————————} \\
\Xi \, ZCL\_Library \\
ZCL\_Component \\
sender : ID\_Component \rightarrow \mathbb{F}_1 \, InteractionPoints \\
receiver : ID\_Component \rightarrow \mathbb{F}_1 \, InteractionPoints \\
type : TYPE \\
buffer : \text{seq } MSG \\
behaviour : BEHAVIOUR \\
\hline
\text{dom } sender \subseteq \text{ran } tasks \lor \text{dom } sender \subseteq \text{ran } groups \\
\text{dom } receiver \subseteq \text{ran } tasks \lor \text{dom } receiver \subseteq \text{ran } groups \\
\forall idcomp : ID\_Component \mid idcomp \in \text{dom } sender \\
\bullet \; sender(idcomp) \subseteq (tasks(idcomp)).interfaces \lor \\
\quad\quad sender(idcomp) \subseteq (groups(idcomp)).interfaces \\
\forall idcomp : ID\_Component \mid idcomp \in \text{dom } receiver \\
\bullet \; receiver(idcomp) \subseteq (tasks(idcomp)).interfaces \lor \\
\quad\quad receiver(idcomp) \subseteq (groups(idcomp)).interfaces
\end{array}
$$

In ZCL, components, connections and architectures (composite components) are considered architectural elements. Components can be viewed as a black boxes entities with a well defined interface described by input and output ports. Components interact via ports and message passing is the only way of communication between components. Therefore, in the original version of ZCL there is not explicit connector. Nevertheless, it exists connections between components ports. An architecture in ZCL is a composite component which joins all the components or other composite components and the connections between them. Modelling LuaSpace's glue codes as ZCL connections does not seem a correct decision, because, as we have already said, it limits the communication between components to message passing. Another important issue is the lack of declaration of required services in CORBA component interfaces. Therefore, we propose an extension to ZCL in which a new architectural element is created - an explicit connector. As a consequence, we propose ports be replaced by *interaction points* at ZCL_Component schema and Port_Attributes to be replaced by *Properties*.

These changes give flexibility to the framework because it is now allowed other forms of communication besides message passing.

The ZCL_Library is a schema specified by a function, *tasks*, which maps an identifier of a component, *ID_Component*, into a ZCL_Component and another one, *groups*, that maps an *ID_Component* into a ZCL_CompositeComponent. The same *ID_Component* can not exist in both sets.

A ZCL_ExplicitConnector is a ZCL_Component and it uses the ZCL_Library, which is not changed by the connector. So, it has a set of interaction points and it is composed of two sets of interaction points (*sender and receiver*), a *buffer* which would be used depending on the *type* of the connector, and a *behavior* by which the connector can be described. The *type* of the connector is used to allow ZCL to deal with different kinds of connectors, such as glue codes, multicast channels, ORB [16], etc.

The framework has a schema to represent an instance of component. In the same way, we have included a schema to represent an instance of an explicit connector. We have also changed some of the operations schemas to adapt them to this new element. Special attention we dedicated to the link operation since we had a component-component connections and now we have component-connector and connector-component attachments.

In section 2.2, we present the producer-consumer application. We now model the same application using ZCL and the proposed extensions.

As we have already said, to create an architecture in ZCL, it is necessary to use the operations of the framework. Initially, we use the operations to create the *producer* and the *consumer* component, their interfaces and to update the library including them. We show below the corresponding operations invocations.

$CL\_Create\_Task[comp\_attr? := \emptyset, itrct\_points := produce, remove]$
$\wedge\ CL\_Create\_InteractionPoint[itrct\_points? := produce, remove]$
$\wedge\ CL\_Update\_LibSimple[nc? := Producer]$

The *consumer* is created using the same sequence of operations. Its interaction points are `retrieve` and `receive_note`.

Having included the components in the library, the architect has to use them in the context and to create their instances. In our case study, we want to create one instance of producer and three instances of consumer. For spaces reasons, we just present the operations which create the instances. In a similar way, we activate the instances.We have the following operations invocations:

$CL\_Create\_Instance[node? := prod, component? := Producer]$
$CL\_Create\_Instance[node? := cons1, component? := Consumer]$
$CL\_Create\_Instance[node? := cons2, component? := Consumer]$
$CL\_Create\_Instance[node? := cons3, component? := Consumer]$

Before linking the interaction points, we have to include the connector in the library and to create an instance of it. This is done invoking the appropriate operations as we have done to create components.

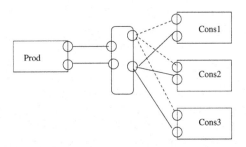

Fig. 4. Producer-Consumer

To link a component to a connector the *ZCL_Link* operation is used. It receives the pair (component instance, interaction point) and the pair (connector instance, interaction point). An interaction point is independent from the others. Therefore, the operation must be invoked as many times as the quantity of interaction points.

In Figure 4, it is illustrated the structure of the created architecture. In this Figure, we can see a dotted line which represents the invocation of the retrieve function by the consumer. As already said in section 2.2, sometimes the consumer is not interested in retrieving an item. In this case, we have to unlink the corresponding interaction points in the architecture. This is done by invoking the *ZCL_Unlink* operation which have the same parameters than *ZCL_Link*.

In summary, ZCL components can be considered components (or scripts) in LuaSpace. ZCL architectures model LuaSpace configuration programs that can contain components, scripts and glue codes. Component provided services of LuaSpace are equivalent to interaction points in ZCL. In LuaSpace there are many facilities to model interactions between components [20], such as: glue code, generic connector and events. In ZCL, all these elements are represented by the ZCL_ExplicitConnector abstraction, which deals with different *types* of connector, allowing the specification of the *behaviour* of them.

Dynamic reconfiguration is expressed in ZCL through operations over architectural elements, as described in section 2.1. The equivalence of ZCL operations for dynamic reconfiguration and LuaSpace reconfiguration support are execution issues and it is under development. Observe that as well as ZCL, LuaSpace addresses ad-hoc and planned reconfiguration [2].

Table 1 summarizes the correspondence between structural issues of ZCL and of LuaSpace.

4   Related Works

Although nowadays the importance of joining ADLs and Component-based development is broadly treated in several works, in this section we just present two approaches which address this issue.

Table 1. Summary of equivalences

Structural Issues	ZCL	LuaSpace
System Topology	Components, connectors and composite components	Components, scripts and glue codes
Interfaces	interaction points	provided services
Component interactions	Connectors	Glue code, Generic Connector and Lua event
Dynamic Reconfiguration	ad-hoc and planned	ad-hoc and planned

4.1 C2

In [16], we can find a work related to our, in which the authors use ADLs to describe *middleware-induced architectural styles* and provide an evaluation of ADLs in order to show their suitability for defining middleware-induced architectural styles. The authors mention the idea of implementing, in long term, an environment that supports the definition of architectures by providing a library of styles induced by specific middlewares. This environment would be able to partially automate the implementation of the architecture on the corresponding middleware.

The authors want to capture the architectural assumptions induced by middlewares in terms of middleware-induced styles. The middlewares Regis and C2, which ADLs (Darwin and C2SADEL) have been specifically defined, are considered. The characteristics that components, connectors and configurations of instances must have to be compliant with a specific middleware are considered to define and to specify a middleware-induced style. A similar approach considering layered style and CORBA middleware can be found in [17]. Two middlewares were chosen: JEDI and C2. They were specified using the ADLs ARMANI, Rapide, Darwin, Wright, and Aesop. In this way, some requirements ADLs should have to specify middleware-induced styles were identified [16]:

- ADLs should be able to define styles and provide a mechanism for exploiting a style in the definition of an architecture;
- ADLs must support the specification of some general topological constraints that must be respected by any specific instantiation of the component and connector types defined in the style;
- ADLs must support the description of the behavior of components and connectors, because topological constraints are not enough to define styles;
- An important requirement for both connectors and components is the possibility of refining their internal structure in terms of the composition of other components and connectors. So, ADLs must support the co-existence of different levels of abstraction in an architecture;
- An special conclusion was taken related to connectors. Connectors have been specified explicitly. Nevertheless, in general, the semantics associated to explicit connectors does not seem appropriate to model more modern kinds of

connectors, such as event dispatchers, ORBs, and multicast channels. Therefore, it is necessary to define an intermediate, artificial connector type to
attach the "real" connectors to the actual components of a C2 architecture.

Our goal is quite different from the one of the work described above in the
sense we want to allow the modeling of a system to which it is known to be
executed in a specific middleware - LuaSpace. More than that, we want this
modeling to be specified using ZCL. Nevertheless, we can consider the conclusions listed above about ADLs to evaluate how ZCL is supposed to support
"LuaSpace-oriented" specifications. We want to guarantee that the system modeled in ZCL can be implemented in LuaSpace. However, in this paper, we are
not proposing an automatic implementation of the modeling system.

4.2 Darwin

Darwin [7] supports the definition of architectures in terms of components, services and bindings. Components are described by interfaces that declares the
provided and required services. Systems are specified in Darwin by describing
the set of component instances and the set of bindings between required and
provided services.

[9] describes the use of Darwin to structure systems using CORBA objects.
This work mentions that object interaction and interface compatibility are the
concern of ORB and the CORBA bus and the Interface Definition Language
(IDL), while the structure of an application is supported by an ADL. We think
that this ADL does not address architectural mismatches [8] between components, once it supposes that interface compatibility is a issue supported by
CORBA bus. CORBA bus is the mediator of the communication and facilitates transparent access to remote components but the configuration language
is used to determine the components involved in the communication. We argue
that there is a level - the configuration level - between the bus and the architecture description. At this level it is possible to determine the overall structure of
the application and to address interface incompatibility as well as to dynamically
reconfigure the application.

In the mapping from Darwin to CORBA, the Darwin compiler translates a
Darwin component specification to the IDL interface. Each provision in the Darwin specification is translated into a read only attribute of the object reference
type. Each requirement is similarly mapped into an attributed which is not read
only because it is set externally to reflect the binding of the component instance.

In our work, there is no compiler to translate ZCL to LuaSpace. We define
the mapping of each architectural entities into configuration elements.

5   Final Remarks

In this paper we evaluate the mapping of an ADL to an environment for
component-based application development that uses a scripting language and

associated tools for configuring an application. We identify the common terminology of the two research areas involved: software architecture and configuration-based development. We focus on the mapping of the structural properties of ZCL and LuaSpace. We also propose an extension to ZCL in order to address its differences to LuaSpace, regarding modeling components interconnections. The definition of the behavioral aspects are under development. We are analyzing the correspondence of the states treated by the ZCL execution model with the LuaSpace execution issues.

Comparing the features of ZCL with those mentioned by [16] and presented in section 4.1, we can say that ZCL and its extension proposed in this paper, satisfies almost all of them. The only one ZCL still does not satisfy is the refinement of connectors. Composite components in ZCL supports refinement of internal structure of components.

The experience in combining an ADL with a configuration based environment can give clues on how integrating the activities of design and implementation during the lifetime of a software system. In [5] we find a classification of technologies as *component-centric* and *system-centric*. The former are represented by component middleware technologies such as CORBA and JavaBeans. They deal with external component properties (interfaces, binding mechanism, and expectations regarding the runtime environment). The second one focuses on the architecture level in which components are black-box entities. In our work, we address the integration of these two approaches.

References

1. de Paula, V. C. C.: A Formal Framework for Specifying Dynamic Distributed Architectures. PhD Thesis, Federal University of Pernambuco, Brazil, (1999)
2. Young, A. and Magee, J.: A Flexible Approach to Evolution of Reconfiguration Systems. In: Proceedings of the First International Workshop on Configurable Distributed Systems, IEE, pp. 152-163, (1992).
3. de Paula, V. C., Justo, G. R. R. and Cunha, P. R. F.: Specifying and Verifying Reconfigurable Software Architectures In: In: 5th International Symposium on Software Engineering for Parallel and Distributed Systems (PDSE-2000), pp. 21-31, IEEE Computer Society, Limerick, Ireland, June (2000).
4. Spivey, J.M.: The Z Notation, A Reference Manual, Editor Prentice-Hall, (1989)
5. Oreizy, P. and Medvidovic, N. and Taylor, R. and Rosenblum, D.: Software Architecture and Component Technologies: Bridging the Gap, In: Proceedings of the OMG-DARPA Workshop on Compositional Software Architectures, Monterey, CA, January, (1998).
6. Issarny, V. and Bidan, C. and Saridakis, T.: Achieving Middleware Customization in a Configuration-Based Development Environment: Experience with the Aster Prototype, In: Proceedings of the Fourth International Conference on Configurable Distributed Systems, pp. 207-214, Annapolis, Maryland, May, (1998).
7. Magee, J. and Kramer, J.: Dynamic Structure in Software Architectures, In: Proceedings of SIGSOFT'96 Symposium on the Foundations of Software Engineering, San Francisco, CA, October, (1996).

8. Garlan, D. and Allen, R. and Ockerbloom, J.: Architectural Mismatch or Why it's hard to build systems out of existing parts, In: Proceedings of the Seventeenth International Conference on Software Engineering, Seattle, WA, April, (1995).

9. Magee, J. and Tseng, A. and Kramer, J.: Composing Distributed Objects in CORBA, In: Third International Symposium on Autonomous Decentralized Systems - ISADS 97, pp. 9-11, Berlin, Germany, April, (1997).

10. Kramer, J. and Magee, J.: Dynamic Configuration for Distributed Systems, In: IEEE Transactions on Software Engineering, 11(4),pp.424-435, April, (1985)

11. Justo, G. R. R. and Cunha, P. R. F.: Programming Distributed Systems with Configuration Languages, In: International Workshop on Configurable Distributed Systems, London,(1992)

12. Justo, G. R. R. and Cunha, P. R. F.: An Application Framework for Dynamic Distributed Software Architectures, In: 5th International Conference on Advanced Computing (ADCOMP'97. IEEE CS Press, December, (1997)

13. Moriconi, M. and Qian, X.: Correctness and Composition of Software Architectures, In: Proceedings of ACMSIGSOFT'94: Symposium on Foundations of Software Engineering, New Orleans, Louisiana, USA, 164-174, December, (1994)

14. Shaw, M. and Garlan, D.: Software Architecture: Perspectives on an Emerging Discipline, Prentice Hall, (1996)

15. Allen, R.: A Formal Approach to Software Architecture, PhD Thesis, School of Computer Science, Carnegie Mellon University, May, (1997)

16. Di Nitto, E. and Rosenblum, D.: Exploiting ADLs to Specify Architectural Styles Induced by Middleware Infrastructures, In: Proceedings of the 21st International Conference on Software Engineering (ICSE'99), Los angeles, CA, USA, May, (1999)

17. da Silva, L. F. and de Paula, V. C. C.: A Meta-model to Specify Layered Software Architectures, In: Brazilian Symposium on Software Engineering (SBES'2001), October, (2001)

18. Ururahy, C; Rodriguez, N.: Alua: An event-driven communication mechanism for parallel and distributed programming. In: PDCS'99, Fort Lauderdale, Florida, (1999).

19. Ierusalimschy, R, Figueiredo, L, Celes, W.: Lua - an extensible extension language. In: Software: Practice and Experience, 26(6):635-652, (1996).

20. Batista, T. and Rodriguez, N.: Using a Scripting Language to Dynamically Interconnect Component-based Applications. To be submitted the 22th International Conference on Distributed Computing Systems (ICDCS), Viena, Austria,(2002).

21. van der Hoek, A., Heimbigner, D., Wolf, A.: Software Architecture, Configuration Management, and Configurable Distributed Systems: A Ménage a Trois Technical Report CU-CS-849-98, University of Colorado, (1998).

22. Siegel, J.: CORBA: Fundamentals and Programming. John Wiley & Sons,(1996)

23. Batista, T., Chavez, C. and Rodriguez, N.: Dynamic Reconfiguration through a Generic Connector. In: Proceedings of the International Conference on Parallel and Distributed Processing Techniques and Applications (PDPTA'00), CSREA Press, Vol. II, pp 1127 – 1132, Las Vegas, USA, June (2000).

24. Batista, T. and Rodriguez, N.: Dynamic Reconfiguration of Component-based Applications. In: 5th International Symposium on Software Engineering for Parallel and Distributed Systems (PDSE-2000), pp. 32-39, IEEE, Ireland, June (2000)

25. Bellissard, L. and Riveill, M.: Constructions des applications réparties, In: Ecole Placement Dynamique et Répartition de Charge, Juillet,(1996).

26. Cerqueira, R., Cassino, C., Ierusalimschy, R.: Dynamic Component Gluing Across Different Componentware Systems. In: International Symposium on Distributed Objects and Applications (DOA'99), 362-371, OMG, Scotland, September, (1999).

From EDOC Components to CCM Components:
A Precise Mapping Specification

Mariano Belaunde and Mikael Peltier
France Telecom R&D

mariano.belaunde@francetelecom.com
mikael.peltier@francetelecom.com

Abstract. Nowadays, component-oriented approaches are being promoted by tool providers as a way to enhance the modularity and the reuse of software pieces. Moreover, there are distinct levels of abstraction where components can be defined. The EDOC specification [5] is a high-level approach that introduces composition independently of any middleware platform, while the CCM specification [3] extends the CORBA middleware to simplify the implementation of concrete software components. This paper will focus on the problem of how to specify mapping from component abstract models into more concrete component models. Moreover, we will present a model transformation language called MTrans that can be used to specify *comprehensive* mappings that can be automated in an ambiguous way.

1   Introduction

To manipulate, classify and buy "on the shelf" software components - in a similar way as hardware electronic components - is still a myth. Most software engineering tool providers refer to this technology when they present their products. Especially, many component-oriented frameworks are currently deployed in the industry (for instance the EJB framework, which is widely used). Nevertheless, there is a lot of confusion regarding what a software component is. Inter-operability between components, coming from distinct tool providers, is in fact very difficult to achieve because there is not yet a widely accepted and operational standard. Part of the complexity arises from the fact that there are already multiple middleware platforms that coexist today (such as CORBA, COM, and the EJB).

The Model Driven Architecture [1] from the OMG intend to manage this complexity by taking a model centric approach and by distinguishing models that are platform independent (PIM) from models specific to a platform (PSM). The MDA promises to standardize the mappings that will enable inter-operation and integration of components, even when these are implemented on the basis of heterogeneous platforms.

In this paper we will focus on the problem of specifying *executable* mappings between a platform independent component based specification and a platform dependent

R.-D.Kutsche and H. Weber (Eds.): FASE 2002, LNCS 2306, pp. 143-158, 2002.
© Springer-Verlag Berlin Heidelberg 2002

component specification. An *executable* mapping is a mapping specification that can be automated by a tool. To illustrate this point we will show how CCM (CORBA Component Model [3]) component descriptions can be derived from high-level EDOC/CCA (Component Collaboration Architecture [5]) component models. The mapping specification will use the MTrans language, a generic formalism for model transformation, developed by France Telecom. This language is based on meta-modeling techniques and intends to mix the "confort" of a declarative language and the efficiency of the procedural style.

In the second section we will present the CCM and the EDOC concepts and point out what are the most relevant differences. The third section will focus on the available approaches used today to specify mappings and we will look in particular the advantages of using meta-modeling techniques. In section four we will describe the general motivation and the fundamental concepts of the MTrans language. In the next section an "EDOC to CCM" executable mapping specification will be presented, first informally and then described formally in terms of the MTrans language.

The last section will point out the future work on the topic of mapping component specifications and will assess some of the expectations in respect of the standardization.

2   CCM Components versus EDOC Components

During the last past four years the OMG has put considerable effort on standardizing the area of software components. The Corba Components [3] adopted specification reflect an attempt to integrate most of the EJB concepts in the context of the CORBA middleware. More recently, the "UML profile for EDOC" [3] specification, which is in the process to be adopted, proposed a high-level component-oriented approach for building enterprise distributed systems. Unlike CCM, an EDOC specification is "platform independent", meaning that it may be implemented in distinct platforms, such as the Microsoft COM, or CORBA. In this section we will describe both of the two frameworks. This will help to understand the mapping specification presented in section 6.

2.1   The CORBA Component Model (CCM)

The Corba Component Model is a very ambitious specification that aims at simplifying the problem of building transactional, robust and secure enterprise systems. In contrast with traditional monolithic transactional systems, it promotes modularity and the reuse of the standardized CORBA services, such as security, notification, transaction and persistence. The CCM specification includes a conceptual model of composition (see the metamodel excerpts in Figure 1), a programming model, a deployment and an execution model. By providing a well-defined environment that manages *containers* and *home* factories for the components, the programmer can focus on the required business functionality rather than dealing with all the non-functional behavior aspects (such as security).

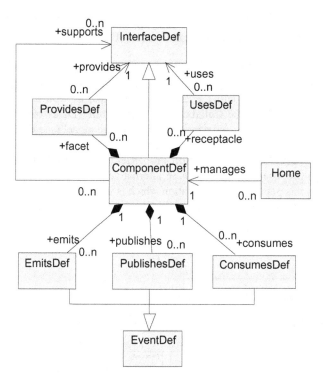

Fig. 1. The CCM metamodel

The CORBA interface definition language (CORBA-IDL) has been enhanced to address the new fundamental types needed for components. A *CCM component* declares the interfaces that are provided (facets) and the interfaces that are used (receptacles) using named ports. In addition a component declares ports for receiving asynchronous events as well as ports for emitting or publishing events. Finally, a component may define the properties that are needed for its configuration.

Surprisingly, composition in CCM is not recursive: a component cannot be defined as a composition of other "small" components. However, an assembly type can be declared to gather a set of CCM components "working together". An assembly descriptor (described using an XML vocabulary) declares the way how components instances are connected together through their respective ports. Also, it can provide collocation constraints on the component instances (either the components execute on a single node, either they are driven in a single process).

2.2   The EDOC Component Model

The RFP (Request for Proposal) "UML Profile for EDOC" [2] called for a standard way to use UML for designing distributed enterprise systems, with the assumption that the design will adopt a component-oriented approach and that it will be "mappable" to the existing software component frameworks (i.e. the CCM, the EJB, etc.).

The final submission, recommended to adoption in September 2001 is a "melting-pot" of distinct interesting works, but containing also a lot of inconsistencies. There are specific UML profiles for modeling event-driven systems, as well as for business process. Anyway, the Enterprise Collaborative Architecture (ECA) which is part of the EDOC submission, has proposed a general composition model (see Figure. 2), that summarizes well the state of the art on components: recursion in composition, port specification using protocols, configuration properties, etc. In addition, a graphical notation has been proposed to be used as an alternative to the standard UML icons. Figures 3 and 4 in this paper uses this notation which is more appropriate to figure out the component structure.

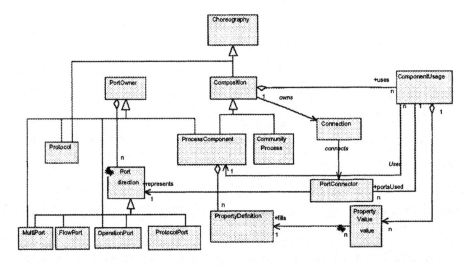

Fig. 2. The EDOC/ECA metamodel

An ECA component has an external view that includes the declaration of ports. A port is simple or composite (containing sub-ports). It plays either the role of an "initiator" or the role of a "responder". The interaction through the ports needs to conforms with a protocol specification. A protocol may imply complex interactions between the two parties. A protocol *choreography*, which is represented by an activity diagram in UML, is used to describe the ordering of the messages. Note that an interface (a collection of synchronous operations) is treated as a particular case of a protocol. A *community* is a special kind of composite that reflects a collaboration of top-level component instances. Figure 3 shows a community with three components.

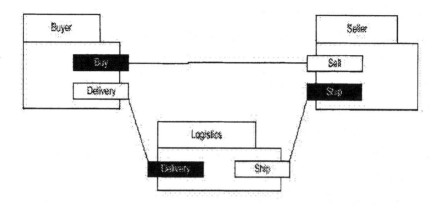

Fig. 3. The Buyer/Seller community

An ECA component may expose its internal structure (its *inside*) or it may declare a "performer" role that implements it. In the former case, the internal view of the component is described as a collaboration of other component instances (*usages* of other components). The connections between the ports of the component instances are explicitly described. A choreography may be used to describe in detail the behavior of this collaboration.

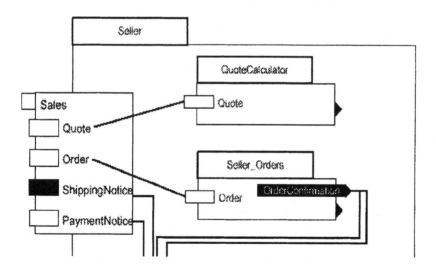

Fig. 4. A partial view of a "seller" component

3   Techniques for Specifying Mappings

A transformation is a process which is used to produce coded data in a format towards another format. This transformation can either consist of an one-to-one relation (correspondence) between elements either be more complex and involve intermediary computations to realize the transformation.

3.1   Current Approaches

The need for specifying mappings between models has increased dramatically today in the object modeling community. This is due at least to two main reasons:

- The UML graphical notation often serves as a *concrete notation* in specific domains. This is made possible because of the extensibility mechanism in UML that permits to extend the semantics while preserving the notation core. However, independently of the usage of the UML diagrams, designers have often a metamodel of the domain concepts. Thus, a mapping specification is needed to show how this domain concepts maps into the UML concepts. The Software Process Engineering Management [4], the "UML profile for EDOC" [5] and the "UML profile for EAI" [6] are examples of OMG specifications providing both a metamodel and a UML profile.

- The MDA promotes the separation between platform independent models and platform dependent. This requires to specify very precisely the mapping between models located at distinct levels. As an example, the "UML profile for EDOC" submission has proposed some non-normative technology mappings, such as   "EDOC to EJB" and "EDOC to CCM"[1].

How do the mapping between a source and target models be specified today in the specifications produced by the OMG?. There are distinct approaches, but all of them are more informal than formal. The SPEM and EDOC submissions, use tables providing the correspondences between the concepts. We will typically find some explanation in natural language accompanied with a three column table in the form: *source-entity/map-comment/target-entity*.

This approach is suitable when the transformations are really simplistic, for instance, in the case of UML profiles, when each domain concept is translated using a single UML stereotype. But in general, things are more complex. In order to really take advantage of all the UML diagramming capabilities, a domain concept may be showed in different places with a distinct identity (in SPEM an activity is represented either as an operation, or as an action state, or as a use case, etc.). There are also many complex short-cuts conventions that are difficult to specify precisely using tables.

In the "UML for EAI" submission [15], in addition to this correspondence tables, the mapping rules are further refined by means of "invariant constraints". For example

---

[1] The mapping presented in section 6 reuses parts of the proposal included in this specification.

"The name of the terminal is the name of the target end of the association". This approach is interesting. The constraints are expressed in English but we could imagine that they can also be translated as OCL invariants (with some extensions to the OCL language). This formal specification could be used to check that a program has performed correctly the mapping. However it will be very difficult (probably impossible) to generate automatically the program itself!

To summarize, it is really difficult to specify precise mappings formally (and even harder if we want these to be readable!). In general the semi-formal mapping provided in the OMG specifications are useful to understand the fundamentals of the mapping. But in the perspective of an implementation, they offer a limited help to human programmers (and even less to an automated engine). A lot of implicit information need to be re-interpreted by the programmer. This includes for instance, the determination of the ordering to accomplish the transformation (the visiting strategy).

3.2   Towards an Executable Mapping Specification

An executable mapping specification is something that ideally should be a pure "declarative" language. However, our feeling is that a compromise is needed between "the procedural" and "declarative" paradigm in order to have a highly expressive, predictable, understandable formalism that could be automated in an efficient way.

Our focus is on executable formalisms that operate with object oriented model definitions. There are examples of other non OO approaches, like those based on XML and XSLT[2], or those based on EBNF production rules[3].

From now on, there a lot of pragmatic solutions for model transformations that mix declarative and procedural aspects. For instance, in a UML Case tool, such as the Objecteering [12], or a transformation engine such as Scriptor [13], a dedicated language is used to inspect and create the model elements (in compliance with the UML metamodel). Transformations rules are written for each UML meta-class using either pseudo-formal navigation expressions, either templates with placeholders. Furthermore, it is possible to derive automatically this transformation rules from models representing design patterns. A very important work in the topic of design pattern application has been achieved with the UMLAUT framework [9].

Anyway, in the context of our research project, we were more interested in an explicit and executable object oriented formalism, tool independent, that would not be dependent on a unique metamodel. In other words, what we were looking for was a kind of OCL extension for model transformation based on the MOF. The MOF provides a

---

[2] There are a lot of limitations that appear when using XSLT processors to transform models rendered as XML documents (using the XMI standard).

[3] The productions rules for XML schemas in [16] are expressed in this way. The rules are precise and unambiguous.

very simple object-oriented meta-language that is used to define other languages (metamodels). The MOF constructs are in fact those commonly used in *class-diagrams*: classes with attributes, binary associations with cardinalities in both ends, class inheritance and so on. Full object-orientation, genericity and good integration with UML graphical notation are the main advantages that emerge from this approach.

A lot of research is being carried out today to apply meta-modeling techniques to model transformation. There were also some interesting results in the last past years. In particular, we would mention the approach taken by R.Lemesle [10], which proposes a prolog-like declarative language with selection clauses and conclusions. The implementation was based on the sNets formalism [11] which was used to encode the MOF *metametamodel* concepts as well as the rules.

3.3   How to Go from an Abstract Model to a Concrete Model

When going from an abstract model of a system into another more concrete model of the same system, the transformation process requires in general additional information to be provided. This includes:

- Decisional choices to set distinct mapping alternatives. For example: what security level will be needed in the concrete system?
- Enrichment of the source model in order to take in account aspects not originally expressed in the source model but that are relevant to the target.

There are different techniques to provide this additional information. For instance global parameters may be passed to the transformation engine. In UML models, *tagged values* are often used to annotate the source model with additional data. Another approach is to use distinct inter-related models as the input for the transformation. A security model and architectural model may, for instance, be linked with the domain specific model to be transformed.

4   The Mtrans Language

MTrans is a textual formal formalism to express transformations on models. It's an executable formalism in the sense that it has unambiguous execution semantics and can be automated by a tool. Access to the source model elements and the assignment of the target model elements is expressed in the terms of the concepts and the properties existing in the source and target metamodels. MTrans reuses the navigation capabilities of OCL, a formal and pure expression language used to define constraints on OO models.

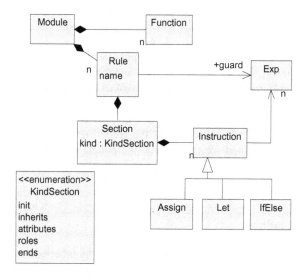

Fig. 5. Main syntax constructs in Mtrans

4.1   Foundations

A MTrans specification is made of a set of *rules* and a set of *function definitions*[4] (see fig 4). A rule indicates how an instance of the target metamodel is created and how its attributes and roles are assigned in the context of an instance of the source metamodel. A rule has an optional name and contains distinct sections. In each section there are instructions. The 'init' section contains initial computations that are performed before creating the destination instance. The 'attributes' and 'roles' sections are used to assign the properties of the destination instance (which is created at the end of the 'init' section). A rule may have additional parameters (other than the implicit 'self' contextual source instance).

A MTrans specification declares one or more rules serving as entry-points. Multiple entry points allow either to perform multiple passes, or to apply the transformations to separate parts of the model. A rule may invoke another rule. This is done using the *new* operator. *Entry-points* and *new* operations allow the MTrans programmer to have an explicit full control on the flow of execution.

A rule can inherit from one or more other rules. The destination type needs to be compliant with the destination types of the inherited rules. The inherited rules are executed

---

[4] OCL definitions (expressed with the 'def' keyword) are a special kind of function definition in Mtrans.

after creating the destination instance and before the execution of the property assignment.

Rule inheritance permits the reuse of code that populates the properties of the *destination* model. In contrast, a *function definition* is used to reuse the code that inspects the *source* model. A rule, for instance, cannot be invoked in a function body. As in OCL, a MTrans function has a context argument (referred as 'self'). It may be of any known type, including classes from the source model, as well as basic data-types and structured data-types (sequences, sets, etc.). All the predefined OCL definitions (such as the set of operations defined for collections like *collect* and *select*) can be used in function bodies.

4.2   Special Situations

- An *abstract* rule is a rule that can only be used by inheritance.
- A rule may not specify its destination. In such case no instance is created in the target model and only the 'init' section is available. The instructions in the 'init' section serves only to invoke other rules in inner source elements. This is often useful to entry-point rules.
- A rule may not specify its source instance. In such case the first parameter acts as the contextual argument (referred as 'self'). This is useful to create, for instance, pre-defined destination elements that are not necessarily linked with a source element.
- A function can be declared as *external*. In this case the body is not present, meaning that the implementation is provided elsewhere. This is useful for implementing predefined functions that will be linked afterwards to the transformation MTrans engine.

4.3   Advantages of an Explicit Execution Strategy

MTrans is obviously not a "pure" declarative language; instead it's a mixture of "declarative" and "procedural" formalism. A MTrans specification is in fact a *program* with a specialized structure that clearly shows what is its intent. We believe that an explicit execution strategy[5] brings many advantages in terms of the precision and the capacity to express complex situations. In non trivial transformations, it's often useful to visit a model element more than once[6]. Since we know what transformations were made before, it is possible to reference the destination instances already created. The *resolve* operation is used to obtain all the destination instances created from a source

---

[5] A strategy describes how we want to apply the different steps of the transformation process.
[6] Section 5.2 shows an example of this: The ECA community is visited twice, once for creating all the CCM component types and a second time for creating all the connections in the CCM assembly.

instance (this is similar to the *co-reference* mechanism found in [10]). Note also that without an explicit execution flow, the rules inheritance mechanisms, used for rule reuse, would have an ambiguous semantics.

4.4   Special Rules and Conventions in MTrans

It is not always easy for a human reader to understand OCL expressions that involves a long chain of iterative operations. In MTrans, to minimize this problem there are some special rules and some short-cut conventions (abbreviations) that make things appear simpler to the end-user of the language.

- "***Do nothing on abort***": In the assignment instruction 'myattr= self.x.y' the assignment will take place only if the access to the x and y fields is successful;

- "***Chained assignments***": The instruction 'myrole=a;b;c;' specifies that *myrole* will merge the results of the three expressions in a single list;

- "***Filtering notation***": The expression x[filtering-expression], where x is a sequence, expresses that the resulting list will be filtered according to the filtering condition (which is expressed in terms of an implicit iterator). It I s equivalent to use in OCL a *select* operation.

- ***Implicit macros***: The filtering expression x[M] where M is a metaclass, expands as x[iterator.isOclType(M)] (only instances of type M are accepted)[7].

- "***pipeline operations***": The instruction x->f(), where x is a collection, results on calling once the 'f' function if f is declared as having a collection as the context argument, or results in calling n times the 'f' function if 'f' declares a non collection context argument. This convention applies also to the *'new'* operator to invoke a rule on each element of the list. Note that in OCL there is a similar convention for 'x.propertyname' where x denotes a collection.

- ***Dynamic casting***: When defining and initializing local properties definitions (using the *'let'* keyword) the type is not mandatory. However, the full signature is mandatory when defining functions signatures.

---

[7] In MTrans disambiguation rules are used to prevent potential conflicts that may arise. In standard OCL the [] operator is also used for accessing class-associations instances.

5   Mapping from EDOC to CCM

5.1   General Principles of the Mapping

The main issue when mapping an EDOC model into a CCM model is how to deal with the EDOC recursive composition. An EDOC component may be defined as a composition of other components, while, in CCM, an assembly cannot act as a part for another composite. When going from an EDOC model to a CCM model, we have then to decide what to do with the *inside* of a composite EDOC component. Many options are possible. For the purpose of this presentation, we assume the following mapping strategy: each EDOC component, whether it's a top-level or an inner one's, is translated as a CCM component type. Furthermore, the whole EDOC community is mapped as a single CCM assembly that declares all the needed connections between the CCM component instances. In order not to loose component encapsulation, each CCM component acts as a proxy for all the CCM components resulting from its "inside". To achieve this we need to perform a deep traversal on the ports structure of each top-level EDOC component and distinguish between ports that are used for "internal" communication from those that are used for "external" communication. Depending on the port mode (synchronous/asynchronous) and the port role (initiator/responding) we generate either sink events, source/published events, facets (provided interfaces which contain operations reflecting the synchronous flows) and receptacles (used interfaces reflecting consumed flows). [8]

5.2   A Formal Specification of the EDOC to CCM Mapping

In this section we present some excerpts of the *executable* mapping specified using MTrans. This mapping is directly expressed in terms of the EDOC and the CCM meta-models (described in Figure 1 and Figure 2)[9].

The first stage in the transformation process is to inspect in two passes the top-level Buyer/Seller community (see Figure 3). The first pass (rule R1) creates the CCM assembly structure while the second one (rule R2) creates CCM *home* instances for each EDOC component found in the community.

```
R1 entrypoint rule Assembly from CommunityProcess {
            -- We do not present this part in the paper -- }
R2 entrypoint rule undefined from CommunityProcess {
    init:
        self.uses.processComponent[unique]->new HomeDef(); }
```

---

[8] The principles for mapping ECA flow ports are presented in the EDOC to CCM mapping found in [3]. Although the way how to manage port composition remains very vague.

[9] Another approach could be to use the UML profile for EDOC and the UML profile for CCM. However the mapping based on the specific meta-models is easier to understand.

The rule R3, which is invoked by rule R2, performs then a deep traversal on the EDOC components. Recursion stops when no *inside* is found in the component (when 'self.uses' aborts in (1)). CCM components are instantiated and linked to the *home* that is in charge to manage it.

```
R3 rule HomeDef from ProcessComponent {
   init :
      self.uses.processComponent[unique]->new HomeDef();        (1)
   roles:
      manages = self.new ComponentDef();
   }
```

The Rule R4, invoked in rule R3, specifies how the CCM components are build from EDOC components. The logic here is a bit more complex. The various kind of CCM ports are populated according to the principles exposed in section 6.1. Ports used for external communication are generated in a different way than ports dedicated to the interaction with the internal components. Note that for an external *consuming* CCM port there is a corresponding proxy *emitting* port. For clarity, many other details of the mapping have been omitted here, such as mapping the configuration properties, the transaction parameters, and so on.

```
R4 rule ComponentDef from ProcessComponent {
  init:
    let ax_out =self.port->allAsyncInitiatorFlowPorts();
    let ax_in = self.port->allAsyncResponderFlowPorts();
    let sx_in = self.port[hasResponderSyncPorts()];
    let sx_out = self.port[hasInitiatorSyncPorts()];
    let pp = self.proxyPorts();
    let ap_out = pp.allAsyncInitiatorFlowPorts();
    let ap_in = pp.allAsyncResponderFlowPorts();
    let sp_in = pp[hasResponderSyncPorts()];               (2)
    let sp_out = pp[hasInitiatorSyncPorts()];
    macro multiple = portUsage.outgoing->size>1;
  roles :
    emits = ax_out[!multiple]->new[External]EmitsDef();
            ap_in[!multiple]->new[Internal]EmitsDef();
    publishes = ax_out[multiple]->new[External]PublishesDef();
               ap_in[multiple]->new[Internal]EmitsDef();
    consumes = ax_in->new[External] ConsumesDef();
               ap_out-> new[Internal] ConsumesDef();
    receptacle = sp_out->new [External] UsesDef();
                sp_in->new [Internal] UsesDef();
    facet = sp_in->new[External]ProvidesDef();             (3)
            sp_out->new[Internal]ProvidesDef();
}
```

The R5 rule, described below, is invoked in rule R4 for each external and top-level port that contains at least one inner synchronous and responder sub-port (see the marks (2) and (3) in rule R4). The purpose of the R5 and R6 is to generate all the provided interfaces that are useful to a CCM component to be used from its outside. An operation is generated for each synchronous and responder sub-port belonging to the current source port. Note that the list of the sub-ports is passed as a parameter to the rule R7.

```
R5 rule [External] ProvidesDef from Port {
    roles:
        provides = self.new InterfaceDef(allSyncResponderPorts());
    }
R6 rule InterfaceDef from Port {
    parameters:
        plist : Set(OperationPort);
    roles:
        contents = plist->new OperationDef();
    }
```

All the utility functions, such as *allAsyncInitiatorFlowPorts*, used by rule *R4,* can be coded in Mtrans using the navigability facilities (in a similar way as in OCL). Alternatively, a function can be implemented directly as a native function using the target language of the compiler (such as Java or Python).

5.3   Back to the Buyer/Seller Example

The MTrans specification described in 6.2 has been applied to the Buy/Seller provisioning example (figures 3 and 4).
Below we present the structure of the resulting CCM model.

```
HomeDef Home_Seller {
        manages:
            ref ComponentDef Seller;
}
ComponentDef Seller {
        emits :
            EmitsDef QuoteRequestInternal { type=... }
            EmitsDef Quote { type= DataQuote ... }
            . . .
        consumes :
            ConsumesDef QuoteRequest { type=... }
            ConsumesDef QuoteInternal { type=... }
            . . .
}
HomeDef Home_QuoteCalculator {
        manages:
            ref ComponentDef QuoteCalculator;
}
Component QuoteCalculator {
        emits:
            EmitsDef Quote { type=DataQuote... }
        consumes:
            ConsumesDef QuoteRequest { type=... }
}
. . .
```

6   Conclusions and Future Work

Component-oriented specifications can be introduced at distinct levels of abstraction during the software development cycle. Thus a EDOC/ECA model is likely to be used at an "analysis" level while a CCM based description could be used later at "design" phase, reflecting the specific architecture decisions. Obviously, for an organization that have to maintain distinct models on their systems, it is an important issue to reduce the gap between models located at distinct level of abstractions. Moreover, in the context of the OMG Model Driven Architecture, the problem of the mapping between distinct models has been identified as being very important. We can expect that a standard for model transformation will emerge from the OMG organization in a near future.

Nowadays, mapping specifications are often defined informally. Although this kind of description is useful to understand the global meaning of the transformation process, it is not sufficient to avoid ambiguities arising from its interpretation. Moreover, an informal mapping can not be executed without an explicit programming effort.

The MTrans language has been designed to address this problem. This formalism is based on the OCL language, is tool independent and it can be used with any MOF compliant metamodel. A former partial implementation of the MTrans language has been achieved on the top of a XSLT processor. The tool was used to transform SPEM models expressed in UML into SPEM models expressed in the terms of the specific SPEM metamodel. It was also used to assist the production of deployment descriptors from CCM-like component specifications (in the context of the European EURESCOM project P924). We are currently developing a new implementation of the MTrans engine, which will be based on the *Univers@lis* model repository tool [8]. Among some of the new properties that could be addressed in a new version of the MTrans formalism we would mention an explicit support for transformation *patterns* and an enrichment of the navigational operations that could be based on techniques existing in OO databases (such as the OQL language which is the counterpart of SQL for relational databases).

References

1. OMG, *«Model-Driven Architecture»*, document ormsc/2000-11-05, November 2000.
2. OMG, *«RFP: UML Profile for Enterprise Distributed Object Computing»*, document ad/1999-03-10, October 1999.
3. OMG, *«CORBA Components»*, document orbos/1999-07-02, August 1999.
4. OMG, *«The Software Process Engineering Metamodel (SPEM)»*, document ad/2001-06-05, June 2001.
5. OMG, *«A UML Profile for Enterprise Distributed Object Computing»*, document ad/2001-08-19, August 2001.

6. OMG, *«UML Profile and Interchange Models for Enterprise Application Integration (EAI)»*, document ad/2001-09-17, September 2001.
7. Meta Integration Technology, *«Meta Integration Model Bridge»*, http://www.metaintegration.net/
8. M.Belaunde, "A pragmatic approach for building a user-friendly UML: Repository", UML'99 conference. Web Site: http://universalis.elibel.tm.fr/index.html
9. W.M. Ho, J-M Jézequel, A. Le Guennec and F. Pennaneac'h, *«UMLAUT: An extensible UML transformation framework»*, Technical Report 3775, INRIA, October 1999.
10. R. Lemesle, *«Transformation rules based on meta modeling»*, Proceedings of the Second International Enterprise Distributed Object Computing Workshop (San Diego), November 1998.
11. J.Bezivin, J.Lanneluc, R.Lemesle *«sNets, the Core formalism for an Object-Oriented Tool»*, 1995.
12. Softeam, "Objecteering.UML Case Tool"; http://www.softeam.fr/
13. Softmaint, "The *Scriptor transformation engine"* http://www.softmaint.com/
14. OMG, *«Meta Object Facility, version 1.3»*, document ad/2000-04-03, March 2000.
15. OMG, *"UML Profil for EAI"*, OMG document ad/2001-08-02.
16. OMG, *"XML Schemas for XMI"*, OMG document ad/2000-08-14.

All the OMG documents referenced here are available from the OMG website using the url: http://www.omg.org/cgi-bin/doc?<doc-id>.

Engineering Modelling Languages:
A Precise Meta-Modelling Approach

Tony Clark1 [1)], Andy Evans [2)] , and Stuart Kent [3)]

[1)] Department of Computer Science, King's College London, UK
anclark@dcs.kcl.ac.uk

[2)] Department of Computer Science, University of York, UK
andye@cs.york.ac.uk

[3)] Computing Laboratory, University of Kent at Canterbury, UK
s.j.h.kent@ukc.ac.uk

Abstract. MMF uses meta-modelling techniques to precisely define modelling languages. The approach employs novel technology based on package specialisation and templates. MMF is being applied to the UML 2.0
revision initiative and is supported by a tool.

1   Introduction

This paper describes a Meta-Modelling Framework (MMF) that addresses many of
the deficiencies in the current definition of The Unified Modeling Language (UML)
[18]. The facility comprises a language (MML) for defining modelling notations, a
tool (MMT) that checks and executes those definitions, and a method (MMM) consisting of a model based approach to language definition and a set of patterns
embodying good practice in language definition. The development of MMF by the
pUML group ([14]) is ongoing and has been supported by IBM and Rational Inc.
The work reported in this paper is a simplified version of the work described in out
initial submission to the UML 2.0 revision initiative [13] [4] which is expected to be
completed in 2002. This paper describes the components of MMF and uses them to
develop a simple modelling language.

1.1   A Method for Meta-Modelling (MMM)

The UML is a collection of notations, some visual some textual. These notations
currently have a loose mapping to an abstract syntax (which is imprecisely defined),
which in turn is given an informal semantics written in natural language. The UML
needs to become a precisely defined *family* of modelling languages, where a modelling language comprises a notation (concrete syntax), abstract syntax and semantics.

Software Engineers define languages as a collection of models with mappings
between them. Typically a language consists of models for concrete syntax, abstract
syntax and for the semantic domain. The MMF approach applies OO modelling to
the definition of OO modelling languages. Each language component is defined as a
package containing a class diagram. Package specialization is employed to support

R.-D. Kutsche and H. Weber (Eds.): FASE 2002, LNCS 2306, pp. 159-173, 2002.

reusable, modular, incremental language design. OCL [20] [15] is used to define well-formedness constraints on the language components. Mappings between language components are defined in terms of OCL constraints on associations between model elements.

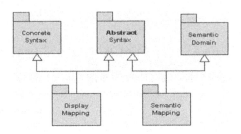

The MMF approach uses two key features of OO modelling technology: *package specialization* and *templates*. Package specialization permits (possible partial) definitions of model elements in a super-package to be consistently specialized in a sub-package. Templates are parametric model elements; supplying model elements as parameter values *stamps out* the template to produce a fresh model element. Templates provide a means of representing reusable modelling patterns; the MMF approach uses templates to capture patterns that occur repeatedly in OO modelling languages thereby providing a framework for defining language families.

This technology is not specific to MMF, UML has package specialization and parametric model elements and in particular the Catalysis approach [7] advocates the use of these features as part of an OO method. Algebraic specification languages such as Clear and OBJ and abstract programming languages such as ML and Haskell provide a means of constructing libraries of parametric components and organising systems by combining these components in different ways. However, MMF has provided the most precise definition of these concepts within the scope of OO modelling to date.

1.2   A Language for Meta-Modelling (MML)

MML is a static OO modelling language that aims to be small, meta-circular and as consistent as possible with UML 1.3. MML achieves parsimony by providing a small number of highly expressive orthogonal modelling features. The complete definition of MML is beyond the scope of this paper; the reader is directed to [2], [3] and [9] for an overview of the MMF approach, to [3] for the meta-circular definition of MML and to [5] and [6] for its formal definition. The rest of this section gives an overview of the main features of MML which are an OCL-like expression language; class definitions; package definitions and templates.

1.2.1   A Basic Expression Language

MML consists of a basic expression language which is based on OCL. The language provides a basic collection of data types including integers, booleans and strings together with standard operations over values of these types. MML supports sets and sequences together with a small number of standard OCL iteration constructs; the following denotes 5 (the full list of iteration constructs is defined in [6]):

```
Set{1,2,3}->select(x | x > 1)->iterate(y n = 0 | n + y)
```

1.2.2   Class Definitions

MML classes define the structure, behaviour and invariants of their instances. The following defines a class of people.

```
class Person
  name : String; age : Integer; married : Boolean;
  children : Set(Person); parents : Set(Person);
  init(s:Seq(Instance)):Person
    self.name := s->at(0) []
    self.age := s->at(1) []
    self;
  averageChildAge():Integer
    self.children->iterate(c a=0 | a+c.age)/self.children->size;
  inv
    IfMarriedThenOver15 self.married implies self.age >= 16;
    OnlyTwoParents self.parents->size = 2
end
```

The definition of the class Person shows a number of MML features. In general, an MML definition consists of a name and an expression. A class definition introduces a new name whose scope is the class definition and relative to the package in which the class is defined using the '::' operator, for example SomePackage::Person.

A class has a number of attributes each of which is a definition consisting of a name and a type. A class definition has a number of method definitions each of which have typed parameters, a return type and a body. The body of a method is an expression which provides the return value when the method is called by sending an instance of the class a message. The init method of a class is automatically invoked when a new instance of the class is created. A class definition has a number of invariant constraint definitions following the keyword inv. Each constraint consists of a name and a boolean expression. The constraints express well formedness properties of the instances of the class. For example, in order to be married a person must be aged 16 or over.

1.2.3   Association Definitions

Classes may be associated to show logical dependency between instances of the classes. Currently MML supports only binary associations. A binary association consists of the two classes being associated, the name of the association and two association ends (one for each class). An association end is a definition consisting of a name and a multiplicity. The multiplicity constraint the number of instances of the attached class that can be associated with an instance of the class attached to the other end. For example, suppose that the children and parents attributes of the Person class were defined via an association (at most 2 parents, but any number of children):

```
association Family
  parents : Person mult: 2
  children : Person mult: *
end
```

1.2.4   Package Definitions

Packages are used in MML to group definitions of model elements. MML provides a powerful package specialization mechanism that allows packages to inherit from parent packages and to consistently specialize all of the inherited contents. For example:

```
package People
  class Person
    // as given above
  end;
  association Family
    // as given above
  end
end
```

Note that the association Family refers to the class Person as defined in the package People. Now, suppose that we want to extend the notion of being a person with an employer:

```
package Employment extends People
  class Person yearsInService : Integer end;
  class Company name : String end;
  association Works
    company : Company mult: 1
    employees : Person mult: *
  end
end
```

The package Employment extends the package People and therefore includes all of the definitions from People. A package is a *name space* and we may refer to two different classes called Person: People::Person and Employment::Person. Employment::Person contains all the definitions from People::Person extended with a new attribute named yearsInService. A package may only contain one definition with any given name. Therefore the association named Family in the package Employment must refer to the extended definition of Person. All definitions given by People have been *consistently extended* in Employment. The notion of consistent extension for model elements defined in a package is similar to the idea of *virtual methods* in C++. Package specialization supports multiple inheritance. Packages may be nested in which case the for package specialization outlined above hold for the nested packages.

1.2.5   Templates

A *template* is a parametric model element. When parameters are supplied to the template the result is a new model element. The supplied parameter values are model elements that are used by the template to construct, or *stamp out*, the new model element. Templates are used to capture patterns of recurring structure, behaviour and constraints that occur in models. Templates differ from specialization, which also captures patterns, in that there is no dependency between the template and the result of stamping it out. Specialization captures patterns in terms of (abstract) model elements that are specialized rather than stamped out. The process of specialization can lead to dependencies both between a super-model element and its sub-model elements and can also lead to sibling dependencies between different sub-model elements. Templates are not a replacement for specialization; they offer a new tool to the modeller that should be used where appropriate.

Suppose that we wish to capture the notion of containment. This involves two classes: a *container* and a *contained element*. Suppose also that all containers provide access to their contained elements via a method with the same name as the contained element class. Finally, suppose that we know all contained elements are named and that the container cannot contain two different elements with the same name. This can be expressed as a template in MML:

```
package Contains(Container,n1,m1,Contained,n2,m2)
  class <<Container>>
    <<n2>>():Set(<<Contained>>) self.<<n2>>
    inv
      <<"Every" + Contained + "HasADifferentName">>
        self.<<n2>>->forAll(c1 c2 | c1.name = c2.name implies c1 = c2)
  end;
  association <<Container + Contains>>
    <<n1>> : <<Container>> mult: <<m1>>
    <<n2>> : <<Contained>> mult: <<m2>>
  end
end
```

The package template Contains is defined to have six parameters. Container is the name of the container class, Contained is the name of the contained element class, n1 is the name used by an instance of the contained class to refer to its container and n2 is the name used by an instance of the container class to refer to its contents. The parameters m1 and m2 are the appropriate multiplicities for the containment. Throughout the body of the template definition literal names may be turned into expressions that are evaluated by enclosing them in << and >>. The names are supplied as strings and therefore the string concatenation operator + is used to construct new names. Suppose that we wish to express the containment relationship between a person and their children:

```
package People
  extends Container("Person","children",*,"Person","parents",2)
  class Person ...atribute and method definitions... end
end
```

Stamping out the container template produces a new package that can be used as the parent package of People. Defining the parents and children attributes this way has not saved much effort, however the template can be reused when defining the Employment package:

```
package Employment
 extends Companies, People,
  Container("Company","employees",*,"Person","employer",1)
end
```

1.3   A Tool for Meta-Modelling (MMT)

MMT is a prototype tool written in Java that supports the MMF approach. MMT consists of a virtual machine that runs the MML calculus which is a simple object-based calculus that supports higher order functions. All the MML examples contained in this paper are derived from MML code running on MMT (some slight simplifications have been applied). MMT defines MML by loading a collection of meta-circular boot files written in MML. The definitions in this paper have been loaded and checked in MMT which provides a flexible environment for inspecting and flattening definitions of packages and classes. A full description of MMT is outside the scope of this paper.

2   The Definition of a Simple Modelling Language

SML is a static modelling language that consists of packages and classes with attributes. Packages can contain both packages and classes. Classes contain attributes. An attribute has a name and a type. SML supports inheritance: packages may have super-packages, classes may have super-classes and attributes may have super-attributes. The meaning of SML package models is given by snapshots that contain objects. Each object is a container of slots which are named values. A package is a *classifier* for snapshots that contain sub-snapshots and objects corresponding to the packages and classes in the package. The structure of the syntax, semantic domain and semantic mapping for SML follows standard patterns that occur in modelling languages. The following sections show how these patterns can be captured as templates and then how SML can be defined by stamping out the templates.

2.1   Templates for SML Definition

2.1.1   Named Model Elements

Most modelling elements in SML are named. Like Java, MMT makes use of a toString method when displaying objects:

```
package Named(Model)
   class <<Model>>
     name : String;
     toString():String
       "<" + self.of.name + self.name + ">"
   end
end
```

2.1.2   Cloning Model Elements

Packages may have parents. A child package is defined to contain all the model elements defined by the parent package. A given model element is defined in a single name space; a package provides the name space for all of its elements. Therefore, when a model element is inherited from a parent package, the element must be copied and the containing name space must be updated to be the child package. The process of inheriting a copy of a model element and updating its containing name space is referred to as *cloning*. The cloning pattern occurs in two distinct stages: (1) a model element is shallow copied (no copying of slots) and the containing name space is updated; (2) the slots are copied.

```
package Clonable(Container,Contained)
   class <<Contained>>
     clone(nameSpace:<<Container>>):<<Container>>
       let o = self.copy()
           ms = self.of.allMethods()
           cs = ms->select(m | m.name = "cloneAux")
       in o.<<Container>> := nameSpace []
          cs->collect(m | (m.body)(o,nameSpace)) [] o
       end
   end
end
```

The Clonable template is defined above and is used to declare a clonable model element. The definition uses knowledge about the MML meta-level in order to copy an instance of the container class. Every object has a method named 'copy' that produces a shallow copy of the receiver. The template updates the value of the container to be the name space supplied to 'clone' and then invokes all of the methods defined by the container class named 'cloneAux'. Each method will deal with copying the slots of the new object 'o'.

2.1.3   Name Spaces

```
class <<Container>>
  <<"locallyDefines"+Contained>>(name:String):Boolean
    self.<<Contained+"s">>()->exists(m | m.name = name);
  <<"localLookup"+Contained>>(name:String):Set(<<Contained>>)
    self.<<Contained+"s">>()->select(m | m.name = name);
  <<"defines"+Contained>>(name:String):Boolean
    self.<<"all"+Contained+"s">>()->exists(m | m.name = name);
  <<"lookup"+Contained>>(name:String):<<Contained>>
    if self.<<"locallyDefines"+Contained>>(name)
    then self.<<"localLookup"+Contained>>(name).selectElement()
    else if self.<<"defines"+Contained>>(name)
         then self.<<"all"+Contained+"s">>()->select(m |
            m.name = name).selectElement()
         else state.error("NameSpace::lookup")
         endif
    endif
end
```

A *name space* is a container of named model elements that provides a protocol for accessing the elements by name. The template defined above is a simple notion of name space in which contained elements are assumed to own their own names. The template defines a name space lookup protocol involving local lookup and inherited lookup. The template therefore represents a mixin that requires the container to define a pair of methods for the contained elements that returns the local contains and the inherited contents.

2.1.4   Containers

```
package Contains(Container,Contained)
   class <<Container>>
     <<Contained + "s">>():Set(<<Contained>>)
       self.<<Contained + "s">>
     cloneAux(me:<<Container>>,nameSpace:<<Container>>)
       me.<<Contained + "s">> :=
         (me.<<Contained + "s">>()->collect(x |
           x.clone(nameSpace.<<"lookup" + Container>>(me.name))))
       end;
   association <<Container + Contained>>
     <<Container>> : Contains::<<Container>> mult: 1
     <<Contained + "s">> : Contains::<<Contained>> mult: *
   end
end
```

Many model elements in SML contain other model elements. The contains template defines a method for accessing the contained elements; providing method access allows the contained elements to be encapsulated. A variation of Contains is Self-Contains which has a single parameter. SelfContains is used to express model elements that can contain other model elements of the same type. A root self container contains itself; the method providing access to the contained elements of a self container removes the 'self' from the elements it returns (thereby satisfying the round trip constraint and also preventing cycles occurring when processing the contained elements).

The template defines a method for cloning the contained elements when a container instance is cloned. The cloneAux method is supplied with the model element to clone (me) and the current name space (nameSpace) containing the model element. Each contained element is passed its name space by looking up the appropriate model element in nameSpace. In the absence of package specialization, the nameSpaces passed to model elements when they are cloned will be the appropriate copy of the original nameSpace container for the element. However, if a package is specialized, nameSpaces may be extended in which case the cloning mechanism will guarantee that the most specific definition is supplied to clone as the containing name space.

2.1.5   Specialization

```
package Specializable(Model)
   class <<Model>>
     parents : Set(<<Model>>);
     allLocalParents() : Set(<<Model>>)
       self.parents->iterate(parent P = self.parents |
         P->union(parent.allLocalParents()))
   end
 end
```

In SML packages may be extended to contain new definitions; classes can be extended to contain new attributes, methods and constraints. Specialization may occur explicitly when the modeller defines a package to extend a super-package or defines a class to extend a super-class. Specialization may occur implicitly when the container of a model element m specializes another container that defines a model element m' such that m and m' have the same name. Every specializable model element must have a set of parents of the same type. The method allLocalParents is the transitive closure of the parents relation.

The contents of a container are defined by its parents: the local parents, as defined above, and any parents which are inherited from its own container:

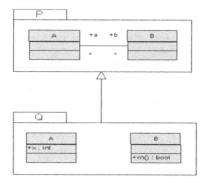

Package P defines classes A and B and a binary association between them. The binary association has ends named a and b causing two attributes to be added to the classes at opposite ends of the association. Package Q defines two classes A and B with an attribute and an operation respectively. Package P is the parent of package Q. In order to compute the attributes of Q::A we must first compute its parents. A has no parents in Q but since the container of Q::A has parents we must inspect P in order to check whether it defines a class named A. We find it does and that P::A has an attributes named b. Therefore Q::A defines an attribute named b. The type of Q::A::b is a class called B which must be referenced with respect to the container of Q::A, namely Q. We find that Q defines Q::B and therefore the type of Q::A::b is Q::B. If we repeat this process for Q::B we find that Q::B defines Q::B::a whose type is Q::A. If we *flatten* the package inheritance the result is as follows:

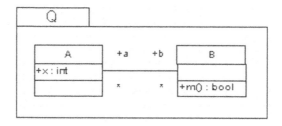

A specializable container requires both the container and the contained model elements to be specializable. The complete set of parents for the contained model elements are defined by computing both the local parents (the transitive closure of the parents relation) and the inherited parents via the container. The contents of a container are computed with respect to *all* parents of the container. The template for specializable containers is:

```
package SpecializableContainer(Container,Contained)
   extends Specializable(Container),Specializable(Contained)
   class <<Container>>
     <<"all" + Contained + "s">>() : Set(<<Contained>>)
     self.allParents()->iterate(parent S = self.<<Contained+"s">>() |
       S->union(parent.<<"all"+Contained+"s">>()->reject(c |
         self.<<"locallyDefines + Contained>>(c.name))->collect(c |
           c.clone(self))))
     inv
       <<Contained + "sHaveDifferentNames">>
       self.<<"all" + Contained + "s">>()->forAll(c1 c2 |
         c1.name = c2.name implies c1 = c2)
   end;
   class <<Contained>>
     allParents() : Set(<<Contained>>)
       self.allLocalParents()->union(self.allInheritedParents());
     allInheritedParents() : Set(<<Contained>>)
       if self.<<Container>> = self
       then Set{}
       else self.<<Container>>.allParents()->iterate(parent S = Set{} |
         S->union(parent.<<"all"+Contained+"s">>()->select(m |
           m.name = self.name)))
       endif
   end
 end
```

All the contained elements of a specializable container are constructed as follows. Firstly all the parents of the container are constructed (recall that the parents of a model element will include both the locally defined parents and the parents inherited from the container's container). The locally defined contents are merged with the contents of all the parents after removing any parent contents that are shadowed locally. Finally, all inherited contents must be cloned in order that they are correctly contained.

2.1.6   Relations

```
package Relation(Name,Domain,Range)
   class <<Name>>
     left : <<Domain>>;
     right : <<Range>>
   end
end
```

A relation has a name and holds between a class of domain elements and a class of range elements. A relation is essentially an *association class* that defines a constraint on pairs of domain and range instances.

2.1.7   Instantiation

A key feature of the MMF approach is the definition of modelling languages in terms of their abstract syntax and *semantic domain*. The abstract syntax is a model of the legal sentences of the language. The semantic domain is a model of the legal meanings that sentences can take. A language definition is completed by a model of the mapping between the abstract syntax and the semantic domain.

The relation between abstract syntax and semantic domain is referred to as *instantiation*. In general the instantiation relation between a model element and its instances may be aribitrary (expressions denote values, classes denote objects, state machines denote filmstrips, etc). However, if we know the structure of the abstract syntax and semantic domain then this places structure on the instantiation relationship. This structure can be expressed as templates.

Consider the following diagram:

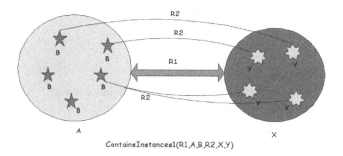

ContainsInstances1(R1,A,B,R2,X,Y)

The diagram shows a typical instantiation relationship between two containers called ContainsInstances1. The instantiable model elements are shown on the left of the diagram and the instances are shown on the right. Elements of type A contain elements of type B and elements of type X contain elements of type Y. Elements of type A have instances of type X and elements of type B have instances of type Y. We wish to express the instantiation constraint that in order for an X to be classified as an instance of an A (R1) every Y that the X contains must be an instance of some B that the A contains (R2).

This form of instantiation relationship occurs between packages and snapshots where every object in the snapshot must be an instance of some class in the package, however not all classes need to be instantiated in the snapshot. This relationship is defined as a template:

```
package ContainsInstances1(
    R1,ModelContainer,ModelContained,
    R2,InstanceContainer,InstanceContained)
  extends
    Relation(R1,ModelContainer,InstanceContainer),
    Relation(R2,ModelContained,InstanceContained)
  class <<R1>>
```

```
  left : <<ModelContainer>>;
  right : <<InstanceContainer>>
  inv
    <<"InstancesOf"+ModelContainer+
          "ContainsInstancesOf"+ModelContained>>
    self.right.<<InstanceContained + "s">>()->forAll(i |
      self.left.<<"all" + ModelContained + "s">>()->exists(m |
        <<R2>>.new(Seq{m,i}).check() = Set{}))
  end
end
```

Other instantiation relationships are possible. For example, if we view slots as the instances of attributes and objects as the instances of classes then classes contain attributes and objects contain slots. An object is a well formed instance of a class when all the attributes have instances. This relationship can be defined as a template which we will call ContainsInstances2. Finally, there is an instantiation relationship which is defined as follows:

```
package ContainsInstances(R1,A,B,R2,X,Y)
  extends
    ContainsInstances1(R1,A,B,R2,X,Y),
    ContainsInstances2(R1,A,B,R2,X,Y)
end
```

2.1.8   Relationships between Attributes

```
package RelateAtt(R,Domain,Range,DomainAtt,RangeAtt,Pred)
  extends Relation(R,Domain,Range)
  class <<R>>
    inv
      <<"Relate"+Domain+"::"+DomainAtt+"To"+Range+"::"+RangeAtt>>
      Pred(self.left.<<DomainAtt>>,self.right.<<RangeAtt>>)
    end
end;
package SameName(R,Domain,Range)
  extends RelateAtt(R,Domain,Range,"name","name",=)
end;
package TypeCorrect(R,Domain,Range)
  extends RelateAtt(R,Domain,Range,"type","value",check)
end
```

An attribute relation involves a domain class and a range class. The relation specifies the domain and range attributes that are to be associated and also specified the predicate that will be used to check the values of the attributes. The invariant constraint in RelateAtt simply applies the predicate to the values of the slots in domain and range objects. SameName associates a domain and range object by requiring that they have the same values for the slot 'name'. In SML this constraint is required when associating the attributes of a class with the slots of an instance of the class. TypeCorrect associates a domain class with an attribute named 'type' and a range class with an attribute named 'value'. The predicate is satisfied when all the invariant constraints of the type return true for the value.

2.2   Definition of SML

We have described the MMF approach to language definition which is to model all components of the languages and to employ object-oriented techniques to achieve modularity and reuse. The previous section has used the novel technology of package specialization and templates to define a library of modelling language patterns. This section shows how the patterns can be used to construct a simple modelling language called SML.

2.2.1   Abstract Syntax

```
package AbstractSyntax
  extends
    SelfContains("Package"), SpecializableContainer("Package","Pack-
age"),
    SpecializableContainer("Package","Class"),
    SpecializableContainer("Class","Attribute"),
    Specializable("Attribute"),
    Contains("Package","Class"), Contains("Class","Attribute"),
    Clonable("Package","Class"), Clonable("Package","Package"),
    Clonable("Class","Attribute"),
    Named("Package"), Named("Class"), Named("Attribute"),
    NameSpace("Package","Package"), NameSpace("Package","Class"),
    NameSpace("Class","Attribute")
  class Attribute
    type : Class
    cloneAux(me:Attribute_,nameSpace:Class)
      me.type := (nameSpace.Package.lookupClass(me.type.name))
  end
end
```

The definition of the abstract syntax model for SML is given above. It is interesting to note that the MMF approach achieves a declarative specification of the model in terms of its properties explicitly listed in the 'extends' clause for the package. For example, we know that a package has the properties of a specializable container, that a package contains both packages and classes, and so on. If we were to define the abstract syntax as the result of flattening this definition, many of these properties would be implicit and therefore difficult to extract.

2.2.2   Semantic Domain

```
package SemanticDomain
  extends
    SelfContains("Snapshot"),
    Contains("Snapshot","Object"),Contains("Object","Slot"),
    Named("Snapshot"), Named("Slot")
  class Slot value : Object end
end
```

The domain is much simpler than the abstract syntax model. In our work using templates to define a UML 2.0 infrastructure we have a much richer semantic domain (for example, snapshots, objects and slots have parents). One of the benefits of the

MMF approach is that we can easily refactor the structure of a model in terms of its properties by adding new templates to the 'extends' clause of the package.

2.2.3   Semantic Mapping

```
package SemanticMapping
  extends
    AbstractSyntax, SemanticDomain,
    ContainsInstances1(
      "PackXSnap","Package","Class",
      "ClassXObj","Snapshot","Object"),
    ContainsInstances(
      "ClassXObj","Class","Attribute",
      "AttXSlot","Object","Slot"),
    SameName("AttXSlot","Attribute","Slot")
    TypeCorrect("AttXSlot","Attribute","Slot")
  end
```

The semantic mapping includes all of the elements from the abstract syntax and semantic domain and then constructs relations between them. For example, the relation PackXSnap is defined to check that every object contained in a snapshot is an instance of some class in the corresponding package.

3   Conclusion and Future Work

This paper has described the MMF approach to engineering Modelling Languages. The approach separates the issues of how to model syntax and semantics domains and allows languages to be developed from modular units. The approach also supports reusable patterns for language engineering. The paper has illustrated the approach with a small modelling language. MMF aims to provide coherent methods, technology and tools for engineering modelling languages. The core technology is not new, the methods for defining languages are well developed, the technology has its roots in Catalysis [7] and has been developed further in [5] and [8]. The novelty in MMF arises from bringing these otherwise disparate technologies together within a single consistent object-oriented framework. The MMF approach does not use a formal mathematical language to express the semantics of the languages; however, it is sufficiently expressive to support the infrastructure of these approaches and therefore can benefit from many of the results such as [1] and [17]. The MMT tool is still under development. Other tools exist, such as Argo and USE [16] [11] that can be used to model languages; however, unlike MMT, these tools tend to have a fixed meta-model.

We are applying the approach to the definition of rich and expressive visual modelling languages, such as [12] and [10]. In particular, the syntax employed in these diagrams is more sophisticated than that typically employed in UML. We are engaged in the UML 2.0 revision process [4] [19], and using MML ideas to help redefine aspects of UML with one of the main submission teams. The interested reader is directed to [4] which contains many examples of templates in a diagram format. But perhaps our most ambitious plans are in applying the MMF approach to realise the OMG MOdel Driven Architecture (MDA) initiative.

References

[1]   Bottoni P., Koch M., Parisi-Presicce F., Taentzer G. (2000) Consistency Checking and Visualization of OCL Constraints. In Evans A., Kent S., Selic B. (eds) UML 2000 proceedings volume 1939 LNCS, 278 -- 293 , Springer-Verlag.

[2]   Clark A., Evans A., Kent S. (2000) Profiles for Language Definition. Presented at the ECOOP pUML Workshop, Nice.

[3]   Clark A., Evans A., Kent S, Cook S., Brodsky S., (2000) A feasibility Study in Rearchitecting UML as a Family of Languages Using a Precise OO Meta-Modeling Approach. Available at http://www.puml.org/mmt.zip.

[4]   Clark A., Evans A., Kent S. (2001) Initial submission to the UML 2.0 Infrastructure RFP. Available at http://www.cs.york.ac.uk/puml/papers/uml2submission.pdf

[5]   Clark A., Evans A., Kent S. (2001) The Specification of a Reference Implementation for UML. Special Issue of L'Objet on Object Modelling, 2001.

[6]   Clark A., Evans A., Kent S. (2001) The Meta-Modeling Language Calculus: Foundation Semantics for UML. ETAPS FASE Conference 2001, Genoa.

[7]   D'Souza D., Wills A. C. (1998) Object Components and Frameworks with UML -- The Catalysis Approach. Addison-Wesley.

[8]   D'Souza D., Sane A., Birchenough A. (1999) First-Class Extensibility for UML - Packaging of Profiles, Stereotypes, Patterns. In France R. & Rumpe B. (eds) UML '99 proceedings volume 1723 LNCS, 265 -- 277, Springer-Verlag.

[9]   Evans A., Kent S. (1999) Core meta-modelling semantics of UML -- The pUML approach. In France R. & Rumpe B. (eds) UML '99 proceedings volume 1723 LNCS, 140 -- 155, Springer-Verlag.

[10]   Howse J., Molina F., Kent S., Taylor J. (1999) Reasoning with Spider Diagrams. Proceedings of the IEEE Symposium on Visual Languages '99, 138 -- 145. IEEE CS Press.

[11]   Hussmann H., Demuth B., Finger F. (2000) Modular Architecture for a Toolset Supporting OCL In Evans A., Kent S., Selic B. (eds) UML 2000 proceedings volume 1939 LNCS, 278 -- 293 , Springer-Verlag.

[12]   Kent S. (1997) Constraint Diagrams: Visualizing Invariants in Object-Oriented Models. In Proceedings of OOPSLA '97, 327 -- 341.

[13]   UML 2.0 Infrastructure Request for Proposals, available from http://www.omg.org/uml

[14]   The pUML Home Page http://www.puml.org.

[15]   Richters M., Gogolla M. (1999) A metamodel for OCL. In France R. & Rumpe B. (eds) UML '99 proceedings volume 1723 LNCS, 156 -- 171, Springer-Verlag.

[16]   Richters M., Gogolla M. (2000) Validating UML Models and OCL Constraints. In Evans A., Kent S., Selic B. (eds) UML 2000 proceedings volume 1939 LNCS, 265 -- 277, Springer-Verlag.

[17]   Richters M., Gogolla M. (2000) A Semantics for OCL pre and post conditions. Presented at the OCL Workshop, UML 2000.

[18]   Object Management Group (1999) OMG Unified Modeling Language Specification, version 1.3. Available at http://www.omg.org/uml.

[19]   The UML 2.0 Working Group Home Page http://www.celigent.com/omg/adptf/wgs/uml2wg.html.

[20]   Warmer J., Kleppe A. (1999) The Object Constraint Language: Precise Modeling with UML. Addison-Wesley.

AToM³: A Tool for Multi-formalism and Meta-modelling

Juan de Lara[1,2] and Hans Vangheluwe[2]

[1] ETS Informática
Universidad Autónoma de Madrid, Madrid, Spain
Juan.Lara@ii.uam.es
[2] School of Computer Science
McGill University, Montréal, Québec, Canada
hv@cs.mcgill.ca

Abstract. This article introduces the combined use of *multi-formalism* modelling and *meta-modelling* to facilitate computer assisted modelling of complex systems. The approach allows one to model different parts of a system using different formalisms. Models can be automatically converted between formalisms thanks to information found in a *Formalism Transformation Graph* (FTG), proposed by the authors. To aid in the automatic generation of multi-formalism modelling tools, formalisms are modelled in their own right (at a meta-level) within an appropriate formalism. This has been implemented in the interactive tool AToM³. This tool is used to describe formalisms commonly used in the simulation of dynamical systems, as well as to generate custom tools to process (create, edit, transform, simulate, optimise, ...) models expressed in the corresponding formalism. AToM³ relies on graph rewriting techniques and graph grammars to perform the transformations between formalisms as well as for other tasks, such as code generation and operational semantics specification.

Keywords: Modeling and Simulation, Meta-Modeling, Multi-Formalism Modeling, Automatic Code Generation, Graph Grammars.

1 Introduction

Modeling complex systems is a difficult task, as such systems often have components and aspects whose structure as well as behaviour cannot be described in a single formalism. Examples of commonly used formalisms are *Bond Graphs*, *Discrete EVent system Specification* (DEVS) [25], *Entity-Relationship* diagrams (ER) and *State charts*. Several approaches are possible:

1. A single *super-formalism* may be constructed which subsumes all the formalisms needed in the system description. This is neither possible nor meaningful in most cases, although there are some examples of formalisms that span several domains (e.g. Bond Graphs for the mechanical, hydraulic and electrical domains.)

R.-D. Kutsche and H. Weber (Eds.): FASE 2002, LNCS 2306, pp. 174–188, 2002.
© Springer-Verlag Berlin Heidelberg 2002

2. Each system component may be modelled using the most appropriate formalism and tool. To investigate the overall behaviour of the system, *co-simulation* can be used. In this approach, each component is simulated with a formalism-specific simulator. Interaction due to component coupling is resolved at the trajectory (simulation data) level. It is no longer possible to answer symbolic, higher-level questions that could be answered within the individual components' formalisms.

3. As in co-simulation, each system component may be modelled using the most appropriate formalism and tool. In the *multi-formalism* approach however, a single formalism is identified into which each of the components may be symbolically transformed [23]. The formalism to transform to depends on the question to be answered about the system. The Formalism Transformation Graph (see Figure 1) suggests DEVS [25] as a universal common modelling formalism for simulation purposes. It is easily seen how multi-formalism modelling subsumes both the super-formalism approach and the co-simulation approach.

Although the model transformation approach is conceptually appealing, there remains the difficulty of interconnecting a plethora of different tools, each designed for a particular formalism. Also, it is desirable to have problem-specific formalisms and tools. The time needed to develop these is usually prohibitive. This is why we introduce *meta-modelling* whereby the different formalisms themselves as well as the transformations between them are modelled explicitly. This preempts the problem of tool incompatibility. Ideally, a meta-modelling environment must be able to generate customised tools for models in various formalisms provided the formalisms are described at the meta-model level. When such a tool relies on a common data structure to internally represent models, irrespective of formalism, transformation between formalisms is reduced to the transformation of these data structures.

In this article, we present AToM³ [1], a tool which implements the above ideas. AToM³ has a meta-modelling layer in which different formalisms are modelled graphically. From the meta-specification (in the Entity Relationship formalism), AToM³ generates a tool to process models described in the specified formalism. Models are internally represented using *Abstract Syntax Graphs* (ASGs). As a consequence, transformations between formalisms are reduced to graph rewriting. Thus, the transformations themselves can be expressed as graph grammar models. Although graph grammars [6] have been used in very diverse areas such as graphical editors, code optimisation, computer architecture, etc. [8], to our knowledge, they have never been applied to formalism transformation.

2   Preliminaries

2.1   Multi-formalism Modelling

For the analysis and design of complex systems, it is not sufficient to study individual components in isolation. Properties of the system must be assessed by looking at the *whole* multi-formalism system.

In figure 1, a part of the "formalism space" is depicted in the form of a *Formalism Transformation Graph* (FTG). The different formalisms are shown as nodes in the graph. The arrows denote a homomorphic relationship "can be mapped onto", using symbolic transformations between formalisms. The vertical dashed line is a division between continuous and discrete formalisms. The vertical, dotted arrows denote the existence of a solver (simulation kernel) capable of simulating a model.

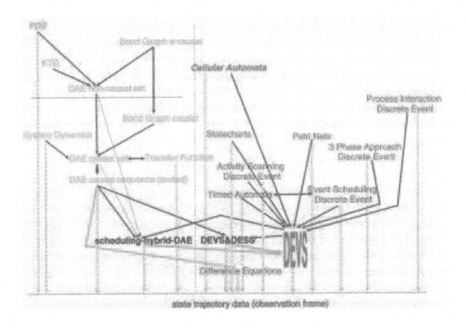

Fig. 1. Formalism Transformation Graph

2.2 Meta-modelling

A proven method to achieve the required flexibility for a modelling language that supports many formalisms and modelling paradigms is to model the modelling language itself [5] [22]. Such a model of the modelling language is called a meta-model. It describes the possible structures that can be expressed in the language. Taking the methodology one step further, the meta-modelling formalism itself may be modelled by means of a meta-meta-model. This meta-meta-model specification captures the basic elements needed to design a formalism. Table 1 depicts the levels considered in our meta-modelling approach.

Formalisms such as the ER or UML class diagrams [16] are often used for meta-modelling. To be able to fully specify modelling formalisms, the meta-formalism may have to be extended with the ability to express constraints (lim-

Table 1. Meta-modelling levels

Level	Description	Example
Meta-Meta-Model	Model that describes a formalism that will be used to describe other formalisms.	Description of Entity-Relationship Diagrams, UML class Diagrams
Meta-Model	Model that describes a simulation formalism. Specified under the rules of a certain Meta-Meta-Model	Description of Deterministic Finite Automata, Ordinary differential equations (ODE)
Model	Description of an object. Specified under the rules of a certain ODE Meta-Model	$f'(x) = -\sin x, f(0) = 0$ (in the ODE formalism)

iting the number of meaningful models). For example, when modelling a Deterministic Finite Automaton (DFA), different transitions leaving a given state must have different labels. This cannot be expressed within ER alone. Expressing constraints is most elegantly done by adding a constraint language to the meta-modelling formalism. Whereas the meta-modelling formalism frequently uses a graphical notation, constraints are concisely expressed in textual form. For this purpose, some systems [22], including AToM³ use the Object Constraint Language OCL [19] used in the UML.

2.3   Graph Grammars

In analogy with string grammars, graph grammars can be used to describe graph transformations, or to generate sets of valid graphs. Graph grammars are composed of rules, each mapping a graph on the left-hand side (LHS) to a graph on the right-hand side (RHS). When a match is found between the LHS of a rule and a part of an input graph, the matching subgraph is replaced by the RHS of the rule. Rules may also have a condition that must be satisfied in order for the rule to be applied, as well as actions to be performed when the rule is executed. A rewriting system iteratively applies matching rules in the grammar to the graph, until no more rules are applicable. Some approaches also offer control flow specifications. In our tool, rules are ordered based on a user-assigned priority.

The use of a model (in the form of a graph grammar) of graph transformations has some advantages over an implicit representation (embedding the transformation computation in a program) [4]:

- It is an abstract, declarative, high level representation. This enables exchange, re-use, and symbolic analysis of the transformation model.
- The theoretical foundations of graph rewriting systems may assist in proving correctness and convergence properties of the transformation tool.

On the other hand, the use of graph grammars is constrained by efficiency. In the most general case, subgraph isomorphism testing is NP-complete. However, the use of small subgraphs on the LHS of graph grammar rules, as well as using node labels and edge labels can greatly reduce the search space.

Since we store simulation models as graphs, it is possible to express the transformations shown in the FTG as graph grammars at the meta-level.

For example, suppose we want to transform Non-deterministic Finite Automata (NFA) into behaviourally equivalent DFA. In the latter formalism, the labels of all transitions leaving a state must be distinct. Models in both formalisms can be represented as graphs. Figure 2 shows the NFA to DFA transformation specification in the form of a graph grammar.

In this graph grammar, entities (both states and transitions) are labelled with numbers. RHS node labels are marked with a prime, to distinguish them from the corresponding LHS ones. If two nodes in a LHS and a RHS have the same number, the node must not disappear when the rule is executed. If a number appears in a LHS but not in a RHS, the node must be removed when applying the rule. If a number appears in a RHS but not in a LHS, the node must be created if the rule is applied.

For subgraph matching purposes, we should specify the value of the attributes of the nodes in the LHS that will produce a matching. In the example, all the attributes in LHS nodes have the value $\langle ANY \rangle$, which means that any value will produce a matching. If a LHS matches, then the additional textual condition (if any) is evaluated. This condition can be specified in Python or in OCL. If this condition holds, the rule can be applied.

It is also necessary to specify the value of the attributes once the rule has been applied and the LHS has been replaced by the RHS. This is done by specifying attributes in the RHS nodes. If no value is specified, and the node is not a new node (the label appears in the LHS), by default it will keep its values. It is also possible to calculate new values for attributes, and we certainly must do this if a new node is generated when replacing the LHS by the RHS. In the example, we specify new values in nodes 5' and 6' of rules 3 and 4 respectively.

In the figure, *matched(i)* means "the node in the host graph that matches node i in the rule". The graph grammar rules do the following: rule one removes unreachable nodes; rule two joins two equal states into one; rule three eliminates non-determinism when there are two transitions with the same label departing from the same node, and one goes to a different node while the other goes into the first one; rule four is very similar to the previous one, but the non-determinism is between two different nodes; finally, the last rule removes transitions with the same label departing from and arriving at the same state.

A graph rewriting module for formalism transformation takes as inputs a grammar and a model in a source formalism and outputs a behaviourally equivalent model expressed in a target formalism. In some cases, the output and the input models are expressed in the same formalism, and the application of the graph grammar merely optimises some aspect of the model. Other uses of graph-grammars will be described in section 3.4.

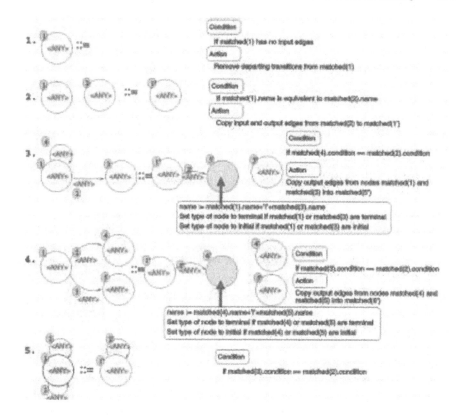

Fig. 2. A graph-grammar to transform NFA into DFA

3   AToM³

AToM³ is a tool which uses and implements the concepts presented above written
in the object-oriented, dynamically typed, interpreted language Python [21]. Its
architecture is shown in figure 3, and will be explained in the following sections.

The main component of AToM³ is the *Processor*, which is responsible for
loading, saving, creating and manipulating models, as well as for generating
code. By default, a meta-meta-model is loaded when AToM³ is invoked. This
meta-meta-model allows one to model meta-models (modelling formalisms) using a graphical notation. For the moment, the ER formalism extended with
constraints is available at the meta-meta-level. When modelling at the meta-
meta-level, the entities which may appear in a model must be specified together
with their attributes. We will refer to this as the semantic information. For example, to define the DFA Formalism, it is necessary to define both *States* and
Transitions. Furthermore, for *States* we need to add the attributes *name* and *type*
(initial, terminal or regular). For *Transitions*, we need to specify the *condition*
that triggers it.

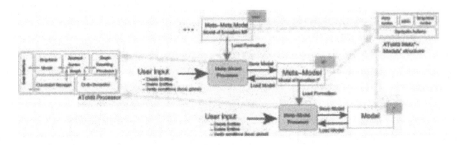

Fig. 3. Meta-... modelling in ATOM³.

AToM³ distinguishes between two kinds of attributes: *regular* and *generative*. *Regular* attributes are used to identify characteristics of the current entity. *Generative* attributes are used to generate new attributes at a lower meta-level. The generated attributes may be *generative* in their own right. Both types of attributes may contain data or code for pre- and post-conditions. Thus, in our approach, we can have an arbitrary number of meta-formalisms as, starting at one level, it is possible to produce *generative* attributes at the lower meta-level and so on. The meta-chain ends when a model has no more *generative* attributes. Attributes can be associated with individual model entities (local) as well as with a model as a whole (global).

Many modelling formalisms support some form of coupled or network models. In this case, we need to connect entities and to specify restrictions on these connections. In our DFA example, *States* can be connected to *Transitions*, although this is not mandatory. *Transitions* can also be connected to *States*, although there may be *States* without incoming *Transitions*. In AToM³, in principle, all objects can be connected to all objects. Usually, a meta-meta-model is used to specify/generate constraints on these connections. Using an ER meta-meta-model, we can specify cardinality constraints in the relationships. These relationships will generate constraints on object connection at the lower meta-level.

The above specification is used by the AToM³ Processor to generate the ASG nodes. These nodes are Python classes generated using the information at the meta-meta-level. The AToM³ Processor will generate a class for each entity defined in the semantic space and another class for the ASG. This class is responsible for storing the nodes of the graph. As we will see later, it also stores global constraints. In the meta-meta-model, it is also possible to specify the graphical appearance of each entity of the lower meta-level. This appearance is, in fact, a special kind of *generative* attribute. For example, for the DFA, we can choose to represent *States* as circles with the state's name inside the circle, and *Transitions* as arrows with the condition on top. That is, we can specify how some semantic attributes are displayed graphically. We must also specify *connectors*, that is, places where we can link the graphic entities. For example, in *Transitions* we will specify *connectors* on both extremes of the arc and in *States* on 4 symmetric points around the circle. Further on, connections between entities are restricted by the specified semantic constraints. For example, a *Transition* must be connected to two *States*. The meta-meta-model generates a Python class for each graphical entity. Thus, semantic and graphical information are separated, although, to be able to access the semantic attributes' values both types of classes (semantic and graphical) have a link to one another.

In the following, we will explore some of the AToM³ features in more detail.

3.1   Constraints and Actions

It is possible to specify constraints in both the semantic and the graphical space:

- In the semantic space, it is not always possible to express restrictions by means of ER diagrams. For example, in DFA's, we would like to require unique *State* names, as well as a unique initial *State* and one or more terminal *States*. Furthermore, *Transitions* departing from the same *State* must have different labels.
- In the graphical space, it is often desirable to have the entities' graphical representation change depending on semantic or graphical events or conditions. For example, we would like the representation of *States* to be different depending on the *States'* type.

Constraints can be *local* or *global*. *Local* constraints are specified on single entities and only involve local attribute values. In *global* constraints, information about all the entities in a model may be used. In our example, the semantic constraints mentioned before must be specified as global, whereas the graphical constraint is local, as it only involves attributes specific to the entity (the type of the State).

When declaring semantic constraints, it is necessary to specify which event will trigger the evaluation of the constraint, and whether evaluation must take place after (post-condition) or before (pre-condition) the event. The events with which these constraints are associated can be *semantic*, such as saving a model, connecting, creating or deleting entities, etc., or purely *graphical*, such as moving or selecting an entity, etc. If a pre-condition for an event fails, the event is not executed. If a post-condition for an event fails, the event is undone. Both types of constraints can be placed on any kind of event (semantic or graphical). *Semantic* constraints can be specified as Python functions, or as OCL expressions. In the latter case, they are translated into Python. *Local* constraints are incorporated in semantic and graphical classes, *global* constraints are incorporated in the ASG class. In both cases, constraints are encoded as class methods.

When modelling in the ER formalism, the relationships defined between entities in the semantic space create constraints: the types of connected entities must be checked as well as the cardinality of the relationships. The latter constraint may however not be satisfied during the whole modelling process. For example, if we specify that a certain entity must be connected to exactly two entities of another type, at some point in the modelling process the entity can be connected to zero, one, two or more entities. If it is connected to zero or one, an error will be raised only when the model is saved, whereas if it is connected to three or more entities the error can be raised immediately. It is envisioned that this evolution of the formalism during the modelling life-cycle will eventually be specified using a variable-structure meta-model (such as a DFA with ER states).

Actions are similar to *constraints*, but they have side-effects and are currently specified using Python only.

Graphical *constraints* and *actions* are similar to the semantic ones, but they act on graphical attributes.

3.2 Types

In AToM^3, attributes defined on entities must have a type. All types inherit from an abstract class named *ATOM3Type* and must provide methods to: display a graphical widget to edit the entity's value, check the value's validity, clone itself, make itself persistent, etc.

As stated before, AToM^3 has two kinds of *basic* types: *regular* (such as integers, floats, strings, lists of some types, enumerate types, etc) and *generative*. There are four types of *generative* attributes:

1. *ATOM3Attribute*: creates attributes at the lower meta-level.
2. *ATOM3Constraint*: creates a constraint at the lower meta-level. The code can be expressed in Python or OCL, and the constraint must be associated to some (semantic or graphical) event(s). It must be specified whether the constraint must be evaluated before or after the event takes place.
3. *ATOM3Appearance*: associates a graphical appearance with the entity at the lower meta-level. Models (as opposed to entities) can also have an associated graphical appearance. This is useful for hierarchical modelling, as models may be displayed inside other models as icons.
4. *ATOM3Cardinality*: generates cardinality constraints on the number of elements connected, at the lower meta-level.

It is also possible to specify *composite* types. These are defined by constructing a type graph [3]. The meta-model for this graph has been built using AToM^3 and then incorporated into the AToM^3 Processor. The components of this graph can be *basic* or *composite* types and can be combined using the *product* and *union* type operators. Types may be recursively defined, meaning that one of the operands of an operator can be an ancestor node. Infinite recursive loops are detected using a global constraint in the type meta-model. The graph describing the type is compiled into Python code using a graph grammar (also defined using AToM^3).

3.3 Code Generation

If a model contains *generative* attributes, AToM^3 is able to generate a tool to process models defined by the meta-information. "Processing" means constructing models and verifying that such models are valid, although further processing actions can be specified by means of graph grammars. These generated tools also use the AToM^3 Processor and are composed of:

- The Python classes corresponding to the entities defined in the semantic space. These classes hold semantic information about the attributes, and local constraints (both defined by means of *generative* attributes in a higher meta-level).
- A Python class used to construct the ASG. It holds the global constraints and a dictionary used to store a list of the nodes in the graph, classified by type. This is useful as operations, such as constraint evaluation can be performed using the *visitor pattern* [12], and the graph can hence be traversed more efficiently.
- Several Python classes to describe the graphical appearance. These classes can have references to semantic attributes, and may also have information about graphical constraints.
- Several Python methods stored in a single file. These methods are added dynamically to the AToM³ Processor class. These methods create buttons and menus that allow the creation of new entities, their editing, connection, deletion, etc.

Models are stored as Python functions that contain the executable statements to instantiate the appropriate semantic and graphical classes and the ASG class. In fact, when these statements are executed, the result is identical to the case where the model is constructed interactively by means of the graphical editor. Thus, if one edits the generated Python code by hand, making it violate some constraint, the AToM³ Processor will detect this and react accordingly when such models are loaded.

Currently we have implemented the ER formalism at the meta-meta-level. Basically, there are two types of entities: *Entities* and *Relationships*. *Entities* are composed of a name (the keyword), a list of *ATOM3Attribute*, a list of *ATOM3Constraint* and an attribute of type *ATOM3Appearance*. *Relationships*, in addition to the above, have a list of *ATOM3Cardinality* which is filled by means of post-actions when an *Entity* is connected to the *Relationship*. By means of pre- and post-conditions, it is ensured that *Entities* can only be connected to *Relationships*, that the names of *Entities* and *Relationships* are unique, etc. With this meta-meta-model it is possible to define other meta-meta-models, such as UML class diagrams as inheritance relationships between classes can be implemented with pre- and post-actions. Note how such an implementation allows for the implementation of various inheritance semantics. Furthermore, target code can be generated in languages (such as C) which do not support inheritance.

Figure 4 shows an example of the ER meta-meta-model in action to describe the DFA Formalism (left side in the picture). This information is used to automatically generate a tool to process DFA models (right side in the picture). On both sides, a dialog box to edit entities is shown. On the right side, the entity that is being edited is a DFA *State*. On the left side, the appearance attribute of an *Entity* is being edited.

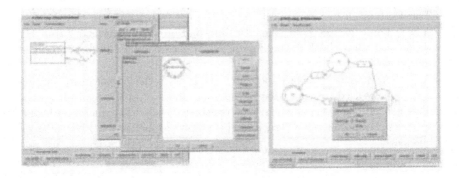

Fig. 4. An example: Generating a tool to process DFA models

3.4   Formalism Transformation

Once a model is loaded, it is possible to transform it into an equivalent model expressed in another formalism provided the transformations between formalisms has been defined. These transformations can be specified as graph grammar[6] models.

In AToM³, graph grammar rules are entities composed of a LHS and a RHS, *conditions* that must hold for the rule to be applicable, some *actions* to be performed when embedding the RHS in the graph and a *priority*. LHS and RHS are models, and can be specified within different formalisms. In figure 2, LHSs are expressed in the NFA formalism, whereas RHSs are expressed in the DFA formalism. For other cases, we can have a mixture of formalisms in both LHS and RHS. For this purpose, we allow opening several meta-models at a time.

Graph grammars are entities composed of a list of rules, an initial action and a final action. The graph rewriting processor orders the rules by priority (lower number first) and iteratively applies them to the input graph until none can be applied. After a rule is applied, the first rule of the list is tried again. The graph rewriting processor uses an improvement of the algorithm described in [6], in which we allow non-connected graphs to be part of the LHS in rules. It is also possible to define a sequence of graph grammars that have to be applied to the model. This is useful, for example to couple grammars to convert a model into another formalism, and then apply model optimisation. Rule execution can either be continuous (no user interaction) or step-by-step whereby the user is prompted after each rule execution.

Figure 5 shows a moment in the editing of the LHS of rule 4 of the graph grammar of figure 2. It can be noted that the dialogs to edit the entities have some more fields when these entities are inside the LHS of a graph grammar rule. In particular, the node label and the widgets to set the attribute value to ⟨*ANY*⟩. RHS nodes have extra widgets to copy attribute values from LHS nodes, and to specify their value by means of Python functions.

Apart from formalism transformation, we use graph-grammars for:

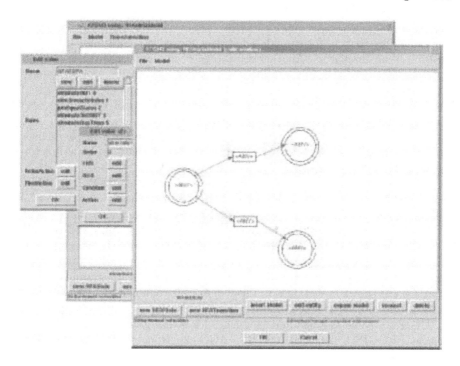

Fig. 5. Editing the LHS of rule 4 of the graph-grammar in Figure 2

- Code generation: graph grammar rules can control the way the ASG is traversed. For example, we use a graph grammar to generate Python code for AToM³ composite types. Other examples can be found at the AToM³ web page [1].
- Simulation: it is possible to describe the operational semantics of models by means of graph-grammars. We have described a simulator for block diagrams in this way.
- Optimisation of models: for example, we have defined a graph-grammar to simplify Structure Charts (SC) diagrams. We usually use this transformation coupled with a graph-grammar to transform Data Flow Diagrams into SC.

4   Related Work

A similar approach is ViewPoint Oriented Software Development [11]. Some of the concepts introduced by the authors have a clear counterpart in our approach (for example, *ViewPoint templates* are similar to meta-models). They also introduce the relationships between ViewPoints, which are similar to our coupling of models and graph transformations.

Although this approach has some characteristics that our approach lacks (such as the work plan axioms), our use of graph transformations allows to express model's behaviour and formalism's semantics. These graph transformations allow us to transform models between formalisms, optimise models, or describe basic simulators. Another advantage of our approach, is that we use meta-modelling, in this way we don't need different tools to process different formalisms (ViewPoints), as we can model them at the meta-level. See also [9] for an approach to integrate heterogeneous specifications of the same system using graph grammars and the ViewPoint framework.

Other approaches taken to interconnecting formalisms are Category Theory [10], in which formalisms are cast as categories and their relationships as functors. See also [24] and [18] for other approaches.

There are other visual meta-modelling tools, among them DOME [5], Multigraph [22], MetaEdit+ [15] or KOGGE [7]. Some of them allow to express formalism' semantics by means of some kind of textual language (for example, KOGGE uses a Modula-2-like language). Our approach is quite different. We express semantics by means of graph grammar models. We believe graph grammars are a natural and general way to manipulate graphs (rather than using a purely textual language). Some of the rationale for using graph grammars in our approach was shown in section 2.3. Also, none of the tools consider the possibility to transform models between different formalisms.

There are some systems and languages for graph grammar manipulations, such as PROGRES [20], GRACE [13], AGG [2]. None of these have a meta-modelling layer.

Our approach is original in the sense that we take the advantages of meta-modelling (to avoid explicit programming of custom tools) and graph transformation systems (to express model behaviour and formalism transformation). The main contribution is thus in the field of multi-paradigm modelling [23] as we have a general means to transform models between different formalisms.

5   Conclusions and Future Work

In this article, we have presented a new approach to the modelling of complex systems. Our approach is based on meta-modelling and multi-formalism modelling, and is implemented in the software tool AToM^3. This code-generating tool, developed in Python, relies on graph grammars and meta-modelling techniques and supports hierarchical modelling.

The advantages of using such an automated tool for generating customised model-processing tools are clear: instead of building the whole application from scratch, it is only necessary to specify –in a graphical manner– the kinds of models we will deal with. The processing of such models can be expressed at the meta-level by means of graph grammars. Our approach is also highly applicable if we want to work with a slight variation of some formalism, where we only have to specify the meta-model for the new formalism and a transformation into a "known" formalism (one that already has a simulator available, for example). We then obtain a tool to model in the new formalism, and are able to convert models in this formalism into the other for further processing.

A side effect of our code-generating approach is that some parts of the tool have been built using code generated by itself (bootstrapped): one of the first implemented features of AToM³ was the capability to generate code, and extra features were added using code thus generated.

Specifying composite types is very flexible, as types are treated as models, and stored as graphs. This means graph grammars can be constructed to specify operations on types, such as discovering infinite recursion loops in their definition, determining if two types are compatible, performing cast operations, etc.

One possible drawback of the approach taken in AToM³ is that even for non-graphical formalisms, one must devise a graphical representation. For example, in the case of *Algebraic Equations*, the equations must be drawn in the form of a graph. To solve this problem, we will add the possibility to enter models textually. This text will be parsed into an ASG. Once the model is in this form, it can be treated as any other (graphical) model.

Currently, the replacement of the basic internal data structure for representing models (graphs) by the more expressive HiGraphs [14] is under consideration. HiGraphs are more suitable to express and visualise hierarchies (blobs can be inside one or more blobs), they add the concept of orthogonality, and blobs can be connected by means of hyperedges.

We also intend to extend the tool to allow collaborative modelling. This possibility as well as the need to exchange and re-use (meta-...) models raises the issue of formats for model exchange. A viable candidate format is XML.

Finally, AToM³ is being used to build small projects in a Modelling &Simulation course at the School of Computer Science at McGill University. It can be downloaded from [1], where some examples can also be found.

Acknowledgement

This paper has been partially sponsored by the Spanish Interdepartmental Commission of Science and Technology (CICYT), project number TEL1999-0181. Prof. Vangheluwe gratefully acknowledges partial support for this work by a National Sciences and Engineering Research Council of Canada (NSERC) Individual Research Grant.

References

1. AToM³ Home page:
   http://moncs.cs.mcgill.ca/MSDL/research/projects/ATOM3.html
2. AGG Home page: http://tfs.cs.tu-berlin.de/agg/
3. Aho, A.V., Sethi, R., Ullman, J.D. 1986. Compilers, principles, techniques and tools. Chapter 6, Type Checking. Addison-Wesley.
4. Blonstein, D., Fahmy, H., Grbavec, A.. 1996. Issues in the Practical Use of Graph Rewriting. Lecture Notes in Computer Science, Vol. 1073, Springer, pp.38-55.
5. DOME guide. http://www.htc.honeywell.com/dome/, Honeywell Technology Center. Honeywell, 1999, version 5.2.1

6. Dorr, H. 1995. Efficient Graph Rewriting and its implementation. Lecture Notes in Computer Science, 922. Springer.

7. J. Ebert, R. Sttenbach, I. Uhe 1997. Meta-CASE in Practice: a Case for KOGGE. Advanced Information Systems Engineering, Proceedings of the 9th International Conference, CAiSE'97 LNCS 1250, S. 203-216, Berlin, 1997. See KOGGE home page at: http://www.uni-koblenz.de/~ist/kogge.en.html

8. Ehrig, H., Kreowski, H.-J., Rozenberg, G. (eds.) 1991. Graph Grammars and their application to Computer Science: 4th International Workshop, Proceedings. Lecture Notes in Computer Science, Vol. 532, Springer.

9. Enders, B.E., Heverhagen, T., Goedicke, M., Troepfner, P., Tracht, R. 2001. Towards an Integration of Different Specification Methods by Using the ViewPoint Framework. Special Issue of the Transactions of the SDPS: Journal of Integrated Design&Process Science, Society for Design&Process Science, forthcoming.

10. Fiadeiro, J.L., Maibaum, T. 1995. Interconnecting Formalisms: Supporting Modularity, Reuse and Incrementality. Proc.3rd Symposium on the Fundations of Software Engineering, G.E.Kaiser(ed). pp.: 72-80, ACM Press.

11. Finkelstein, A., Kramer, J., Goedickie, M. 1990. ViewPoint Oriented Software Development. Proc, of the Third Int. Workshop on Software Engineering and its Applications.

12. Gamma, E., Helm, R., Johnson, R., and Vlissides, J. 1995. Design Patterns, Elements of Reusable Object-Oriented Software. Professional Computing Series. Addison-Wesley.

13. GRACE Home page:
http://www.informatik.uni-bremen.de/theorie/GRACEland/GRACEland.html

14. Harel, D. 1998. On visual formalisms. Communications of the ACM, 31(5):514–530.

15. MetaCase Home Page: http://www.MetaCase.com/

16. Meta-Modelling Facility, from the precise UML group:
http://www.cs.york.ac.uk/puml/mmf/index.html

17. Mosterman, P. and Vangheluwe, H. 2000. Computer automated multi paradigm modeling in control system design. IEEE Symposium on Computer-Aided Control System Design, pp.:65–70. IEEE Computer Society Press.

18. Niskier, C., Maibaum, T., Schwabe, D. 1989 A pluralistic Knowledge Based Approach to Software Specification. 2nd European Software Engineering Conference, LNCS 387, Springer Verlag 1989, pp.:411-423

19. OMG Home Page: http://www.omg.org

20. PROGRES home page:
http://www-i3.informatik.rwth-aachen.de/research/projects/progres/main.html

21. Python home page: http://www.python.org

22. Sztipanovits, J., et al. 1995. MULTIGRAPH: An architecture for model-integrated computing. In ICECCS'95, pp. 361-368, Ft. Lauderdale, Florida, Nov. 1995.

23. Vangheluwe, H. 2000. DEVS as a common denominator for multi-formalism hybrid systems modelling. IEEE Symposium on Computer-Aided Control System Design, pp.:129–134. IEEE Computer Society Press.

24. Zave, P., Jackson, M. 1993. Conjunction as Composition. ACM Transactions on Software Engineering and Methodology 2(4), 1993, 371-411.

25. Zeigler, B., Praehofer, H. and Kim, T.G. 2000. Theory of Modelling and Simulation: Integrating Discrete Event and Continuous Complex Dynamic Systems. Academic Press, second edition.

A Toolbox for Automating
Visual Software Engineering

Luciano Baresi[1] and Mauro Pezzè[2]

[1] Dipartimento di Elettronica e Informazione - Politecnico di Milano
Piazza L. da Vinci 32, I-20133 Milano, Italy
baresi@elet.polimi.it
[2] Dipartimento di Informatica, Sistemistica e Comunicazione
Università degli Studi di Milano - Bicocca
Via Bicocca degli Arcimboldi 8, I-20126 - Milano, Italy
pezze@disco.unimib.it

Abstract Visual diagrammatic (VD) notations have always been widely used in software engineering. Such notations have been used to syntactically represent the structure of software systems, but they usually lack dynamic semantics, and thus provide limited support to software engineers. In contrast, formal models would provide rigorous semantics, but the scarce adaptability to different application domains precluded their large industrial application. Most attempts tried to formalize widely used VD notations by proposing a mapping to a formal model, but they all failed in addressing flexibility, that is, the key factor of the success of VD notations.

This paper presents *MetaEnv*, a toolbox for automating visual software engineering. *MetaEnv* augments VD notations with customizable dynamic semantics. Traditional meta-CASE tools support flexibility at syntactic level; *MetaEnv* augments them with semantic flexibility. *MetaEnv* refers to a framework based on graph grammars and has been experimented as add-on to several commercial and proprietary tools that support syntactic manipulation of VD notations.

1 Introduction

Visual diagrammatic (VD) notations [10] have always been widely used in software engineering. Examples of these notations, which are daily exploited in industrial practice, are Structured Analysis [13], UML [9], SDL [14], IEC Function Block Diagram [21]. Graphical elements make these languages appealing and easy to understand. Users can glance the meaning of their models without concentrating on complex textual descriptions. The graphical syntax of these models is well defined, but the dynamic semantics is not clearly (formally) stated. The same graphical model can be interpreted in different ways, relying on human reasoning as the main means to analyze and validate produced specifications.

Formal models have been widely studied in academia and research laboratories [35]. Formal models would provide powerful formal engines that support automatic reasoning about important properties, but the supplied VD interfaces lack domain specificity [17,27]. The many proposals, which tried to combine graphical notations with formal models, fail in addressing flexibility, i.e., the real problem: They freeze a fixed semantics and over-constrain the VD notation ([16,24]). Consequently, these proposals remained limited to very specific projects and never got any general acceptance.

R.-D. Kutsche and H. Weber (Eds.): FASE 2002, LNCS 2306, pp. 189–202, 2002.

This paper proposes *MetaEnv*, a toolbox that complements domain-specific VD notations with formal dynamic semantics without missing either flexibility, which is the key factor for the success of VD notations, or formality, which is the base of the benefits of formal methods. *MetaEnv* works with VD notations that can be ascribed with an intuitive operational dynamic semantics [18]. It improves VD notations by adding analysis capabilities, and fostering customizability of the associated semantics. Meta-CASE technology provides flexibility at syntactic level [29], and thus supply the concrete syntax and visualization capabilities; *MetaEnv* provides a formal engine to execute and analyze designed models according to the chosen semantics. Users can both exploit already defined semantics and define their own interpretations. In both cases, they gain all benefits of a formal engine without being proficient in it.

MetaEnv is based on the approach for defining customizable semantics for VD notations described in [6,4]. It supports the definition of formal dynamic semantics through rules that define both a High-Level Timed Petri Net (HLTPN), which captures the semantics associated with the model, and proper visualizations of executions and analysis results. Rules can easily be adapted to new needs of software engineers who may want to change or extend the semantics of the adopted VD notation. This paper presents the conceptual framework of *MetaEnv*, its software architecture, and the results of a set of experiments performed with prototypes. Experiments have been carried out on integrating our prototype with both commercial tools (Software through Pictures [2], ObjectMaker [28], and Rose [32] and in-house user interfaces implemented in tcl-tk, Java, and MATLAB/SIMULINK.

2 Technical Background

In *MetaEnv*, a VD notation consists of two sets of rules: *Building rules* and *Visualization rules*. Building rules define both the abstract syntax, i.e., the syntactic elements and their connectivity, and the operational semantics of each element, i.e., the corresponding HLTPN. Visualization rules translate execution and analysis from HLTPNs to the VD notation.

Building rules are pairs of attributed programmed graph grammar productions [30]. These rules work on the abstract syntax, that is, models are described as directed graphs with typed nodes and arcs, and represent admissible operations for designing models with the chosen VD notation. For each rule, the first production belongs to the *Abstract Syntax Graph Grammars* (ASGG) and describes the evolution of the abstract syntax graph; the second production is part of the *Semantic Graph Grammar* (SGG) and defines the operational semantics as modifications to the associated HLTPN. For example, Figure 1 presents a simple building rule taken from a formalization of Structured Analysis [8]. The rule defines how to connect a Process (P) to an input port (I) (connected to a data flow) through an input consumption (IC) element. The two productions are represented graphically using a Y: the left-hand side indicates the elements on which the production applies; the right-hand side indicates the elements introduced by applying the production; the upper part indicates how new elements are connected to the graph. The same identifiers associated with nodes in the left-hand and right-hand sides indicate that the two objects are kept while applying the production. The Abstract Syntax production of Figure 1(a) adds a node of type InCons (IC) and an edge of type belong (b). It adds also an edge of type connect (c) between the added IC node and each I node that is connected to the P node through a b edge. The textual attributes indicate that the newly created node (node 2) has three attributes: *name*, *type*, and *action*. The value of the attribute name is the concatenation of the name of node 1 (the node of type P) and the string IC, the value of attribute type is the string InCons, and the value of attribute action is provided externally (typically by the user).

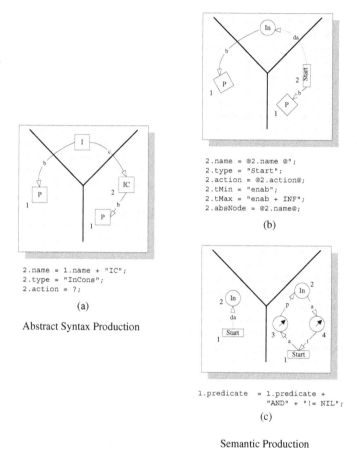

2.name = 1.name + "IC";
2.type = "InCons";
2.action = ?;

(a)

Abstract Syntax Production

2.name = @2.name @";
2.type = "Start";
2.action = @2.action@;
2.tMin = "enab";
2.tMax = "enab + INF";
2.absNode = @2.name@;

(b)

1.predicate = 1.predicate +
              "AND" + "!= NIL";

(c)

Semantic Production

Figure 1. A simple *Building Rule*

The corresponding Semantic production of Figure 1(b) adds a transition of type Start and two nodes of type arc (graphically identified with an arrow in a circle) between the newly created Start transition and all In places that belong to the semantic representation of the process. Special edges, called sp-edges, represent sub-production invocations and are drawn using dashed lines. The sp-edge of Figure 1(b) triggers the sub-production illustrated in Figure 1(c) that substitutes each da sp-edge with a pair of arcs. Notice that nodes of type arc represent HLTPN arcs and edges define the connectivity among nodes.

Semantic HLTPNs allow VD models to be formally validated through execution, reachability analysis and model checking. Visualization rules translate obtained results in terms of suitable visualization actions on the abstract elements.

```
VisRule va = new VisAction();

if (tr.type() == "Start") {
    foreach pl in tr.preSet() {
        Animation an = new Animation();
        an.setEntityId(pl.getAbsId());
        an.setAnimType("readFlow");
        va.addAnimation(an);
    }
    Animation an = new Animation();
    an.setEntityId(tr.getAbsId());
    an.setAnimType("start");
    an.setAnimPars("executing");
    an.addAnimation(an);
}
```

Figure 2. A simple Visualization rule

For example, the rule of Figure 2 describes how the firing of a transition of type Start is visualized in terms of Structured Analysis. Start transitions (see the building rule of Figure 1) correspond to starting process executions. When transition tr is fired, the visualization action (va) defines how to animate the data flows, which correspond to the places (pl) in the preset of tr, and the process corresponding to the transition itself. In particular, action va associates animation readFlow to all selected data flows and animation start to the process.

3   *MetaEnv*

MetaEnv consists of a set of tools that integrate CASE technology with an HLTPN (High Level Timed Petri Nets) engine to augment current CASE tools with analysis and validation capabilities.

MetaEnv is built around a layered architecture (Figure 3). Its components can easily be organized in *concrete*, *abstract*, and *semantic* components according to the level at which they work on the VD notation.

Concrete components are the *CASE Tool* and the *Concrete Interface*. The interface allows *MetaEnv* to be plugged in the chosen CASE Tool. The only constraint *MetaEnv* imposes is that the CASE Tool must be a service-based graphical editor [33]: It must supply a set of services that *MetaEnv* can use to properly store and animate user models. These services are used by the Concrete Interface that connects the CASE tool to the inner components of *MetaEnv*. This interface defines a two-way communication channel: It transforms user models in suitable invocation sequences of building rules and animation actions in concrete visualizations.

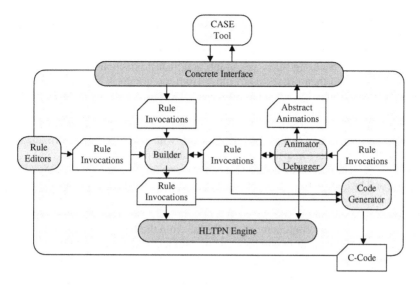

Figure 3. Architecture of *MetaEnv*

To transform user models in invocation sequences of building rules, the concrete interface can use different policies. The simplest solution is that user actions are immediately translated into rule invocations. Alternatively, the interface can adopt a generative approach that reads complete user models and then defines the sequence according to a predefined partial order among building rules. A detailed analysis can be found in [4].

The data flow in the opposite direction transforms the abstract animations produced by visualization rules in concrete animations. Abstract animations describe visualizations of notation elements in a plain and tool-independent way. The interface adds all details that depend on the specific tool. Differently from all other *MetaEnv* components, the concrete interface varies according to the CASE tool that "imposes" the communication means, supplied services and actual implementation. *MetaEnv* requires only that building and visualization rules be defined in a special purpose format.

Abstract components are a *Builder*, an *Animator/Debugger*, and a *Rule Editor*. The *Builder* is a graph grammar interpreter that applies building rules according to the application sequence defined by the concrete interface and it builds both the abstract model (i.e., the abstract representation of the user model) and the HLTPN that correspond to the current model. The *Animator/Debugger* applies visualization rules to place markings and transition firings from the HLTPN engine. For example, it transforms the execution of the HLTPN, that is, a sequence of transition firings, into a sequence of abstract visualizations. The debugger allows users to control the execution of their models as if they were using a "standard" debugger: They can set breakpoints and watch-points, chose step-by-step execution, and trace the execution. All these services, which are set through the CASE tool, are transformed in terms of constraints on the sequence of abstract animations. A step-by-step execution becomes an execution that stops after each abstract animation; a break point on a specific element of the model means that the execution is suspended at the first abstract animation that involves the selected element.

Both the *Builder* and the *Animator/Debugger* read their rules from external repositories that store all required rules. Rule editors are the personalization-oriented user interfaces of *MetaEnv*. They let users define new rules, but they are not part of the run-time environment. Building rules, i.e., graph grammar productions, are defined with a graphical editor and then processed to move from the graphical representation to the required textual format. Visualization rules can be designed with any textual editor. The use of these editors requires proficiency not only in the particular VD notation, but also in HLTPNs to be able to ascribe meaningful semantics. Most users will never cope with designing new rules; they will do their experiments with already existing formalizations or they will ask experts for special-purpose formalizations.

The *Code Generator* is an abstract/semantic component because it uses inputs from both layers. The code generator automatically produces ANSI C code from VD models. Again, it does not use the concrete representation, but it starts from the HLTPN to get the code semantics and the abstract representation to get a reasonable way to partition the code. Topology and computations are "read" from the HLTPN, while modules and functions are defined according to the structure of the abstract model. Differently from other proposals (for example, [12]), which supplies the code together with the abstract machine to execute it, this component produces raw code to be compiled and linked using standard C compilers.

The Semantic component is the *HLTPN Engine*. It defines, executes and analyzes the HLTPNs obtained through the builder. *MetaEnv* reuses a light version of Cabernet [31] as Petri net tool. Other Petri net tools or even other formal engine would be usable as well. The layered and component-based architecture of *MetaEnv* allows for experiments with different formal engines without rebuilding the system from scratch. The interfaces and the services provided by/required from the engine are clearly stated and thus plugging in a new engine is quite easy.

4   Experimental Validation

The approach described in this paper has been validated by plugging prototype implementations of *MetaEnv* in different front-ends. The integration of the prototype with a front-end requires the selection of the CASE tool and the selection of a set of rules to formally define the addressed VD notation. The experiments described in this section aim at showing the flexibility of *MetaEnv* both in interfacing with different CASE tools and in formalizing different VD notations. The flexibility in interfacing with different CASE tools has been shown by both choosing commercial CASE tools and implementing special-purpose concrete interfaces developed using different languages. The commercial CASE tools used in the experiments are Software through Pictures [2], ObjectMaker [28], and Rational Rose [32]. The special-purpose interfaces described in this section have been developed using tcl-tk, MATLAB-SIMULIK, and Java. The capability of adapting to different VD notations has been shown by both formalizing de-facto standard notations and developing ad-hoc VD notations to address specific needs. The standard VD notations addressed in the experiments include Structured Analysis [13], the Unified Modeling Language (UML) [9], and Function Block Diagram (FBD) [21]. The special-purpose VD notations described in this section are Control Nets, a variant to timed Petri nets for the design of control systems, and LEMMA, a VD notation for modeling diagnostic and therapeutic medical processes. All experiments are summarized in Table 1 that lists the different VD notations, the CASE tools (ad-hoc interfaces) that we used (defined), and the number of building rules required to ascribe the formal semantics.

Table 1. Summary of experiments

Structured Analysis	StP, ObjectMaker	50
Function Block Diagram	Ad-hoc interface (MATLAB)	40
UML	Rose	20
Control Nets	Ad-hoc interface (tcl-tk)	30
LEMMA	Ad-hoc interface (tcl-tk, Java)	10

In all cases, the cost of plugging *MetaEnv* in exiting CASE tools, and providing rules for the chosen VD notation, is negligible with respect to the cost of developing a new specific graphical editor. The flexibility of the obtained environments permitted also the experimentation with different semantics without significant extra costs, while ad-hoc "semantic" editors would have hardly be adapted to new semantics.

The following sections briefly overview the main results.

4.1 Structured Analysis

The first VD notation considered in the experiments was Structured Analysis (SA) [13]. SA was chosen because of the variety of uses and related interpretations as well as supporting CASE tools. *MetaEnv* was plugged in two different CASE tools: Software through Pictures (StP) [2] and ObjectMaker [28]. In both cases *MetaEnv* was integrated by filtering the information stored in the repository of the two tools. StP was also connected using the open interface provided by the tool. The integration with the repository works off-line, i.e., the HLTPN is built after completing the models. The integration with the open interface allows the construction of the HLTPN incrementally. We provided a family of rules for addressing the main variants of SA, as described in [8].

The effect of combining different interpretations for the same notation is illustrated in Figure 4 that presents a sample of alternative semantics for a process, i.e., a functional transformation. The figure presents the semantics for a process with two input flows and one output flow. Semantics (a) and (b) define an atomic instantaneous functional transformation. Semantics (c) defines a functional transformation with duration that can be interrupted. Semantics (a) requires exactly one input to execute the transformation, while semantics (b) and (c) require both inputs. All different semantics can be given by simply selecting suitable building rules, as discussed in [8].

An interpretation of the SA-RT dialect proposed by Hatley and Pirbhai [19] was used for modeling and analyzing the hard real-time component of a radar control system by Alenia [1].

4.2 Function Block Diagrams

The second standard VD notation considered in the experiments was IEC Function Block Diagram (FBD), one of the graphical languages proposed by the IEC standard

---

[1] The experiment was conducted within the ESPRIT IDERS Project (EP8593).

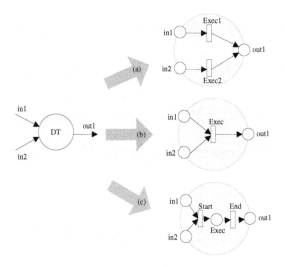

Figure 4. Different semantics for an SA process

1131-3 [21] for designing programmable controllers. FBD was chosen because it presents different challenges. In particular FBD is used at a much lower abstraction level than Structured Analysis, and the IEC standard is mostly limited to the syntax, while the semantics of the components is highly programmable to adapt the notation to different platforms and applications. Another interesting option of FBD is the possibility of adding new syntactic elements (blocks) provided with proper semantics according to user needs. We formalized FBD by providing rules for defining different libraries of components and a library manager that allows new libraries to be added and existing libraries to be modified by producing suitable rules. The possibility of adding rules to *MetaEnv* to modify or create a formalization greatly facilitated the construction of libraries and the library manager. The formalization supported by *MetaEnv* requires the description of a block usually given as Structured Text (ST)[2] to be formalized by means of a HLTPN. Figure 5 shows two alternative semantics (HLTPNs) for a simple block. In the first case, the textual description is mapped in the action of a single transition. In the second case, the action is semantically described with two alternative transitions.

MetaEnv was interfaced with an ad-hoc editor, **PLCTools**, developed with MAT-LAB/SIMULINK. PLCTools and *MetaEnv* are integrated through CORBA in a way that allows only generative construction of HLTPNs. Formal FBD was used to model and analyze controllers of electrical motors developed by Ansaldo[3].

4.3   UML

We are currently applying the approach to the Unified Modeling Language (UML) [9]. UML has been chosen because the semantics derived from the object-oriented nature of the notation includes aspects that radically differ from the hierarchical approach of

---

[2] ST is another standard language of IEC1131-3.
[3] The experiment was conducted within the ESPRIT INFORMA project (EP23163).

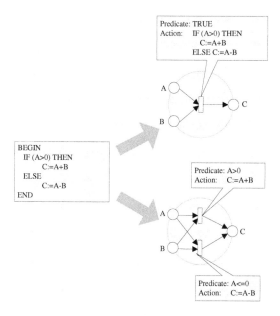

Figure 5. Alternative ways for expressing the semantics of an FBD block

both SA and FBD. Moreover, the different diagrammatic notations provided within UML allow alternative descriptions of the same elements, thus raising consistency and completeness issues. This led us to consider the UML meta-model as integration means, choice that significantly impacted the definition of the abstract representation.

The work aims at analyzing mainly the dynamic behavior of UML models. HLPTNs are used to animate and validate the dynamics of object interactions (mainly class diagrams and collaboration diagrams). Static aspects (e.g., the consistency among classes) are not covered by these experiments.

In this case, *MetaEnv* has been plugged in Ratioal Rose by interfacing with the data repository, as done for StP and Object-Maker. The rules defined so far (only a subset of all rules needed to formalize UML) formalize class and Statecharts diagrams partially. We are currently extending the set of rules to cope with other UML diagrams and we are applying the formalization to significant examples. Details can be found in [7] where we used the "formalized" UML to model the well-known problem of dining philosophers. Figure 6 sketches the *Forks* that philosophers should use and the corresponding HLTPN, where methods are rendered using pairs of places (one for the "request of execution" and one for the results) and the internal semantics mimics a state diagram.

4.4   Control Nets

Control Nets have been defined for designing embedded control systems. Control nets enrich Petri nets with a higher-level VD notation to identify subnets to be reused in further developments. The notation is open, i.e., new elements can be added to the set of reusable components by simply defining their syntax, their external ports and

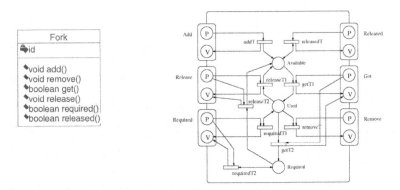

Figure 6. Class *Fork* and its HLTPN semantics

the corresponding HLTPN. In this case, *MetaEnv* has been integrated with a special-purpose interface implemented in tcl-tk. The obtained CASE tool has been successfully used to model and analyze the controller of a robot arm developed by Comau; details can be found in [11].

4.5   LEMMA

The last experiment reported in this paper is the use of *MetaEnv* for giving operational semantics to LEMMA (a Language for Easy Medical Model Analyses) [5]. LEMMA is a notation for specifying, executing, and analyzing clinical diagnostic and therapeutic processes, which has been developed jointly with the 4th Institute of General Surgery in Rome (Italy). Doctors usually describe diagnostic and therapeutic processes informally. Formal notations represent a barrier for doctors who are not able to take advantage from formal analysis. LEMMA conjugates the high expressiveness of VD notations with the rigor of formal methods necessary to simulate and analyze defined models. The lack of experience of doctors with formal methods made it very hard to freeze the specification notation. *MetaEnv* made it possible to incrementally adapt the toolset to the evolving requirements of doctors, who modified or added new elements to the notation while modeling new processes and learning the expressiveness and usefulness of LEMMA. Figure 7 shows the evolution of the semantic model of medical laboratories involved in the analysis required during diagnostic and therapeutic processes. Model (a) simply describes the two possible outcomes of a medical analysis. Model (b) describes the limited resources and capacity of the laboratory and thus allows more accurate evaluation of the timing aspects of the processes.

The toolbox has been implemented by plugging *MetaEnv* in graphical interfaces generated with tcl-tk and Java. The tool-box has been used at the 4th Institute of General Surgery in Rome to model and analyze the diagnostic process of colon-rectal cancer.

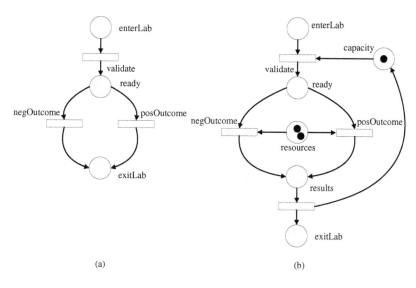

(a)   (b)

Figure 7. Two different models of medical laboratories

5   Related Work

Meta-CASE technology, according to the taxonomy presented in [22], introduces customizable environments, that is, tools that offer a set of core functionalities to define, tailor and extend VD notations. To the best of authors' knowledge all these tools are repository-based. All information is stored in a repository in predefined and fixed format; customization deals only with the way this information is presented to users. For example, *MetaEdit+* [23] is based on an object repository that contains all the information about available - both built-in and user defined - notations. Users can exploit all supported notations at the same time; it is the repository that enforces and ensures consistency among them. The repository supplies also data for model reporting and code generation. *ObjectMaker* [28] supplies two different tools for customizing the information stored in the repository. The tool developer kit customizes the notation syntax, the syntactic and static semantic checks, and the way models are stored in the repository. The method maker guides users while defining new notations at a higher abstraction level: Notations are specified by filling built-in forms, customizing general-purpose diagrams, and answering specific questions.

ToolBuilder [25] is organized around the object repository LINCOLN. It supplies both a general-purpose CASE tool, which allows users to manipulate the data stored in the object repository, and a tool for designing new notations and generating the rules required by the CASE tool. A new notation consists of a data model and a frame model. The data model describes how data are organized; the frame model defines the view hierarchy.

Software through Pictures [2] offers a family of products: Stp/SE for structured analysis, StP/UML for object modeling, and StP/IM for information modeling). They all are built around a centralized repository and share the same engine called StPCore. StPCore supplies the access to the centralized repository, an API to the graphical interfaces, a predefined framework to associate notations with static semantics, and the control of client-server interaction through messages and notifications. All information is stored according to a simple meta-model called Persistent Data Model (PDM). PDM cannot be extended, but users can define new "views" on the data stored according to this format. The graphical interfaces can be customized by means of textual rules that specify notation elements, syntactic checks, and system answers to user actions.

Metaview [15] is organized around a layered architecture. The meta-model is defined using an extension to entity-relationship data model. At this level users specify notation elements and the constraints among them. Graphical symbols are defined at the environment level. Conceptual tables define the notation symbols and conceptual constraints ensure the consistency among them. The user level defines the concrete interfaces.

All tools described so far privilege the syntax and static semantics of VD notations. They supply appealing features to define or modify the syntax of VD notations, but analysis capabilities are limited to the syntactic correctness and static constraints among data. In contrast, we do not concentrate on these aspects, but we aim at supplying customizable formal semantics to existing notations and tools and thus we consider that all these tools could easily be complemented by *MetaEnv*, but they do not provide the same functionality.

Examples of research prototypes are *GENGED* [3] and *DIAGEN* [3] that allow users to define specialized graphical editors. GENGED is based on algebraic specifications and algebraic graph grammars; DIAGEN is based on hyper-edge graph grammars. The first approach "formalizes" the definition of symbols and links used within the language; the second approach addresses also animation of designed models, but again they both do not address dynamic semantics.

A slightly different approach is taken by *Dome* [20], which does not limit itself to syntactical aspects, but let users define the semantics of their blocks using Scheme, a Lisp-like language. In this case, the main difference with respect to our approach is the difficulty associated with the customization of semantic aspect and the need of using a predefined interface to interact with the tool. Again, even if Dome moves in the same direction as we did, the use of Petri nets for designing the semantics and the freedom of using existing CASE tools, instead of just one tool, are the key differences between our approach and Dome.

Other "semantic" customizable tools (for example, [26]) offer large-grained components to program computer aided generation, analysis, verification, and testing of complex systems. They do not aim at letting users customize graphical notations, but they offer large-grained components to program complex systems in a graphical way. In this context, meta-modeling capabilities allow users to define new building blocks by combining existing ones. The user notation is always the same; no customization of the graphical interfaces is permitted.

Finally, we can mention [1,34]: two theoretical frameworks for defining graphical notations from concrete aspects to semantics. They supply a hierarchy of graph grammars to concentrate on concrete and abstract syntax aspects, but the semantics is relegated to textual annotations in natural language.

5.1 Conclusions and Future Work

This paper presented *MetaEnv* and its supporting methodology to add formal semantics to VD notations. *MetaEnv* does not significantly reduce the flexibility and adaptability of VD notations and thus it can be seen as a means to smoothly introduce formal methods in industrial practice. The experiments briefly outlined in the paper demonstrate the suitability of the approach in different application domains. Differently from other approaches, *MetaEnv* neither significantly alters the formalized VD notation nor limits its flexibility. Moreover, *MetaEnv* can be adapted to different environments with a small effort and thus it can be used in situations that could not be efficiently addressed with expensive solutions due to the limited scope of the notation or of the chosen interpretation in the specific situation.

References

1. M. Andries, G. Engels, and J. Rekers. *How to Represent a Visual Program?* In Proceedings of International Workshop on Theory of Visual Languages (1996).
2. Aonix. Structure Environment: Using the StP/SE Editors (1998).
3. R. Bardohl, M. Minas, A. Schuerr, and G. Taentzer. *Application of graph transformation to visual languages.* Handbook of Graph Grammars and Computing by Graph Transformation, volume II: Applications, Languages and Tools, pp. 105-180 (1999).
4. L. Baresi. *Formal Customization of Graphical Notations.* PhD thesis, Dipartimento di Elettronica e Informazione – Politecnico di Milano, 1997. in Italian.
5. L. Baresi, F. Consorti, M. Di Paola, A. Gargiulo, and M. Pezzè. *LEMMA: A Language for an Easy Medical Models Analysis.* Journal of Medical Systems - Plenum Publishing Co., 21(6):369-388 (1997).
6. L. Baresi, A. Orso, and M. Pezzè. *Introducing Formal Methods in Industrial Practice.* In Proceedings of the 20th International Conference on Software Engineering, pp. 56-66. ACM Press (1997).
7. L. Baresi and M. Pezzè. *On Formalizing UML with High-Level Petri Nets.* In G. Agha and F. De Cindio (eds.) *Concurrent Object-Oriented Programming and Petri Nets* (a special volume in the Advances in Petri Nets series); 2001, pages 271-300. Volume 2001 of Lecture Notes in Computer Science.
8. L. Baresi and M. Pezzè. *A formal Definition of Structured Analysis with Programmable Graph Grammars.* In *Proceedings of AGTIVE99:*, volume 1779 of *Lecture notes in Computer Science*, pages 193–208. Springer/Verlag, 1999.
9. G. Booch, J. Rumbaugh, and I. Jacobson. *The Unified Modeling Language User Guide.* The Addison-Wesley Object Technology Series (1998).
10. M. Burnett and Marla J. Baker. *A Classification System for Visual Programming Languages.* Journal of Visual Languages and Computing, pp. 287-300 (1994).
11. A. Caloini, G. Magnani, and M. Pezzè. *A Technique for Designing Robotic Control Software Based on Petri Nets.* IEEE Transactions on Control Systems (1997).
12. CJ International. IsAGRAPH 3.3 Documentation (1999).
13. T. De Marco. *Structured Analysis and System Specification.* Prentice-Hall (1978).
14. O. Fargemand and A. Olsen. *Introduction to SDL-92.* Computer Networks and ISDN Systems, 26:1143-1167 (1994).
15. P. Findeisen. The Metaview System. Technical report, University of Alberta (Canada) (1994).
16. R. B. France and M. M. Larrondo-Petrie. *From Structured Analysis to Formal Specifications: State of the Theory.* In Proceedings of Computer Science Conference, pp. 249-256. ACM Press (1994).

17. J.A. Goguen and Luqi. *Formal Methods and Social Context in Software Development*. In 6th International Conference on Theory and Practice of Software Development (TAPSOFT'95), number 915 in Lecture Notes in Computer Science, pp. 62-81. Springer-Verlag, (invited talk), Aarhus (Denmark) (1995).

18. D. Harel and B. Rumpe. *Modeling Languages: Syntax, Semantics and All That Stuff - Part I: The Basic Stuff*. Faculty of Mathematics and Computer Science, The Weizmann Institute of Science, Israel, MCS00-16, September 2000.

19. D. J. Hatley and I. A. Pirbhai. *Strategies for Real-Time System Specification*. Dorset House, New York (1987).

20. Honeywell. Dome Extensions Manual (ver. 5.2.2) (1999).

21. IEC. *Part 3: Programming Languages, IEC 1131-3*. Technical report, International Electrotechnical Commission - Geneva (1993).

22. A. S. Karrer and W. Scacchi. *Meta-Environments for Software Production*. Technical report, University of Southern California, Atrium Laboratory (1994).

23. S. Kelly, K. Lyytinen, and M. Rossi. *MetaEdit+ A Fully Configurable Multi-User and Multi-Tool CASE and CAME Environment*. In Proceedings of CAiSE'96, volume 1080, pp. 1-21. Springer-Verlag, Lecture Notes in Computer Science (1996).

24. C. Kronlof, editor. *Method Integration - Concepts and Case Studies*. John Wiley & Sons (1993).

25. Lincoln Software Limited. *What is a Meta-Tool?* (white paper), see
    http://www.ipsys.com/mc-wp.htm

26. Luqi. Real-time constraints in a rapid prototyping language. Computer Languages, 18(2):77-103 (1993).

27. T.S.E. Maibaum and B. Rumpe. *Automated Software Engineering: Special Issue on Precise Semantics for Software Modeling Techniques* Volume 7, Issue 1, Kluwer Academic Publishers, March 2000.

28. Mark V Systems. ObjectMaker User's Guide (1997).

29. METACase Consulting. ABC To Metacase Technology. Technical report (1999).

30. M. Nagl. *Set theoretic approaches to graph grammars*. In H. Ehrig, M. Nagl, G. Rozenberg, and A. Rosenfeld, editors, Graph Grammars and Their Application to Computer Science, volume 291 of Lecture Notes in Computer Science, pp. 41-54. Springer-Verlag (1987).

31. M. Pezzè. *Cabernet: A Customizable Environment for the Specification and Analysis of Real-Time Systems*. Technical report, Dipartimento di Elettronica e Informazione, Politecnico di Milano, Italy (1994).

32. Rational Software Corporation. Rational Rose 2001: User's Manuals (2001).

33. S. Reiss. *Connecting Tools using Message Passing in the FIELD Program Development Environment*. IEEE Software, pp. 57-67 (1990).

34. J. Rekers and A. Schuerr. *A Graph Based Framework for the Implementation of Visual Environments*. In Proceedings of VL'96 12th International IEEE Symposium on Visual Languages. IEEE-CS Press (1996).

35. H. Saiedian. *An Invitation to Formal Methods*. IEEE Computer, pp. 16-30 (1996).

Enriching OCL Using Observational Mu-Calculus*

Julian Bradfield, Juliana Küster Filipe, and Perdita Stevens

Laboratory for Foundations of Computer Science
University of Edinburgh, JCMB, King's Buildings
Edinburgh EH9 3JZ, United Kingdom
{jcb,jkf,Perdita.Stevens}@dcs.ed.ac.uk

Abstract. The Object Constraint Language is a textual specification language which forms part of the Unified Modelling Language[8]. Its principal uses are specifying constraints such as well-formedness conditions (e.g. in the definition of UML itself) and specifying *contracts* between parts of a system being modelled in UML. Focusing on the latter, we propose a systematic way to extend OCL with temporal constructs in order to express richer contracts. Our approach is based on observational mu-calculus, a two-level temporal logic in which temporal features at the higher level interact cleanly with a domain specific logic at the lower level. Using OCL as the lower level logic, we achieve much improved expressiveness in a modular way. We present a unified view of invariants and pre/post conditions, and we show how the framework can be used to permit the specification of liveness properties.

1 Introduction

In *contract-based design*, the designer not only identifies the parts that the system should have but also specifies explicitly the contracts that those parts should obey. The contract for a part specifies what the developer of that part (who may be someone doing more detailed design, or someone programming) must ensure; it simultaneously specifies what clients of that part may assume. The use of contracts thus provides a process by which dependencies between parts of the system may be made explicit and managed. Commonly used examples of contracts are class invariants, and pre- and post-condition pairs. Contracts today are usually written in natural language or code.

One of the aims of the Object Constraint Language, OCL, is to provide the designer who is modelling a system in the Unified Modelling Language, UML with a language for expressing such contracts which is at the same time formal (and so, unambiguous and possibly open to verification and analysis) and easy to use. There are well-known problems with OCL1.x, and the language is currently undergoing a careful revision. In part, this paper is motivated by a desire to disambiguate certain aspects of the OCL language and its use, such

---

* Work reported here was supported by the EPSRC grant GR/R16891, and EPSRC Advanced Fellowships held by Bradfield and Stevens.

R.-D. Kutsche and H. Weber (Eds.): FASE 2002, LNCS 2306, pp. 203–217, 2002.

as when exactly a class invariant is required to hold. More ambitiously, we aim
to provide an expressive framework to allow designers to write contracts which
have a temporal character: that is, contracts which specify certain aspects of the
ongoing behaviour of a part of a system under particular dynamic interaction
conditions.

To achieve this we need to extend OCL. It is a challenge to do this in a clean,
understandable way which is amenable both to practical use and, eventually, to
verification. Temporal logics such as the modal mu-calculus are well-suited to
describing dynamic properties such as deadlock, liveness, fairness, etc., but they
only provide means of specifying such properties; they do not provide means
for expressing static properties, such as those currently expressible in OCL.
In practice we believe it will be essential to be able to write constraints which
flexibly combine both aspects. Here are some simple examples of things we would
like to express; later we will show how they are expressed in our proposed logic.
Each example is in the context of an object o of class C:

1. after o receives message $m(p, r)$ it will eventually send message $n(r)$ to object
   p, unless p and r are the same object;
2. each time o receives message $t()$ it will return a positive integer which is larger
   than the one it returned in response to the previous instance of message $t()$.

In order to combine the dynamic power of the mu-calculus with the static
expressiveness of OCL, we propose to use the two-level logic *observational mu-calculus*, with standard OCL as the instantiation of the lower level logic. The
resulting logic, $\mathcal{O}\mu(\text{OCL})$, is extremely powerful, whilst being designed with
verification in mind. Using it directly does, however, require an understanding
of temporal logic with fixpoints which it would be unrealistic to expect most
developers to be interested in acquiring. We suggest that it is useful to design
"templates" of standard usage, with their own developer-friendly syntax, which
are then translated into $\mathcal{O}\mu(\text{OCL})$. In this paper we define and translate one
such template for specifying liveness constraints. Moreover, we show that the
existing OCL contract-types, invariants and pre- and post-conditions, can also
be regarded as such templates and translated into $\mathcal{O}\mu(\text{OCL})$.

This paper is structured as follows. The next section describes the state of
the art in OCL extensions. Section 3 introduces an example illustrating some
requirements which cannot currently be captured adequately by OCL, but which
can be described using a new *after/eventually* template described informally in
Section 4. Section 5 describes the logic, $\mathcal{O}\mu(\text{OCL})$, which forms the framework
we use, and shows how it is an instantiation of a two-level logic $\mathcal{O}\mu$. Section
6 demonstrates how OCL templates are translated into $\mathcal{O}\mu(\text{OCL})$. The paper
finishes with some conclusions and discussion on future work.

2   State of the Art in OCL Extensions

In this section we describe various proposals to extend OCL in order to allow it to
express contracts involving dynamic constraints. There are also many proposals
for non-OCL-based contract notations, but for reasons of space we do not discuss

them here, given that we are specifically interested in capitalising on the existing acceptance of OCL.

[9] introduces a temporal extension of OCL in order to describe safety and liveness constraints of reactive and distributed systems. It adds some basic temporal logic operators to the grammar of OCL, such as until and always. However, there are problems: the main one is that OCL only allows query operations in expressions, whereas general operations are used in the paper, and needed by many of the desired properties. Another approach [6] extends OCL in order to express constraints involving changes of state, and introduces operators initially and eventually, applied to properties. It also changes the meaning of @pre; in standard OCL this is used only in postconditions, to refer to values before the invocation of the operation being specified (c.f. VDM's hook). In this approach it can be used in invariants as well, and means "the value of a property in every pre-state of an operation". Given that this means *any* operation, it is not clear how to interpret this so as to make @pre useful for anything but specifying that certain elements of an object's state never change. Both of these approaches are interesting, but in neither case are the new features defined precisely.

A dynamic extension in [7] adds so-called action clauses to OCL. The motivation is to be able to express dynamic constraints involving events, signals or the invocation of operations. An action clause can appear in an operation specification or with an invariant of a classifier. In the first case, it allows us to express that when an operation is executed it triggers the execution of other operations. In the second case, it specifies, for instance, that when certain conditions hold an object has to send events to given objects. Action clauses express some interesting dynamic properties, but their semantics is not entirely understood. The paper has influenced the OCL2.0 proposal [1].

Catalysis is a methodology for component-based software design which uses a textual constraint language similar to OCL but slightly more expressive [5]. For instance, it is possible to refer to operations in a postcondition. This means that we can specify that the effect of an operation is to invoke another operation. Furthermore, such an operation invocation can be either synchronous (the invoked operation is written within brackets [[operation(...)]]) or asynchronous (it is further prefixed with sent).

Finally, a different approach is taken in [4] which defines the logic BOTL and its transition system semantics. BOTL does not extend OCL by temporal operators itself. Rather what it does is translate a part of OCL v 1.1 into an object-based version of CTL. This means that temporal extensions of OCL in the sense of CTL could be translated into BOTL as well, but such extensions are not provided. The motivation for BOTL is model checking of existing OCL constraints. A strength of the work is that its concepts are clearly and precisely defined. In particular, it provides a semantic model which we shall reuse with minor modifications.

3   Example

In this section we will demonstrate various contracts which can, and cannot, be expressed using OCL. We use a variant of the (in)famous dining philosophers example. Consider the fragment of a class diagram in Figure 1.

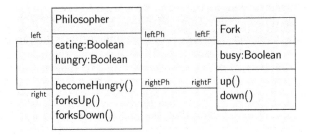

Fig. 1. Class diagram for dining philosophers

Using operations in the interface, clients of class Philosopher (e.g. instances of other classes in the design, not shown in this fragment) can instruct a philosopher to become hungry, or to pick up or put down both forks. Notice that a philosopher may pick up either fork separately using the interface of class Fork, but it is not possible for an outside client to instruct the philosopher to do so. Associations between Philosopher and Fork link a philosopher with her right and left forks. The association between Philosopher and itself records the philosopher's place at the table; she will have someone on her left and on her right.

The UML class diagram given above does not give us a full description of our intended society of philosophers sharing forks around a table; there are many ways in which developers working in accord with this diagram could make decisions which we might regard as unfortunate. For example, there is nothing yet to forbid an implementation which deadlocks, or which starves certain philosophers, or even one which violates the familiar rules of the problem such as the arrangement of philosophers and forks. To reduce this scope for error, we can add further requirements as OCL constraints. We now give a few examples of OCL constraints, before concentrating on further requirements which we cannot currently express in OCL.

First, we write a class invariant on Philosopher recording that a philosopher's right and left neighbours are different from herself; this ensures that there are at least two Philosophers!

context Philosopher **inv:**

    self.left <> self and self.right <> self

Furthermore, adjacent philosophers share a fork:

context Philosopher **inv:**

    self.leftF = self.left.rightF

Therefore we want the implementation to prevent adjacent philosophers from being able to eat at the same time:

context Philosopher **inv**:
    self.eating=false or self.left.eating=false

The following OCL constraint describes the pre- and postconditions of the operation up() of class fork.

context Fork::up()
    pre: self.busy=false
    post: self.busy=true

This list of contracts is by no means exhaustive: we could continue adding OCL constraints to our model. However, many requirements are inexpressible in OCL. We will provide developer-friendly syntax for certain liveness conditions, including the following paradigmatic examples[1]:

(1) If a philosopher is hungry then she will eventually be eating.
(2) If a philosopher is instructed to pick up the forks (i.e. receives message forksUp()) she will eventually pick up her left fork (i.e. send message up() to the appropriate fork).

To make our new syntax precise, we will also introduce the logic $\mathcal{O}\mu(\text{OCL})$ in which a much larger class of temporal constraints can be expressed.

4   A New Template

In this section we demonstrate the use of our new *after/eventually* (AE) template. It is a template in the sense that it is a standard framework in which to express a particular liveness property, parameterised on certain OCL expressions. The template and its OCL contents are then translated together into our logic $\mathcal{O}\mu(\text{OCL})$. Thus the developer using the template does not have to understand the $\mathcal{O}\mu(\text{OCL})$ logic; at the same time, the wholesale embedding of OCL into $\mathcal{O}\mu(\text{OCL})$ allows the translation to be very simple, and should help tools to provide understandable feedback based on verification of $\mathcal{O}\mu(\text{OCL})$ formulae. (A common problem with verification based on translations of user-friendly languages into less user-friendly underlying syntax is that it is difficult for a tool to give feedback in terms which are understandable to the user; by avoiding translating OCL itself we hope to minimise such problems.) If an expert developer requires the full flexibility of the language – or perhaps some intermediate sublanguage, such as a CTL-like syntax for a subset of $\mathcal{O}\mu(\text{OCL})$– there is of course no obstacle to a tool providing it.

Thus, the template presented here is merely one example of a possible use of the extra temporal power provided by the use of $\mathcal{O}\mu$, which is explained in the next section; in Section 6 we give the translation.

---

[1] Of *requirements*: meeting them may depend on more than one component's design.

```
context Classifier:
    after: oclExpression
    eventually: oclExpression
```

Like an invariant or a pre/post-condition pair, an AE template is written in the context of a type, typically a classifier such as a class or a component from a UML model. As there, "self" may be used to refer to the instance of this type to which the contract is being applied.

The **after:** clause expresses some trigger for the contract: once the condition it expresses becomes true, the contract specifies a guarantee that the condition expressed in the **eventually:** clause will eventually become true. Notice that there is, in this particular example template, no intention that the **eventually:** clause should be required to become true immediately; the subtlety of this template is precisely that it is able to talk about consequences at a distance.

The oclExpressions must be either of OCL type Boolean, or may have special forms which extend OCL1.x, but which we expect to be standard in OCL2.0. The **eventually:** clause is permitted to contain an expression like self.left.leftF.up(), specifying that self sends message up() to object self.left.leftF. This is an OCL action expression, as described in the OCL2.0 proposal [1]. Similarly, the **after:** clause may simply name an operation of the Classifier in whose context the template is being used, possible also naming its arguments. For example, **after:** forksUp() is to be read as "after self *receives* the message forksUp()"; in UML terms it represents an event, not an action. We call such an expression an OCL event expression: [1] does not currently include these, but as they go naturally with action expressions we believe that the final proposal will do so. ([1] will certainly be revised before OCL2.0 is finalised, as there are still significant semantic ambiguities in the current draft; indeed, we are committed to contribute to that revision.) These considerations are purely syntactic: the AE template is translated as a whole into $\mathcal{O}\mu(\mathrm{OCL})$, where the notions are clearly distinguished. In this paper we have chosen to keep our example template very simple: the rationale for allowing OCL event expressions in **after:** but not in **eventually:** and vice versa for OCL action expressions is the philosophy that the developer of a part cannot reasonably be expected to control the events which eventually happen to the part, only the actions eventually done by the part. Technically, however, any use of events, actions and boolean conditions can be translated.

We can now record the example contracts from Section 3. (1) becomes:

```
context Philosopher:
    after: self.hungry=true
    eventually: self.eating=true
```

In this case both clauses are Boolean constraints, already legal in OCL1.x. Notice that we have not specified any limit on the length of time a philosopher can be hungry and not eating, merely that it is not infinite. (2) becomes:

context Philosopher:

    after: forksUp()

    eventually: self.leftF.up()

Again, we are deliberately not stating that self.leftF.up() is an immediate reaction to the receipt of message forksUp(). The specifier may reasonably choose to use the AE template here in order not to tie the developer down too tightly, and to avoid the problems inherent in specifying what is meant by "immediate", even informally. (Is internal computation permitted between the trigger and its consequence? At least this must be allowed in practice. But what about the sending of a message to self? The sending of a message to another object? And so on.) One natural possibility in a synchronous system where the trigger is the receipt of a message is to specify that the consequence must have happened before the message is replied to; this too is easy to express in $\mathcal{O}\mu(\text{OCL})$.

Note the use of an OCL event expression in the **after:** clause and of an OCL action expression in the **eventually:** clause. We distinguish them here by context; if OCL2.0 follows our expectations and standardises both, it may choose a different syntax which of course we could adopt.

We have only specified that the left fork will be picked up. As there is no objection to several contracts applying to the same classifier, we could also apply the corresponding contract for the right fork; both would apply and both forks would be picked up. Alternatively, we could have permitted the contracts to be combined, getting

context Philosopher:

    after: forksUp()

    eventually: self.leftF.up() and self.rightF.up()

that is, combining two OCL action expressions with the OCL and. However, the implications of forming complex expressions using OCL action expressions have not been considered in the OCL2.0 proposal, and it may be considered undesirable to allow this at all. Because of this uncertainty, we choose not to permit such combinations for now; at the same time, the probability of wanting greater power of combination later is a reason for defining OCL event expressions rather than allowing events to be discussed only implicitly, as they are at present in pre/post conditions. (We could alternatively have defined a second template, perhaps *pre/eventually*, to be written in the context of a particular operation; this would be similar to what is done in [5] for what they call asynchronous action invocations in postconditions. Then we would not have needed to invent OCL event expressions to express (2). Pragmatically, we prefer the solution presented here, but either could equally well be translated to $\mathcal{O}\mu(\text{OCL})$.)

5   Observational Mu-Calculus

The modal mu-calculus has a long history of being used to describe properties of systems whose behaviour evolves over time. It is a very simple, concise language, which at the same time has sufficient expressiveness to capture a wide range of useful properties. For this reason it has often been used as the target of translations from more user-friendly languages; the specifier writes in some suitable syntax, which is then translated into mu-calculus and verified there. It is a logic defined on labelled transition systems, so that the semantics of a formula is a set of states of the system. As well as the boolean operators, the mu-calculus incorporates two features, modalities and fixpoints, each of which appears in two (dual) forms. The *modalities* provide the means of exploring a labelled transition system locally; they are $\langle a \rangle \Phi$ (from the current state, there is a transition labelled a which leads to a state where Φ holds) and $[a]\Phi$ (from the current state, any transition labelled a leads to a state where Φ holds). Adding these modalities gives Hennessy–Milner logic, which can express simple "finite" properties, but cannot say things about behaviour which continues for unboundedly many steps. The *fixpoints* ($\mu X.\Phi(X)$ and $\nu X.\Phi(X)$) add this power. For a detailed discussion of their meaning and power we refer the reader to references such as [3]; here it suffices to say that they allow the expression of safety properties (something bad is guaranteed not to happen), liveness properties (something good is guaranteed to happen) and indeed a wide class of fairness properties (e.g. provided this thing keeps happening, so will that thing).

In specifying contracts within UML models, these kinds of properties are among those that we need. We also, however, need smooth ways to combine the kinds of properties we can talk about in OCL with the kinds of properties we can talk about in mu-calculus. Notice that we do not simply want the union of these classes of properties: greater power is needed to express requirements such as that a service provider will always respond to a service request by making a request of a third party, where the parameters of that new request are related to those of the original request in some way which can be specified in OCL. The examples given in Section 1 are also of this kind. Semantically, what we say in OCL needs to be entwined with what we say in mu-calculus. However, from the point of view of the specifier, we need to maintain a clear separation.

5.1   The Calculus $\mathcal{O}\mu$(OCL)

Observational mu-calculus ($\mathcal{O}\mu$) is an extension of the modal mu-calculus with some first-order features. It is a two level logic: intuitively, the upper level is the modal mu-calculus, and the lower level can be instantiated with any appropriate domain specific logic, such as OCL—thus we write $\mathcal{O}\mu$(OCL) for $\mathcal{O}\mu$ with OCL as its domain logic. In order to provide a clean separation of domain-dependent logical expressions from purely temporal properties, we confine domain-dependent expressions (for example, OCL expressions) to appear only inside modalities and as 'atomic' formulae of the mu-calculus. To provide expressive power, $\mathcal{O}\mu$ works on transition systems where the transitions are labelled with structured data, and the (domain-dependent) choice of what form the transitions have determines what properties of the system can be referred to in specifications. One can see this both as an instantiation of Milner's thesis that observation is fundamental, and as an instantiation of the thesis that systems should only be accessible through defined interfaces.

The link between the two levels is provided by 'cells'; these are first-order variables, in the sense of hybrid logics, but we call them 'cells' to distinguish them from the fixpoint variables. In the upper level, a cell x appears only implicitly, as a first-order variable passed through the fixpoint operators; in the lower level, a 'cell' is seen as a normal first-order variable of some appropriate model-dependent datatype – for example, an OCL variable.

An $\mathcal{O}\mu$ formula 'observes' a system by evaluating a box or diamond modality, which may import data into the cells. The existential modality has the form: $\langle l, C, \phi \rangle \Phi$, where: C specifies a set of *mutable* cells; l is an *action expression*, which is intuitively an expression that is pattern-matched against the structured transition label and thereby assigns values to the mutable cells mentioned in l; and ϕ is a constraint in the domain-specific logic. The constraint ϕ may refer to cells c, meaning their value after the transition is taken and matched against l, and also, in VDM style, to hooked cells $\overleftarrow{c}$, meaning their value before the transition is taken (hooked cells are syntactic sugar, but useful). Intuitively, a state satisfies the formula if there is a matching transition satisfying the constraints after which Φ is true; the formal semantics is slightly richer.

The formal syntax of $\mathcal{O}\mu$ is:

$$\Phi = \psi \mid \mathbf{T} \mid \mathbf{F} \mid X \mid \Phi \vee \Phi \mid \Phi \wedge \Phi \mid \langle l, C, \phi \rangle \Phi \mid [l, C, \phi] \Phi \mid \nu X. \Phi \mid \mu X. \Phi$$

where ψ is a formula of the lower-level logic (not mentioning hooked cells).

Since the 'cells' are first-order variables which are implicitly passed through fixpoint variables, the meaning of a formula with no free fixpoint variables is a function from cell valuations to sets of states, rather than just a set of states; we write $A \models_{V,\rho} \Phi$ to mean that given a variable valuation V and cell valuation ρ, the state A satisfies Φ.

The formal semantics of the diamond modality is then: $A \models_{V,\rho} \langle l, C, \phi \rangle \Phi$ iff

- $\exists \rho'$ a new cell valuation differing from ρ only in the values of cells in C ($c \notin C \Rightarrow \rho'(c) = \rho(c)$), and
- $\exists a, A'$ such that $A \xrightarrow{a} A'$ and a matches l in context ρ' and $\rho, \rho' \models \phi$ and $A' \models_{V,\rho'} \Phi$

The box operator is dual, and the fixpoint operators have the usual meaning, but taken over states parametrised by cell valuations rather than over states. Formal details may be found in [2].

To define $\mathcal{O}\mu$ in the specific domain of UML models, we need (a) to define the logic used in constraints ϕ, (b) to define the transition system, (c) to define the action expressions and how they match transition labels.

The Low Level Logic OCL. The low level logic used in the constraints ϕ of the modalities is essentially OCL[2], with some re-interpretation to link it to the higher level logic, as follows.

---

[2] A minor complication is that OCL is a three-valued logic. We insist that OCL expressions used in $\mathcal{O}\mu$(OCL) not evaluate to undefined: if they do so, the whole $\mathcal{O}\mu$(OCL) formula is meaningless. This is not too restrictive, especially since undefinedness does not always propagate in OCL.

The $\mathcal{O}\mu$ cells provide the link between the two levels, so OCL variables appear as cells of $\mathcal{O}\mu(\text{OCL})$. By convention we will always have an $\mathcal{O}\mu(\text{OCL})$ cell *self*, which gives the value of the special OCL keyword `self`, and thereby provides a starting point for navigation in the OCL expression. It is then possible, by allowing the value of *self* to change, to write properties whose context changes over time. Similarly, the OCL keyword `result` is tied to an $\mathcal{O}\mu(\text{OCL})$ cell *result*.

The reader familiar with [4] will wonder about the OCL `@pre` construct, which requires a quite complicated translation in that work. It is possible in $\mathcal{O}\mu(\text{OCL})$ to do the same translation, which essentially involves storing the precondition-time values of `@pre`'ed expressions in auxiliary variables and referring to these at postcondition time, but it is not necessary. Because our lower level logic *is* essentially OCL, and will be evaluated by an OCL-based model-checker, we can leave `@pre` alone, and extend its interpretation thus: an `@pre` expression in a constraint is evaluated at the origin state of the transition taken in the modality. Hence in particular when the modality action expression refers to a complete method invocation (defined below), `@pre` has its usual OCL meaning. This makes `@pre` the lower-level analogue of the $\mathcal{O}\mu$ hook, and so we shall write hook and `@pre` interchangeably.

For typographic reasons we shall use normal logical notations (e.g. $\wedge$) instead of always using OCL keywords (e.g. `and`).

The Transition System. The definition of a transition system amounts to a formal semantics for UML, which of course is a major research topic in the community. We will therefore adopt for this paper an abstract high-level semantics, a variation on that of [4]. The state of a system comprises at least the attribute and link values of all the objects in the system, together with the set of currently active method calls, and a unique identifier for each active method call. If the model is sufficiently defined, the state may also include other UML state information.

The transitions represent changes in state as the system evolves, and provide the interface to the specification formulae.

Message passing or method invocation is modelled by communication transitions which may represent a complete invocation, or just the sending of or reply to a message. Each message instance is assigned an identifier, and this is exported in the transition label, along with the source and target of the message. (The source and target are implicit in the state, but we can only observe what is exported in the transition labels.) Communication transitions may, then, be:

- send(*selector*, *source*, *target*, *id*, *arguments*), representing the sending of a message, or
- return(*selector*, *source*, *target*, *id*, *return_value*), representing the reply to a message (where *source* means the sender of the original message)
- *val* = call(*selector*, *source*, *target*, *id*, *arguments*) representing the invocation of a method returning *val*, seen as a single *complete transition*.

The complete transitions deserve further comment. In a fully detailed model (such as verification approaches normally assume) they are derived transitions: a complete transition is generated automatically for each possible sequence of transitions starting and ending with corresponding send and return transitions. However, in a verification approach suitable for tool-supported use during on-going design, it would not be practical to assume that a fully detailed transition system can be generated. A tool might then work with complete transitions without ever representing the underlying transitions from which they would be derived. This might happen for two reasons. First, the user might not have specified the detailed information; the tool would work with any information the user had specified, for example, with pre/post conditions for the operation. (Note that nondeterminism is inherent in working with designs, and also that as the transition systems concerned are infinite or very large, any practical tool would have to be using some form of symbolic representation of the transition system anyway.) Second, the information might be present in the model but not required for the particular task; this is a form of "on the fly" transition system generation.

Finally, we have transitions labelled 'internal', representing some internal computation (including object creation); this may be refined to a more detailed label according to requirements.

It is important to note that we are *not* addressing here the issue of how the transition system is derived from the UML model, but taking it as given. The derivation of a transition system from a model depends on, among other things, the level of detail at which the model is given. Since designs are not concrete systems, and may well be infinite-state, the appropriate representation of transition systems will usually be symbolic; appropriate verification techniques include infinite-state symbolic model-checking, constraint-solving, theorem-proving or abstract games.

Action Expressions. Now we define the *action expressions*. In the following, O is a navigation expression, m is a selector, and $v, d, s, t, a_1, \ldots, a_n$ are expressions of appropriate types, perhaps including cells. The notation $\hat{a}_1$ (etc.) means the value of a_1 in the current cell valuation, i.e. the value to which a_1 evaluates when current cell values are substituted for cells wherever they occur.

- $O.m_d(a_1, \ldots, a_n)$ matches transitions $\text{send}(m, \hat{self}, \hat{O}, \hat{d}, \hat{a}_1, \ldots, \hat{a}_n)$, and is the sending of message $m(a_1, \ldots, a_n)$ with identifier d by the current object to the object O.
- $m_{d,s}(a_1, \ldots, a_n)$ matches transitions $\text{send}(m, \hat{s}, \hat{self}, \hat{d}, \hat{a}_1, \ldots, \hat{a}_n)$, and is the receipt of message $m(a_1, \ldots, a_n)$ by the current object from the object s.
- $\overline{m}_{d,t}(v)$ matches transitions $\text{return}(m, \hat{self}, \hat{t}, \hat{d}, \hat{v})$, and is the receipt of a reply to a message m.
- $O.\overline{m}_d(v)$ matches transitions $\text{return}(m, \hat{O}, \hat{self}, \hat{d}, \hat{v})$, and is the sending to O of a reply to a message m with return value v.
- $v = O.m_d(a_1, \ldots, a_n)$ matches $\hat{v} = \text{call}(m, \hat{self}, \hat{O}, \hat{d}, \hat{a}_1, \ldots, \hat{a}_n)$, a complete transition from the viewpoint of the caller. (Note that v is in principle an expression; in practice, it will usually be just a mutable cell.)
- $v = m_{d,s}(a_1, \ldots, a_n)$ matches $\hat{v} = \text{call}(m, \hat{s}, \hat{self}, \hat{d}, \hat{a}_1, \ldots, \hat{a}_n)$, a complete transition from the viewpoint of the callee.
- τ matches internal computation.

If subscripts or arguments of an action expression are omitted, they are wild cards, and always match; and we write $\star$ as a wild-card *selector*. Thus the action expression $\star$ matches any message receipt action, and $O.\star$ matches any message sent to O. In addition, we adopt the usual practice in modal mu-calculi of allowing sets of action expressions, so that $\{e_1, e_2\}$ matches anything matching e_1 or e_2, and we allow the use of $-$ to mean the complement of a set, so that the action expression $-e$ matches any transition *except* one matched by e, and in particular $-$ matches any action whatsoever. (This notation can be a little confusing: note that according to these rules, $-\star$ matches any action except a message receipt action.)

6 Applying Observational Mu-Calculus

In this section we show how the liveness template we informally presented is expressed in $\mathcal{O}\mu(\text{OCL})$. As a further demonstration of expressiveness, we also show how to express the standard invariants and pre- and post-conditions for operations. Designers can continue to use the familiar syntax, whilst we translate them into the underlying observational mu-calculus representation. In the context of a UML verification tool, this is a foundation for a single coherent verification task.

We begin with translating invariants as this leads to slightly simpler $\mathcal{O}\mu(\text{OCL})$ formulae. An invariant in OCL has the form

context TypeName inv:

  P

where P is an OCL constraint, to be evaluated with reference to a particular instance of TypeName which may be referred to as "self" in P.

A recurring question is "exactly when is an invariant supposed to hold?" It is clear that the answer cannot be literally "always"; for example, in the case of a constraint that self should always be linked to exactly one Foo, this would make it impossible ever to replace one instance of Foo by another. A common compromise [10,4] for use with single-threaded synchronous systems is "whenever no method of self is executing". Adopting this, we translate the above invariant into the $\mathcal{O}\mu(\text{OCL})$ formula:

$$\nu Z.\,(P \wedge [-\star, \varnothing, \mathbf{T}]Z)$$

which can be read as "P is true now and remains so unless we look inside a method call". The "whenever no method of self is executing" condition appears as the action expression $-\star$; the formula correctly asserts invariance because any method call on self is represented by a complete transition (as well as possibly by complex sequences of transitions). If such a formula is to be verified of a design (as opposed to asserted as part of a specification) the transition system obtained from the UML model will of course have to include detailed specification of the behaviour resulting from a message invocation; in this case, the complete transitions are added to the transition system to represent any sequence of transitions which starts with self receiving a message and ends with self replying to that message.

Given a transition system, the $\mathcal{O}\mu(\text{OCL})$ formula is unambiguous. Notice also that although we have used the "whenever no method of self is executing" interpretation of invariant here, any reasonable variant can also be encoded in observational mu-calculus.

Next we consider operation pre- and post-conditions.

context TypeName::m(par1:Type1,...,parn:Typen):ReturnType
  pre: P
  post:Q

Parameters can be used in P and Q, and **result** in Q. This is expressed as

$$\nu Z.\,([result = m(par1,\dots,parn), C_1, \neg \overleftarrow{P} \vee \neg Q]\mathbf{F} \wedge [-, \varnothing, \mathbf{T}]Z)$$

where C_1 is $\{par1,\dots,parn,result\}$. This can be read as 'it is always impossible to do an m action such that either P fails before it or Q fails after it'. Note the constraint $\neg \overleftarrow{P} \vee \neg Q$: this is because an OCL precondition is a guard as well as a Hoare precondition. Note also that we have assumed that pre-/postconditions come in pairs: OCL in fact allows pre- and postconditions to be stated independently, for which the natural meaning is to conjoin all the stated preconditions and conjoin all the stated postconditions, and then interpret as above.

The concise expression of a pre-/postcondition property depends on the presence of the complete 'call' transitions. However, we should note that if such transitions are not included in the system, it is still possible to express the property, albeit with a considerably more complex formula.

The translation of our new AE template differs according to the type of clause. For the version where both the after and eventually clauses have boolean expressions, we have:

context Classifier:
  after: P
  eventually: Q

becomes

$$\nu Y.\,([-, \varnothing, P \wedge \neg \overleftarrow{P}]\mu Z.\,(Q \vee (\langle -, \varnothing, \mathbf{T}\rangle\mathbf{T} \wedge [-, \varnothing, \mathbf{T}]Z)) \wedge [-, \varnothing, \mathbf{T}]Y)\ .$$

In the version with action and event, we have:

context Classifier:
  after: e
  eventually: a

becomes

$$\nu Y.\,([e, C, \mathbf{T}](\mu Z.\,[-a, \varnothing, \mathbf{T}]Z) \wedge [-, \varnothing, \mathbf{T}]Y)$$

where C includes a cell for any argument to the OCL event expression e. As it happens our examples did not include arguments: but, for example, if e is request(r) then C becomes $\{r\}$, so that our matching rules ensure that the actual parameter of the invocation of result is saved, in a cell called r, across any transition matching e. Thus a is able to mention r; for example, it might be self.collaborator.otherRequest(r+1).

We omit the obvious analogues for the mixed cases.

Finally, we show how to express in $\mathcal{O}\mu(\text{OCL})$ some of the properties not expressible in either OCL or our new template: the property 'after o receives message $m(p, r)$ it will eventually send message $n(r)$ to object p, unless p and r are the same object' is expressed as

$$\nu Y.\, ([m(p, r), \{p, r\}, p \neq r]\mu Z.\, [-p.n(r), \varnothing, \mathbf{T}]Z) \wedge [-]Y$$

and the property 'each time o receives message $t()$ it will return a positive integer which is larger than the one it returned in response to the previous instance of message $t()$' is expressed as

$$\nu Z.\, [x = t(), \{x\}, x \leq \overline{x}]\mathbf{F} \wedge [x = t(), \{x\}, \mathbf{T}]Z \wedge [-(y = t()), \{y\}, \mathbf{T}]Z$$

where $x = 0$ in the initial cell valuation.

7 Conclusion and Future Work

In this paper we have presented logical foundations for adding temporal expressiveness to OCL, together with an example of how these might be used in practice to support richer contracts. Of course, the *after/eventually* template discussed here only represents one small application of the logic; it is not intended to be exhaustive but rather to illustrate that the technique can be used in a way which will be understandable to developers without special logical knowledge. There is a vast range of possible templates which could be developed and translated into $\mathcal{O}\mu(\text{OCL})$; experimentation will probably be required to determine which are useful in practice. For example, we might consider

- after/immediately: as mentioned in Section 4, we might wish to define a template which specifies self's immediate reaction to a certain stimulus, but will have to specify carefully what is meant by "immediately".
- provided/infinitely often: we might wish to define a template which specifies that provided some condition continues to hold (or perhaps, to hold infinitely often), some other condition will be true infinitely often. Such conditions are used in specifying *fairness*: it is often unreasonable to expect a part to continue to work no matter what, because it legitimately relies on correct functionality of some other part, but one wishes to specify that under fair conditions, i.e. when the relied-upon parts do work (often enough) the part will work correctly.

We have not discussed verification issues extensively in this paper but in fact the observational mu-calculus was designed with verification in mind. Considerable further work is needed, but in brief, we intend to extend the Dresden OCL kit to support the extra template described here, and to add a translator module to produce $\mathcal{O}\mu$ formulae from these templates. Alongside this we may extract a CCS process representing a labelled transition system from a UML model saved as XMI. Both the formula and the CCS process could then be fed into the Edinburgh Concurrency Workbench, which would use its existing abstraction techniques to check whether or not the process satisfies the formula. Because $\mathcal{O}\mu$ incorporates OCL as its lower-level logic, the translation can be kept quite simple which should enable us to give meaningful feedback to the user on the basis of this verification.

References

1. Boldsoft, Rational Software Corporation, and IONA. Response to the UML2.0 OCL RfP. http://www.klasse.nl/ocl/subm-draft-text.html, August 2001.
2. J.C. Bradfield and P. Stevens. Observational mu-calculus. In *Proceedings of FICS'98*, 1998. An extended version is available as BRICS-RS-99-5.
3. J.C. Bradfield and C.P. Stirling. Modal logics and mu-calculi: an introduction. In J.A. Bergstra, A. Ponse, and S.A. Smolka, editors, *Handbook of Process Algebra*, chapter 4, pages 293–330. Elsevier, 2001.
4. D. Distefano, J.-P. Katoen, and A. Rensink. On a temporal logic for object-based systems. In S. F. Smith and C. L. Talcott, editors, *Formal Methods for Open Object-based Distributed Systems*, pages 305–326. Kluwer, 2000.
5. D. D'Souza and A.C. Wills. *Objects, Components, and Frameworks with UML: The Catalysis Approach*. Object Technology Series. Addison-Wesley, 1999.
6. A. Hamie, R. Mitchell, and J. Howse. Time-based constraints in the Object Constraint Language. Technical Report CMS-00-01, University of Brighton, 2000.
7. A. Kleppe and J. Warmer. Extending OCL to include actions. In S. Kent and A. Evans, editors, *UML'2000 - The Unified Modeling Language: Advancing the Standard, Third International Conference, York, UK, October 2-6, 2000*, volume 1939 of *LNCS*, pages 440–450. Springer, 2000.
8. OMG. *Unified Modeling Language Specification version 1.4 draft*, February 2001. OMG document 01-02-14 available from www.omg.org.
9. S. Ramakrishnan and J. McGregor. Extending OCL to support temporal operators. In A. Ulrich, editor, *ICSE'99 Workshop on Testing Distributed Component-based Systems*, Los Angeles, California, USA, May 1999.
10. J. Warmer and A. Kleppe. *The Object Constraint Language: Precise Modelling with UML*. Object Technology Series. Addison-Wesley, 1999.

Formal Verification of UML Statecharts with Real-Time Extensions[*]

Alexandre David[1], M. Oliver Möller[2], and Wang Yi[1]

[1] Department of Information Technology, Uppsala University
{adavid,yi}@docs.uu.se,
[2] ▥BRICS Basic Research in Computer Science, Aarhus University
omoeller@brics.dk

Abstract. We present a framework for formal verification of a real-time extension of UML statecharts. For clarity, we restrict ourselves to a reasonable subset of the rich UML statechart model and extend this with real-time constructs (clocks, timed guards, and invariants). We equip the obtained formalism, called *hierarchical timed automata* (HTA), with an operational semantics. We outline a translation of one HTA to a network of flat timed automata, that can serve as input to the real-time model checking tool UPPAAL. This translation can be used to faithfully verify deadlock-freedom, safety, and unbounded response properties of the HTA model. We report on an XML-based implementation of this translation, use the well-known pacemaker example to illustrate our technique, and report run-time data for the formal verification part.

1   Introduction

Computer-dependent systems are experiencing an enormous increase in complexity. Maintaining consistency and compatibility in the development process of industrial-sized systems makes it necessary to describe systems on various levels of detail in a coherent way. Modern software engineering answers the challenge with powerful modeling paradigms and expressive yet abstract formalisms. Object orientation concepts provide—among many other features—a consistent methodology to abstract away from implementation details and achieve a high level view of a system.

Modeling languages, like UML, go a step further. They describe high-level structure and behavior, rather than implementations of solutions. Thus they help organizing design and specifications in different views of a system, meeting the needs of developers, customers, and implementors. In particular, they capture a notion of *correctness*, in terms of requirements the system has to meet. Formal methods typically address *model correctness*, for they operate on a purely mathematical formalization of the model. This makes it possible to prevent errors inexpensively at early design stages.

For real-time systems correctness does not only depend on functionality but also timeliness. This adds another dimension of complexity and make early validation an even more crucial step. Industrial CASE tools, e.g., VisualState™ [19],

---

[*] Supported by the European AIT-WOODDES project, No IST-1999-10069.

R.-D. Kutsche and H. Weber (Eds.): FASE 2002, LNCS 2306, pp. 218–232, 2002.
© Springer-Verlag Berlin Heidelberg 2002

exemplify how implementations benefit from high level analysis. One particularly interesting part of a complete model is the behavioral view, since it captures the dynamics of a system. The action and inter-action of components is often non trivial. Therefore a variety of formalisms allow *execution* of the model, that unfolds and visualizes system behavior.

The UML statechart formalism focuses on the control aspect, where event communication and data determines possible sequences of states. Often the behavior is dependent on real-time properties [5] and is therefore supported by industrial tools like Rhapsody [18,6]. The generated traces of the system model can be validated to coincide with the intuitive understanding of the system. However, we feel that in order to talk about correctness of a system the notion of a *formal requirement* is needed, that is either fulfilled or violated.

High-level requirements have to be communicated among collaborators with often very non-homogeneous backgrounds. It is desirable to express requirements in a simple yet powerful language with a clearly defined meaning. In this paper we use a formal *logical* language for this purpose, equipped with constructs to express real-time properties, namely *timed computation tree logic* TCTL [8]. Logically expressed properties are completely unambiguous, and automated validation and verification is possible for a reasonable class of systems. If the system does not satisfy a required logical formula, this reflects a design flaw.

In addition, it is necessary to establish sanity properties of the model, like deadlock freedom. If a behavioral model can enter a deadlock state, where no further changes are possible, the behavior of an implementation is typically (flawfully) unspecified. Simulators, e.g., ObjectGeode [16], can execute behavioral descriptions and can help to *validate* systems, i.e., discover design flaws, if they occur in a simulation session. Similar to testing, simulators cannot show the absence of errors. In contrast, *formal verification* establishes correctness by mathematical proof. If a model satisfies a property, there is no way to misbehave, at least not for the model.

Properties only carry over safely to the implementation under certain assumptions, e.g., that a local hardware bus can be accessed in below $2\mu s$. These values can often be included as parameters.

Related Work. Statecharts have been analyzed by means of model-checking earlier. In [17] a formal semantics in terms of clocked transition systems is given, that allows to benefit from the analysis tools developed for this formalism. However, this work treats time in a discrete lock-step fashion.

In [13] a formalization of UML statecharts is presented. The formalization is given in terms of an operational semantics and is implemented in the vUML tool that uses the model-checker SPIN [9]. However the timing aspects are not treated in this approach.

In contrast, we propose dense time extensions of statecharts for formal verification purposes. As a prerequisite, we give formal syntax and semantics. Then we sketch a translation of our (hierarchical) formalism into a parallel composition of timed automata, that serve as input to the UPPAAL verification tool. We establish deadlock-freedom and TCTL safety and (unbounded) response properties of a pacemaker model. The detailed version of the paper is found in [4].

Organization. Section 2 gives the formal syntax of our statechart restriction, extended with real-time constructs. Section 3 contains the formal semantics. In Section 4 we sketch a translation of our formalism to the UPPAAL tool. Section 5 reports on formal verification of the pacemaker example and gives run-time data for the tool executions. Section 6 summarizes and outlines further work.

2   Hierarchical Timed Automata

In this section we define the formal syntax of hierarchical timed automata. This is split up in the data parts, the structural parts, and a set of well-formedness constraints. Before we present the formal syntax we introduce some restrictions on the UML statecharts.

2.1   A Restricted Statechart Formalism

In this paper we address the formal verification of a restricted version of the UML statechart formalism. We add formal clocks in order to model timed behavior.

Unlike in the UML, where statecharts give rise to the incarnation of objects, we treat a statechart itself as a behavioral entity. The notion of thread execution is simplified to the parallel composition of state machines. Relationships to other UML diagrams are dropped.

Our formalism does not support exotic modeling constructs, like synchronization states. Some UML tools allow to use C++ as an action language, i.e., C++ code can be arbitrarily added to transitions. Formal verification of this is out of scope of this work, we restrict ourselves to primitive functions and basic variable assignments. Event communication is simplified to the case, where two parts of the system synchronize via handshake.

Some of the restrictions we make can be relaxed, as explained in the Future Work Section 6. What we preserve is the essence of the statechart formalism: hierarchical structure, parallel composition at any level, synchronization of remote parts, and history.

2.2   Data Components

We introduce the data components of hierarchical timed automata, that are used in guards, synchronizations, resets, and assignment expressions. Some of this data is kept local to a generic super-state, denoted by l. A *super-state* is a state containing other states.

Integer Variables. Let V be a finite set of integer variables. We later define their scope locally.

Clocks. Let $\mathcal{C}$ be a finite set of clock variables. The set $\mathcal{C}(l) \subseteq \mathcal{C}$ denotes the clocks local to a super-state l. If l has a history entry, $\mathcal{C}(l)$ contains only clocks, that are explicitly declared as *forgetful*. Other locally declared clocks of l belong to $\mathcal{C}(root)$.

Channels. Let *Ch* a finite set of synchronization channels. $Ch(l) \subseteq Ch$ is the set of channels that are local to a super-state l, i.e., there cannot be synchronization along a channel $c \in Ch(l)$ between one transition inside l and one outside l.

Synchronizations. *Ch* gives rise to a finite set of channel synchronizations, called *Sync*. For $c \in Ch$, $c?$, $c! \in Sync$.

Guards and Invariants. A data constraints is a boolean expression of the form $A \sim A$, where A is an arithmetic expression over V and $\sim \in \{<, >, =, \leq, \geq\}$. A clock constraint is an expression of the form $x \sim n$ or $x - y \sim n$, where $x, y \in \mathcal{C}$ and $n \in \mathbb{N}$ with $\sim \in \{<, >, =, \leq, \geq\}$. A clock constraint is downward closed, if $\sim \in \{<, =, \leq\}$. A guard is a finite conjunction over data constraints and clock constraints. An invariant is a finite conjunction over downward closed clock constraints. *Guard* is the set of guards, *Invariant* is the set of invariants. Both contain additionally the constants **true** and **false**.

Assignments. A clock reset is of the form $x := 0$, where $x \in \mathcal{C}$. A data assignment is of the form $v := A$, where $v \in V$ and A an arithmetic expression over V. *Reset* is the power set of clock resets and data assignments.

2.3   Structural Components

We give now the formal definition of our hierarchical timed automaton.

Def 1 *A hierarchical timed automaton is a tuple* $\langle S, S_0, \delta, \sigma, V, \mathcal{C}, Ch, \mathrm{Inv}, T \rangle$ *where*

- S *is a finite set of locations.* $root \in S$ *is the root.*
- $S_0 \in S$ *is a set of initial locations.*
- $\delta : S \rightarrow 2^S$. δ *maps l to all possible sub-states of l. δ is required to give rise to a tree structure. We readily extend δ to operate on sets of locations in the obvious way. If $\delta(l) \neq \varnothing$, then l is called a super-state.*
- $\sigma : S \rightarrow \{AND, XOR, BASIC, ENTRY, EXIT, HISTORY\}$ *is the type function for locations.*
- $V, \mathcal{C}, Ch$ *are sets of variables, clocks, and channels. They give rise to Guard, Reset, Sync, and Invariant as described in Section 2.2.*
- $\mathrm{Inv} : S \rightarrow \mathrm{Invariant}$ *maps every locations l to an invariant expression, possibly to the constant* **true**.
- $T \subseteq S \times (\mathrm{Guard} \times (\mathrm{Sync} \cup \{\varnothing\}) \times \mathrm{Reset} \times \{\mathbf{true}, \mathbf{false}\}) \times S$ *is the set of transitions. A transition connects two locations l and l', has a guard g, (optionally) a synchronization s, an assignment r (including clock resets), and an urgency flag u. We use the notation $l \xrightarrow{g,s,r,u} l'$ for this and omit g, s, r, u, when they are necessarily absent (or **false**, in the case of u).*

Notational Conventions. We use the predicate notation *TYPE(l)* for *TYPE* $\in$ $\{AND, XOR, BASIC, ENTRY, EXIT, HISTORY\}$, $l \in S$. E.g., *AND(l)* is true, exactly if $\sigma(l) = AND$. The type *HISTORY* is a special case of an entry. We use *HENTRY(l)* to capture simple entry or history entry, i.e., *HENTRY(l)* stands for *ENTRY(l)* $\vee$ *HISTORY(l)*.

We define the parent function

$$\delta^{-1}(l) \stackrel{def}{=} \begin{cases} n, \text{ where } l \in \delta(n) \text{ if } l \neq root \\ \varnothing \hspace{3.2cm} \text{otherwise.} \end{cases}$$

We use $\delta^*(l)$ to denote the set of all nested locations of a super-state l, including l. δ^{-*} is the set of all ancestors of l, including l. Moreover we use $\delta^{\times}(l) \stackrel{def}{=} \delta^*(l) \backslash \{l\}$. We introduce $\tilde{\delta}$ to refer to the children, that are proper locations.

$$\tilde{\delta}(l) \stackrel{def}{=} \{n \in \delta(l) \mid BASIC(n) \vee XOR(n) \vee AND(n)\}$$

We use $V^+(l)$ to denote the variables in the scope of location l: $V^+(l) = \bigcup_{n \in \delta^{-*}(l)} V(n)$. $\mathcal{C}^+(l)$ and $Ch^+(l)$ are defined analogously.

2.4   Well-Formedness Constraints

We give only the major well-formedness constraints to ensure consistency, grouped according to the syntactic categories variables, entries, and transitions.

Variable Constraints. We explicitly disallow conflict in assignments in synchronizing transitions:
It holds that $l_1 \xrightarrow{g,c!,r,u} l_1'$, $l_2 \xrightarrow{g',c?,r',u'} l_2' \in T \Rightarrow vars(r) \cap vars(r') = \varnothing$, where $vars(r)$ is the set of integer variables occurring in r. We require an analogous constraint to hold for the pseudo-transitions originating in the entry of an *AND* super-state. Static scope: For $l \xrightarrow{g,s,r,u} l' \in T$, g, r are defined over $V^+(\delta^{-1}(l)) \cup \mathcal{C}^+(\delta^{-1}(l))$ and s is defined over $Ch^+(\delta^{-1}(l))$.

Entry Constraints. Let $e \in S$, $HENTRY(e)$. If $XOR(\delta^{-1}(l))$, then T contains exactly one transition $e \xrightarrow{} l'$. If $AND(\delta^{-1}(l))$, then T contains exactly one transition $e \xrightarrow{r} e_i$ for every proper sub-state $l_i \in \tilde{\delta}(\delta^{-1}(l))$, and $e_i \in \delta(l_i)$.

Transition Constraints. Transitions have to respect the structure given in δ and cannot cross levels in the hierarchy, except via connecting to entries or exits. The set of legal transitions is given in Table 1. Transitions $l \xrightarrow{g,s,r,u} l'$ with $HENTRY(l)$ or $EXIT(l')$ are called *pseudo-transitions*. They are restricted in the sense, that they cannot carry synchronizations or urgency flags, and only either guards or assignments. For $HENTRY(l)$, only pseudo-transitions of the form $l \xrightarrow{r} l'$ are allowed. For $EXIT(l')$, only pseudo-transition of the form $l \xrightarrow{g} l'$ are allowed. For $EXIT(l) \wedge EXIT(l')$, this is further restricted to be of the form $l \rightarrow l'$.
    The syntax does not support directly a transition to a composite state such as *XOR* or *AND* state. The syntax has only explicit entries and such a transition, with an associated entry marked *default*, is only a convenient notation. The same applies for a transition from a composite state, it happens actually from a default exit that is connected to all the nested states. Figure ?? shows these convenient notations.

Table 1. Overview over all legal transitions $l \xrightarrow{g,s,r,u} l'$

	Comment	l	l'	Constraint
		$BASIC$	$BASIC$	
Internal transitions	Internal	$BASIC$	$EXIT$	$\delta^{-1}(l) = \delta^{-1}(l')$
		$HENTRY$	$BASIC$	
Entering transitions	Entering	$BASIC$	$HENTRY$	
	and fork	$HENTRY$	$HENTRY$	$\delta^{-1}(l) = \delta^{-2}(l')$
Exiting transitions	Exiting	$EXIT$	$BASIC(l)$	
	and join	$EXIT$	$EXIT$	$\delta^{-2}(l) = \delta^{-1}(l')$
Changing transitions	Changing	$EXIT$	$HENTRY$	$\delta^{-2}(l) = \delta^{-2}(l')$

3   Operational Semantics of HTAs

We present the operational semantics of our hierarchical timed automaton model.
A *configuration* captures a snapshot of the system, i.e., the active locations, the
integer variable values, the clock values, and the history of some super-states.
Configurations are of the form (ρ, μ, ν, θ), where

- $\rho : S \to 2^S$ captures the control situation. ρ can be understood as a partial,
  dynamic version of δ, that maps every super-state s to the set of active sub-
  states. If a super-state s is not active, $\rho(s) = \varnothing$. We define $Active(l) \stackrel{def}{=} l \in$
  $\rho^\times(root)$, where $\rho^\times(l)$ is the set of all active sub-states of l. Notice that
  $Active(l) \Leftrightarrow l \in \rho(\delta^{-1}(l))$.
- $\mu : S \to (\mathbb{Z})^*$. μ gives the valuation of the local integer variables of a super-
  state l as a finite tuple of integer numbers. If $\neg Active(l)$ then $\mu(l) = \lambda$
  (the empty tuple). If $Active(l)$ then we require that $|\mu(l)| = |V(l)|$ and μ is
  consistent with respect to the value of shared variables (i.e., always maps
  to the same value). We use $\mu(l)(a)$ to denote the value of $a \in V(l)$. When
  entering a non-basic location, local variables are added to μ and set to an
  initial value (0 by default). We use the shorthand $0^{V(l)}$ for the tuple $(0, 0 \ldots 0)$
  with arity $|V(l)|$.
- $\nu : S \to (\mathbb{R}^+)^*$. ν gives the real valuation of the clocks $\mathcal{C}(l)$ visible at location
  l, thus $|\nu(l)| = |\mathcal{C}(l)|$. If $\neg Active(l)$ then $\nu(l) = \lambda$.
- θ reflects the history, that might be restored by entering super-states via
  history entries. It is split up in the two functions θ_{state} and θ_{var}, where
  $\theta_{state}(l)$ returns the last visited sub-state of l—or an entry of the sub-state,
  in the case where the sub-state is not basic—(to restore $\rho(l)$), and $\theta_{var}(l)$
  returns a vector of values for the local integer variables.
  There is no history for clocks at the semantics level, all non-forgetful clocks
  belong to $\mathcal{C}(root)$.

History. The predicate $HasHistory(l) \stackrel{def}{=} \exists n \in \delta(l). \; HISTORY(n)$ captures the
existence of a history entry. If $HasHistory(l)$ holds, the term $HEntry(l)$ denotes
the unique history entry of l. If $HasHistory(l)$ does not hold, the term $HEntry(l)$

denotes the default entry of l. If l is basic $HEntry(l) = l$. If none of the above is the case, then $HEntry(l)$ is undefined.

Initially, $\forall l \in S.HasHistory(l) \Rightarrow \theta_{state}(l) = HEntry(l) \wedge \theta_{var}(l) = 0^{V(l)}$.

Reached Locations by Forks. In order to denote the set of locations reached by following a fork, we define the function $Targets_\theta : 2^S \rightarrow 2^S$ relative to θ.

$$Targets_\theta(L) \stackrel{def}{=} L \cup \bigcup_{l \in L} \{n | n \in \theta_{state}(l) \wedge HISTORY(l)\} \cup \{n | l \stackrel{r}{\rightarrow} n \wedge ENTRY(l)\}$$

We use the notation $Targets_\theta(l)$ for $Targets_\theta(\{l\})$, if the argument is a singleton. $Targets_\theta^*$ is the reflexive transitive closure of $Targets_\theta$.

Configuration-Vector Transformation. Taking a transition $t : l \xrightarrow{g,s,r,u} l'$ entails in general 1. executing a join to exit l, 2. taking the proper transition t itself, and 3. executing a fork at l'. If l (respectively l') is a basic location, part 1. (respectively 3.) is trivial. We represent this complex transition by a transformation function $\mathcal{T}_t$, which depends on a particular transition t.

The three parts of this step are described as follows.

1. *join:*
   (ρ, μ, ν, θ) is transformed to $(\rho^1, \mu^1, \nu^1, \theta^1)$ as follows:
   ρ is updated to $\rho^1 := \rho[\forall n \in \rho^\times(l). \ n \mapsto \varnothing]$.
   μ is updated to $\mu^1 := \mu[\forall n \in \rho^\times(l). \ n \mapsto \lambda]$.
   ν is updated to $\nu^1 := \nu[\forall n \in \rho^\times(l). \ n \mapsto \lambda]$.

   If $EXIT(l)$, the history is recorded. Let H be the set of super-states $h \in \rho^\times(\delta^{-1}(l))$, where $HasHistory(h)$ holds. Then
   $$\theta_{state}^1 := \theta_{state}[\forall h \in H. \ h \mapsto HEntry(\rho(h))] \text{ and}$$
   $$\theta_{var}^1 := \theta_{var}[\forall h \in H. \ h \mapsto \mu(h)].$$
   If $\neg EXIT(l)$ or $H = \varnothing$, then $\theta^1 := \theta$.
2. *proper transition part:*
   $(\rho^1, \mu^1, \nu^1, \theta^1)$ is transformed to $(\rho^2, \mu^2, \nu^2, \theta^2) := (\rho^1[l'/l], r(\mu^1), r(\nu^1), \theta^1)$. $r(\mu^1)$ denotes the updated values of the integers after the assignments and $r(\nu^1)$ the updated clocks after the resets.
3. *fork:*
   $(\rho^2, \mu^2, \nu^2, \theta^2)$ is transformed to $(\rho^3, \mu^3, \nu^3, \theta^3)$ by moving the control to all proper locations reached by the fork, i.e., those in $Targets_{\theta^2}^*(l')$. Note that $\rho^2(n) = \varnothing$ for all $n \in \delta^\times(l')$. Thus we can compute ρ^3 as follows:
   $\rho^3 := \rho^2$
   FORALL $n \in Targets_{\theta^2}^*(l')$
       IF $ENTRY(n)$
           THEN $\rho^3(\delta^{-2}(n)) := \rho^3(\delta^{-2}(n)) \cup \{\delta^{-1}(n)\}$
           ELSE $\rho^3(\delta^{-1}(n)) := \{n\}$ $/\star$ *BASIC* $\star/$

μ^3 is derived from μ^2 by first initializing all local variables of the super-states s in $Targets_{\theta^2}^*(l')$, i.e., $\mu^3(V(s)) := 0^{V(s)}$. If $HasHistory(s)$, $\theta_{var}(s)$ is used instead of $0^{V(s)}$. Then all variable assignments and clock-resets along the pseudo-transitions belonging to this fork are executed to update μ^3 and ν^3. The history does not change, θ^3 is identical to θ^2.

Note that parts 1. and 3. correspond to the identity transformation, if l and l' are basic locations.

We define the configuration-vector transformation $\mathcal{T}_t$ for a transition t : $l \xrightarrow{g,s,r,u} l'$:

$$\mathcal{T}_t(\rho,\mu,\nu,\theta) \overset{def}{=} (\rho^3,\mu^3,\nu^3,\theta^3)$$

If the context is unambiguous, we use $\rho^{\mathcal{T}_t}$ and $\nu^{\mathcal{T}_t}$ for the parts ρ^3 respectively ν^3 of the transformed configuration corresponding to transition t.

Starting Points for Joins. A super-state s can only be exited, if all its parallel sub-states can synchronize on this exit. For an exit $l \in \delta(s)$ we note by *PreExitSets(l)* the family of sets of exits. If transitions are enabled to all exits in $X \in PreExitSets(l)$, then all sub-states can synchronize.

Rule Predicates. To give the rules, we need to define predicates that evaluate conditions on the dynamic tree ρ. We introduce the set set of active leaves (in the tree described by ρ), which are the innermost active states in a super-state l:

$$Leaves(\rho, l) \overset{def}{=} \{n \in \rho^\times(l) \mid \rho(n) = \varnothing\}$$

The predicate expressing that all the sub-states of a state l can synchronize on a join is:

$$JoinEnabled(\rho,\mu,\nu,l) \overset{def}{=} BASIC(l) \vee$$
$$\exists X \in PreExitSets(l). \forall n \in Leaves(\rho,l). \exists n' \in X. n \xrightarrow{g} n' \wedge g(\mu,\nu)$$

Note that *JoinEnabled* is trivially true for a basic location l.

For the invariants of a location we use a function $Inv_\nu : S \to \{\textbf{true}, \textbf{false}\}$, that evaluates the invariant of a given location with respect to a clock evaluation ν. We use the predicate $Inv(\rho, \nu)$ to express, that for control situation ρ and clock valuation ν all invariants are satisfied.

$$Inv(\rho,\nu) \overset{def}{=} \bigwedge_{n \in \rho^\times(root)} Inv_\nu(n)$$

We introduce the predicate *TransitionEnabled* over transitions $t : l \xrightarrow{g,s,r,u} l'$, that evaluates to **true**, if t is enabled.

$$TransitionEnabled(t : l \xrightarrow{g,s,r,u} l', \rho,\mu,\nu) \overset{def}{=}$$
$$g(\mu,\nu) \wedge JoinEnabled(\rho,\mu,\nu,l) \wedge Inv(\rho^{\mathcal{T}_t}, \nu^{\mathcal{T}_t}) \wedge \neg EXIT(l')$$

Since urgency has precedence over delay, we have to capture the global situation, where some urgent transition is enabled. We do this via the predicate

UrgentEnabled over a configuration.

$$UrgentEnabled(\rho, \mu, \nu) \stackrel{def}{=} \exists t : l \xrightarrow{g,r,u} l'. \, TransitionEnabled(t, \rho, \mu, \nu) \, \wedge \, u$$
$$\vee \, \exists t_1 : l_1 \xrightarrow{g_1,c!,r_1,u_1} l_1', t_2 : l_2 \xrightarrow{g_2,c?,r_2,u_2} l_2'.$$
$$TransitionEnabled(t_1, \rho, \mu, \nu) \, \wedge$$
$$TransitionEnabled(t_2, \rho, \mu, \nu) \, \wedge \, (u_1 \vee u_2)$$

Rules. We give now the action rule. It is not possible to break it in join, action, and fork because the join can be taken only if the action is enabled and the action is taken only if the invariants still hold after the fork. The predicate *Transition-Enabled* takes into account the join, the action, and the fork conditions. The inferred transition is computed with the configuration-vector transformation.

$$\frac{TransitionEnabled(t : l \xrightarrow{g,r,u} l', \, \rho, \mu, \nu)}{(\rho, \mu, \nu, \theta) \xrightarrow{t} \mathcal{T}_t(\rho, \mu, \nu, \theta)} \; action$$

Here g is the guard of the transition and r the set of resets and assignments. The urgency flag u has no effect here. This rule applies for action transitions between basic locations as well as super-states. In the later case, this includes the appropriate joins and/or fork operations.

The delay transition rule is:

$$\frac{Inv(l)(\rho, \nu + d) \qquad \neg UrgentEnabled(\rho, \mu, \nu)}{(\rho, \mu, \nu, \theta) \xrightarrow{d} (\rho, \mu, \nu + d, \theta)} \; delay$$

where $\nu + d$ stands for the clock assignment ν shifted by the delay d. Time can elapse only if all the invariants stay satisfied and no urgent transition is enabled.

The last transition rule reflects the situation, where two action transitions synchronize via a channel c.

$$\frac{TransitionEnabled(t_1 : l_1 \xrightarrow{g_1,c!,r_1,u_1} l_1', \, \rho, \mu, \nu) \qquad l_1 \notin \delta^\times(l_2)}{TransitionEnabled(t_2 : l_2 \xrightarrow{g_2,c?,r_2,u_2} l_2', \, \rho, \mu, \nu) \qquad l_2 \notin \delta^\times(l_1)} \over (\rho, \mu, \nu, \theta) \xrightarrow{t_1,t_2} \mathcal{T}_{t_2} \circ \mathcal{T}_{t_1}(\rho, \mu, \nu, \theta)} \; sync$$

The order $\mathcal{T}_{t_2} \circ \mathcal{T}_{t_1}$ could equivalently be replaced by $\mathcal{T}_{t_1} \circ \mathcal{T}_{t_2}$ since the assignments cannot conflict with each other (according to the well-formedness constraints on transitions).

If no action transition is enabled or becomes enabled when time progresses, we have a *deadlock* configuration, which is typically a bad thing. If in addition time is prevented to elapse, this is a *time stopping deadlock*. Usually this is an error in the model, since it does not correspond to any real world behavior.

Our rules describe all legal sequences of transitions. A *trace* is a finite of infinite sequence of legal configurations that start at the initial configuration S_0 with all variables and clocks set to 0. Any two subsequent configurations are connected according to one of the transition rules. For our purposes it suffices to associate a hierarchical timed automaton semantically with the (typically infinite) set of all derivable traces.

4   Translation of Hierarchical Timed Automata to UPPAAL Timed Automata

In this section we outline the procedure for translating one hierarchical timed automaton to a parallel composition of (flat) UPPAAL timed automata [12]. We use the model of a pacemaker as a running example. We implemented our procedure in Java.

4.1   UPPAAL Timed Automata

UPPAAL [12] is a tool box for modeling, verification and simulation or real-time systems developed jointly by Uppsala University and Aalborg University. It is appropriate for systems that can be described as collection of non-deterministic parallel processes. The model used in UPPAAL is the timed automaton and corresponds to the flat version of our hierarchical timed automaton where each process is described as a state machine with finite control structure, real-valued clocks and integers. Processes communicate through channels and (or) shared variables [11]. The tool has been successfully applied in many case studies [14,15,7].

4.2   Flattening a Hierarchical Timed Automaton

Syntactically, HTAs are generated by a template mechanism that has to be instantiated. The number of templates can be substantially smaller than the number of super-states in the hierarchical state machine.

On the topmost level, conceptually under an implicit root, we find a parallel composition of instantiated templates. Each corresponds to a super-state S_i, that can itself instantiate templates in sub-states and so on. This gives rise to an *instantiation tree*, which expresses the actual behavior of the hierarchical timed automaton.

The translation proceeds in three phases:

1. *Collection of instantiations:* the hierarchical instantiation tree is traversed and for every hierarchical super-state, the skeleton of a (flat) template is constructed.
2. *Computation of global joins:* transitions originating from super-states can require a cascade of sub-state exits—called *global join*—in order to be taken. All combinations of possible start configurations are computed; this yields a guard condition, that evaluates to **true** if an only if one such cascade can be taken to completion.
3. *Post-processing channel communication:* if a transition in the hierarchical timed automaton formalism starts at a super-state S and carries a synchronization, it cannot synchronize with a transition *inside* S. Since the sub-state/super-state relation is lost in the translation, we resolve this scope conflict explicitly. We do so by introducing duplications of channels and transitions.

Every super-state S in the hierarchical timed automaton model corresponds exactly to one UPPAAL timed automaton $\hat{S}$. We can relate control locations ρ in the hierarchical timed automaton model to a *control vector* $\hat{\rho}$ in the UPPAAL model. This correspondence allows us to trace back an error sequence obtained with the flat

5   Formal Verification of a Cardiac Pacemaker

In this case study, we use a cardiac pacemaker example, as it is described in various UML books, e.g. [5]. We translate our hierarchical timed automaton model of it to an equivalent (flat) UPPAAL timed automata model and report on run-time data of the formal verification of deadlock, one safety, and one liveness property.

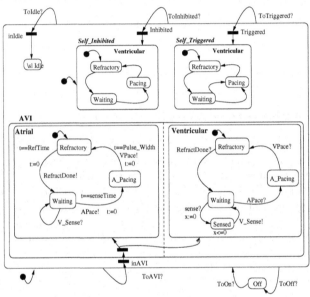

Fig. 1. Overview of our hierarchical timed automaton pacemaker model. Initially, the VVI mode is entered

5.1   The Cardiac Pacemaker Model

The main component of the pacemaker is a *XOR* super-state with the two sub-states *Off* and *On*. If the pacemaker is on, it can be in the different modes *Idle*, AAI, AAT, VVI, VVT, and AVI. The first letter indicates, to which chamber of the heart an electrical pacing pulse is sent (articular or ventricular). The second letter indicates, which chamber of the heart is monitored (articular or ventricular). In the *Self_Inhibited* (I) modes, a naturally occurring heartbeat blocks a pulse from being sent, whereas in the *Self_Triggered* (T) modes a pacing pulse will always occur, either triggered by a timeout or by the heart contraction itself.

For simplicity, we restrict to the operation modes *Idle*, VVT, VVI, and AVI. Of particular interest is the AVI mode, which is described as an *AND* super-state with two parallel sub-states that are entered on demand. Thus, in our example only the ventricular chamber is observed, but a pace signal my be sent either to the ventricular or articular chamber.

Programmer Model. The signals commandedOn! commandedOff! toIdle! toVVI! toVVT! toAVI! are issued by a medical person, called the *programmer* in our context. We do not make assumptions, on how or in which order she issues these signals, but require a time delay of at least DELAY_AFTER_MODESWITCH after each signal. If one of the signals commandedOff! or toIdle! was issued, this is recorded in the binary variable wasSwitchedOff.

Note that we equipped the pacemaker with default exits, thus it can *always* synchronize with these signals.

Composed Model. The complete hierarchical timed automaton model contains in parallel the pacemaker, the programmer, and a model of a heart, that might spontaneously cease beating on its own (not described here).

Table 2. Translations of a hierarchical timed automaton description to an equivalent flat UPPAAL model. For the cardiac pacemaker example, the increases are moderate. Both data formats are described in terms of XML grammars

	HTA model	UPPAAL model
# XML tags	549	1233
# proper control locations	35	45
# pseudo-sates / committed locations	31	62
# transitions	47	174
# variables and constants	33	90
# formal clocks	6	6

5.2 Model-Checking the UPPAAL Model

The automatic translation of the pacemaker model yielded a gentle expansion in size, as recorded in Table 2. The high number of committed location indicates, that most of the additional control structure is purely auxiliary and does not contribute significantly to the state space of the translation.

We used the translation as input to the UPPAAL tool. All run-times were measured on a Sun Enterprise 450 with UltraSPARC-II processors, 300 MHz, It took 0.92 seconds to establish deadlock-freedom. We verified two desirable properties in the obtained hierarchical timed automaton model.

(*i*)   A[] (heart_sub.FLATLINE => (wasSwitchedOff == 1))
(*ii*) A[] (heart_Sub.AfterAContraction =>
            A<> heart_Sub.AfterVContraction)

Property *(i)* is a safety property and establishes, that the heart never stops for too long, unless the pacemaker was switched off by the programmer (in which case we cannot give any guarantees). Property *(ii)* is a response property and states, that after an articular contraction, there will *inevitably* follow a ventricular contraction. In particular, this guarantees that no deadlocks are possible between these control situations.

The latest version of the UPPAAL tool[1] was able to perform the model-checking of both properties successfully in 13.30 respectively 4.11 seconds. The verification of the typically more expensive property *(ii)* was faster, since here we were able to apply a property preserving convex hull over-approximation. This approximation yields false negatives for property *(i)*. We note that using UPPAAL's powerful optimization options, in particular the active clock reduction, reduces also model-checking times drastically.

```
REFRACTORY_TIME   = 50
SENSE_TIMEOUT     = 15

DELAY_AFTER_V = 50
DELAY_AFTER_A =  5

HEART_ALLOWED_STOP_TIME = 135

MODE_SWITCH_DELAY   = 66
```

Fig. 2. Constants that yield property *(i)*

It is worthwhile to mention that validity of property *(i)* is strongly dependent on the parameter setting of the model. We used the constants from Figure 2. If the programmer is allowed to switch between modes very fast, it is possible that she prevents the pacemaker from doing its job. E.g., for `MODE_SWITCH_DELAY = 65` the property *(i)* does not hold any more. In practice it is often a problem to find parameter settings, that entail a safe or correct operation of the system.[2]

6   Conclusion and Further Work

We extract a subset of the behavioral part of UML for the purpose of formal verification. We extend it with real-time constructs, i.e., with real-valued formal clocks, invariants, and timed guards. We use a simple hand-shake synchronizations mechanism to express dependencies among components. For this formalism we give a formal semantics to capture the exact behavior. This makes it possible to translate our hierarchical structure to a flat timed automaton model while preserving properties like timed reachability. We make use of this by applying a mature model-checking algorithm and by this means established time-critical safety and response properties of a pacemaker model.

Our formal extension of statecharts to timed statecharts is about to be finalized in a UML profile in the context of the European AIT-WOODDES project No IST-1999-10069. Here, our proposed method is applied in the verification

---

[1] A release version that supports—among other new features—the possibility to model-check response properties is available since April 2001.

[2] In related work, an extended version of UPPAAL is used to derive parameters yielding property satisfaction automatically, see [10].

part of a design methodology for real-time and embedded systems. Among other tools, the mature UPPAAL model-checking engine is used as a back-end. The runtime data we get from our pacemaker example is encouraging—it suggests that reasonable-sized models are in the reach of algorithmic treatment with formal method tools.

The pacemaker example indicates, that clocks, guards, and invariants are a feasible selection of real-time constructs. Though not necessarily familiar to the designer, these constructs are expressive enough to capture essential real-time behavior and nevertheless stay in a decidable fragment of real-time properties. For every real-time model that can be encoded in our formalism, this opens the way for formal and fully automated algorithmic verification in many interesting cases. This suggests that real-time temporal logics can be included into the UML requirement specification language.

Future Work. Event communication can be coded by hand with the help of channel synchronizations and global variables. The inclusion of events into hierarchical timed automata can be expressed by this way. Extensions of the action language to other data types are planned, and the possibility of safe over-approximation of C++ statements has to be investigated.

Since checking real-time temporal logics is computationally hard under various aspects [2,1], it is desirable to try our technique on larger examples from industrial designs. Currently the formal verification part is possible via a translation to a flattened version of the system. However, there is indication that the hierarchical structure can be exploited. We plan to investigate this further in the context of the UPPAAL tool, see [3].

References

1. Luca Aceto and François Laroussinie. Is your Model Checker on Time? In *Proc. 24th Int. Symp. Math. Found. Comp. Sci. (MFCS'99), Szklarska Poreba, Poland, Sep. 1999*, volume 1672 of *Lecture Notes in Computer Science*, pages 125–136. Springer–Verlag, 1999.
2. Rajeev Alur and Thomas A. Henzinger. Real-time Logics: Complexity and Expressiveness. *Information and Computation*, 1(104):35–77, 1993. preliminary version appeared in Proc. 5th LICS, 1990.
3. Tobias Amnell, Gerd Behrmann, Johan Bengtsson, Pedro R. D'Argenio, Alexandre David, Ansgar Fehnker, Thomas Hune, Bertrand Jeannet, Kim G. Larsen, M. Oliver Möller, Paul Pettersson, Carsten Weise, and Wang Yi. UPPAAL - Now, Next, and Future. In *Proc. of the Summer School on Modelling and Verification of Parallel Processes (MOVEP'2k), Nantes, France, June 19 to 23, 2001*.
4. Alexandre David and M. Oliver Möller. From HUPPAAL to UPPAAL: A Translation from Hierarchical Timed Automata to Flat Timed Automata. Research Series RS-01-11, BRICS, Department of Computer Science, University of Aarhus, March 2001. see http://www.brics.dk/RS/01/11/.
5. Bruce Powel Douglass. *Real-Time UML, Second Edition - Developing Efficient Objects for Embedded Systems*. Addison-Wesley, 1999.
6. David Harel and Eran Gery. Executable Object Modeling with Statecharts. *IEEE Computer*, 7(30):31–42, July 1997.

7. Klaus Havelund, Arne Skou, Kim G. Larsen, and Kristian Lund. Formal Modelling and Analysis of an Audio/Video Protocol: An Industrial Case Study Using UPPAAL. In *Proc. of the 18th IEEE Real-Time Systems Symposium*, pages 2–13. IEEE Computer Society Press, December 1997.

8. Thomas. A. Henzinger, Xavier Nicollin, Joseph Sifakis, and Sergio Yovine. Symbolic Model Checking for Real-Time Systems. *Information and Computation*, 111(2):193–244, 1994.

9. Gerand J. Holzmann. The Model Checker SPIN. *IEEE Transactions on Software Engineering*, 23(5):279–295, May 1997.

10. Thomas S. Hune, Judi Romijn, Mariëlle Stoelinga, and Frits W. Vaandrager. Linear parametric model checking of timed automata. Research Series RS-01-5, BRICS, Department of Computer Science, University of Aarhus, January 2001. 44 pp.

11. Paul Pettersson Kim G. Larsen and Wang Yi. Model-Checking for Real-Time Systems. In *Proc. of the 10th International Conference on Fundamentals of Computation Theory*, volume 965 of *Lecture Notes in Computer Science*, pages 62–88. Springer–Verlag, 1995.

12. Kim G. Larsen, Paul Pettersson, and Wang Yi. UPPAAL in a Nutshell. *Int. Journal on Software Tools for Technology Transfer*, 1(1–2):134–152, October 1997.

13. Johan Lilius and Ivan Porres. Formalising UML State Machines for Model Checking. In *UML'99 - The Unified Modeling Language*, volume 1723 of *Lecture Notes in Computer Science*, pages 430–445. Springer–Verlag, October 1999.

14. Magnus Lindahl, Paul Pettersson, and Wang Yi. Formal Design and Analysis of a Gear Controller. In *Proc. of the 4th International Workshop on Tools and Algorithms for the Construction and Analysis of Systems.*, volume 1384 of *Lecture Notes in Computer Science*, pages 281–297. Springer–Verlag, 1998.

15. Henrik Lönn and Paul Pettersson. Formal Verification of a TDMA Protocol Start-Up Mechanism. In *Proc. of IEEE Pacific Rim International Symposium on Fault-Tolerant Systems*, pages 235–242, 1997.

16. ObjectGeode is a commercial product of Verilog. Documentation and whitepapers are available from
http://www.telelogic.com/ObjectGeode/Geode_Articles.asp.

17. Carsta Petersohn and Luis Urbina. A timed semantics for the STATEMATE implementation of statecharts. In John Fitzgerald, Cliff B. Jones, and Peter Lucas, editors, *FME'97: Industrial Applications and Strengthened Foundations of Formal Methods (Proc. 4th Intl. Symposium of Formal Methods Europe, Graz, Austria, September 1997)*, volume 1313 of *Lecture Notes in Computer Science*, pages 553–572. Springer–Verlag, September 1997. ISBN 3-540-63533-5.

18. Rhapsody is a commercial product of I-Logix. Documentation and whitepapers are available from http://www.ilogix.com/quick_flinks/white_papers/index.cfm.

19. visualState™ is a commercial product of IAR Systems. Detailed information is available from http://www.iar.com.

An Authoring Tool for Informal and Formal Requirements Specifications

Reiner Hähnle, Kristofer Johannisson, and Aarne Ranta

Chalmers University of Technology, Department of Computing Science
S-41296 Gothenburg, Sweden
{reiner,krijo,aarne}@cs.chalmers.se

Abstract. We describe foundations and design principles of a tool that supports authoring of informal and formal software requirements specifications simultaneously and from a single source. The tool is an attempt to bridge the gap between completely informal requirements specifications (as found in practice) and formal ones (as needed in formal methods). The user is supported by an interactive syntax-directed editor, parsers and linearizers. As a formal specification language we realize the Object Constraint Language, a substandard of the UML, on the informal side a fragment of English. The implementation is based on the Grammatical Framework, a generic tool that combines linguistic and logical methods.

1 Introduction

The usage of formal and semi-formal languages for requirements specifications is becoming more widespread. Witness, for example, the Java Modeling Language (JML) [11], closely related to which is the ESC/Java specification language used in Extended Static Checking [12], the constraint language Alloy [9], and the Object Constraint Language (OCL) [15,21]. The OCL is not only used in meta-modeling to supply a precise semantics for UML diagrams, but also in requirements specification. A subset of the OCL is also used in iContract [10], the JAVA variant of design-by-contract, as an assertion language.

Although these languages make an effort to be more "user-friendly" than earlier formal notations that were based on set theory and predicate logic, it still takes a considerable effort to master them and use them effectively. Moreover, it should not be forgotten that the by far most popular language, wherein software specifications are still written today is natural language (NL).

None of the approaches mentioned above offers support for authoring, understanding, and maintaining formal specifications. We consider this deficiency to be a serious obstacle to routine usage and further development of formal and semi-formal methods. Specifically, the following problems have to be addressed, if formal and semi-formal notations are to become a standard item in the software engineer's toolbox:

Authoring. Support is needed for authoring well-written, well-formed formal specifications. A syntax-directed editor is of help along with specification templates.

R.-D. Kutsche and H. Weber (Eds.): FASE 2002, LNCS 2306, pp. 233–248, 2002.

Maintenance. Large and complex expressions in any formal language are not easy to read, even if, like OCL, this language was designed to enhance readability. In realistic scenarios, numerous and complex expressions have to be maintained and, therefore, understood by people who did not necessarily author them or are even familiar with formal languanges.

Mapping Different Levels of Formality. No specification language fits all needs. For different audiences and purposes it is important to have renderings in, say, NL, OCL, and first-order logic. For effective communication parts of these must be mappable into each other efficiently and with a clear semantics.

Synchronisation. If a system is specified in languages of differing level of precision, it is important to propagate changes consistently. For example, any change in an OCL constraint should be instantly reflected in the corresponding NL description. It will not do to perform these changes manually.

In this paper we suggest a solution to the problems just outlined. We show that a systematic connection between specification languages on differing levels of precision is possible. We concentrate on OCL and NL as specification languages, but the method is not limited to this configuration.

Our approach is based on the Grammatical Framework (GF) [18], a flexible mechanism that allows to combine linguistic and logical methods. The key idea is to specify (i) an abstract syntax for a specification language (in our case roughly corresponding to OCL) together with semantic conditions of well-formedness and type-correctness, and (ii) concrete syntaxes for all supported notations (in our case, concrete OCL expressions as well as a fragment of English). For each set of abstract/concrete syntaxes the GF system then implements algorithms for parsing, linearization, translation, type checking, and a graphical syntax editor. The abstract grammar is much richer than the usual context-free OCL grammar [15] and, together with the syntax editor, enables interactive editing of templates for frequently needed specifications. The result is an authoring system for requirements specifications that supports creation and maintenance of informal and formal specifications from a single source.

In Section 2 we walk through an example that serves as motivation and at the same time demonstrates what can be done with our system. In Section 3 we give some background on the GF formalism that is necessary to understand Section 4, where the implementation is discussed in detail. In Section 5 we evaluate our approach and we show how the problems outlined above are addressed in our system. The paper is rounded off with brief sections on related work, on future work, and by concluding remarks.

The latest prototype of our system can be downloaded from
`http://www.cs.chalmers.se/~krijo/GF/specifications.html`.

2   Motivating Example

As a motivating example we will consider a standard queue data structure—a class `Queue`—and show how to use our system for developing specifications of this class in OCL and natural language.

2.1 A Class for Queues

For the purpose of this example, we need to specify the interface of a class `Queue` for
integer queues (we need not
consider implementation details). We use standard OCL
types in doing this (see figure
on left). This class should be straightforward. We have an operation `enqueue` for
enqueueing an integer on the queue and an operation `dequeue` for removing the
first integer of the queue. The return value of `enqueue` is simply the value of its
argument. We also have an operation `getFirst` for inspecting the first element
of the queue. The operation `asSequence` gives us a `Sequence` (standard OCL
type) with all the elements from the queue, in their correct order. This operation
is included for specification purposes; in an actual implementation of the class,
`asSequence` is not required.

Queue
`enqueue(i: Integer): Integer`
`dequeue(): Integer`
`getFirst(): Integer {query}`
`size(): Integer {query}`
`asSequence(): Sequence(Integer) {query}`

Note also that all operations which do not affect the state of the queue ("observer methods" or "queries") have been tagged with `{query}`, using standard
UML notation.

2.2 Using the GF-Based System

Our system is based on the GF system (described in Section 3) with grammars
for OCL and English (Section 4). It features an interactive editor for formulating
constraints in OCL and English:

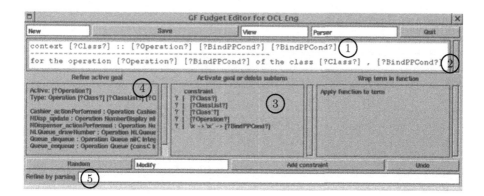

Fig. 1. The Interactive Editor

Suppose that we want to author a postcondition for the method `enqueue` of
the class `Queue` in the interactive editor. Figure 1 shows what the editor looks
like after a few initial steps.

In this screen-shot we see the beginning of a postcondition for an operation. The main part of the window shows the postcondition in OCL ① and in English ②, and also an abstract (internal to GF) representation ③. To complete this postcondition, we select a subgoal (that is, metavariable or placeholder) of the form [?...?] and then select one of the possible refinements in the lower left subwindow ④, until there are no more subgoals to fill in. In the example, the next logical step is to specify the operation for which the current postcondition is intended, that is, enqueue. So we select the subgoal [?Operation?] and the refinement enqueue. Figure 2 shows the result.

Now a new subgoal [?BindPPCond?] is active, and new refinements appear in the lower left menu. The subgoal [?Class?] was automatically filled in with Queue, since this was the only correct refinement left after we chose the operation enqueue. The system is able to infer this automatically.

Note that we edit the postcondition in OCL and in English in parallel. Every change is instantly reflected in both the OCL and the English version. What is actually going on is that we are editing the abstract representation, which is linearized to English and OCL. This means that the user of the editor can produce OCL constraints, even though he or she only understands the English form of the constraint.

There are also other ways to interact with the editor. Aside from choosing refinements from a menu to fill in a subgoal, we can simply enter a string (at ⑤ in Figure 1) in English or OCL which will be parsed by the GF editor. We can also wrap a term in a function, that is, perform bottom-up editing instead of top-down.

As will be seen in Section 3, the interactive editor is merely one part of GF: having grammars for OCL and English means that we also have a parser for OCL and for a fragment of English as well as a translator between OCL and this fragment of English.

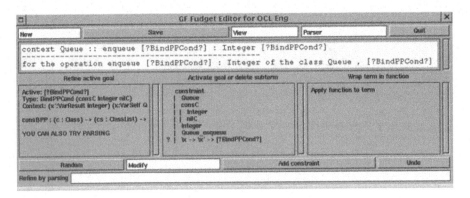

Fig. 2. The Interactive Editor—one editing step later

2.3   More Examples

We present some more constraints for methods in the **Queue** class authored with our system and highlight some of the problems that had to be solved in order to obtain a smooth rendering in English. In the OCL versions of the constraints only line breaks and spaces were inserted by hand (this is a current limitation). The formatting of the English version of the constraints was achieved by including LATEX commands in the English grammar.

Operation getFirst

OCL: `context Queue::getFirst() : Integer`
`      pre:  self.size() > 0`
`      post: result = self.asSequence()->first`
English: for the operation getFirst() : Integer of the class Queue, the following precondition should hold:
        the size of the queue is greater than zero
    and the following postcondition should hold:
        the result is equal to the first element of the queue

The meaning of the OCL constraint **self** depends on the context. In these examples, **self** refers to an instance of **Queue**, since we are formulating constraints for an operation of the class **Queue**. In English, **self** corresponds to an anaphoric expression, which in this particular case is "the queue".

The operation **asSequence** can be seen as a way of converting a **Queue** to an OCL **Sequence**. While this type cast is necessary in OCL, it is not that interesting in English. It is therefore omitted, so the OCL expression `self.asSequence()` simply corresponds to "the queue" in English.

Operation dequeue

OCL: `context Queue::dequeue() : Integer`
`      pre: self.size() > 0`
`      post: (self.size() > 0 implies self.asSequence() =`
`          self.asSequence@pre() -> subSequence(2, self.size() + 1))`
`      and result = self.getFirst@pre()`
English: for the operation dequeue() : Integer of the class Queue, the following precondition should hold:
        the size of the queue is greater than zero
    and the following postconditions should hold:
        – if the size of the queue is greater than zero, then the queue is equal to the subsequence of the queue at the start of the operation which starts at index 2 and ends at the index equal to the size of the queue plus one
        – the result is equal to the first element of the queue at the start of the operation

Here we see that a sequence of conjuncts in OCL (such as **x and y and ...**) can be displayed as an itemized list in English. This implies that we need to have the word "postconditions" in plural form (in contrast to the **getFirst** example, where we have "postcondition"). We can also note that @pre in OCL simply corresponds to "at the start of the operation" in English.

The OCL operation subSequence requires its second argument to be greater than or equal to its first argument – it never returns an empty sequence. This explains why we use the condition that the size of the queue is greater than zero in the first postcondition.

3   Grammatical Framework

The Grammatical Framework (GF) is a framework for defining grammars and working with them [18]. It is used for defining special-purpose grammars on top of a semantic model, which is expressed in type theory [13]. Type theory is a part of GF, the abstract syntax part. The concrete syntax part tells how type-theoretical formulas are translated into a natural language or a formal notation.

The first application of GF was in a project on Multilingual Document Authoring at Xerox Research Centre Europe [4]. The idea in multilingual authoring is to build an editor whose user can write a document in a language she does not know (for example, French), while at the same time seeing how it develops in a language she knows (for example, English). From the system's point of view, the object constructed by the user is a type-theoretical formula, of which the French and English texts are just alternative views.

The GF programming language, as well as the tools supporting multilingual authoring, are designed to be generic over both the subject matter and the target language. While prototypes have been built for documents such as tourist information and business letters, the most substantial application so far has been natural-language rendering of formalized proofs [5]. Software specifications are another natural GF application, since it is usually clear how specifications are expressed in type theory. Most uses of type theory as a specification language have been based on the Curry-Howard isomorphism, but we will here use it for OCL specifications.

3.1   Abstract Syntax

GF, like other logical frameworks in the LF [6] tradition, uses a higher-order type theory with dependent types. In this type theory, it is possible to define logical calculi, as well as mathematical theories, simply by type signatures. The type-theoretical part of a GF grammar is called the abstract syntax of a language.

To take an example, we first define the types of propositions and proofs, where the type of proofs depends on proposition.

```
cat Prop ; Proof Prop ;
```

We then define implication as a two-place function on propositions, and the implication introduction rule is a function whose argument is a function from proofs of the antecedent to proofs of the succedent:

```
fun Imp  : Prop -> Prop -> Prop ;
fun ImpI : (A,B:Prop) -> (Proof A -> Proof B) -> Proof (Imp A B)
```

As usual in functional languages, GF expresses function application by juxtaposition, as in `Proof A`, and uses parentheses only for grouping purposes.

3.2   Concrete Syntax

On top of an abstract syntax, a concrete syntax can be built, as a set of linearization rules that translate type-theoretical terms into strings of some language. For instance, English linearization rules for the two functions above could be

```
lin Imp A B = {s = "if" ++ A.s ++ "then" ++ B.s} ;
lin ImpI A B c = {s = "assume" ++ A.s ++ "." ++ c.s ++ "." ++
                      "Hence" ++ "if" ++ A.s ++ "then" ++ B.s} ;
```

As shown by these examples, linearization is not just a string, but a record of concrete-syntax objects, such as strings and parameters (genders, modes, etc.), and parameter-dependent strings. Notice that linearization rules can generate not only sentences and their parts, but also texts. For instance, a proof of the implication $A\&B \to A$ as generated by the rules above, together with a rule for conjunction elimination, is a term that linearizes to the text:

> Assume A and B. By the assumption, A and B. *A fortiori*, A. Hence if A and B then A.

Different languages generally have different types of concrete-syntax objects. For instance, in French a proposition depends on the parameter of mode, which we express by introducing a parameter type of modes and defining the linearization type of `Prop` accordingly:

```
param  Mode = Ind | Subj ;
lincat Prop = {s : Mode => Str} ;
```

The French linearization rule for the implication is

```
lin Imp A B =
     {s = table {m => si (A.s ! ind) ++ "alors" ++ B.s ! m}} ;
```

which tells that the antecedent is always in the indicative mode and that the main mode of the sentence is received by the succedent. One may also notice that *si* is not a constant string, but depends (in a way defined elsewhere in the grammar) on the word following it (as in *s'il vous plaît*).

   Finally, in formal logical notation, linearization depends on a precedence parameter:

```
lincat Prop = {s : Prec => Str} ;
lin Imp A B = {s = mkPrec p0 (A.s ! p1 ++ "->" ++ A.s ! p0)} ;
```

where the function `mkPrec` (defined elsewhere in the concrete syntax) controls the usage of parentheses around formulas.

The examples above illustrate what is needed to achieve genericity in GF. In the abstract syntax, we need a powerful type theory in order to express dependencies among parts of texts, such as in inference rules. In the concrete syntax, we need to define language-dependent parameter systems and complex structures of grammatical objects using them.

3.3 Functionalities

GF helps the programmer of grammar applications by providing framework-level functionalities that apply to any GF grammar. The main functionalities are **linearization** (translation from abstract to concrete syntax), **parsing** (translation from concrete to abstract syntax), **type-checking** of abstract-syntax objects, **syntax editing**, and **user interfaces** (both line-based and graphical). Although these functionalities apply generically to all grammars, it is often useful to customize them for the task at hand. For this end, the GF source code (written in Haskell) provides an API for easy access to the main functionalities.

4   Implementation

4.1 Classes and Objects

In this section we give a general idea of how we have implemented GF grammars for OCL and natural language (at present English). We begin by defining categories and functions for handling standard object-oriented concepts such as classes, objects, attributes and operations:

```
cat Class;
cat Instance (c : Class);
```

There is a category (type) `Class` of classes, and a dependent type `Instance`, hence, for every class `c` there is a type `Instance c` of the instances of this class. OCL expressions are represented as instances of classes (and we can of course see an instance of a class as an object).

Classes are introduced by judgements like the following:

```
fun Bool : Class; Integer : Class; Real : Class;
```

This means that we have type checking in the abstract grammar: for example, where a term of type `Instance Bool` is expected, we cannot use a term of type `Instance Integer`.

The linearizations of these functions to OCL is easy: for `Integer` we simply take `lin Integer = {s = "Integer"}`, and so on. In English, a class can be linearized either as a noun (which can be in singular or plural form, say, "integer" or "integers") or as an identifier of a class ("Integer"). In GF we handle this by using parameters, as explained in Section 3.

Subtyping (inheritance) between classes is handled by defining a subtype relation and a coercion function:

```
cat Subtype (sub, super : Class);
fun coerce : (sub,super:Class) -> Subtype sub super ->
    Instance sub -> Instance super;
```

The function `coerce` is used for converting an instance of a class c into an instance of any superclass of c. The arguments to this function are the classes in question, a proof that the subtyping relation holds between the classes, and finally an instance of the subclass. The result is an instance of the superclass. For every pair of classes in OCL's subtyping relation we introduce a term (a proof) of the type `Subtype`, e.g.:

```
fun intConformsToReal : Subtype Integer Real;
```

The linearization of `coerce` is interesting: since the whole point is to change the type (but not the meaning) of a term, the linearization rule will leave everything as it is. For both OCL and English we have:

```
lin coerce _ _ _ obj = obj;
```

GF converts to context free grammars to realize parsing, and this makes this rule circular (it has the form `Instance -> Instance`). This means that we cannot use our grammars to parse OCL or English with the GF system as it is now. We will have to implement custom modifications for coercion rules.

4.2 Attributes, Operations, and Queries

For operations and attributes we have three categories:

```
cat Attribute (c,a : Class);
    Operation (c:Class) (args:ClassList) (returns:Class);
    OperationQ (c:Class) (args:ClassList) (returns:Class);
```

Attributes are simple enough: the two arguments to `Attribute` give the class to which the attribute belongs, and the type (class) of the attribute itself, respectively. For operations, we need to know if they have side-effects, i.e. whether they are marked with `{query}` in the underlying UML model or not. This explains why there are two categories for operations. The first argument of these categories is, again, the class to which they belong. The second argument is a (possibly empty) list of the types of the arguments to the operation, the third argument is the return type (possibly void) of the operation. The use of lists makes these categories general (they can handle operations with any number of arguments), but this generality also makes the grammar a bit more complex at places.

Here is how we use an UML attribute or query method (a term of type `OperationQ`) within an OCL expression:

```
fun valueOf : (c, result:Class) -> (Instance c) ->
    Attribute c result -> Instance result;
  query : (c:Class) -> (args:ClassList) -> (ret:Class) ->
    Instance c -> OperationQ c args ret  -> InstList args ->
    Instance ret;
```

The arguments to `query` are, in turn: the class of the object we want to query, a list of the classes of the arguments to the query, the return type of the query, the object we want to query, the query itself, and finally a list of the arguments of the query. The result is an instance (an object) of the return type.

The linearization to OCL is fairly simple:

```
lin query _ _ ret obj op argsI =
    dot1 obj (mkConstI (op.s ++ argsI.s ! brackets));
```

What happens here is that the list of arguments is linearized as a comma-separated list enclosed in parentheses (`argsI.s ! brackets`), then we put the name of the query (`op.s`) in front, and finally add the object we query and a dot (`dot1` ensures correct handling of precedence), so we end up with something like `obj.query(arg1, arg2, ...)`.

For the English linearization, we have the problem of having one category for all queries, regardless of the number of arguments they depend on. Our solution is to give a custom "natural" linearization of queries having up to three arguments (this applies to all query operations in `Queue`). For instance, the linearization of the query `getFirst` produces "the first element of the queue". For `asSequence` we take, as could be observed in Section 2, simply "the queue". The implementation is based on the following:

```
param Prep = To | At | Of | NoPrep;
lincat OperationQ = {s : QueryForm => Str;
        preps : {pr1 : Prep; pr2 : Prep; pr3 : Prep}};
```

The idea is that the linearization of a query includes up to three prepositions which can be put between the first three arguments. If there are more than three arguments, these prepositions are ignored and we choose a more formal notation like "query(arg1, arg2, ...) of the queue".

4.3   Constraints

For handling OCL constraints (invariants, pre- and postconditions) we introduce a category `Constraint` and various ways of constructing terms of this type. The simplest form of constraint is an invariant for a class:

```
cat Constraint;
fun invariant : (c:Class) -> (VarSelf c -> Instance Bool) ->
    Constraint;
```

To construct an invariant we supply the class for which the invariant should hold: the first argument of **invariant**. We require a boolean expression (a term of type **Instance Bool**) which represents the actual invariant property. An additional complication is that we want to be able to refer to (the current instance of) the class c in this boolean expression—in terms of OCL this means to use the variable **self**. This accounts for the type of the second argument, **VarSelf c -> Instance Bool**, which can be thought of as a term of type **Instance Bool** where we have access to a bound variable of type **VarSelf c**. This bound variable can only be used for one purpose: to form an expression **self** of the correct type:

```
fun self : (c:Class) -> VarSelf c -> Instance c;
```

The linearization of **invariant** is simple, and we show the linearizations for both OCL and English:

```
lin invariant c e = {s = "context"++c.s++"inv:"++e.s};
lin invariant c e = {s = ["the following invariant holds
    for all"] ++ (c.s ! cn pl) ++ ":" ++ e.s} ;
```

Notice the choice of the plural form of a class: c.s ! cn pl produces, for example, "queues", for **Queue**.

For formulating pre- and postconditions of an operation, we use the same technique employing bound variables. In this case one bound variable for each argument of the operation is required, besides the ones for **self** and **result**.

4.4   The OCL Library and User Defined Classes

The grammar has to include all standard types (and their properties) of OCL. Just as an example, we show the **Sequence** type and some of its properties:

```
fun Sequence : Class -> Class;
    subSequence : (c:Class) -> Instance (Sequence c) ->
      (a,b : Instance Integer) -> Instance (Sequence c);
    seqConforms2coll : (c:Class) ->
      Subtype (Sequence c) (Collection c);
```

The operations of **Sequence** (or any standard OCL type) are not terms of type **OperationQ**, they are simply modelled as functions in GF. This is very convenient, but it also means that the grammar does not allow to express constraints for the standard OCL operations. User defined operations, however, must permit constraints, so they are defined using **Operation** and **OperationQ**. Here are some operations of the class **Queue** from Section 2:

```
fun Queue : Class;
    Queue_size : OperationQ Queue nilC Integer;
    Queue_enqueue : Operation Queue (consC Integer nilC) Integer;
```

Note the use of the constructors **nilC** and **consC** to build lists of the types of the arguments to the operations.

5   Evaluation

5.1   Advantages

Our approach to building an authoring tool has a number of advantages for the development of requirements specifications:

Single Source Technology. Each element of a specification is kept only in one version: the annotated syntax tree of the abstract grammar. Concrete expressions are generated from this on demand. In addition, edits made in one concrete representation, are reflected instantly in all others. This provides a solution to the maintenance and synchronization problems discussed in Section 1. The following two items address the mapping problem:

Semantics. The rules of abstract and concrete GF grammars can be seen as a formal semantics for the languages they implement: for each pair of concrete languages, they induce a function that gives to each expression its "meaning" in the other language. Working with the syntax directed editor, which displays abstract and concrete expressions simultaneously, makes it easy for users to develop an intuition for expressing requirements in different specification languages.

Extensibility. GF grammars constitute a declarative and fairly modular formalism to describe languages and the relationships among them. This makes it relatively easy to adapt and extend our implementation.

These positive features rest mainly on the design principles of GF. From an implementor's point of view, the GF base provides a number of additional advantages. The fact that GF is designed as a *framework* is crucial:

Tools. GF provides a number of functionalities for each set of abstract and concrete grammars as detailed in Section 3.3 and an interactive syntax directed editor coming with a GUI. In particular, we have a parser for full OCL incorporating extensive semantic checks.

Development Style. The declarative way, in which knowledge about specific grammars is stored in GF, permits a modern, incremental style of development: rapid design-implementation-test cycles, addition of new features on demand, and availability of a working prototype almost from the start, are a big asset.

5.2   Limitations

GF gives a number of functionalities for free, so that applications can be built simply by writing GF grammars. The result, however, is not always what one would expect from a production-quality system. Software built with GF is more like a prototype that needs to be optimized (more accurately: the grammars can be retained, but the framework-level algorithms must be extended). In the case of specification authoring, we encountered the following limitations:

Parsing. The generic GF parsers are not optimized for parsing formal languages like OCL, for which more efficient algorithms exist. More seriously, the parser has to be customized to avoid the circularity problem due to instance coercions (Section 4.1).

Compositionality. Texts generated by GF have necessarily the same structure as the corresponding code. One would like to have methods to rephrase and summarize specifications.

The Need for Grammars. All new, user-defined concepts (classes and their features) have to be defined in a GF grammar. It would be better to have the possibility to create grammars dynamically from UML class diagrams given in some suitable format (for example, in the UML standard exchange format XMI [20]); this can be done in the same way as GF rules are generated from Alfa declarations [5].

A general limitation, which is a problem for *any* natural-language interface, is:

Closedness. Only those expressions that are defined in the grammar are recognized by the parser.

This means a gap persists between formal specifications and informal legacy specifications. One could imagine heuristic natural language processing methods to rescue some of this material, but GF does not have such methods at present.

Finally, an obstacle to the applicability of syntax-directed editors for programming languages, for which special techniques are required [19], is the phenomenon that top-down development as enforced by stepwise refinement is usually incompatible with the direction of the control flow. The latter, however, is more natural from an implementor's point of view. This problem does not arise in the context of specifications due to their declarative nature.

6   Related Work

We know of no natural-language interfaces to OCL, but there are some earlier efforts for specifications more generally: Holt and Klein [7] have a system for translating English hardware specifications to the temporal logic CTL; Coscoy, Kahn and Théry [3] have a translator from Coq code (which can express programs, specifications, and proofs) into English and French. Both of these systems function in batch mode, and they are unidirectional, whereas GF is interactive and bidirectional. Power and Scott [16] have an interactive editor for multilingual software manuals, which functions much like GF (by linearizations from an underlying abstract representation), but does not have a parser. In all these systems, the grammar is coded directly in the program, whereas GF has a separate grammar formalism. The mentioned systems are fine-tuned for the purposes that they are used for, and hence produce or recognize more elegant and idiomatic language. But they cannot be dynamically extended by new forms of expression. An idea from [3] that would fit nicely to GF is optimization by factorization: For example, *x is even or odd* is an optimization of *x is even or x is odd*.

The context free grammar of OCL 1.4 [15] is a concrete grammar, which is not suitable as a basis for an abstract grammar for both OCL and English. Furthermore, it provides no notion of type correctness. A proposal for OCL 2.0 [14] addresses these problems: both an abstract and a concrete grammar are included, as well as a mechanism for type correctness. However, these grammars are partly specified by metamodelling, in the sense that UML and OCL themselves are used in the formal description of syntax and semantics. It is, therefore, not obvious how to construct a GF grammar directly based on the OCL 2.0 proposal.

A general architecture for UML/OCL toolsets including a parser and type checker is suggested in [8], but informal specifications are not discussed there.

7 Future Work

Besides overcoming the limitations expressed in Section 5.2, we will concentrate on the following issues:

Integration. For our authoring tool to be practically useful, it must be tightly integrated with mainstream software development tools. In the KeY project [1] a design methodology plus CASE-tool is developed that allows seamless integration of object-oriented modeling (OOM) with program development, generation of formal specifications, as well as formal verification of code and specifications. The KeY development system is based on a commercial UML-CASE tool for OOM. Following, for example, [8] we will integrate our tool into KeY and, hence, into the CASE tool underlying KeY. Users of the CASE tool will be able to use our authoring tool regardless of whether they want to do formal reasoning.

Stylistic Improvements. To improve the style of texts, we plan to use techniques like factorization [3] and pronominalization [17], which can be justified by type-checked definitions inside GF grammars. To some extent, such improvements can be even automatized. However, one should not underestimate the difficulty of this problem: it is essentially the same problem as taking a piece of low-level code and restructuring it into high-level code.

More and Larger Case Studies. We started to author a combined natural language/OCL requirements specification of the API of the Java Collections Framework based on textual specifications found there.

Further Languages. It is well-known how to develop concrete grammars for other natural languages than English. Support for further formal specification langages besides OCL might require changes in the abstract grammar or could even imply to shift information from the abstract to the concrete grammars. It will be interesting to see how one can accomodate languages such as Alloy or JML.

Improve Usability. The usability of the current tool can be improved in various ways: the first are obvious improvements of the GUI such as context sensitive pop-up menus, powerful pretty-printing, active expression highlighting, context-sensitive help, etc. A conceptually more sophisticated idea is to enrich the abstract grammar with rules that provide further templates for frequently required kinds of constraints. For example, a non-terminal `memberDeleted` could guide the user in writing a proper postcondition specifying that a member was deleted from a collection object. This amounts to encoding *pragmatics* into the grammar.

Increase Portability. The GUI of GF's syntax editor is written with the Haskell Fudgets library [2]. We plan to port it to JAVA. This is compatible with the KeY system, which is written entirely in JAVA.

8 Conclusion

We described theoretical foundations, design principles, and implementation of a tool that supports authoring of informal and formal software requirements specifications. Our research is motivated by the gap between completely informal specifications and formal ones, while usage of the latter is becoming more widespread. Our tool supports development of formal specifications in OCL: it features (i) a syntax-directed editor with (ii) templates for frequently needed elements of specifications and (iii) a single source for formal/informal documents; in addition, (iv) parsers, (v) linearizers for OCL and a fragment of English, and (vi) a translator between them are obtained.

The implementation is based on a logico-linguistic framework anchored in type theory. This yields a formal semantics, separation of concrete and abstract syntax, separation of declarative knowledge and algorithms. It makes the system easy to extend and to modify.

In summary, we think that our approach is a good basis to meet the challenges in creating formal specifications outlined in the introduction.

Acknowledgements

We would like to thank Wojciech Mostowski and Bengt Nordström for the careful reading of a draft of this paper, for pointing out inaccuracies, and for suggestions to improve the paper.

References

1. W. Ahrendt, T. Baar, B. Beckert, M. Giese, E. Habermalz, R. Hähnle, W. Menzel, and P. H. Schmitt. The KeY approach: Integrating object oriented design and formal verification. In M. Ojeda-Aciego, I. P. de Guzmán, G. Brewka, and L. M. Pereira, editors, *Proc. JELIA*, LNAI 1919, pages 21–36. Springer, 2000.
2. M. Carlsson and T. Hallgren. *Fudgets—Purely Functional Processes with applications to Graphical User Interfaces*. PhD thesis, Department of Computing Science, Chalmers University of Technology, 1998.
3. Y. Coscoy, G. Kahn, and L. Thery. Extracting text from proofs. In M. Dezani-Ciancaglini and G. Plotkin, editors, *Proc. Second Int. Conf. on Typed Lambda Calculi and Applications*, volume 902 of *LNCS*, pages 109–123, 1995.
4. M. Dymetman, V. Lux, and A. Ranta. XML and multilingual document authoring: Convergent trends. In *COLING, Saarbrücken, Germany*, pages 243–249, 2000.
5. T. Hallgren and A. Ranta. An extensible proof text editor. In M. Parigot and A. Voronkov, editors, *Logic for Programming and Automated Reasoning, LPAR*, LNAI 1955, pages 70–84. Springer, 2000.
6. R. Harper, F. Honsell, and G. Plotkin. A framework for defining logics. *JACM*, 40(1):143–184, 1993.
7. A. Holt and E. Klein. A semantically-derived subset of English for hardware verification. In *Proc. Ann. Meeting Ass. for Comp. Ling.*, pages 451–456, 1999.
8. H. Hussmann, B. Demuth, and F. Finger. Modular architecture for a toolset supporting OCL. In A. Evans, S. Kent, and B. Selic, editors, *Proc. 3rd Int. Conf. on the Unified Modeling Language*, LNCS 1939, pages 278–293. Springer, 2000.

9. D. Jackson. Alloy: A lightweight object modelling notation.
   `htpp://sdg.lcs.mit.edu/~dnj/pubs/alloy-journal.pdf`, July 2000.
10. R. Kramer. iContract—the Java Designs by Contract tool. In *Proc. Technology of OO Languages and Systems, TOOLS 26*. IEEE CS Press, Los Alamitos, 1998.
11. G. T. Leavens, A. L. Baker, and C. Ruby. Preliminary design of JML: A behavioral interface specification language for Java. Technical Report 98-06i, Iowa State Univ., Dept. of Computer Science, Feb. 2000.
12. K. R. M. Leino, G. Nelson, and J. B. Saxe. ESC/Java user's manual. Technical Note #2000-002, Compaq Systems Research Center, Palo Alto, USA, May 2000.
13. B. Nordström, K. Petersson, and J. M. Smith. Martin-löf's type theory. In S. Abramasky, D. Gabbay, and T. Maibaum, editors, *Handbook of Logic in Computer Science*, volume 5. Oxford University Press, 2000.
14. Object Modeling Group. *Response to the UML 2.0 OCL RfP*, Aug. 2001. `htpp://cgi.omg.org/cgi-bin/doc?ad/01-08-01`.
15. Object Modeling Group. *Unified Modelling Language Specification, version 1.4*, Sept. 2001. `htpp://www.omg.org/cgi-bin/doc?formal/01-09-67`.
16. R. Power and D. Scott. Multilingual authoring using feedback texts. In *COLING-ACL 98*, Montreal, Canada, 1998.
17. A. Ranta. *Type Theoretical Grammar*. Oxford University Press, 1994.
18. A. Ranta. Grammatical framework homepage, 2000. `htpp://www.cs.chalmers.se/~aarne/GF/index.html`.
19. T. Teitelbaum and T. Reps. The Cornell program synthesizer: A syntax-directed programming environment. *CACM*, 24(9):563–573, 1981.
20. Unisys Corp. et al. *XML Metadata Interchange (XMI)*, Oct. 1998. `ftp://ftp.omg.org/pub/docs/ad/98-10-05.pdf`.
21. J. Warmer and A. Kleppe. *The Object Constraint Language: Precise Modelling with UML*. Addison-Wesley, 1999.

Introducing Context-Based Constraints

Felix Bübl

Technische Universität Berlin, Germany
Computergestützte InformationsSysteme (CIS)
fbuebl@cs.tu-berlin.de
http://www.CoCons.org

Abstract Software evolution is a major challenge to software development. When adapting a system model to new, altered or deleted requirements, existing requirements should not unintentionally be violated. One requirement can affect several possibly unassociated elements of a system. A new constraint technique is introduced in this paper: One *context-based constraint* (CoCon) specifies a requirement for those system (model) elements that belong to the related context. The constrained elements are indirectly selected via their meta-information. Thus, verifying compliance with requirements can be supported automatically when a system's model is modified, during (re-)configuration and at runtime.

1 Introduction: Continuous Engineering

1.1 Continuous Engineering Requires 'Design for Change'

The context for which a software system was designed changes continuously throughout its lifetime. **Continuous software engineering** (CSE) is a paradigm discussed in [18] for keeping track of the ongoing changes and to adapt legacy systems to altered requirements as addressed in the KONTENG[1] project. The system must be prepared for adding, removing or changing requirements. The examples in this paper concentrate on component-based software systems because this rearrangeable software architecture is best suited for CSE.

New methods and techniques are required to ensure consistent modification steps in order to safely transform the system from one state of evolution to the next without unintentional violating existing dependencies or invariants. This paper focuses on recording requirements via constraints in order to protect them from unwanted modifications. However, an enhanced notion of 'constraint', introduced in section 3, is needed for this approach.

1.2 Focus: Requirements Specification in System Models

This paper proposes to express important requirements via a new specification technique that facilitates their consideration in different levels of the software

---

[1] This work was supported by the German Federal Ministry of Education and Research as part of the research project KONTENG (Kontinuierliches Engineering für evolutionäre IuK-Infrastrukturen) under grant 01 IS 901 C.

R.-D. Kutsche and H. Weber (Eds.): FASE 2002, LNCS 2306, pp. 249–263, 2002.

development process: some requirements should be reflected in models, some during coding, some during deployment and some at runtime. This paper focuses on specifying requirements in models. Thus, this paper discusses how to write down which *model elements* are affected by a requirement. Obviously, there are no *model* elements during configuration or at runtime. When applying the new approach discussed here during configuration or at runtime, please read model element as *system element during configuration* or *system element at runtime* throughout the paper.

1.3   The New Concept in Brief

The basic idea introduced in this paper can be explained in just a few sentences.

1. Yellow sticky notes are stuck onto the model elements. They are called 'context properties'because they describe the context of their model element.
2. A new constraint mechanism refers to this meta-information for identifying the part of the system where the constraint applies. Only those model elements whose meta-information fits the constraint's 'context condition' must fulfill the constraint. Up to now, no constraint technique exists that selects the constrained elements according to their meta-information.
3. Via the new constraint technique a requirement for a group of model elements that share a context can be protected automatically in system modifications.

This article is an overview on the new constraint technique – much more details are provided in the corresponding technical report ([2]).

2   Introducing Context Properties

This section explains the concept of 'context' used here.

2.1   Describing Indirect Dependencies via Context Properties

A **context property** has a name and a set of values. A formal definition is given in [2]. If its values are assigned to an element, they describe how or where this element is used – they show the context of this element. The name of the context property stays the same when assigning its values to several elements, while its values might vary for each element. For example, the values of the context property 'Workflow' reflect in which workflows the associated element is used, as discussed in section 2.2. A graphical representation is indicated in figure 1. The context property symbol resembles the UML symbol for comments because both describe the model element they are attached to. The context property symbol is assigned to one model element and contains the name and values of one context property specified for this model element. However, it is also possible to use one context property symbol for each context property that is assigned to the same model element. The primary benefit of enriching model elements with context properties is revealed in section 3, where such properties are used to specify requirements.

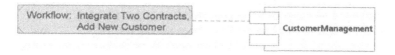

Figure 1. The Context Property Symbol

2.2   General Context Properties

Only three context properties are presented here. The proposed context properties may be ignored and others might be used by the developer as needed in the application domain.

'Workflow' reflects the most frequent workflows and enables the designer to write down requirement specifications for them. If preferred, the term 'Business Process' or 'Use Case' may be used instead of 'Workflow'. For example, a requirement in a system could state that *"all classes needed by the workflow 'Integrate Two Contracts' must be unreadable by the 'Web Server' component"*. This requirement can be written down by identifying all of the classes involved accordingly. This paper suggests taking only the names of the workflows used most often into account for requirement specification. Hiding avoidable granularity by only considering *static aspects of behavior* (= nothing but workflow names) enables developers to ignore details. Otherwise, the complexity would get out of hand. The goal of this paper is to keep the requirement specifications as straightforward as possible.

'Personal Data' signals whether a model element handles data of private nature. Thus, privacy policies, like, *"all components handling Personal Data must be unreadable by the components belonging to the workflow 'Calculate Financial Report' "* can be specified.

'Operational Area' allows for the specification of requirements for certain departments or domains in general, like *"all components handling personal data must be unreadable by all components belonging to the operational area 'Controlling'"*. It provides an organizational perspective.

2.3   Belongs-To Relations

Elements can belong to each other. If, for instance, the model element e is a package, then all the model elements inside this package belong to e. In this case, a context property value assigned to e is automatically assigned to all elements belonging to e. A Belongs-To relation is a directed, transitive relation between elements. One set of values can be assigned to a single element e for each context property cp . This set is called $ConPropVals^{cp,e}$. The Belongs-To relation of the element e_{owner} of the 'Owner'-type to other elements $e_{i,...,j}$ of the 'Part'-type is represented via '**Part** $\xrightarrow{BeTo}$ **Owner**'. A Belongs-To relation has the following impact: $\forall i \leq n \leq j : ConPropVals^{cp,e_{owner}} \subseteq ConPropVals^{cp,e_n}$ — all values of cp assigned to e_{owner} are also assigned to $e_{i,...,j}$.

The values $ConPropVals^{cp,e_{owner}}$ are 'associated with' e_{owner}, and 'assigned to' e_{owner} and all $e_{i,...,j}$ due to the Belongs-To relation. The term 'associated with' is only used for the root element e_{owner}. When implementing a context-property-aware tool, like a modeling tool, only the *associated* values must be made persistent because the derived values can be derived from the associated values as needed.

Some Belongs-To relations are *implicit*. An implicit Belongs-To Relation $e_1 \overset{BeTo}{\longrightarrow} e_2$ exists between the elements e_1 and e_2, if e_1 is part of e_2. For example, all model elements *inside* a package implicitly belong to this package. No model element inside this package does not belong to this package. The fact that e_1 is part of e_2 usually is specified either as composition or aggregation in UML. According to the modeling approach used, other implicit Belongs-To relations can exist. On the contrary, some Belongs-To relations are *explicit*. They must be manually defined, as discussed in [2].

Belongs-To relations create a hierarchy of context property values because they are transitive: if $a \overset{BeTo}{\longrightarrow} b \overset{BeTo}{\longrightarrow} c$ then $a \overset{BeTo}{\longrightarrow} c$. Thus, a context property value associated with c automatically is assigned to b and a. This Belongs-To hierarchy provides a useful structure. It enables the designer to associate a context property value with the element that is as high as possible in the Belongs-To hierarchy. It must be associated only once and usually applies to many elements. Hence, redundant and possibly inconsistent context property values can be avoided, and the comprehensibility is increased.

2.4   Additional Features of Context Properties

This section briefly outlines two more features of context properties. Details are explained in [2]. The context property value assigned to an element can also depend on other influences. For instance, the value can depend on the current state at runtime or on other context property values assigned to the same element.

Usually, the context property values assigned to an element have to be defined manually. Nevertheless, values of **system properties**, like 'the current user' or 'the current IP-address', can only be queried from the middleware platform during configuration or at runtime. This paper focuses on *semantic* context properties that are not automatically available due to the underlying middleware platform.

2.5   Research Related to Context Properties

Many techniques for writing down meta-information exist The notion of context or container properties is well established in component runtime infrastructures such as COM+ EJB, or .NET. Context properties are similar to tagged values in UML - on the design level, tagged values can be used to express context properties. In contrast to tagged values, the values of a context property must fulfill some semantic constraints. For example, the values of one context property for one model element are not allowed to contradict. E.g., the values of 'Personal Data' must not be both 'Yes' and 'No' for the same model element. Furthermore, not every value may be allowed for a context property. For instance, only the few names of existing workflows are valid values of the context property Workflow.

UML diagrams can express *direct* dependencies between model elements via associations. In contrast, context properties allow the specification of *indirect* dependencies between otherwise unassociated model elements that share the same context. A context property groups model elements that share a context. Existing grouping mechanisms like *inheritance*, *stereotypes* ([1]) or *packages* are not used because the values of a context property associated with one model element might vary in different configurations or even change at runtime. The instances of a model element are not supposed to change their stereotype or package during (re-)configuration or at runtime. One context property can be assigned to different types of model elements. For example, the values of 'Workflow' can be associated both with 'classes' in a class diagram and with 'components' in a component diagram. Using packages or inheritance is not as flexible. According to [13], stereotypes can group model elements of different types via the baseClass attribute, too. However, this 'feature' has to be used carefully and the instances of an model element are not allowed to change their stereotype. Context properties are a simple mechanism for grouping otherwise possibly unassociated model elements - even across different views or diagram types.

3   Introducing Context-Based Constraints (CoCons)

This section presents a new constraint technique for requirements specification.

3.1   A New Notion of Invariants

One requirement can affect several possibly unassociated model elements in different diagrams. A **context-based constraint** (CoCon) specifies a requirement for a group of model elements that share a context. The shared context is identified via the context property values assigned to these elements. If these values comply with the CoCon's context condition then their elements share same context. The metamodel in figure 2 shows the abstract syntax for CoCons. The metaclasses 'ModelElement' and 'Constraint' of the UML 1.4 'core' package used in figure 2 are explained in [13].

CoCons should be preserved and considered in model modifications, during deployment, at runtime and when specifying another – possibly contradictory – CoCon. Thus, a CoCon is an *invariant*. It describes which parts of the system must be protected. If a requirement is written down via a CoCon, its violation can be detected *automatically* as described in section 3.5.

As proposed in section 2.2, a context property 'Workflow' is assigned to each model element. Thus, a CoCon can state that "*All classes belonging to the workflow 'Integrate Two Contracts' must be unreadable by the component*

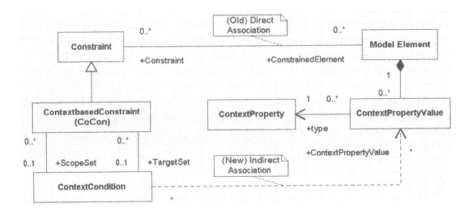

Figure 2. The CoCon Metamodel

'*Customer Management*'" (**Example A**). This constraint is based on the context of the classes – it is a *context-based constraint*. Another requirement might state that "*the class 'Employee' must be unreadable by any class whose context property 'Operational Area' contains the value 'Field Service'* " (**Example B**).

3.2   New: Indirect Selection of Constrained Elements

One CoCon applies to model elements that share a context. The shared context is expressed using a '**context condition**' that selects model elements via their context property values. It describes a (possibly empty) *set* of model elements. A context condition may be restricted to model elements of one metaclass – in examples A and B, the context condition is restricted to 'classes' – no model elements of other metatypes, e.g. 'components', are selected even if their context property values otherwise fit the context condition. A **range** can limit the number of model elements that are denoted by a context condition. The range mechanism is not discussed in this paper – it is needed to specify 'flexible Co-Cons'. Two different kinds of sets can be selected by a context condition:

On the one hand, a context condition can determine the '**target set**' containing the elements that are checked by the CoCon. In example A, the target set is selected via "*all classes belonging to the workflow 'Integrate Two Contracts*'". On the other hand, a context condition can select the 'scope set' that represents the *part of the system*, where the CoCon is enforced. In example A, the scope of the CoCon is a single model element – the component 'Customer Management'. Nevertheless, the scope of a CoCon can be a '**scope set**' containing any number of elements, as illustrated in example B.

Both target set elements and scope set elements can be selected either directly or indirectly: Set elements can be *directly* associated to a CoCon by naming the model element(s) or by using the keyword `this` as in OCL. In example A, the CoCon is associated *directly* with the 'Customer Management' component. This unambiguously identifies the only element of the scope set. The new key concept of context-based constraints is **indirect association**. Set elements can be *indirectly associated* with a CoCon via a context condition. The scope set in example B contains all the classes whose context property 'Operational Area' contains the value 'Field Service'. These scope set elements are anonymous. They are not directly named or associated, but described indirectly via their context property values. If no element fulfills the context condition, the set is empty. This simply means that the CoCon does not apply to any element at all. This 'indirect association' is represented as a dotted line in fig. 2 because it is not a UML association with an AssociationStart and an AssociationEnd. Instead, it is a UML dependency. The 'indirectly associated' model elements are selected by evaluating the context condition each time when the system is checked for whether it complies with the CoCon.

As explained in section 2.3, the Belongs-To relation is transitive: if $a \xrightarrow{BeTo}$ $b \xrightarrow{BeTo} c$ then $a \xrightarrow{BeTo} c$. If the context property value v is *associated* with the element e then **transitive closure** $BeTo^*_{v,e}$ contains all elements where v is assigned to due to a Belongs-To relation. If v is associated with c in a $a \xrightarrow{BeTo}$ $b \xrightarrow{BeTo} c$ then $BeTo^*_{v,c} = \{a, b\}$ (if no other elements than a and b belong to c). A context condition selects an element if the context property values *assigned to* this element ($ConPropVals^{cp,e}$) match the context condition. The transitive closure $BeTo^*_{v,e}$ must be considered when evaluating a context condition. Many algorithms exist for calculating a transitive closure. A well-known one is the Floyd-Warshall algorithm. It was published by Floyd ([8]), and is based on one of Warshall's theorems ([17]). Its running time is cubed in the number of elements.

A CoCon can have two context conditions in different roles: one describing *which* model elements are controlled by the CoCon (contained in the target set), and one describing *where (In which parts of the system? Only in the scope set)* the target elements are checked for whether or not they comply with the CoCon. Yet, in some cases the names 'target set' and 'scope set' do not seem appropriate. Mixing example A and example B, a CoCon could state that "*All classes belonging to the workflow 'Integrate Two Contracts' (Set_1)* must be unreadable by *all classes whose context property 'Operational Area' contains the value 'Field Service' (Set_2)*". In this paper, Set_2 is called the scope set. Nevertheless, which part of the system is the scope in this example? Should those elements of the system be called 'scope' which are unreadable(Set_1), or does 'scope' refer to all elements (in Set_2) that cannot read the elements in Set_1? Should Set_1 be called 'scope set one' and Set_2 'scope set two' or is it better to name one of them 'target set'?Unfortunately, there is no intuitive answer yet. Perhaps better names will be invented in the future. But, for most CoCon types (see [2]) the names 'target set' for Set_1 and 'scope set' for Set_2 fit well.

3.3 Handling Conflicts within CoCon Type Families

In this paper, only CoCons of the '**UnreadableBy**' type are discussed due to space limitations. They specify that the target set elements cannot be accessed by the CoCon's scope set elements. Many other CoCon types are discussed in [2]. A *CoCon type family* groups CoCon types. For instance, the UnreadableBy CoCon belongs to the family of Accessibility CoCon types. Conflicting requirements can be automatically detected via *CoCon family specific constraints*. In the case of UnreadableBy CoCons, the CoCon family specific constraints are:

1. No element of the target set may be both ReadableBy and UnreadableBy any element in the scope set.
2. No model element of the target set may be UnreadableBy itself.

One kind of context conditions exists that doesn't refer to context property values: the **joker** context condition simply selects *all* model elements regardless of their context. A context-based constraint is called **simple**, if either its target set or its scope set contains *all* elements of the whole system via an unrestricted joker condition or if it contains exactly one directly associated element. Conflicts may arise if several CoCons of the same CoCon type family apply to the same element. Defining a CoCon's **priority** can prevent these conflicts. If several CoCons of the same CoCon type family apply to the same model element then only the CoCon with the highest priority is checked. If this CoCon is invalid because its scope set is empty then the next CoCon with the second-highest priority is checked. The value of the priority attribute should be a number. This paper does not attempt to discuss priority rules in detail, but it offers the following suggestion: a **default CoCon** which applies to all elements where no other CoCon applies should have the lowest priority. Default CoCons can be specified using a joker condition as introduced in section 3.1. CoCons using two context conditions should have *middle priority*. These constraints express the basic design decisions for *two possibly large* sets of elements. CoCons with one context condition have *high priority* because they express design decisions for *one possibly large* set of elements. CoCons that select both the target set and the scope set *directly* should have the *highest priority* – they describe exceptions for some individual elements.

A CoCon **attribute** can define details of its CoCon. Each attribute has a name and one or more value(s). This paper only discusses two general attributes that can be applied to *all* CoCon types: A CoCon can be named via the attribute **CoConName**. This name must be unique because it is used to refer to this CoCon. Moreover, the **Priority** of a CoCon can be defined via an attribute.

3.4 A Textual Language for CoCon Specification

This section introduces a textual language for specifying context-based constraints. The standard technique for defining the syntax of a language is the Backus-Naur Form (BNF), where ":\:=" stands for the definition, "Text" for a nonterminal symbol and "**TEXT**" for a terminal symbol.

This paper only discusses one CoCon type: the UnreadableBy CoCons enforce access permission. The model elements in its target set are unreadable by all the model elements in its scope set. In the BNF rules, 'UnreadableBy' is abbreviated 'UR'. Furthermore, all rules concerning concatenation via a separator (',', 'OR' or 'AND') are abbreviated: "(Rule)+^{Separator}" represents "Rule {Separator Rule }*".

URCoCon	::= URElementSelection+^{OR} **'MUST BE UnreadableBy'** URElementSelection+^{OR} ['**WITH**' URAttribute+^{AND}]
URElementSelection	::= URContextCondition | URDirectSelection | **'THIS'**
URDirectSelection	::= **'THE'** URRestriction ElementName
URContextCondition	::= Range (URRestrictions | **'ELEMENTS'**) ['**WHERE**' ContextQuery+$^{AND\ or\ OR}$]
Range	::= **'ALL'** | Number | '[' LowerBoundNumber ',' UpperBoundNumber ']'
ContextQuery	::= ContextPropertyName Condition (ContextPropertyValue | SetOfConPropValues)
SetOfConPropValues	::= ('{' (ContextPropertyValue)+^{Comma}'}') | ContextPropertyName
Condition	::= **'CONTAINS'** | **'DOES NOT CONTAIN'** | '=' | '!=' | '<' | '>' | '<=' | '>='
URAttribute	::= ('**CoConNAME** =' Name) | ('**PRIORITY** =' PriorityValue)

The URContextCondition rule allows for the *indirect* selection of the elements involved. In contrast, the ElementName rule *directly* selects elements by naming them. The URRestriction(s) rules depend the CoCon type and on the modeling approach used – [2] defines them as "'**Components**' | '**Interfaces**')+" for the 'UML Components' approach ([4]).

The ConditionExpression describes (one or more) set(s) of *RequiredValues*^{cp}. A context condition selects *e*, if for each context property *cp* used in the context condition the *RequiredValues*$^{cp} \subseteq ConPropVals^{cp,e}$. Besides '**CONTAINS**' ($\subseteq$), this paper suggests other expressions like '!=' (does not equal) and '**DOES NOT CONTAIN**' ($\not\subseteq$). Only simple comparisons (inclusion, equality,...) are used in order to keep CoCons comprehensible. Future research might reveal the benefits of using complex logical expression, such as temporal logic.

Different kinds of context conditions can be defined in *simple CoCons*. On the one hand, a simple CoCon can have a joker condition instead of a context condition. A joker condition can be defined by omitting the 'WHERE ...' clause in the URContextCondition rule. For instance, '*ALL COMPONENTS* MUST BE ...' is a joker condition. On the other hand, a simple CoCon can be specified via the terminal symbol 'THIS' in the URElementSelection rule. 'THIS' in CCL has the same semantic as 'this' in OCL (see [5, 16]). If the CoCon is directly associated with an model element via an UML association then 'THIS' refers to this model element.

3.5 'Privacy Policy' Example of Using UnreadableBy CoCons

In this section, an UnreadableBy CoCon illustrates the case where the target set and the scope set of a CoCon can overlap. Moreover, the example shows how to detect whether a system model complies with a CoCon. A requirement might state that *"All components belonging to the operational area 'Controlling' are not allowed to access components that handle personal data"*. This statement can be specified as a CoCon in this way:

```
ALL COMPONENTS WHERE 'Personal Data' EQUALS 'Yes'
MUST BE UnreadableBy
ALL COMPONENTS WHERE 'Operational Area' CONTAINS 'Controlling'
```

If a component has the value 'Yes' in its context property 'Personal Data' *and* the value 'Controlling' in its context property 'Operational Area' then it belongs *both* to the target set and to the scope set of the CoCon. This is absurd, of course. It means that this component cannot read itself. The CoCon is valid, but the system model does not comply with this CCL specification. Such bad design is detected via the CoCon type family specific constraint number two in section 3.3. Every component involved in this conflict must be changed until *either* handles personal data *or* belongs to the 'Controlling'. It must not belong to *both* contexts. If it is not possible adjust the system accordingly, then it cannot comply with the requirement.

3.6 Present Research Results

A CoCon language consists of different CoCon types. Up to now, two CoCon languages exist: The **D**istribution **C**onstraint **L**anguage **DCL** supports the design of distributed systems as described in [3]. It was developed in cooperation with the Senate of Berlin, debis and the Technical University of Berlin. DCL concepts have been implemented at the Technical University of Berlin by extending the tool 'Rational Rose'. A prototype is available for download in German only. It turned out that Rose's extensibility is inadequate for integrating DCL concepts.

The context-based **C**omponent **C**onstraint **L**anguage **CCL** introduced in [2] consists of CoCon types that describe requirements within the logical architecture of a component-based system. It is currently being evaluated in a case study undertaken in cooperation with the ISST Fraunhofer Institute, the Technical University of Berlin and the insurance company Schwäbisch Hall. The UnreadableBy CoCon discussed in this paper is one of CCL's many CoCon types.

UML *profiles* provide a standard way to use UML in a particular area without having to extend or modify the UML metamodel. A profile tailors UML for a specific domain or process. It does not extend the UML by adding any new basic concepts. Instead, it provides conventions for applying and specializing standard UML to a particular environment or domain. Hence, a UML profile for CoCons can only be developed in future research if the CoCon concepts can be covered with current UML mechanisms and semantics. New metatypes are suggested in figure 2. Usually, this would go beyond a true 'profile' of UML. However, the new metatype 'ContextBasedConstraint' only *specializes* the 'Constraint' metatype. 'ContextCondition' is a utility class that only illustrate the difference between the existing metatypes and the new one. Thus, the integration suggested is based on standard UML concepts and refines them in the spirit of UML profiles. It falls into the category of lightweight formal methods.

In the winter semester 2001/02 a 'CCL-plugin' for the open source UML editor 'ArgoUML' wasimplemented at the TU Berlin in order to specify and to automatically protect CoCon specifications during modeling. It is available at `ccl-plugin.berlios.de` and demonstrates how the standard XMI format for representing UML in XML must not be changed in order to save or load models containing CoCons. Hence, CoCons can be integrated into UML without modifying the standard.

3.7 Comparing OCL to Context-Based Constraints

According to [10, 15], three kinds of constraints exist: preconditions, postconditions and invariants. Typically, the *Object Constraint Language OCL* summarized in [16] is used for the constraint specification of object-oriented models. One OCL constraint refers to (normally one) *directly identified* element, while a context-based constraint can refer both to directly identified and to (normally many) indirectly identified, *anonymous and unrelated* elements. A CoCon selects the elements involved according to their meta-information. In the UML, tagged values are a mechanism similar to context properties for expressing meta-information. There is no concept of selecting the constrained elements via their tagged values in OCL or any other existing formal constraint language.

An OCL constraint can only refer to elements that are directly linked to its scope. On the contrary, a CoCon scope is not restricted. It can refer to elements that are not necessarily associated with each other or even belong to different models. When specifying an OCL constraint it is not possible to consider elements that are unknown at specification time. In contrast, an element becomes involved in one context-based constraint simply by having the matching context property value(s). Hence, the target elements and the scope elements can change without modifying the CoCon specification.

Before discussing another distinction, the OMG meta-level terminology will be explained briefly. Four levels exist: Level 'M_0' refers to a system's objects at runtime, 'M_1' refers to a system's model or schema, such as a UML model, 'M_2' refers to a metamodel, such as the UML metamodel, and 'M_3' refers to a meta-metamodel, such as the Meta-Object Facility (MOF).

If an OCL constraint is associated with a model element on level M_i, then it refers the instances of this model element on level M_{i-1} — in OCL, the 'context' [5] of an invariant is an *instance* of the associated model element. If specified in a system model on M_1 level, an OCL constraint refers to *runtime* instances of the associated model element on level M_0. In order to refer to M_1 level, OCL constraints must be defined at M2 level (e.g. within a stereotype). On the contrary, a CoCon can be verified automatically on the *same* meta-level where it is specified. All CoCons discussed in this paper are specified *and* verified on M_1 level because this paper focuses on using them during design. For example, if a CoCon states that *"package 'X' must contain all classes belonging to the operational area 'field service'"*, then the model should be checked for whether it violates this CoCon already during design. Using OCL, the designer may create a stereotype «contains-all-classes-belonging-to-the-field-service» and assign a constraint to this stereotype on the M2 level. As discussed before, there is no formal constraint language for selecting a model element due to its metadata. Hence, the constraint must be written down in natural language and cannot be verified automatically. Even if OCL constraints could iterate over all model elements in all diagrams and select those fulfilling the context condition, modifying the *meta*model each time the requirements change is not appropriate.

There used to be a lot of interest in machine-processed records of *design rationale*. According to [11], the idea was that designers would not only record the results of their design thinking, but also the reasons behind their decision. Thus, they would also record their justification for why it is as it is. CoCons record design decisions that can be automatically checked. They represent certain relevant requirements in the model. The problem is that designers simply don't like writing down design decisions. The challenge is to make the effort of recording the rationale worthwhile and not too tedious for the designer. As a reward for writing down essential design decisions via CoCons they reap the benefits summarized in section 4.3.

4   Conclusion

4.1   Applying CoCons in the Development Process

In this section the application of CoCons throughout the software development process is sketched. **During requirements analysis** the business experts must be asked specific questions in order to find out useful context properties and CoCons. They may be asked about which business exist rules for which context. Examples: *"Which important workflows exist in your business? And for each workflow, which business objects belong to this workflow and which requirements belong to this workflow"*. Then it is possible to state that all business objects belonging to workflow 'X' must comply with requirement 'Y'. Currently a CoCon-aware method for requirements analysis is being developed at the Technical University of Berlin in cooperation with Eurocontrol, Paris.

The benefits of considering both requirements and architecture when **modeling** a system are discussed in [12]. The application of CoCons during modeling is currently being evaluated in a case study being carried out in cooperation with the ISST Fraunhofer Institute, the TU Berlin and the insurance company Schwäbisch Hall. This paper cannot discuss how to verify or 'proof' CoCon specifications *automatically* because for each CoCon type and for each abstraction level in the development process different requirement verification mechanisms are necessary. Please refer to the verification of CoCons integrated into the Design Critiques ([14]) mechanism of ArgoUML via the CCL Plugin.

During deployment a CoCon-aware configuration file checker can automatically protect requirements. Likewise, the notion of contextual diagrams is introduced in [7] in order to cope with the intrinsic complexity of configuration knowledge. A deployment descriptor checker for Enterprise Java Beans is currently being developed at the TU Berlin.

The people who need a new requirement to be enforced often neither know the details of every part of the system nor do they have access to the complete source code. By using CoCons, developers don't have to understand every detail ('glass box view') or modify autonomous parts of the system in order to enforce a new requirement on them. Instead, context properties can be assigned *externally* to an autarkic component and communication with this component can be monitored *externally* for whether it complies with the CoCon specification **at runtime**. A prototypical framework is currently beeing integrated into an application server at the TU of Berlin in cooperation with BEA Systems and the Fraunhofer ISST. Thus, legacy components or 'off the shelf' components can be forced to comply with new requirements.

4.2   Limitations of Context-Based Constraints

Taking only the tagged values of a model element into consideration bears some risks. It must be ensured that theses values are always up-to date. Whoever holds the responsibility for the values must be trustworthy. Confidence can be assisted with encryption techniques. Within one system, only one ontology should be used. For instance, the workflow 'New Customer' must have exactly this name in every part of the system, even if different companies manufacture its parts. Otherwise, string matching gets complex when checking a context condition.

Context properties are highly abstract and ignore many details. For instance, this paper disregards the dependencies between context property values. Handling dependent context property values is explained in [2]

4.3   Benefits of Context-Based Constraints

In contrast to grouping techniques, e.g. packages or stereotypes, context properties facilitate handling of overlapping or varying groups of model elements that share a context even across different model element types or diagrams. Hence, one requirement referring to several, possibly unassociated model elements can now be expressed via one constraint. Context properties allow *subject-specific, problem-oriented views* to be concentrated on. For instance, only those model elements belonging to workflow 'X' may be of interest in a design decision. Many concepts for specifying metadata exist and can be used instead, if they enable a constraint to select the constrained elements via their metadata.

Decision making is an essential activity performed by software architects in designing software systems. The resulting design must satisfy the requirements while not violating constraints imposed on the problem domain and implementation technologies. However, in complex domains, no one architect has all the knowledge needed to make a complex design. Instead, most complex systems are designed by teams of stakeholders providing some of the needed knowledge and their own goals and priorities. The 'thin spread of application domain knowledge' has been identified by [6] as a general problem in software development. In complex domains even experienced architects need knowledge support. For instance, they need to be reminded which of the requirements apply to which part of the system. The model should serve as a document understood by designers, programmers and customers. CoCons can be specified in easily comprehensible, straightforward language. They enforce a system's compliance with requirements. Even the person who specifies a requirement via CoCons must not have complete knowledge of the system due to the indirect association of CoCons to the system parts involved. CoCons associate relevant requirements with related elements of the system's model.

In software engineering, it has long been recognized that inconsistency is a fact of life. Evolving descriptions of software artefacts are frequently inconsistent, and tolerating this inconsistency is important if flexible collaborative working is to be supported. The abstract meta-information belonging to a model element can be ascertained out is an early lifecycle activity. When identifying the context property values the model element must not be specified in full detail. Metadata can supplement missing data based on experience or estimates.

Maintenance is a key issue in *continuous software engineering*. CoCons help to ensure consistency during system evolution. A context-based constraint serves as an invariant and thus prevents the violation of design decisions during later modifications of UML diagrams. It assists in detecting when design or context modifications compromise intended functionality. It helps to prevent unanticipated side effects during redesign and it supports collaborative design management. The only constant in life is change, and requirements tend to change quite often. This paper suggests improving the adaptability of a system model by enforcing conformity with meta-information. This meta-information can be easily adapted, whenever the context of a model element changes. In this case, some CoCon specifications may apply anew to this model element, while others may cease to apply. Furthermore, the CoCon specifications themselves can also be modified if requirements change. Each deleted, modified or additional CoCon can be automatically enforced and any resulting conflicts can be identified as discussed in [2]. It is changing contexts that drive evolution. CoCons are context-based and are therefore easily adapted if the contexts, the requirements or the configuration changes – they improve the traceability of contexts and requirements. CoCons can be verified during modeling, during deployment and at runtime. They facilitate description, comprehension and reasoning at different levels and support checking the compliance of a system with requirements automatically. According to [9], automated support for software evolution is central to solving some very important technical problems in current day software engineering.

References

[1] Stefan Berner, Martin Glinz, and Stefan Joos. A classification of stereotypes for object-oriented modeling languages. In B.Rumpe and R.B.France, editors, *2nd International Conference on the Unified Modeling Language, Colorado, USA*, volume 1723 of *LNCS*, pages 249–264. Springer, 1999.

[2] Felix Bübl. The context-based component constraint language CCL. Technical report, Technical University Berlin, available at http://www.CoCons.org, 2002.

[3] Felix Bübl and Andreas Leicher. Desiging distributed component-based systems with DCL. In 7th *IEEE Intern. Conference on Engineering of Complex Computer Systems ICECCS, Skövde, Sweden.* IEEE Computer Soc. Press, June 2001.

[4] John Cheesman and John Daniels. *UML Components.* Addison-Wesley, 2000.

[5] Steve Cook, Anneke Kleppe, Richard Mitchell, Jos Warmer, and Alan Wills. Defining the context of OCL expressions. In B.Rumpe and R.B.France, editors, *2nd International Conference on the Unified Modeling Language, Colorado, USA*, volume 1723 of *LNCS*. Springer, 1999.

[6] Bill Curtis, Herb Krasner, and Neil Iscoe. A field study of the software design process for large systems. *Comm. ACM*, 31(11):1268–1287, 1988.

[7] Alexander Felfernig, Gerhard Friedrich, Dietmar Jannach, and Markus Zanker. Contextual diagrams as structuring mechanism for designing configuration knowledge bases in UML. In A. Evans, S. Kent, and B. Selic, editors, *3rd International Conference on the Unified Modeling Language, York, United Kingdom*, volume 1939 of *LNCS*. Springer, 2000.

[8] Robert W. Floyd. Algorithm 97 (shortest path). *Communications of the ACM*, 5(6):345, 1962.

[9] Tom Mens and Theo D'Hondt. Automating support for software evolution in UML. *Automated Software Engineering*, 7(1):39–59, 2000.

[10] Bertrand Meyer. *Object-Oriented Software Construction.* Prentice-Hall, 1988.

[11] Thomas P. Moran and John M. Carroll, editors. *Design Rationale : Concepts, Techniques, and Use (Computers, Cognition, and Work).* Lawrence Erlbaum Associates, Inc., 1996.

[12] Bashar Nuseibeh. Weaving the software development process between requirements and architecture. In *Proceedings of ICSE-2001 International Workshop: From Software Requirements to Architectures (STRAW-01) Toronto, Canada*, 2001.

[13] OMG. UML specification v1.4 (ad/01-02-14), 2001.

[14] Jason E. Robbins and David F. Redmiles. Software architecture critics in the argo design environment. *Knowledge-Based Systems. Special issue: The Best of IUI'98*, 5(1):47–60, 1998.

[15] Clemens Szyperski. *Component Software - Beyond Object-Oriented Programming.* Addison-Wesley, Reading, 1997.

[16] Jos B. Warmer and Anneke G. Kleppe. *Object Constraint Language – Precise modeling with UML.* Addison-Wesley, Reading, 1999.

[17] Stephan Warshall. A theorem on boolean matrices. *Journal of the ACM*, 9(1):11–12, 1962.

[18] Herbert Weber. Continuous engineering of information and communication infrastructures (extended abstract). In Jean-Pierre Finance, editor, *Fundamental Approaches to Software Engineering FASE'99 Amsterdam Proceedings*, volume 1577 of *LNCS*, pages 22–29, Berlin, March 22-28 1999. Springer.

Formal Requirements Engineering Using Observer Models

Andreas Nonnengart, Georg Rock, and Werner Stephan

German Research Centre for Artificial Intelligence
Stuhlsatzenhausweg 3, 66123 Saarbrücken, Germany
nonnenga,rock,stephan@dfki.de

Abstract. Today we are confronted with an enormous variety of formal software engineering approaches and tools. Among these are many that address the critical early stages of software development. However, only little attention has been paid to the integration of different specialised approaches and to the overall development process.
In this paper we present a technique for formal requirements analysis (observer models) that deals with particular perspectives on a system rather than with particular aspects of it.
A realistic gasburner example illustrates the overall approach.

1   Introduction

Thirty years ago (in the early seventies of the last century) the question what are formal methods was easy to answer. However, code verification in Hoare style systems failed not only because of its inability to cope with complexity but also because this restricted approach did not meet important needs of software engineering. Meanwhile the situation has drastically changed. We are confronted with an enormous variety of formal approaches and tools. Among these are many that address the critical early stages of software development. Although much progress has been made with respect to fully automatic methods little attention has been paid to the integration of different specialised approaches and to the overall development process.

Formal techniques for requirements analysis often deal with a particular aspect of the system to be designed. Examples of such aspects are properties of information flow, correctness of (cryptographic) protocols, and real time behaviour. In this paper we concentrate on real time analysis as one view on a system among others. It is not difficult to imagine a system that separates different applications by controlling the flow of information between them using authentication protocols as one of the security mechanisms and that in addition has to satisfy certain real time requirements.

Although it is well known that many severe errors occur already in the early stages of the development process it is the case also for later design stages like architectural design and implementation that they have to be treated formally if one aims at high assurance levels. For example, according to level EAL5 of

R.-D. Kutsche and H. Weber (Eds.): FASE 2002, LNCS 2306, pp. 264–278, 2002.

Common Criteria (CC) [7], a formal high-level design and a "correspondence proof" with resect to the so-called functional specification has to be provided. In the case of real time systems one has to define *how* the intended global behaviour is realized by separating the control component from its environment and by making assumptions (delays, cycle time) explicit. This scenario is described in section 3. Therefore, a number of particular views for requirements analysis have to be linked to a single abstract systems specification (`System Design Spec.`) that serves as a starting point for the refinement process (see Figure 1).

Rather than having a `satisfies` relation between a specification and a collection of simple properties that have to be established, requirements analysis will be based on its own descriptions (views) and postulated properties that refer to these descriptions. The description of a particular view will not necessarily use the same terminology as the system specification and often application specific formalisms and tools will allow for an efficient analysis. For establishing information flow properties a technique called non-interference, which is based on closure properties of sets of (system) traces, has to be used [8]. The analysis of protocols is based on a different kind of traces [10] that include steps of an attacker. A number of tools, like for example the one described in [9], have been used in this area. The real time view can be implemented by Hybrid Automata [2] or by Timed Automata [3]. Again, tools like HyTech [4] provide efficient techniques to establish real-time properties.

In the following we present a general technique called *observer models* to link abstract descriptions of the real time behaviour of a system to a system specification consisting of a control component, an environment, and a clock by means of an *observer mapping*. After an outline of the general technique we shall illustrate our approach using the specification of a controller for a gasburner (together with an environment and a clock) and a Hybrid Automaton that describes the global realtime behaviour of the system.

2   Observer Models for Realtime Properties

Requirements of a system to be developed are specified and analysed by possibly several different formalisms that are specific for a particular view on that system. The choice of the formalisms can be influenced by several factors: preferences or expertise of the user, special features that need certain constructs of the specification language, system support, and the re-use of already existing specifications. In Figure 1 each view is represented by an `Observer-Spec`$_i$ following its own description technique and formalism. One of these specifications might contain a global description of the runs of a protocol while another view concentrates on realtime properties. In the following we shall assume that the realtime view is given by Hybrid Automata [2].

As already mentioned above a view will also include properties, called `OS-Properties`$_i$ in Figure 1, that have to be established from the observer specification. Realtime requirements can be formulated and proven using tools like HyTech [4]. Note that we consider Hybrid Automata as a kind of comprehensive

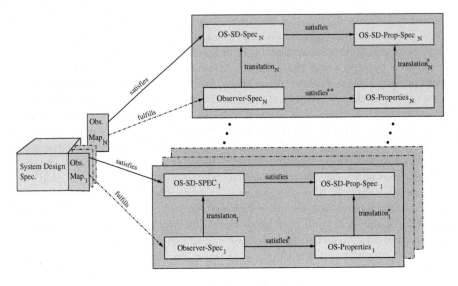

Fig. 1. Observer Models

description of the entire system behaviour with respect to time constraints. As can be seen from our example, the description is *global* in the sense that it does not distinguish between the control system and its environment. States of the Hybrid Automaton therefore do not directly correspond to internal states of the controller. They rather describe certain situations that might occur in a run of the three components (controller, environment, clock) together. To demonstrate this we will start an example scenario in section 3 using the specification of a gasburner controller.

To integrate various views into a common formal development the Observer-Spec$_i$ and the OS-Properties$_i$ first have to be translated into the language of the System Design Spec. The resulting specifications are called OS-SD-Spec and OS-SD-Prop-Spec. The translation of Hybrid Automata into the specification language of VSE is described in [11,12]. The language used in VSE[6,5] is VSE-SL. This is similar to TLA but with some extensions concerning among others the handling of shared variables and the handling of assumption commitment specifications.

It can be shown that the satisfies relation between OS-SD-SPEC$_i$ and OS-SD-Prop-Spec$_i$ holds, if and only if the satisfies relation holds between Observer-Spec$_i$ and OS-Properties$_i$. First of all this means that results obtained by using a tool like HyTech can be safely integrated into the overall development. However, since the language of OS-SD-Spec and OS-SD-Prop-Spec is more expressive (than that of Hybrid Automata) requirements specifications that are still "in the style of Hybrid Automata" but more general than these can be used in this context if one is inclined to use deductive techniques instead of model-checking. As an example one might wish to consider state transitions where one of the parameters (like speed) changes arbitrarily.

We are still left with the problem of establishing a link between the system specification and the particular realtime view we have defined. This is done by a mapping (called Obs. Map$_i$ in Figure 1) that (in the case of realtime requirements) interprets a given state of the interleaved computation of the controller, environment, and clock as a state of the (translation of the) Hybrid Automaton. It thereby turns the entire controller scenario into a model (in the sense of Hybrid Automata). For this we need to be sure that the translation faithfully preserves the semantics of Hybrid Automata.

In the following we present an instantiation of the general methodology that uses an abstract and global specification of the realtime behaviour of a gasburner scenario by a Hybrid Automaton on the one side and the specification of a controller that is connected to an environment by sensors and actors on the other. We outline the proof, that the automaton really describes the behaviour of the technical scenario with respect to a given mapping.

3   General Specification Scheme for Observer Models

The general scenario (see Figure 2), which we shall instantiate using a realistic yet abstract gasburner specification consists of three components: an environment, a controller and an observer/clock component. Which role do the individual components play now? Generally, given a system design one cannot decide always accurately, which parts are to be assigned to the environment and which parts belong to the controller itself. In the application of formal methods we are often interested in the safety critical parts of the system to be developed. The other parts are considered to be irrelevant for the safety of the system. These parts could consist for example of monitoring units[1]. The fact is substantial that the control, which is to be refined later or at least is applicable for a refinement, should contain all the safety critical parts.

The behaviour of the environment is determined by the specification of its interfaces. I.e. the environment has to supply the values needed on the various interfaces (in time). To guarantee the right functioning of the system in this case we have to make assumptions about the correct behaviour of the environment[2]. These assumptions can be used in the proof of the postulated properties of the system. If the environment component does not only exist as an interface definition, but also as a component with accurately specified behaviour, then one can prove these assumptions about the environment using the behaviour of the environment. Of course the type, range, and depth of the specification of

---

[1] Of course this is not always a uncritical unit. Just think of flight control that show the pilot the actual status of the plane.

[2] If one is interested in fault-tolerant systems, the possible faults can be described in the specification of the environment, so that the control system must detect these and behave accordingly.

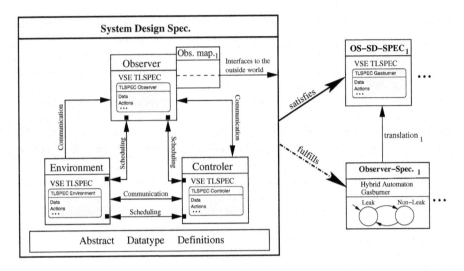

Fig. 2. General scenario (Observer model instantiated)

both the environment and controller depends on the properties that should be fulfilled.

The environment and the system/controller are specified as usual temporal logic specifications. Both components can be structured into subcomponents.

The specification of the observer/clock component differs in some sense from these usual specifications. One of the tasks of the observer is that it holds the time. But this fact does not influence the method described here.

The essential part of the observer is that it observes the system parts that are built from the Controller and the Environment components. These observations are filtered by the observer and communicated to the outside world. This filtration of the behaviour of the whole system constitutes a special view on the system that will be a realtime view in our example described in section 4. This is indicated by the right part of Figure 2 consisting of Observer-Spec$_1$ (instantiated by the Hybrid Automaton Gasburner) and the translation of this gasburner into a VSE specification (see OS-SD-SPEC$_1$ in Figure 2). The languages used in the real specification are VSE-SL (VSE-Specification Language) and Hybrid Automata as indicated in Figure 2.

In what follows, the general scenario is replaced by the real scenario of the gasburner.

4   Gasburner as Realtime Observation

The real scenario is included in the general one in Figure 2 by giving the instantiations for the Observer, Environment, and Controller components (that are the TLSPECS `Environment`, `Controller` and `Observer` respectively) and by giving instantiations for the `System Design Spec`, OS-SD-SPEC$_1$ and Observer-Spec$_1$

from Figure 1. A screenshot of the VSE development graph[5,6] of the implementation of the real scenario is given in Figure 3. In Figure 3 the composition of the environment, the controller and the observer is combined to the `gasburner` component representing the real gasburner.

Next we want to show that the VSE-observation (the VSE specification resulted from the translation of the hybrid gasburner into VSE[11] shown in Figure 3 as the temporal logic specification `gasprop`[3] is satisfied by the combined `gasburner`. That way the VSE-observation represents a complex realtime property of this gasburner.

The definitions of the datatypes are located in the theories `def1`, `def2`, `def3`, and `Definition` in Figure 3. They define the possible values of the flexible variables of the component specifications.

In what follows we describe the scheduling of the three components and the specification of the components itself.

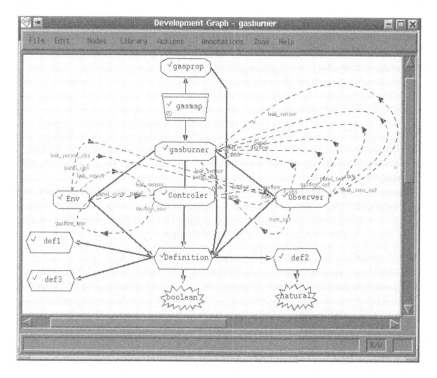

Fig. 3. Development Graph of the real Gasburner

---

[3] This has its correspondence in the general scenario given in Figure 2 in the `OS-SD-SPEC`[1] specification.

4.1   Scheduling

The scheduling between the components of the gasburner, i.e. the environment, the controller, and the observer is realised with the help of the shared variable who. In the absence of such a scheduling variable, component steps are simply interleaved. Combining the components without scheduling would result in a situation where we did not know what component computes next. In particular we would not know when the observer makes its next observation. In order to define an observer component that is not too complicated and in order to guarantee that the observer makes an observation when significant changes happen we have introduced a scheduling where the computation of the components starts with the Observer followed by the Controller. After this first phase the computing order of the components is: Environment, Observer, Controller. Of course, there are other possibilities to schedule the components. One of these is to start with an initial sequence consisting of Observer, Controller and again the Observer and after that the repeated computation order is Environment, Observer, Controller, and Observer. It has revealed that this scheduling results in a more complicated behaviour description of the observer and in more complicated proofs. The implementation of the scheduling can be taken from the description of the various components shown in Figures 7, 4 and 5.

4.2   Environment

The specification of the environment is shown in Figure 5. It consists of the definition of the possible initial states and the actions the environment can take[4]. Note that, because of the initialisation shown in Figure 5, the VSE-observation's initial state is leaking.

The action the environment can take is described in the ACTIONS-slot by the action env_act. The environment is specified such that the panel can change arbitrarily, but the leak_sensor representing the sensor to measure whether unburned gas flows out has to work correct. This means that in a situation in which the panel is off or the gasflow is blocked the sensor is expected to deliver the right values. Specifying the environment this way results in the assumption that the environment is expected never to fail. Faulty sensors are excluded from the model[5].

4.3   Controller

The TLSPEC of the controller is given in Figure 4. Again, its initial state description forces the gasburner observation to start in the leaking state.

The actions the controller can take are described in the ACTIONS slot by A1 through A7. The actions are disjunctively connected to a single action A1toA7.

---

[4] The doubling of the variables has technical reasons. It simulates an identical output sent to several components.

[5] Faulty sensors can be specified giving them the possibility to change non-deterministically. Such problems do not concern us in this paper, though.

```
TLSPEC Controller
 USING Definitions
 DATA INTERNAL cstate : OnOff_t
      OUT timer : nat; gasflow_env, gasflow : gas_t
      IN leak_sensor : bool; now : nat; panel : OnOff_t
      SHARED INOUT who : schedule_t
 ACTIONS
 A1 ::= cstate = on AND panel = off AND leak_sensor = F AND
        cstate' = off AND gasflow' = blocked AND
        gasflow_env' = blocked AND UNCHANGED(timer)
 A2 ::= cstate = on AND panel = off AND leak_sensor = T AND
        cstate' = off AND gasflow' = blocked AND
        gasflow_env' = blocked AND timer' = now
 A3 ::= cstate = on AND panel = on AND leak_sensor = F AND
        UNCHANGED(cstate, gasflow, gasflow_env, timer)
 A4 ::= cstate = on AND panel = on AND leak_sensor = T AND
        cstate' = off AND gasflow' = blocked AND
        gasflow_env' = blocked AND timer' = now
 A5 ::= cstate = off AND panel = on AND now >= timer + (30 * c) AND
        cstate' = on AND gasflow' = run AND gasflow_env' = run AND
        UNCHANGED(timer)
 A6 ::= cstate = off AND panel = on AND now < timer + (30 * c) AND
        UNCHANGED(cstate, gasflow, gasflow_env, timer)
 A7 ::= cstate = off AND panel = off AND
        UNCHANGED(cstate, gasflow, gasflow_env, timer)
 A1to7 ::= who = contr AND who' = env AND A1 OR A2 OR ... OR A7
 /*Definition of the behaviour of the gasburner */
 SPEC INITIAL gasflow = run AND gasflow_env = run AND
              cstate = on AND timer = 0 AND who = obs
      TRANSITIONS [A1to7] {gasflow, gasflow_env, timer, cstate}
 TLSPECEND
```

Fig. 4. Specification of the Controller

Since in every moment of execution only one of these actions is enabled, only this very action can be taken unless the controller stutters.

Up to now we have specified the controller together with its environment. By adding a clock component that mimics the flow of time (the change of the variable now) we end up in a system for which we can prove certain realtime properties.

As described in section 1 our methodology is different. It is not our aim to prove single realtime properties of a system, rather we want to check its entire realtime behaviour. How this is realised is explained in the next sections.

4.4   Observer

As can be recognised by looking at the specification of the controller and the environment, a simple refinement mapping [1] is not enough to prove the refine-

```
TLSPEC Env
 PURPOSE  "Specification of the Environment"
 USING Definitions
 DATA OUT panel_contr, panel_obs : OnOff_t
      OUT leak_sensor_obs, leak_sensor : bool
      IN gasflow_env : gas_t
      SHARED INOUT who : schedule_t
 ACTIONS
 env_act ::= /*scheduling*/
             who = env AND who' = obs AND
             (/*switch the gasburner on or off*/
              (panel_contr' = on AND panel_obs' = on) OR
              (panel_contr' = off AND panel_obs' = off)) AND
             /*Environment behaves correct*/
             IF (panel_obs' = off OR gasflow_env = blocked)
             THEN (leak_sensor' = F AND leak_sensor_obs' = F)
             ELSE (leak_sensor' = T AND leak_sensor_obs' = T) OR
                  (leak_sensor' = F AND leak_sensor_obs' = F) FI
 SPEC INITIAL leak_sensor = T AND leak_sensor_obs = T AND
             panel_obs = on AND panel_contr = on AND who = obs
      TRANSITIONS [env_act] {panel_obs, panel_contr, who,
                             leak_sensor, leak_sensor}
 TLSPECEND
```

Fig. 5. Specification of the Environment

ment. One reason for that is that in a refinement mapping only those variables can be mapped that are known in the actual state. In this sense a refinement mapping is a filter that maps the states of the implementing system to the states of the implemented system. The refinement model described here uses the usual refinement mapping extended by an observer component. The observer component together with the refinement mapping represents an external observer filtering the observed behaviour and mapping these filtered behaviours to special observer behaviours represented in our case by the translated hybrid gasburner shown in section 4.5. As already mentioned in section 1 observations may look at the system from different angles. This could be a data flow perspective or, as in our example here, a realtime perspective. The responsibility of the observer is to map the states of the real gasburner to the (virtual) states of the translated hybrid gasburner. In the easiest case the mapping only consists of a variable mapping which simply renames or recomputes the values of the variables according to certain given functions. The mapping of the variable **state** of the translated hybrid gasburner is somewhat more complicated since there is no immediate correlation between variables of the implementing system and the variable **state**. Moreover, the mapping does not only depend on the actual state of the implementing system but also on some other information given by the behaviour of the observer. This situation is illustrated in Figure 6. Some of the steps of the hybrid gasburner in Figure 6 relate to stuttering steps and some

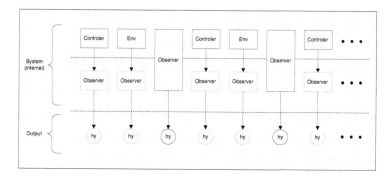

Fig. 6. Refinement Relation

relate to real steps. Thus the Observer calculates steps of the hybrid gasburner from the steps of the environment and the controller. In addition the observer makes the clock available to all the system components.

We now come to the actual specification of the observer (given in Figure 7). In its specification it should be avoided to rebuild the specification of the hybrid gasburner shown in section 4.5. This can be accomplished by certain syntactical restrictions on the observer's actions. For instance only the variables of the controller and the environment are allowed in the enabling conditions.

The observer has to handle the following situations that might occur in the hybrid gasburner: The system is in its initial state and gas flows out of the nozzle without being burned, the system changes from leaking to non-leaking, the system remains leaking or it changes from non-leaking to leaking. To recognise these situations in the observer component it is not enough to only have a look at the values of the input variables in the actual state. Looking at these variables the observer could not recognise whether there was a situation change from leaking to non-leaking or not. In order to detect all these situation changes the observer stores parts of the previous observation in internal variables (`gas_int` and `leak_sens_int`).

Let us have a more detailed look at one of the possible situations. Assume that the condition `leak_to_non_leak` (see Figure 7) is satisfied. This means that the actual values of the variables `gasflow` and `leak_sens` are `blocked` and `F`, respectively. Moreover, assume that the previous observations of the observer where that there was a running gas flow and a leak, i.e. `gas_int` is `run` and `leak_sens_int` is `T`. This situation indicates that the system happened to be in a leaking situation and changed to a non-leaking situation. The observer reacts on this change by setting the `state` variable to `non_leak` and by resetting the variable `x` to `0`. This corresponds exactly to the behaviour of the hybrid system in such a situation. That way the behaviour of the hybrid gasburner is filtered out of the behaviour of the controller and the environment.

```
TLSPEC Observer
 USING Definitions
 DATA IN panel_obs:OnOff_t;leak_sensor:bool;gasflow:gas_t;timer:nat
      SHARED INOUT who:schedule_t
      OUT panel_out:OnOff_t;leak_sens_out:bool;gasflow_out:gas_t;
          now, now_out:nat;x,t_obs:nat;state:state_t
      INTERNAL leak_sens_int:bool;gas_int:gas_t
 ACTIONS
 /*Condition for the initial phase*/
 init_cond :: = leak_sens = T AND leak_sens_int = T AND
                gasflow = run AND gas_int = run
 /*Condition for the leaking to non_leaking phase*/
 leak_to_non_leak ::= gasflow =blocked AND gas_int = run AND
                      leak_sens = F AND leak_sens_int = T
 /*Condition for the non_leaking to leaking phase*/
 non_leak_to_leak ::= gasflow =run AND leak_sens = T AND
                      leak_sens_int = F
  /*Special case for initial phase*/
 obs1 ::= state' = leaking AND unchanged(x, ...,gas_int, now, now_out)
 /*leaking to non_leaking action*/
 obs2 ::= state' = non_leaking AND x' = 0 AND t_obs' = t_obs AND
          now' = now AND now_out' = now_out AND gas_int' = gasflow
          AND leak_sens_int' = leak_sens
 /*non_leaking to leaking action*/
 obs3 ::= state' = leaking AND x' = 0 AND
          now' = now AND now_out' = now_out AND t_obs' = t_obs AND
          leak_sens_int' = T AND gas_int' = run
 /*Action describing the remaining in non_leaking state. Enabled if:
   not init_cond AND not leak_to_non_leak AND not non_leak_to_leak*/
 obs4 ::= state' = non_leaking AND x' = x + 1 AND now' = now + 1 AND
          now_out' = now_out + 1 AND t_obs' = t_obs AND
          leak_sens_int' = leak_sens AND gas_int' = gasflow
 /*Observer action with scheduling and setting of output variables*/
 obs_act ::= who = obs AND who' = contr AND gasflow_out' = gasflow AND
             panel_out' = panel_obs AND leak_sens_out' = leak_sensor AND
             IF init_cond THEN obs1
             ELSE IF leak_to_non_leak THEN obs2
                  ELSE IF non_leak_to_leak THEN obs3 ELSE obs4
                     FI FI FI
 SPEC INITIAL who = obs AND panel_out = on AND leak_sens_out = T AND
              gasflow_out = run AND gas_int = run AND leak_sens_int = T
              AND now = 0 AND now_out = 0 AND x = 0 AND t_obs = 0 AND
              state = leaking
      TRANSITIONS [obs_act] {now, gasflow_out, panel_out,
                             leak_sens_out, who, leak_sens_out}
 TLSPECEND
```

Fig. 7. Specification of the Observer

4.5   The Gasburner as VSE Specification

As usual we illustrate hybrid automata as annotated graphs. The hybrid gas-burner is then picturised as follows:

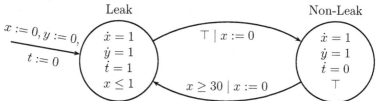

The meaning of the variables of the hybrid gasburner is as follows. y accumulates overall time. x represents a control clock that guarantees that the system remains for at most 1 time unit within location Leak and for at least 30 time units within location Non-Leak. t counts leakage time, i.e. the amount of time the system resides within Leak.

The translation of the hybrid gasburner (see [11]) then results in the VSE gasburner specification:

```
TLSPEC gasburner
 PURPOSE  "Specification of the gasburner. "
 USING definition
 DATA OUT x, y, t : nat
      OUT state : state_t
 ACTIONS
 phi_1 ::= state = leaking AND state' = non_leaking AND
           x' = 0 AND UNCHANGED(y, t)
 phi_2 ::= state = non_leaking AND state' = leaking AND
           x >= 30 * c AND x' <= c AND x' = 0 AND UNCHANGED(y, t)
 phi_1_star ::= state = leaking AND state' = non_leaking AND
                NOT x + 1 <= c AND x' = 0 AND UNCHANGED(y, t)
 psi_1 ::= state = leaking AND  state' = leaking AND
           x + 1 <= c AND y' = y + 1 AND
           x' = x + 1 AND t' = t + 1
 psi_2 ::= state = non_leaking AND state' = non_leaking AND
           x' = x + 1 AND y' = y + 1 AND UNCHANGED(t)
 SPEC INITIAL x = 0 AND y = 0 AND t = 0 AND state = leaking
      TRANSITIONS [phi_1, phi_2, phi_1_star, psi_1, psi_2]
                  {x, y, t, state}
      FAIRNESS WF(phi_1_star) {x, y, t, state},
               WF(psi_1) {x, y, t, state},
               WF(psi_2) {x, y, t, state}
 SATISFIES Safety
TLSPECEND
```

This VSE gasburner specification constitutes the **gasprop** TLSPEC given in Figure 3 and represents a complex realtime property we want to prove from the **gasburner**.

4.6   Example Behaviour of the Real Gasburner

This section mainly consists of the table shown in Figure 8 that provides a
possible initial part of the behaviour of the real gasburner (see the upper part
of the table) including the mapping done by the observer component and the
refinement mapping[6]. The table shows how the filter consisting of the observer
component works and therefore how it maps the behaviour of the real gasburner
to the hybrid gasburner (see the lower part of Table 8). The proof given in
section 4.8 finally states that every behaviour of the real gasburner is mapped
to a behaviour of the hybrid gasburner and so that the refinement relation is
established. For readability we use the abbreviations n_l for **non_leaking** and bl

	init	obs	contr	env	obs	contr	env	obs	contr	env	obs	...
cstate	on	on	off	off	off	off	off	off	of	off	off	...
timer	0	0	0	0	0	0	0	0	0	0	0	...
gasflow	run	run	bl	bl	bl	bl	bl	bl	bl	bl	bl	...
panel	on	on	on	on	on	on	on	on	on	on	on	...
leak_sens	T	T	T	F	F	F	F	F	F	F	F	...
now	0	0	0	0	0	0	0	1	1	1	2	...
gas_int	run	run	run	run	bl	bl	bl	bl	bl	bl	bl	...
leak_sens_int	T	T	T	T	F	F	F	F	F	F	F	...
y	0	0	0	0	0	0	0	1	1	1	2	...
x	0	0	0	0	0	0	0	1	1	1	2	...
t	0	0	0	0	0	0	0	0	0	0	0	...
state	1	1	1	1	n_l	n_l	n_l	n_l	n_l	n_l	n_l	...

Fig. 8. Example behaviour with refinement mapping

for **blocked** in Table 8. If we just consider the lower part we can see that this is
also a possible behaviour of the hybrid gasburner.

4.7   Handling of the Constant c

The constant c, as introduced in [11], plays a special role in the example presented
here. It is used to get an exact discretisation of the continuous behaviour of
the original hybrid gasburner. Moreover, it is used in the specification of the
Controller (see Figure 4) in the actions A5 and A6.

The role of the natural constants c is the same as in the translation of hybrid
automata into VSE [11]. It makes the system independent from the chosen time
unit. Let us assume, for example, the value of c is 10. Then the clock has to
make 300 steps, before the barrier is reached. If, however, c is 1000 the clock has

---

[6]   The refinement mapping is shown in the development graph of the real gasburner
in Figure 3. It consists of a mapping of the variables to be implemented to terms
constructed from the variables of the implementing system

to tick 30.000 times to reach the barrier. I.e. if we consider seconds as the basic time unit then steps take $\frac{1}{10}$ of a second or a millisecond, respectively.

However, the real proof of the (safety) properties is done independent from specific values of the constant c. Therefore it is valid for all possible integer values and thus for all granularities (even the infinitesimal).

4.8   Refinement Proof

In this chapter we shall sketch the refinement proof indicated in Figure 3 by a VSE `satisfies`-link. The proof is done locally to the observer component. During the proof one immediately realises that assumptions about the behaviour of the environment of the observer are needed. These assumptions deal with two different proof situations. First, we have to know whether we are in a leaking or a non-leaking state. We insert this knowledge by the following invariants into the proof.

$$\Box(intern(observer) \land init\_cond \to state = leak)$$
$$\Box(intern(observer) \land leak\_non\_leak \to state = leak)$$
$$\Box(intern(observer) \land non\_leak\_leak \to state = non\_leak)$$
$$\Box(intern(observer) \land non\_leak\_non\_leak \to state = non\_leak)$$

The definitions of $init\_cond$, $leak\_non\_leak$, non_leak_leak and $non\_leak\_non\_leak$ are given below.

$$
\begin{aligned}
init\_cond \qquad &\; \widehat{=}\; leak\_sens = T \land leak\_sens\_int = T \land gasflow = run \\
&\quad \land gas\_int = run \\
leak\_non\_leak \quad &\; \widehat{=}\; gasflow = bl \land gas\_int = run \land leak\_sens = F \\
&\quad \land leak\_sens\_int = T \\
non\_leak\_leak \quad &\; \widehat{=}\; leak\_sens = T \land leak\_sens\_int = F \land gasflow = run \\
non\_leak\_non\_leak &\; \widehat{=}\; \neg(init \lor leak\_non\_leak \lor non\_leak\_leak)
\end{aligned}
$$

The formula $intern(observer)$ represents the internal behaviour of the observer component, i.e. the behaviour of the observer without the hiding quantification.

In the second proof situation we need knowledge about the behaviour of the controller in the `non_leak_leak` situation. Again this knowledge is inserted by the following assumptions:

$$\Box((leak\_sens = T \land leak\_sens\_int = F \land gasflow = run)$$
$$\to now \geq timer + 30 * c)$$
$$\Box((leak\_sens = T \land leak\_sens\_int = F \land gasflow = run) \to x = now - timer$$

It is evident that the proofs of these assumptions need knowledge about the controller component as well as about the scheduling. Finally, the proof is performed locally to the observer component and is exported as a lemma to the global proof obligation.

5   Conclusion and Future Work

We have presented a methodology, observer models, for formal requirements engineering. Its applicability is illustrated with the help of a realistic gasburner example that is presented in detail.

One of the open issues in this context is the question how to refine a specification without doing the whole proof work again. This problem seems to be very similar to that of refinement in the security area, for example in protocol analysis.

References

1. Martín Abadi and Leslie Lamport. The Existence of Refinement Mappings. *Theoretical Computer Science*, 82(2):253–284, May 1991.
2. R. Alur, C. Courcoubetis, N. Halbwachs, T. A. Henzinger, P.-H. Ho, X. Nicollin, A. Olivero, J. Sifaksi, and S. Yovine. The algorithmic analysis of hybrid systems. *Theoretical Computer Science*, 138:3–34, 1995.
3. R. Alur and D. L. Dill. A theory of timed automata. *Theoretical Computer Science*, 126:183–235, 1994.
4. T. A. Henzinger and P.-H. Ho. HyTech: The cornell hybrid technology tool. In P. Antsaklis, A. Nerode, W. Kohn, and S. Sastry, editors, *Hybrid Systems II*, pages 265–293. Springer Verlag, Lecture Notes in Computer Science, vol. 999, 1995.
5. D. Hutter, B. Langenstein, J. H. Siekmann C. Sengler, W. Stephan, and A. Wolpers. Deduction in the verification support environment (vse). In *Formal Methods Europe (FME)*, LNCS. Springer, 1996.
6. Dieter Hutter, Heiko Mantel, Georg Rock, Werner Stephan, Andreas Wolpers, Michael Balser, Wolfgang Reif, Gerhard Schellhorn, and Kurt Stenzel. VSE: Controlling the complexity in formal software developments. In D. Hutter, W. Stephan, P. Traverso, and M. Ullmann, editors, *Proceedings Current Trends in Applied Formal Methods, FM-Trends 98*, Boppard, Germany, 1999. Springer-Verlag, LNCS 1641.
7. U. Institute and o Standards. Common criteria for information technology security evaluation, 1999.
8. Heiko Mantel. Possibilistic definitions of security - an assembly kit. In *Proceedings of the 13th IEEE Computer Security Foundations Workshop*, Cambridge, England, 2000. IEEE Computer Society Press.
9. Catherine Meadows. The NRL protocol analyzer: An overview. *Journal of Logic Programming*, 26(2):113–131, 1996.
10. Jonathan K. Millen. CAPSL: Common authentication protocol specification language. The MITRE Corporation, Technical Report MP 97B48, 1997. http://www.csl.sri.com/~millen/capsl.
11. A. Nonnengart, G. Rock, and W. Stephan. Expressing Realtime Properties in VSE-II. In *ESA Workshop on On-Board Autonomy*, volume WPP-191, pages 447–454, October 2001.
12. A. Nonnengart, G. Rock, and W. Stephan. Using Hybrid Automata to Express Realtime Properties in VSE-II. In Ingrid Russel and John Kolen, editors, *Proceedings of the Fourteenth International Florida Artificial Intelligence Research Society Conference*, pages 640–644. AAAI Press, 2001.

Automatic Generation of Use Cases from Workflows: A Petri Net Based Approach

Oscar López[1], Miguel A. Laguna[2], and Francisco J. García[3]

[1] Technological Institute of Costa Rica, San Carlos Regional Campus, Costa Rica
olopez@infor.uva.es
[2] Department of Informatics, University of Valladolid, Spain
mlaguna@infor.uva.es
[3] Department of Informatics and Automatics, University of Salamanca, Spain
fgarcia@usal.es

Abstract. This paper presents automatic generation of use cases as an alternative both to speeding up requirements elicitation and formalizing the obtained use cases to approach the requirements reuse. We propose a framework for requirements documentation as use cases that might be included in coarse grain reusable structures. In order to effectively integrate the software requirements in reusable components, adequate models promoting reusability are required. Hence, we accomplish the requirement elicitation through a process using Workflows and Petri nets. This process gives an analytical treatment to system requirements which are stored in a repository.

Keywords: Requirement engineering, use cases, workflow, Petri nets, requirements reuse.

1 Introduction

Requirements engineering triggers the software development process by producing a document containing both the necessities of stakeholders and a characterization of the software that is going to be created in a specific domain [17,13]. However, it seems that the activities of requirements engineering take too much time, thus postponing the code production. Therefore, nowadays, research is aimed at developing methods and tools to adequately document the system requirements as well as to shorten the requirements process.

Requirements reuse is an approach which can contribute to improve and quicken the requirements engineering process by systematically using existing requirements documents. Although it has received little attention [21,13], reusing early software products and processes can improve the requirements engineering process [5,20]. If the developers can benefit from requirements reuse then it is possible both to increase the productivity and to reduce the error probability in requirements specifications.

Besides its potential benefits in software engineering, requirements reuse faces as principal trade-off its difficulties to enact, to process and hence to reuse, the requirements. The documentation of the requirements is originally oriented to being a means of communication between users and analysts. For this reason, it is represented with diverse notations and formats. This diversity implies the need for particular actions to

R.-D. Kutsche and H. Weber (Eds.): FASE 2002, LNCS 2306, pp. 279–293, 2002.

analyze requirements documents and their organization in a repository of reusable artifacts [5]. The systematic requirements reuse requires two specific actions. First, to define the adequate way to model and store specifications. Second, to define a process for selecting and adapting the reusable requirements.

In the Research Group in Reuse and Object Orientation (in Spanish, GIRO), at the University of Valladolid, Spain, we have proposed a component model called *mecano* [8]. A mecano is a coarse grain reusable element consisting of a set of fine grain elements which correspond to distinct levels of abstraction and are associated by inter-level and intra-level relations. We shall integrate the requirements documentation as an essential part of the mecano structure. System requirements documents give a characterization of the software component to be applied to a specific domain. Thus this documentation should cover representation and comprehension of the environment and the essential functions of the software product [19] in a traceable format and without ambiguity [10]. Software requirements based on natural language give us poor results in requirements specification because of its shortages, such as ambiguity, poor scalability and traceability [14]. So, we aim to establish a method to formally define requirements that promote reusability at the requirement level of abstraction.

In this paper we supply an approach to model system requirements and to store them as reusable elements (assets) on the analysis level. We look for an adequate representation for requirements facilitating comprehension, retrieval, and adaptation. From the initial system functionality based on user job we collect system requirements as scenarios for interaction between the users and the system. These scenarios are expressed as use cases looking on a syntactic and semantic formalism. The starting point is an administrative workflow [9] represented as a Case Graph (CG) that leads to the automatic generation of use cases. These use cases are stored in a repository of reusable components.

The rest of the paper is arranged as follows: Section 2 presents a reference framework for the generation of use cases and assets. In section 3 we specify the modeling process applying workflows as starting point to automate software requirements elicitation with use cases. Section 4 relates our work to other known studies. Section 5 concludes the paper and focuses on future work.

2   A General Framework for Use Cases Generation

When defining software requirements, users and analysts are related to each other within a complex communication scheme. Users are not usually sure enough about the required functionality. Therefore, system analysts or requirement engineers should correctly specify functionality through an iterative process [19]. A strong approach is needed to support user-analyst interaction and to make sure user requirements are discovered and expressed in a correct, precise, unambiguous, verifiable, traceable and modifiable form.

In addition to the difficulties of correctly obtaining user requirements from system analysis, it is accepted that the best performance of software reuse is associated with an early comprehension of system functionality. Hence, it is strongly recommended to have a process model for requirement elicitation as presented in Figure 1. This model is situated in the discrete event systems, according to Silva [18], because we are interested in the evolution of the states regardless of when the system reaches a particular state, or how long it remains in that state. In other words, requirement modeling is based on state sequences within the system. As a result, we use Petri nets in both process modeling and system requirements modeling to supply formal support for verification of the system, as has been proved in [6,14].

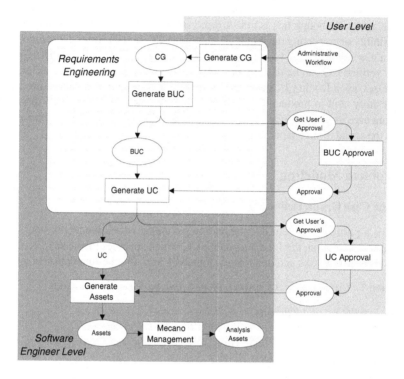

Fig. 1. General framework, arranged as a Petri net, for deriving analysis assets from a workflow

The process model includes two levels in requirement elicitation: The user level, and the software engineer level. The former has an external view (black box) of the system. The latter has an internal view (white box) of the system. Inside the Software Engineer Level one finds the Requirement Engineer View, which acts as an interface between user and engineer levels. In this way, we have arranged a general frame for the normalization of requirements elicitation.

The initial point is an administrative workflow containing the information flow. This workflow reflects the information changing from its entry into the system until it is outputted with the corresponding modifications. Workflows have been used to express business logic as recommended by the Workflow Management Coalition (WfMC) [22]. We obtain a preliminary description from the user job by a specific requirements documentation technique known as Document-Task diagram (DTd) [4]. When rigorously applied, the DTd satisfies WfMC standards indicating which tasks have to be performed in what order to transform the relevant information. In this way, our proposed methodology gives us a preliminary definition of system requirements.

The Requirements Engineering job consists of modeling the system functionality as a CG which is described in Section 3. From this CG the requirement engineer gets a set of business use cases (BUC Graphs), which require user approval to generate a set of use cases (UC Graphs). Again, use cases must be approved by the user in order to be used to generate assets. Although this is not shown, validation and verification activities gives the possibility of correcting the initial version of the CG, and if required, the process can ask for a new release of the CG and, consequently, new BUC Graphs and UC Graphs.

The verified CG can be used by the software engineer to obtain assets as templates of use cases, as in Durán [7]. These assets are sent to a mecano manager to iterate with the repository, and to produce the corresponding mecanos for storing in a repository. Obtaining use cases as templates, as well as the iteration process with the repository, is beyond the scope of this paper.

3   Problem Modeling

3.1   The Case Graph Definition

A DTd is a particular system documentation technique which models business logic. By adding information, the DTd becomes a CG which specifies the tasks to be done in a given order. Both tasks and documents, joined by arcs, are the foundation of a CG.

Definition 1. *Case Graph: A Case Graph is a four-tuple (D,T,A,E), where:*

- *D is a finite set of documents*
- *T is a finite set of tasks, $(D \cap T = \emptyset)$, $T^p = \{T_{(AA)}, T_{(AO)}, T_{(OA)}, T_{(OO)}\}$ is a disjointed partition of T. That is, in a Case Graph there are four types of tasks.*
- *A is a set of arcs, $A \subseteq ((D \times T) \cup (T \times D))$*
- *E : $D \cup T \rightarrow \Sigma^+$ is a label function which relates a distinct label to each document and to each task. Σ^+ is a finite set of labels.*

Tasks are the transition points between documents, and there are four different kinds of tasks (AA, OA, AO, OO). Each task contains a list of internal sub-tasks. Graphical icons of tasks are shown in Figure 2.A. We have chosen a representation showing requirements for a task to be executed in an organizational context. To execute a task, both required inputs (input documents) and pre-conditions must be met. Carrying out a task leads to both output documents and holding the post-condition. Sometimes a temporal event is also required in order to execute a task. Additionally, each task has an associated operator who is directly responsible and in charge of the same task. Graphical representation of tasks is shown in Figure 2.B.

The different kinds of tasks have distinctive behavior. The AA type requires all its input documents to be enabled, and its triggering leads to all its output documents. The OA is enabled with one of its input documents, and its triggering leads to all its output documents. The AO requires all of its input documents to be enabled, and its triggering leads to one of its output documents. The OO type is enabled with one of its input documents, and its triggering leads to one of its output documents.

We have represented the four basic types of routing in CGs. These types of routing are shown in Figure 2.C. Sequential actions and parallel actions may be described using AA tasks. Nevertheless, conditional actions and iterative actions require different arrangements of AA, OA, AO, and OO tasks.

To formally treat the resulting CGs, we need to standardize the behavior of the tasks. The Petri nets, which have been applied to express the workflow semantics [6], can help us to supply formal support for the analysis of CGs. In this way, the tasks are visualized as Petri net transitions. Documents are represented by Petri net places. The Petri net marking represents the sequence of states. As OA, AO, and OO tasks become AA tasks, the CG becomes a Petri net. Figure 2.D graphically shows this transformation of OA, AO and OO tasks into AA tasks, and next in algorithm 2 we give its formal expression.

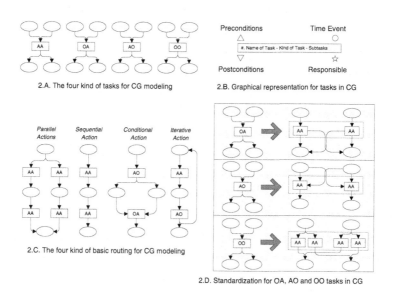

2.A. The four kind of tasks for CG modeling

2.B. Graphical representation for tasks in CG

2.C. The four kind of basic routing for CG modeling

2.D. Standardization for OA, AO and OO tasks in CG

Fig. 2. Representation for tasks, transformations and action flows for Case Graph modeling

To illustrate how to apply our approach for deriving use cases, we have taken a DTd from a real case of a Spanish Electrical Enterprise. It is represented as a CG as shown in Figure 3. We take four general processes - Request Process, Resolution Process, Execution Process, and Refund Process - taking place in two organizational units represented by two different internal actors - Control Centre (CC), and Local Operator (Op)- which are responsible for the actions. There are seven external actors: Particular Customer, Area Agent, Requester, Security Committee, Affected Customer, Enterprise Organizations, and Tax Organizations.

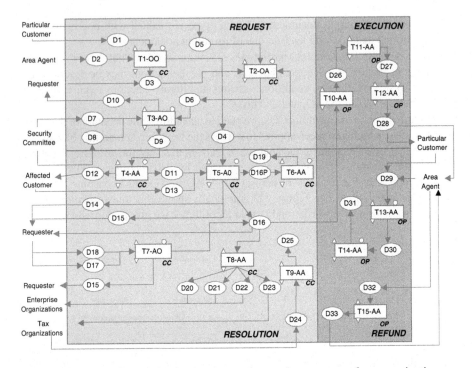

Fig. 3. Graphs of Cases for four processes in two departments of an organization

3.2   BUC Graphs and UC Graphs

Because the Case Graph represents system functionality, it might indicate what the interaction between users and the system is. Jacobson [12] differentiates two types of interaction as use cases: Business Use Cases (BUC), and Use Cases (UC). According to our framework, BUC and UC are generated from a CG as BUC Graphs and UC Graphs, respectively.

Both BUC Graphs and UC Graphs reflect possible sequences of interaction between actors and system. A BUC Graph corresponds to an external actor. A UC Graph corresponds to an internal actor. Both BUC Graphs and UC Graphs contain paths in which the action flow can follow.

Definition 2. Path: *Let G= (D,T,A,E) be a Case Graph, $N = \{n_i, i = 1..n$, such that $n_i \in D \cup T\}$. The R path from a node n_1 to n_k is a sequence $(n_1, n_2, .., n_k)$ such that $(n_j, n_{j+1}) \in A, \forall j \in \{1..k-1\}$.*

This definition means that a path is any logical sequence of action in the current system. This sequence is formed by documents and tasks that should be joined by arcs inside the CG. For example, in Figure 3, the sequence D3,T2,D6,T3,D10 is a path.

Tasks are the transition points in documents. Each task has two associated sets of documents, previous documents and post documents. Formally, these two sets are defined as follows:

Definition 3. Previous Documents and Post Documents: *Let G= (D,T,A,E) be a Case Graph, the set of previous documents of task t ($t \in T$) is defined by $°t = \{d_i \in D \mid \exists x \in A, x$ connects d_i to $t\}$. Analogously, the set of post documents of task t ($t \in T$) is defined by $t° = \{d_i \in D \mid \exists x \in A, x$ connects t to $d_i\}$. Similarly, the notations $°p$ and $p°$ mean the set of previous transitions and post transitions of place p ($p \in P$).*

To assure the consistency of the BUC Graphs and the UC Graphs, we should guarantee that all nodes are achievable. It is a strongly connected Case Graph when a path exists that connects any two points in the graph.

Definition 4. Strongly connected: *Let G= (D,T,A,E) be a Case Graph. G is strongly connected if $\forall x \in N, \forall y \in N, N = \{n_i, i = 1..n,$ such that $n_i \in D \cup T\}$, then a path exists leading from x to y.*

According to Cockburn [3], use cases describe how users use the system. Our Case Graph should describe possible interaction flows between users and the system. Consequently, the term *Case Sequence* needs to be defined.

Definition 5. Case Sequence: *Let G= (D,T,A,E) be a Case Graph. G is a Case Sequence (CS) if:*

1. *The set D has two special documents **i** and **o**. The place **i** is a source place, $°i = \emptyset$. The place **o** is a sink place, $o° = \emptyset$.*
2. *If a task t' is added to T, t' connects the documents o and i (i.e. $\{o,t',i\}$ is the path from o to i), then the resulting Case Graph is strongly connected.*
3. *No symmetric associations exist between documents and tasks. In other words, $\forall t_i \in T, °t_i \cap t°_i = \emptyset$ is satisfied.*

This definition of Case Sequence is coincident with the Workflow Net definition given by Van der Aalst [6], specifically regarding conditions 1 and 2. We have added the condition 3 in order to avoid potential deadlocks and/or livelocks in our Case Sequence definition. Adopting this Workflow Net definition we are sufficiently sure about the soundness property of a procedure modeled by a Case Sequence.

We can now define a BUC Graph and a UC Graph. A BUC Graph is a Case Graph that contains all the possible case sequences for an input document from an external actor. A UC Graph is a CG containing all possible case sequences for an internal actor inside a BUC Graph.

Definition 6. BUC Graph: *Let G= (D,T,A,E) be a Case Graph. G is a BUC Graph if it contains all the possible case sequences for an input document from an external actor.*

Definition 7. UC Graph: *Let G= (D,T,A,E) be a Case Graph. G is an UC Graph if:*

1. *It contains case sequences which correspond to an internal actor inside a BUC Graph.*
2. *All the tasks of G are of the AA kind. That is, $T = T_{(AA)}$ so $(T_{(AO)} \cup T_{(OO)} \cup T_{(OA)}) = \emptyset$ is satisfied.*

Twelve BUC Graphs have been identified in our case study, one for each input document, and are presented in Figure 4. This figure also represents 10 UC Graphs (the different shadowed areas). The CG contains a set of BUC_i Graphs. Each BUC_i Graph is a set of UC_i Graphs. Both a BUC_i Graph and a UC_i Graph consist of internal structures and external interfaces. The shared documents and the shared tasks are considered part of the external interfaces. The internal structures are the same as in a Case Graph, according to definitions 1 to 7.

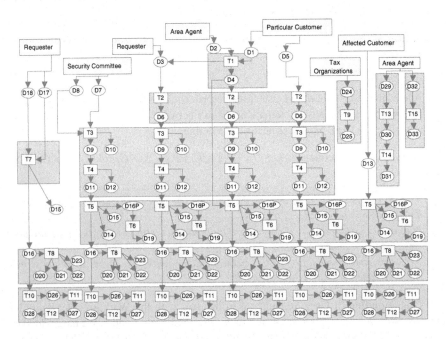

Fig. 4. Case Sequences for four processes in two departments of an organization

3.3   The Modular Case Graph

Since the same document could be directed to, or directed from, distinct tasks, the documents and tasks can be shared by different sequences of case. This means that different sequences of case can be intersected.

While BUC Graphs can share documents and tasks, UC Graphs can only share documents. Each UC Graph indicates the way the information is handled through different case sequences inside a BUC Graph. Because information is handled by tasks, these are not sharable between UC Graphs.

Shared documents acting as connection points between UC Graphs leads the Case Graph to be viewed as a modular structure.

Definition 8. Modular Case Graph: *A Modular Case Graph (MCG) is a set* $\{G_i = (D_i, T_i, A_i, E_i), i = 1 \ldots n\}$ *where:*

- *Each G_i is a UC Graph*
- *All T_i must be disjointed for every G_i*
- *The same label must not be used for documents and tasks, thus, $\forall G_i, \forall G_j, \neg \exists d \in D_i, \neg \exists t \in T_j$ such that $E_i(d) = E_j(t)$*

A process must be carried out on the CG in order to obtain the MCG. This process is composed of factorization of the GC and refining and transforming tasks. It leads to the discovery of common blocks across the BUC Graphs.

Factorization of the CG. The factorization leads to the specification of the common blocks of CG. Identifying these common blocks leads to the factorized expression of the CG without changing the particular structure of each BUC Graph. Consequently, only strictly necessary abstractions of use cases can be done to specify the system functionality.

Algorithm 1. Factorization of the CG: *Let M= (D,T,A,E) be a Case Graph.*

1. *Let S be $\{CS_d, d \in D$ such that CS_d is a Case Sequence corresponding to the external document d $\}$.*
2. *For every $CS_d \in S$*
   (a) *Let T_{cs_d} become $\bigcup_{i=1}^{n} T_{cs_{di}}$ such that $T_{cs_{di}}$ is the task set of the CS corresponding to document d and internal actor i*
3. *Let $T^{\sim}_{cs_{di}}$ be recursively defined as follows:*
   (a) *$T^{\sim}_{cs_{d1}} = T_{cs_{d1}}$*
   (b) *$\forall i = 2..n, T^{\sim}_{cs_{di}} = T_{cs_{di}} \setminus \bigcup_{j=1}^{i-1} T^{\sim}_{cs_{dj}}$*
4. *Let every $T^{\sim}_{cs_{di}}$ and the associated documents, arcs and labels be a preliminary UC Graph*

This algorithm allows a factorization of CG to be obtained. Every CS belonging to a specific CG is divided into fragments. These fragments are formed by the $T^{\sim}_{cs_{di}}$ and the associated documents, arcs and labels. Each fragment is taken as a preliminary UC Graph because each of these blocks may contain different kinds of tasks. In this way a factorized form of the initial CG is obtained.

Following our example, we obtain the common blocks to different BUC Graphs which are shown in Figure 4. It can be BUC Graphs without common blocks. For example, the ones corresponding to D24, D29, and D32 documents. The other BUC Graphs have common structures. The factorized form of the CG is shown in Figure 5.

The distinct blocks from Figure 5 are only previous to every UC Graph because each of these blocks has to be transformed until it contains only AA tasks. The transformation process from OA, AO, and OO tasks to AA tasks implies refining tasks combining only AA tasks. We propose this job be done automatically. Modular Case Graphs (MCG) will result from this transformation. We must point out that the model of Figure 5 is only a base for the MCG.

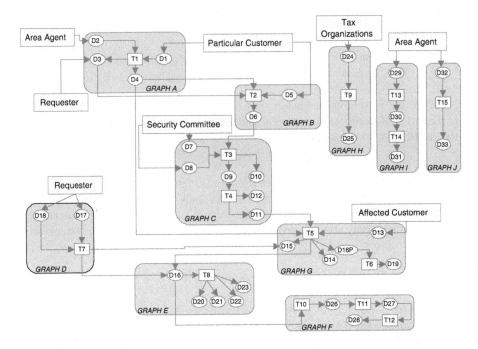

Fig. 5. Factorization of BUC Graphs for the processes of the organization

Refining and Transforming Tasks. Use cases can be extracted automatically from a factorized Case Graph. Hence we propose an algorithmic process for refining and transforming the tasks if required. This process should lead to the expression of factorized Case Graphs by combining UC Graphs. This must take the kind, precondition, and post condition of each task into account. Moreover, it is necessary to know how many documents are being input, and how many are being output in each task.

Algorithm 2. Refining and Transforming Tasks: *Let M= (D,T,A,E) be a Case Graph.*

1. *For every $t \in T$ do*
   (a) *Case of $t \in T_{(OA)}$*
      i. *Let t become $\{t_{(AA)s}\}$ such that $s = 1, 2, \ldots, j$; where $j = |{}^o t|$, $t_{(AA)s}$ is an AA task*
      ii. *Every $d \in {}^o t$ is connected to a distinct $t_{(AA)s}$ such that ${}^o t_{(AA)s} = 1$*
      iii. *Every $d \in t^o$ is connected to each $t_{(AA)s}$ such that $t_{(AA)s}{}^o = |t^o|$*
      iv. *Let $T = T \backslash \{t\} \bigcup \{t_{(AA)s}\}$*
   (b) *Case of $t \in T_{(AO)}$*
      i. *Let t become $\{T_{(AA)s}\}$ such that $s = 1, 2, \ldots, j$; where $j = |t^o|$, $t_{(AA)s}$ is an AA task*
      ii. *Every $d \in {}^o t$ is connected to each $t_{(AA)s}$ such that ${}^o t_{(AA)s} = |{}^o t|$*
      iii. *Every $d \in t^o$ is connected to a distinct $t_{(AA)s}$ such that $t_{(AA)s}{}^o = 1$*
      iv. *Let $T = T \backslash \{t\} \bigcup \{t_{(AA)s}\}$*

(c) *Case of* $t \in T_{(OO)}$

    i. *Let t become* $\{T_{(AA)s}\}$ *such that* $s = 1, 2, \ldots, j$; *where* $j = |{}^{o}t| \times |t^{o}|$, $t_{(AA)s}$ *is an AA task*

    ii. *Every* $d \in {}^{o}t$ *is connected to* $|t^{o}|$ *distinct* $t_{(AA)s}$ *such that* ${}^{o}t_{(AA)s} = 1$

    iii. *Every* $d \in t^{o}$ *is connected to* $|{}^{o}t|$ *distinct* $t_{(AA)s}$ *such that* $t_{(AA)s}{}^{o} = 1$ *and* $\forall t_{(AA)s1}, t_{(AA)s2}$ *if* ${}^{o}t_{(AA)s1} = {}^{o}t_{(AA)s2}$ *and* $t_{(AA)s1}{}^{o} = t_{(AA)s2}{}^{o}$ *then* $t_{(AA)s1} = t_{(AA)s2}$

    iv. *Let* $T = T \backslash \{t\} \bigcup \{t_{(AA)s}\}$

2. *Take every* $t \in T$ *as a chain of generic tasks*

This algorithm 2 allows the OA, AO, and OO tasks to be transformed following the pattern given in Figure 2.D. The behaviour of the algorithm depends on the type of task to be refined or transformed. The OA tasks are refined to as many sub-tasks as there are inputs, each input is connected to one sub-task, each sub-task is also connected to all outputs. The AO tasks are refined to as many sub-tasks as there are outputs, each input is connected to all sub-tasks, each sub-task is also connected to one output. The OO tasks are refined to as many sub-tasks as the product of the amount of inputs and outputs, each input is connected to as many sub-tasks as outputs in the mother task, each sub-task is also connected to an output from every input document.

In this way, the refining and transforming process for each task leads to a Case Graph expressed in terms of the AA standard. If all blocks are expressed with only AA tasks then the definition of a UC Graph is satisfied. If each UC Graph corresponds to a Petri net then the entire Modular Cases Graph is also a Petri net. On the other hand, the validation and verification activities lead to the adjustment of the tasks if required.

The algorithm 2 establish also each task is formed by a chain of generic sub-tasks. If we consider each task as a chain of sub-tasks then we refine each one as this sequence of sub-tasks. Once again, following the example, let us consider data from table 1. We consider each task to be formed by the chain: *Verify, Process, and Generate.*

Table 1. Data for refining the T1 and T2 tasks of the Case Graph of an organization

Task Name	Details	Kind of Task	Responsible
T1: Fill out unloading form	*Verification of* precondition *Processing* data and establish postcondition *Generate* D3 or D4	OO	Control Centre
T2: Receive unloading form	*Verification of* precondition *Processing* data and establish postcondition *Generate* D6	OA	Control Centre

These generic sub-tasks allow the set of steps for use cases to be obtained. The *Verification* sub-task is directly related to precondition and to inputs. The *Process* sub-task is in charge of establishing the post-condition. The *Generate* sub-task is in charge of producing the output of the mother task.

3.4   Obtaining Use Cases

As established in definition 6, the BUCs are obtained as graphs containing all case sequences. An external actor inputting a document starts each sequence. Then, in definition 7, we affirm that obtaining the use cases requires transforming OA, AO, and OO tasks to AA tasks. In algorithms 1 and 2 we establish how to process the CG to obtain an MCG. Finally, having refined and transformed tasks, use cases may be derived and expressed as a template. To do this, we can follow the marking of the Petri net. Some standards for naming intermediate documents must be defined. It is also necessary to decide upon the general naming of use cases to write them as a template, as proposed by Durán [7].

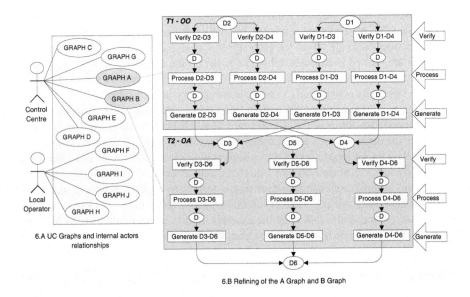

Fig. 6. Relationship between UC Graphs and actors, and refining of the A and B Case Graphs

Figure 6.A shows the relationships between the distinct UC Graphs and the internal actors. Figure 6.B shows A and B cases containing T2 and T3 transformed tasks according to what was established in algorithm 2. One can see that figure 6.B contains all different flows of sequential actions corresponding to the A Graph and B Graph, after refined the T1 and T2 tasks.

Use cases, written as templates, or expressed as a Petri net, have to be sent to a Mecano Manager to finally become adjust assets under the corresponding semantic of the repository. In this way, it is possible to conform the mecanos for reuse, as established by García [8]. On the other hand, expressing use cases under Petri net semantics should lead to establishing a way to organize the requirements of a domain. The definition of these mechanisms both to organize the requirements and write them as templates are being addressed in our future work.

4 Related Work

Few studies have looked at reusing software at requirements level. Besides it is known that requirements from domains and similar tasks are more likely to show similarities than other software elements [21], the requirements reuse has received relatively little attention. A tool and methodological support is necessary to reuse the software requirements [1]. Complex structures to accomplish the requirements related to design and code have been proposed [8]. Nevertheless, to integrate requirements assets and design assets and code assets, it is necessary to find out how to adequately model them. Requirements are modeled with a diversity of techniques so we aimed at normalization to ensure requirements reusability when stored in a repository. The normalized requirements when related to assets of different levels of abstraction provide a large grain interface to increase the abstraction level of the reuse process.

Software requirements have to be treated adequately inside a reuse strategy. Requirements have to be previously classified to be retrieved when developers send their queries. Classification and retrieval of general assets have been approached with schemes and methods based on text, ontology or facets. However, requirements contain knowledge from both the domain and the development process. The complexity of this knowledge forces the application of sophisticated techniques for requirements classification and retrieval [5]. To efficiently answer the queries by selecting, composing or generating elements, a robust strategy based on software requirements reuse is required.

Common classification and retrieval techniques show limited utility in representing requirements for reuse [5]. Some different alternatives based on knowledge representation [15] and analogical reasoning [16] to reuse the requirements from a knowledge base have been proposed. These techniques place emphasis on the semantics of requirements documents and it demands artificial intelligence applications to acquire and manage the encoded knowledge in requirements documentation. Other techniques are based on meta-models [17], evolutionary development [2] and formal methods [23] all of which emphasize the process for development and maintenance of the reusable requirements. Cybulski [5] has proposed a set of techniques based on structural properties of documents and tasks emphasizing the way to enact and use the requirements in the life cycle of requirements engineering.

Scenarios approaches like use cases (UC) and business use cases (BUC) [12,11] are helpful and widely accepted in requirements elicitation. They offer several advantages in overcoming natural language shortcomings. Particularly, the UC approach solves scalability and traceability shortcomings, and it supplies facilities for description. Nevertheless, according to Lee, Cha and Kwon [14], the UC approach does not correct natural language ambiguity. We also believe that use cases do not supply facilities for organizing software requirements to software development with reuse.

5   Conclusions and Future Work

To integrate system requirements in complex reuse structures, adequate models to promote requirements reusability are required. In the present paper we have proposed a method to automatically obtain analysis assets as use cases from an administrative workflow. We have shown that use cases can be generated from a workflow modeling the information flow in a business domain.

We have applied an elicitation process of system requirements through a Case Graph and a Petri net. The established process leads to formalized analysis assets taking part in a reusable component called mecano. With formalized functionality we are in a position to support different analysis to systematically investigate the component behaviour. Furthermore, from sets of use cases we hope to establish ways to organize the information about system requirements.

Proposed CG is an unambiguous alternative to model business dynamics with little information. The CG represent activity flows by a control scheme formalizing the requirements elicitation process and accomplishing scalability and traceability. However, this CG based approach should be proven and validated in the definition of system requirements. We expected their functionality, representing a domain and founded on Petri net theory, will be applicable for obtaining good performance in managing the requirements information.

Our middle term objective is to integrate different requirements notations within requirements reuse strategy. We have found the Petri net approach useful to obtain a precise expression of system requirements from workflow. However, classical Petri nets have shown such net explosion in system modeling as we look for a more compact representation. We are working on a high level Petri net based approach, specifically coloured Petri nets, to represent analysis assets. Our next job will also supply:

- A tool to automatically generate use cases from Case Graphs.
- A model to support organization of system requirements in a domain.

Acknowledgments

This work is sponsored by the DOLMEN Project within CICYT-TIC2000-1673-C06-05, Ministry of Technology and Science, Spain. Oscar López wishes to thank the Spanish Agency for International Cooperation (AECI) and the Ministry of Technology and Science of Costa Rica.

References

1. K. Barber, S. Jernigan, and T. Graser. Increasing opportunities for reuse through tool and methodology support for enterprise-wide requirements reuse and evolution, 1999.
2. Roberto Bellinzona, Maria Grazia Fugini, and Vicki de Mey. Reuse of specifications and designs in a development information system. In N. Prakash, C. Rolland, and Barbara Percini, editors, *Information System Development Process*, pages 79–96, Amsterdam, 1993. North-Holland.
3. A. Cockburn. *Writing Effective Use Cases*. Addison-Wesley, Boston, 2000.

4. Collonges, Huges, and Laroche. *Merisse. Methode de conception*. Dunod, France, 1987.
5. Jacob L. Cybulski. Patterns in software requirements reuse. Technical report, Department of Information Systems. University of Melbourne, July 1998.
6. V. d. Aalst. The Application of Petri Nets to Workflow Management. Eindhoven, University of Technology, Netherland, URL: `http://wwwis.win.tue.nl/~wsinwa/jcsc/jcsc.html`, 1997.
7. A. Durán, B. Bernárdez, M. Toro, R. Corchuelo, and J.A. Pérez. Expressing customer requirements using natural language requirements templates and patterns. In *Modern Applied Mathemathics Techniques in Circuits, Systems and Control*, pages 337–342, Atenas, Greece, 1999. World Scientific and Engineering Society Press.
8. Francisco José García, Antonio Barras, Miguel Ángel Laguna, and José Manuel Marqués. Product line variability support by FORM and mecano model integration. In *ACM Software Engineering Notes*, To appear 2002.
9. Dimitrios Georgakopoulos, Mark F. Hornick, and Amit P. Sheth. An overview of workflow management: From process modeling to workflow automation infrastructure. *Distributed and Parallel Databases*, 3(2):119–153, 1995.
10. IEEE. *IEEE Software Engineering Standard Collection. 1999 Edition*. IEEE Computer Society Press, 1999.
11. Ivar Jacobson, Grady Booch, and James Rumbaugh. *The Unified Software Development Process*. Object Technology Series. Addison-Wesley, 1999.
12. Ivar Jacobson, M. Christerson, Patrik Jonsson, and G. Övergaard. *Object-Oriented Software Engineering: A Use Case Driven Approach*. Addison-Wesley, 1992. (Revised 4th printing, 1993).
13. I. Kotonya, G.; Sommerville. *Requeriments Engineering: Processes Techniques*. USA Wiley, 1997.
14. Woo Jin Lee, Sung Deok Cha, and Yong Rae Kwon. Integration and analysis of use cases using modular Petri nets in requirements engineering. *IEEE Transactions on Software Engineering*, 24(12):1115–1130, December 1998. Special Issue: Scenario Management.
15. M. Lowry and R. Duran. Knowledge-based software engineering. In *The Handbook of Artificial Intelligence*, pages 241–322, Massachusetts, 1989. A. Barr, P.R. Cohen, and E.A. Feigenbaum, Editors. Addison-Wesley.
16. N. Maidenand and A. Sutcliffe. Exploting reusable specification through analogy. *Communications of ACM*, 35(4):55–64, 1993.
17. Colette Rolland and Naveen Prakash. From conceptual modelling to requirements engineering. Technical Report Series 99-11, CREWS, 1999.
18. Manuel Silva. *Las Redes de Petri en la Automática y la Informática*. Editorial AC, Madrid, España, 1985.
19. I. Sommerville. *Software Engineering*. Addison-Wesley, USA, 6th edition, 2001.
20. A. Sutcliffe, N. Maiden, S. Minocha, and D. Manuel. Supporting scenario-based requirements engineering. *IEEE Transactions on Software Engineering*, 24(12), December 1998.
21. Axel van Lamsweerde. Requirements engineering in the year 00: A research perspective. In *22nd. International Conference on Software Engineering*, Limerich, June 2000. ACM Press.
22. WfMC. The workflow management coalition. Terminology and Glossary. Document Number WFMC-TC-1011. United Kingdom, 65 pages. feb 99.
23. M.R. Wirsing, R. Hennicker, and R. Stabl. Menu - an example for the systematic reuse of specifications. In *2nd European Software Engineering Conference*, pages 20–41, Coventry, England, 1989. Springer-Verlag.

Meta-modeling Techniques Meet
Web Application Design Tools

Luciano Baresi, Franca Garzotto, Luca Mainetti, and Paolo Paolini

Dipartimento di Elettronica e Informazione - Politecnico di Milano
Piazza L. da Vinci 32, I-20133 Milano, Italy
{baresi,garzotto,mainetti,paolini}@elet.polimi.it

Abstract Web-based hypermedia systems are becoming more and more sophisticated, new modeling requirements constantly arise, and design models must constantly evolve. Since design tools should complement models to support an efficient design process, model evolution raises a technological issue: Design tools must be modified when their underlying model changes. This is why the paper proposes a general approach to efficiently update design tools in response to model evolutions. The key ideas are: a) the description of a hypermedia model in terms of a general meta-model, powerful enough to express the semantics of current and future design constructs; b) the transformation of a hypermedia design tool into a meta-CASE tool, able to cope with model updates without requiring to be redefined and rebuilt from scratch.
The approach is presented by discussing a case study, that is, the feasibility study to transform our design toolkit, Jweb, into a meta-CASE tool (Jweb3). This tool will support the latest version of our model (called W2000), and will easily evolve with the model it supports. We discuss the adoption of the OMG meta-modeling standards MOF and XMI as enabling technology, we present a sample of the representation of W2000 in terms of MOF, and we sketch the architecture of the under-implementation Jweb3.

1 Introduction

Web-based hypermedia systems are becoming more and more sophisticated: New modeling requirements constantly arise, and hypermedia design models must constantly evolve. An example of this evolution is HDM (Hypertext Design Model). Since its first definition in 1991 [8], HDM has originated a family of variants (HDM2 [7], HDM-lite [6]) and, more recently, W2000 [2]. W2000 has been defined in response to the transformation of Web-based hypermedia from read-only navigational "repositories" to complex applications that combine navigation and operations in a sophisticated way. W2000 enriches the latest version of HDM with concepts and notations for modeling richer information structures as well as operations and services accessible through the Web. It exploits the Unified Modeling Language UML [13] and its customizability to ascribe W2000 with a standard graphical syntax.

Along with HDM, we have been developing Jweb [3], a CASE toolbox that assists Web application designers during the whole development process: from conceptual design to semi-automatic generation of final applications. Jweb provides a set of tools that enables the designer to specify, document, reuse, and prototype their design choices in

R.-D. Kutsche and H. Weber (Eds.): FASE 2002, LNCS 2306, pp. 294–307, 2002.

an efficient way. It has been evolving with the HDM family, but always a step beyond. We have experimented that the evolution of a CASE tool is not as easy as the evolution of the model it supports, and originates an almost chronic misalignment. This is why, before starting the development of Jweb3, the latest version of our toolbox, which should fully support W2000, we decided to investigate new solutions.

In this paper, we present the first results of the feasibility study that we conducted to pave the ground to Jweb3. We started from the schema editor, which has been always the first and most important tool in the Jweb chain of tools [1], trying to meet the two following requirements:

- Jweb3 should smooth the chronic misalignment between models and tools. It should be able to absorb possible changes in the underlying W2000 model without imposing that all tools be rebuilt from scratch.
- Since W2000 is based on UML, the prototype schema editor should exploit the modeling features of commercial UML CASE tools, like Rational Rose [15] or SoftTeam Objecteering [17], without constraining the whole toolbox to adopt strange and proprietary format to store produced artifacts.

The former requirements can be tackled using meta-CASE technology. Standard CASE tools support fixed notations, whose definition is hard-coded in the tool. Even slight changes in the notation would require that the tool(set) be rebuilt from scratch. Meta-CASE tools, in contrast, separate editing facilities from the definition of the notation they support and thus foster flexibility and evolvability. Meta-CASE technology has been widely adopted by several software engineering environments, but to the best of authors' knowledge, it is new in the domain of hypermedia model: We do not know other "meta" approaches to which our proposal can be compared. The advantage in terms of flexibility is counterbalanced by the need of supplying the tool with a rigorous description of the supported notation. The latter requirement imposes to adopt UML tools that are customizable and support a vendor-independent common format to seamlessly exchange UML specifications among different tools.

In this paper, we adopt "standard" OMG (Object Management Group) to find a solution to both problems: XMI (XML Metadata Interchange [14]) solves the first requirement, while MOF (Meta-Object Facility [12]) solves the second problem. XMI is the XML-based stream format for metadata interchange. It is useful for storing artifacts in a vendor-independent format and all newer UML tools support it. MOF is the standardized model for meta-data definition, that is, for describing the fundamental concepts with which applications work. MOF can be used to define special-purpose notations for particular application domains. These definitions can then drive subsequent implementation steps, serve as basis for connecting independent software components, or be used as oracle (i.e., reference) for assessing the correctness of specifications that should be compliant with it.

The adoption of MOF-XMI as underlying enabling technology for Jweb3 would transform Jweb in a meta-CASE tool that would allow us to update all modeling tools each time a new version of W2000 is released. A rigorous definition of the notation (i.e., of the meta-model) would provide a precise framework to accomplish all versions

---

[1] The schema editor is the CASE component that assists the designer to model the data, navigation, presentation, and operations that belong to the application.

and customizations of W2000 and would shorten the update effort from months to days. Nevertheless, the adoption of this technology requires an in-depth and critical analysis due to its novelty and continuous evolution.

All major UML tools are good at letting designers manipulate UML models visually and export them using XMI-UML. MOF can proficiently be used to specify the W2000 meta-model, i.e., it can act as meta-meta-model for W2000. What is still missing is the semantic validation, that is, the crosscheck of a W2000 model (for a particular application) against its meta-model. This paper proposes a solution based on Schematron [2] ([1]) to let W2000 designers validate their models within the framework described so far. Even if the emphasis of the paper is on W2000 and Jweb, all identified solutions are general enough to be adapted to other – mainly object-oriented – design models and tools, in particular if object oriented (such as OOHDM [16], WebML [4] or similar).

The rest paper is organized as follows. Section 2 describes the feasibility study. Section 3 sketches a fragment of the W2000 meta-model, defined using the technology presented in Section 2. Section 4 describes how Jweb3 will exploit meta-modeling by proposing a first high-level architecture, and Section 5 briefly lists our current and future work and concludes the paper.

1.1   OMG Terminology

To explain our approach, it is important to clarify the OMG terminology (summarized in Table 1), and give the terms models and meta-models a different meaning with respect to traditional Web and database design. According to the OMG, a notation (e.g., UML) is based on a meta-model, which can be used to design different models (i.e., definitions of particular applications). This is against usual database or Web design jargon, where an OMG meta-model is called model (e.g., the ER model or the HDM model), and an OMG model is called schema (of a particular application).

Table 1. OMG hierarchy

OMG Levels	OMG terminology	DBterminology	Examples
3	Meta-meta-model	Meta-model	MOF
2	Meta-model	Model	W2000 (UML)
1	Model	Schema	Web-based conference manager
0	Object	Instance	Papers, authors, etc.

2   Feasibility Study

Before updating (rebuilding) the Jweb toolset to make it become fully compliant with W2000, we decided to start a feasibility study to better understand the key features of

---

[2] Schematron is a structural schema language that differs from other schema languages since it not based on grammars but on finding tree patterns in the parsed document. This approach allows for the definition of simple and powerful validation engines.

the new toolbox. We wanted the new tool-suite to supply developers with a UML-like graphical notation for application schema design, and we wanted also to find better solutions to the severe problem of lack of flexibility and extensibility, i.e., the chronic misalignment between Jweb and HDM evolutions.

As to the first aspect, we decided to probe the possibilities of using existing UML CASE tools as temporary front-ends for the forthcoming schema editor. The idea was not to select "the best" available tool, but simply do some experiments and delay the implementation of a special-purpose editor to better refine W2000 constructs. As side effect, this implied that we did not want to work with proprietary formats to store models (W2000 schemas), but we needed a cross-platform standard to be able to change the front-end according to our needs.

Flexibility and extensibility required something more sophisticated than the XML-DTD solution used so far. The DTD description of HDM revealed to be insufficient and did not support tool evolution seamlessly. We did not try to find independent solutions to the two problems, but we decided to exploit the OMG novel way to meta-modeling to find a cumulative solution.

When we think of meta-modeling, we have first to recall that a CASE tool can roughly be schematized as software that supports a given notation and allows developers to create design artifacts according to that notation. Using the OMG jargon, we can say that each model (i.e., artifact) must be compliant to a given meta-model (i.e., notation). This definition allows us to decompose a CASE tool into a provider of modeling features, which depends on the supported meta-model, and a consistency checker between defined models and their meta-model. Meta-CASE tools ([18]) do a similar job at a meta-meta-level. Meta-CASE tools let the developer define his own meta-model and express the semantics of the primitives of this meta-model in terms of a meta-meta-model. Describing a new modeling feature of a meta-model (e.g., a new primitive for W2000) with a meta CASE tool would require the designer to describe the semantics of the new construct in terms of the meta-meta-model. The key point is that a meta-meta-model (MOF) supplies all modeling features to render extensions and mechanisms to (automatically) update the tools with respect to consistency checking and manipulation operations.

Borrowing and extending this definition, we decided to study how to describe W2000 as a meta-model, how to identify what modeling features are specific to W2000 (with respect to other standard meta-models like pure UML), how to generate meta-model updates automatically, and how to store and distribute designed models in a way that would not be tight to any particular tool vendor and would reserve room for possible changes in the meta-model. As a side effect, a complete and powerful formalization of the meta-model would have served also as rigorous description of W2000 itself.

2.1   W2000 as a Profilable MOF Meta-model

W2000 can be seen as a UML extension (profile, according to the UML terminology) [3]. UML, in fact, supplies ad-hoc features (stereotypes, tagged values, and constraints) to extend the original UML to cope with particular needs and specific application domains.

---

[3] W2000 was born as a by-hand extension to UML. Its rigorous definition as a UML profile is in progress.

Defining W2000 as a UML profile allows us to exploit UML commercial tools, but also XMI-UML, that is, the UML instantiation of XMI [4], which is rapidly becoming the "lingua franca" to exchange UML models in a vendor-independent way. Any XMI-compliant UML tool can then be used as graphical front-end for the schema generator; we have only to implement our UML profile using the features offered by the particular tool. Roughly speaking, we can say that no matter the tool we use to edit a W2000 schema, we should obtain an XML description compliant to an XMI-UML DTD.

The adoption of UML profiles is enough to use UML CASE tools as front-ends for the schema editor, but does not allow semantic checks. Currently, available CASE tools support profiles partially (only Objecteering [17] provides some support): Evolution and consistency checks would not be possible. This is why we decided to adopt MOF (the OMG standard way for designing meta-models) to describe the W2000 meta-model, that is, to give a precise definition of W2000 concepts in terms of a flexible meta-meta-model. This approach allows us to change W2000 the way we want and we have a better means to assess the consistency of our models. Even if MOF is the means for implementing meta-CASE technology, we did not want to get rid of the whole UML and start our description of the W2000 meta-model from scratch. We decided for a compromise solution: The W2000 meta-model reuses many UML concepts, and this means that we can see W2000 as a UML profile and all possible versions of W2000 constructs can always be mapped onto instances of UML primitives, but with respect to conventional UML profiles it satisfies also an additional condition: All concepts (both new and borrowed ones) are defined using MOF. Thus, we can say that W2000 is a profilable MOF meta-model (hereafter, p-meta-model).

The reason for introducing the concept of p-meta-model is that if the UML meta-model can be described in terms of MOF, the opposite does not hold true, i.e., not all meta-models described in MOF can be mapped onto the UML meta-model. Thus we could not be able to check the consistency of a W2000 model (compliant with a "purely UML" definition of W2000 and described using standard UML tools) against the W2000 meta-model (compliant with the MOF-defined meta-model) directly. The comparison would never be possible in the general case, but the profilability of the W2000 meta-model allowed us to think of a translator to make the comparison happen. Besides this, we had to bear in mind evolvability, thus the comparison/validation would have been possible against evolutions of the W2000 meta-model.

2.2   Our Technological Solution

All these requirements led us to define the software architecture for the schema editor of Jweb3, i.e., the editor of W2000 models, as depicted in Figure 1.

The gray box in the upper left corner identifies meta-modeling technology; all other tools belong to the usual modeling chain, which must be enabled by a set of preliminary meta-modeling steps. We start by defining the W2000 p-meta-model: Usually we do this using *Rational Rose* integrated with the *Unisys add-on for XMI* ([19]). This model, stored in XMI-MOF, is the main input to the two meta-modeling tools. The **translator generator** produces a translator from XMI-UML to XMI-W2000 as a set of XSLT

---

[4] XMI-UML means the XMI format for the UML meta-model. XMI can be employed with any meta-model defined using MOF.

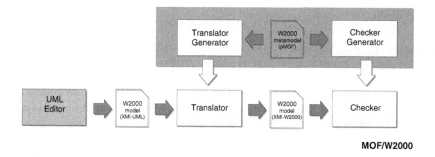

Figure 1. Our proposal

rules. The **checker generator** uses the same meta-model to produce a set of Schematron rules. Schematron can be used to find specific patterns in an XML document; in this case it is used to validate W2000 models against the constraints identified in the meta-model. These tools exploit the *IBM XMI toolkit* ([9]) to produce the DTD needed by XMI-W2000.

Moving to the modeling chain, the designer specifies his W2000 models using his preferred UML editor and stores them in XMI-UML. The translator, through the XSLT rules, transform the XML file compliant to XMI-UML to another XML file, but compliant to XMI-W2000. This file is then the input to the checker that validates it through the Schematron rules. Model validation would have been accomplished using a MOF repository, that is, using a repository that is aware of the "format" its stored models should be compliant with. These repositories should exploit OCL as language to specify constraints and thus the rules that define a valid model. Unfortunately, none of the MOF repositories (for example, dMOF [5]) we used during our experiments fully supported all these features and thus we decided to move to a temporary solution based on Schematron. Also, other more standard technologies, like XPath, XLink, and XQuery, would be applicable, but the supporting frameworks need further attention and analysis before being usable to mimic a MOF repository.

Some excerpts of the meta-modeling process are presented in the next section, but the presented solution deserves two more remarks:

- Even if p-meta-models have been defined to solve a specific problem, that is, to define the meta-model of W2000, they are absolutely general and can be used in all those cases where either we need (want) a MOF definition of an extended UML notation or simply we want to integrate MOF-based and UML-based tools.
- We implemented all logical components of Figure 1 through special-purpose scripts (batch files and javascript) and XSLT sheets, all coordinated by HTML interfaces. We think that this implementation style should better fit evolution and simplify maintenance. More conventional solutions (for example, Java-based solutions) will be investigated in the near future as soon as both the technological and methodological landscapes are more defined and clearer.

3   W2000

This section presents an example application of the p-meta-model of W2000. We present both a simplified p-meta-model and its use for modeling the Web-based conference manager described in [2]. Lack of space obliges us to present some excerpts of both models; the whole formalizations are presented in [10]. We have also to assume that readers are proficient in HDM/W2000. Interested readers are referred to [2,8] for in-depth presentations of both notations.

3.1   A P-Meta-model for W2000

The p-meta-model for W2000 (Figure 2) comprises the three standard UML packages (see the UML meta-model, [13]), and the new *W2000 package*.

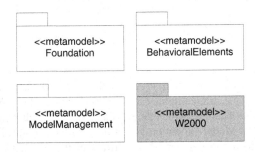

Figure 2. The high-level organization of the W2000 p-meta-model

This organization allows W2000 to share all main modeling elements with UML. The *Foundation* package supplies all basic modeling elements (i.e., classes, attributes, associations, etc.), the *BehavioralElements* package supplies the elements to specify the dynamic behavior of a model, the *ModelManagement* package supplies the means to cope with complexity and organize a model into submodels according to the different viewpoints. The new package, *W2000*, defines how we extended UML to represent W2000 constructs.

The profilability of the p-meta-model implies that all new W2000 concepts be specified as extensions to standard UML elements, that is, W2000 elements are subclasses of standard UML meta-model classes. This organization is partially shown in Figure 3, which collects some excerpts from the W2000 package. Figure 3(a) shows the main elements of the *Information Model Design*: classes Entity and Component are both subclasses of class Class (defined in the *Core* subpackage of the *UML Foundation* package). Both classes are abstract classes because Entity are always specialized in either EntityTypes or SpearEntities, while Components become ComponentTypes or SpearComponents. Types are similar to classes: They will be instantiated as many times as needed in the running application; spear elements correspond to singletons: They specify special-purpose elements singularly instantiated in the application. Figure 3(b), which shows the main elements for *Access Layer Design*, has a similar organization. A `Collection`, abstract concept, comes from a `Class` and is specialized in `SpearCollections` and `CollectionTypes`. Moreover, each collection has a `CollectionCenterType`, which is a subclass of `Center-Type`. Figure 3(c) shows links and nodes, the two main elements as to *Navigation Design*. Once more, `Nodes` must be either `NodeTypes` or `SpearNodes`. `Links` must be either `CollectionLinks` or `SemanticLinks`, or `StructuralLinks`. Collection links relate the elements of a collection with their center, semantic links correspond to semantic associations, and structural links render the component-based decomposition of complex entities.

The whole *W2000* package comprises some 40 different elements, which are special-purpose refinement of UML elements. Besides adding new properties (attributes) to these elements, we defined also some 60 constraints among the elements in the new package. These constraints range from very simple constraints, like: each W2000 model must comprise at least an entity, to more complex constraints. For example: An `AssociationEnd`, which defines the connections of either a `SemanticAssociation` or a `SemanticAssociationCenterType`, must refer to an `EntityType` or a `ComponentType` or a `CollectionType`, or a `CenterType`.

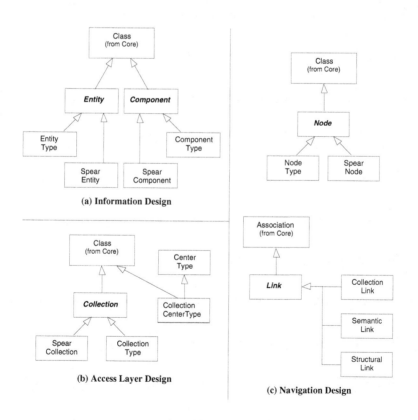

(a) Information Design

(b) Access Layer Design

(c) Navigation Design

Figure 3. Excerpts from the W2000 p-meta-model

To formalize this constraint as a Schematron rule, we have first to recall all dependencies in the p-meta-model:

- `SemantiAssociation` is a specialization of `Association`;
- `AssociationClass` is a specialization of `Association`;
- `SemanticAssociationCenterType` is a specialization of `Association-Class`;
- `EntityType`, `ComponentType`, `CollectionType`, `CenterType` are specializations of `Class`.

All these specializations, together with the knowledge of how XMI works, permit the construction of the Schematron pattern of Figure 4. The name of the pattern simply identifies its meaning. The context defines the "scope" of the rule and identifies the types of the `AssociationEnds` connected to either `SemanticAssociation` or `SemanticAssociationCenterType`, that is, the two specialization of `Association`. The test statement checks that the types of the previously identified ends are compliant with the constraint and outputs a warning in case of violation.

This solution, even if should only be a temporary one, supplies an interesting way for assessing the correctness of XML files with respect to external constraints. It would be redundant in our solution if all technology were available, but could be an interesting way for checking the consistency of XML files that simply come from a DTD.

3.2 An Example W2000 Model

After defining a simplified p-meta-model for W2000, we can show some excerpts of the model of the Web-based management system described in [2]. The goal is not the presentation of W2000 as modeling means for Web application, but rather we want to describe how well known concepts are rendered using the p-meta-model. Interested readers are referred to [10] for a complete specification of the application.

Figure 5 presents the *information model* for the `paper` entity type. The entity is structured in three main components: The `abstract` is always part of the paper and it presents some basic information, like the paper title, authors, and affiliation, along with other information required by the conference, that is, paper id (number) and review status.

The other two components are mutually exclusive: Either we have a `first submission`, or after accepting the paper, we have its `camera-ready version`. The XOR label between the two aggregations codes this dependence. These components reuse also some information already defined in the abstract. Each time an attribute (slot) is reused in a component, we simply refer to its original definition, instead of re-specifying it. This way, we avoid inconsistent redefinitions and we maximize reuse. For example, the paper id is repeated in all components, but the abstract defines it and the others reuse the definition.

When we move to *navigation design*, Figure 6(a), we see that the paper has been decomposed in three nodes. Once more, the main one contains all base information, while the other two nodes correspond to the first submission and camera-ready respectively. The actual contents of these nodes is specified using the keyword body, which make readers refer to the information design to understand the actual contents. For example,

```
<pattern name="SemanticAssociation">
  <rule context="
    //W2000.SemanticAssociation
    /Foundation.Core.Association.connection
    /Foundation.Core.AssociationEnd
    /Foundation.Core.AssociationEnd.type/*
    |
    //W2000.SemanticAssociationCenterType
    /Foundation.Core.Association.connection
    /Foundation.Core.AssociationEnd
    /Foundation.Core.AssociationEnd.type/*
  ">
  <assert test="
    (local-name(id(@xmi.idref))=
                    'W2000.EntityType') or
    (local-name(id(@xmi.idref))=
                    'W2000.SemanticAssociationCenterType') or
    (local-name(id(@xmi.idref))=
                    'W2000.CollectionType') or
    (local-name(id(@xmi.idref))=
                    'W2000.ComponentType')
  ">A SemanticAssociation link only EntityTypes, ComponentType,
    SemanticAssociationCenterType, and CollectionType</assert>
  </rule>
</pattern>
```

Figure 4. Sample Schematron rule

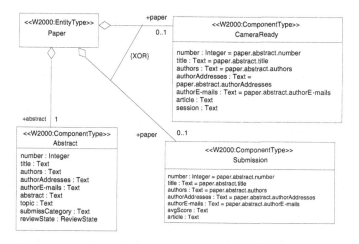

Figure 5. Information model for the *paper* entity type

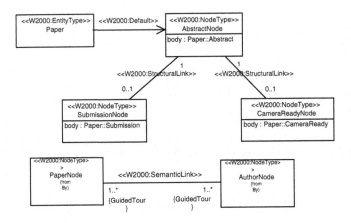

Figure 6. Excerpts from the navigation design

the contents of the AbstractNode node is defined by the body of the Abstract component. The correspondence between nodes and components is not mandatory, but it helps modularize the design. Users are free to specify the contents of nodes as lists of attributes taken from the entities and components that they embody.

Figure 6(b) shows how the user of the Web application can navigate among papers and authors. PaperNode nodes have been defined in Figure 6(a); we assume we have a similar definition for AuthorNode nodes. These two node types are connected through a *semanticLink* object, that is, a kind of association with a navigational semantics. The diagram specifies that given a paper, we can navigate its authors (at least one, but possibly many) through a guided tour. The same is true if we consider an author and we would like to know his papers. We could navigate them using another guided tour.

The few excerpts presented in this section are not enough to demonstrate if W2000 is powerful enough, but they show how each W2000 concept has a clean and neat representation in the p-meta-model and how the concept can be rendered using an UML-like syntax to supply designers with a usable means. Moreover, simple annotations or the use of the dotted notation allow us to trace and relate all concepts to define consistent specifications.

4   Impact on Jweb

Before describing how meta-modeling could affect Jweb and its tools, we have to briefly introduce the toolset and clarify its main components. Jweb assists designers during the whole design process: from information design to prototype and enactment. Figure 7 shows its main logical components: The *editor* lets designers design their applications using HDM/W2000 and produces a HDM/W2000 schema. The *mapper* takes this schema and automatically generates the relational schema for the editorial repository, suitable interfaces for populating the repository, and a general description (XML mapping) of the relational schema. The *configurator* reads the HDM schema, the description of the editorial repository, and the editorial contents and allows for the creation of special-purpose filters to select data; the description of these filters is rendered in XML. The *generator* uses the HDM/W2000 schema, the description of the editorial repository and its contents, together with the filters defined to select data, and generates the run-time database, populating it with the editorial contents suitably filtered. The *engine* reads the contents from the run-time database, presents this contents to users and is responsible for managing the interaction between the user and the application.

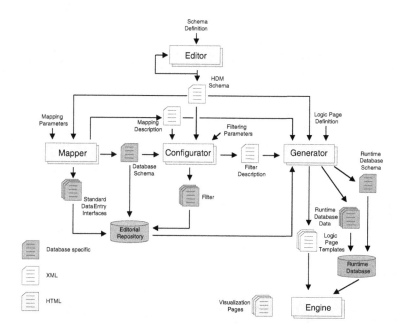

Figure 7. Logical architecture of Jweb

The work done so far concentrated on the *editor*, but since its output (application schema) is then used by all other components, its being meta affects also these other tools. The ideal foreseen situation is that all the meta-tools interact with a centralized repository, which contains the current definition of W2000, that is, its p-meta-model, and through suitable interfaces it allows for the generation of all data needed by the chain of tools. In other words, all tools would play a dual role: They would have a part that belongs to the design process, but their meta component would be in charge of generating/customizing the element according to the specific W2000 p-meta-model in use.

5 Conclusions and Future Work

Our experiments in using meta-modeling technology to support design tools are so far limited to the editor, but starting from the p-meta-model presented in the paper, we induced a non-trivial modification and we studied the impact of these modifications. The main bottleneck was the definition and test of all (new) constraints in Schematron, but all other changes were almost trivial and they could be obtained automatically. This exercise suggested two interesting considerations:

- The availability of a real MOF repository together with a friendlier notation for specifying constraints would further shorten the maintenance process.
- If we had done the same exercise using our standard way, we would have used the following process:
    1. The new meta-model would have been coded directly using a DTD, with suitable comments to explain the meaning of the new/changed features;
    2. The implementer in charge of working on the new editor (component) would have taken this definition as the reference for his work.

Thus, no automatic steps can easily be identified and misunderstandings and errors would be highly possible. In contract, the new approach should pay both in terms of avoiding misunderstandings and errors due to different interpretations, and in the possibility of making several maintenance activities automatic. In conclusion, the feasibility study gave encouraging results as to the use of meta-CASE technology, but it revealed also the extreme youth of available implementations of OMG standards. While waiting for more robust implementations and completing the whole design of Jweb3, we can summarize the feasibility study as follows:

- It gave us the opportunity to identify new technologies for Jweb3 and permitted a thorough analysis of problems (known) and possible solutions (still to be completely identified).
- We defined the family of profilable MOF meta-models (p-meta-models), which are characterized by their intrinsic UML extended notation.
- We exploited XML, UML, MOF, XMI, XSL, and Schematron to implement the software components that support p-meta-models.
- We applied p-meta-models to a first prototype of the new schema editor.
- We defined the first p-meta-model for W2000 and also a first evolution to better understand and evaluate the soundness of our proposal as to evolution and misalignments.

Even if we applied p-meta-models to W2000, they are much more general and can be exploited each time we have a UML extension defined using MOF and we want to integrate MOF-based and UML-based tools.

In the new future, we will continue working on these ideas, trying to simplify our approach and to identify the right compromises between technological and methodological solutions ([11]). We will complete the design and start the implementation of Jweb3. But we are also investigating other possible uses of p-meta-model technology to improve the potentialities of Jweb. For example, we have ideas for two new components: a simulator and a report generator. The former should allow the designer to probe the quality of his models by playing with them before generating the real application. The latter should allow for the customizable generation of design documentation. Both these components will exploit p-meta-models and all needed information will be coded using special-purpose tags in the W2000 p-meta-model.

References

1. Academia Sinica Computer Center. *The Schematron*,
   `http://www.ascc.net/xml/resource/schematron/schematron.html`
2. L. Baresi, F. Garzotto, Paolo Paolini. From Web Sites to Web Applications: New Issues for Conceptual Modeling. In Proceedings WWW Conceptual Modeling Conference, Salt Lake City, October, 2000.
3. M. Bochicchio, R. Paiano, P. Paolini. JWEB: An Innovative Architecture for Web Applications. ICSC 1999: 453-460
4. S. Ceri, P. Fraternali, S. Paraboschi. Web Modeling Language, (WebML): a modeling language for designing Web sites. Proceedings of the 9th. International World Wide Web Conference, Elsevier 2000, pp 137-157
5. DSTC. dMOF User Guide, 2000, v1.01,
   `http://www.dstc.edu.au/Products/CORBA/MOF/`
6. P. Fraternali and P. Paolini. A Conceptual Model and a Tool Environment for Developing More Scalable, Dynamic, and Customizable Web Applications. EDBT 1998: 421-435
7. F. Garzotto, L. Mainetti, P. Paolini. HDM2: Extending the E-R Approach to Hypermedia Application Design. In Proc.12th Int'l Conf. on the Entity-Relationship Approach, Arlington, Tx, Dec. 1993
8. F. Garzotto, P. Paolini, D. Schwabe. HDM - A Model-Based Approach to Hypertext Application Design, TOIS 11(1) (1993), pp.1-26
9. IBM Alphaworks. IBM XMI Toolkit v1.15,
   `http://www.alphaworks.ibm.com/tech/xmitoolkit`
10. V. Miazzo. Strumenti di supporto per Modeling Ipermediale ad elevata dinamicità: ambiente di meta-modeling basato su MOF e UML. Laurea Thesis. Politecnico di Milano, February 2001. In Italian.
11. J. Nanard and M. Nanard. Hypertext Design Environment and the Hypertext Design Process, Communications of the ACM, Vol.38, No.8, Aug.1995, pp. 49-56.
12. OMG. Meta Object Facility Specification, version 1.3, March 2000.
13. OMG. Unified Modeling Language Specification version 1.4, Beta 1, November 2000.
14. OMG. XML Metadata Interchange (XMI) version 1.1, November 2000.
15. Rational Software. Rational Rose. `http://www.rational.com/rose`
16. D. Schwabe, G. Rossi. An object-oriented approach to web-based application design. Theory and Practice of Object Systems (TAPOS), Special Issue on the Internet, v. 4#4, pp.207-225, October, 1998
17. Softeam. Objecteering UML Modeler and Profile Builder, `http://www.softeam.fr`
18. J. Tolvanen. ABC to Metacase Technology. MetaCase Consulting Ltd, white paper, July 1999
19. Unisys. Unisys Rose XMI Tool v1.3, `http://www.rational.com`

Formal-Driven Conceptualization and Prototyping of Hypermedia Applications

Antonio Navarro, Baltasar Fernandez-Manjon,
Alfredo Fernandez-Valmayor, and Jose Luis Sierra

Dpto. Sistemas Informaticos y Programacion Universidad Complutense de Madrid
28040 Madrid, Spain
{anavarro,balta,alfredo,jlsierra}@sip.ucm.es

Abstract. In this paper we present an approach that covers the conceptualization and prototyping phases of hypermedia applications development. This approach is based on a formal model, *Pipe*, adequate to characterize present hypermedia applications. Pipe is used to demonstrate the conceptualization and prototyping phases of the Fraternali/Ginige-Lowe process model, providing a new process model called *Plumbing*. This model is the basis of *PlumbingXJ*, where XML is used to represent Pipe structures in a more human-readable manner. The XML descriptions produced are processed by an *Automatic Prototypes Generator* tool that builds a prototype of the hypermedia application. This prototype is used to evaluate the contents and navigational schema of the final application before large-scale production. As a case study we apply our approach to the whole life cycle of a simple Web application.

1 Introduction

Currently the design and maintenance of high-quality Web hypermedia applications is one of the major challenges for the software industry. In most cases, these applications are constructed by simply "building the solution" with little emphasis on the development process [6]. Production of high-quality hypermedia requires new process models dealing with the specific characteristics (e.g. frequent changes in contents) that appear in these applications. Two specific hypermedia process models are those provided by Fraternali [6] and Ginige and Lowe [8]. In these approaches prior to detailed design and development stages, there is a conceptualization phase, intended to clarify the main requirements of the application for both customers and developers.

Although classic *hypermedia representation systems* (reference models, hypermedia models, and methodologies) [4], [5], [7], [9], [10], [12], [13], [14], [19], [23], [24] could be used in the conceptualization phase, recent studies reveal that these systems are not applied in practice [1]. Generally, these were conceived as design tools, providing a very specific representation of the application, which not

R.-D.Kutsche and H. Weber (Eds.): FASE 2002, LNCS 2306, pp. 308-322, 2002.
© Springer-Verlag Berlin Heidelberg 2002

only engages the conceptualization phase, but also the design and implementation stages. This produces designs and implementations excessively tied to the model's expressive power which, in many situations, is contrary to the industry needs. Also, there is little CASE-based support associated with classic models and methodologies.

In this paper we first present *Pipe*, a new hypermedia model specifically conceived to support the conceptualization and prototyping phases in the development of hypermedia applications. This model is intended to be used as a tool to assist in the conceptualization stage. This can encourage the development of independent designing and implementation techniques. Pipe's main characteristics are:

(i)   It supports Dexter's concepts [9] as well as the context and synchronization concepts of the Amsterdam Hypermedia Model [10];

(ii)   It is able to represent the static and/or dynamic linking of contents in the applications [2]; and

(iii)   It has a formalized browsing semantics (i.e. the manner in which the information is to be visited and presented to users [23]) that can be used in the automatic generation of prototypes [15].

None of the prior hypermedia representation systems present all these characteristics simultaneously.

By integrating Pipe main concepts into the Fraternali/Ginige-Lowe process model we obtain *Plumbing*, where conceptualization and prototyping phases are developed using Pipe´s structures. In accomplishing its goal, Plumbing does not compromise any concrete Pipe representation or particular technique in the automatic generation of prototypes.

In our approach we create a more specialized instance of Plumbing using well-defined markup language techniques obtaining *PlumbingXJ*. In PlumbingXJ we use XML [27] to represent the contents and navigational schema provided by Pipe. PlumbingXJ XML documents are the input for a Java based *Automatic Prototypes Generator (APG)*. This generator uses the default Pipe browsing semantics to build a prototype of the hypermedia application. Later, these XML-coded information can be used in the development phase thanks to its applicability as a bridge between heterogeneous data formats [3], [18]. We have refined our previous work [16] by using a well-known process model and limiting its scope of applicability. Expanding APG´s capabilities, PlumbingXJ could be used as a specific development methodology, applying Pipe and XML to the design and development phases, in a way that is similar to that of the Amsterdam Hypermedia Model [10] and SMIL [26].

In this paper, we first present a brief review of the Pipe formal model [17] and how it is integrated into the Fraternali/Ginige-Lowe process model. This process model is then used to create a more specific one using concrete prototyping techniques. These concepts are illustrated by means of its application using the development of a web site as a case study. Finally, the conclusions and ongoing work are presented.

2   Pipe Hypermedia Model

In this section we present the *Pipe* model, a tuple $<CG, NS, CF, BS, PS>$ that characterizes the linked contents (CG), the navigational schema (NS), the relationships between the two former components (*CF*), and the browsing and presentation semantics (*BS* and *PS* respectively) of hypermedia applications.

2.1   Contents Graph (CG)

The *Contents Graph* (*CG*), is the representation of the contents' domain in the hypermedia application, and of the relationships, or links between its content objects. *CG* is a tuple $<C, H, L>$, in which,

- *C* is the set of *Contents* of the application.
- *H* is the set *ancHors* (i.e., specific locations inside the content objects)
- *L* is the set of *Links* of the application.

Since we are interested in a characterization of dynamic applications, there will be cases where the set *L* cannot be characterized by extension, but by intension (e.g., the links established as the result of a query in a form). Therefore, we introduce the *relation function r* (where N is the set of *Natural Numbers*),

$$r: C \times H \times N \to C \times H \qquad (1)$$

This function *r* represents a simplification of the function used, but illustrates the main concepts of our model. We use *r* to define the set of links.

$$L = \{ (s, h, n, r(s, h, n)) \mid (s, h, n) \in C \times H \times N \} \qquad (2)$$

In this manner, the static and dynamic linking between contents can be characterized as pairs of source content and anchor with its *link number* (*(s, h, n)*), and destination content and anchor (*r(s, h, n)*) via the function *r*. Note that in Pipe, the property of being *source* or *destination anchor* is not intrinsic to the anchor definition. It is provided by the *link definition* that assigns this role. This approach is similar to those presented in [5] and [9].

Function *r* acts a *black box* that hides the nature of the content links (static or dynamic) to the browsing semantics. There are several functions and sets that must be defined in order to provide Pipe with its complete characteristics (but, that is outside the scope of this paper.) Also, there is a graphic notation to represent these sets. A complete description can be found in [17].

In particular, this function is an evolution of the *resolution function*, and *access function* described in [9] in order to cope with dynamic contents.

$$resolution: Specifications \to Identifiers \qquad (3)$$
$$access: Identifiers \to Contents$$

These functions are joined to retrieve the contents of the hypermedia applications, that is, to translate from specifications of the contents to the actual contents. The function *r* is the composition of both functions, *r = access ∘ resolution*, being in this case the function *resolution* the *identity* because in Pipe the specifications are themselves identifiers.

The approach represented by function *r* is radically different, for example, to the one provided in [14]. In this work the links have attached information about their navigational and presentational treatment. As we will see, one of the key concepts in Pipe is the radical separation between content-link information and their navigational treatment. In Pipe, this is represented by the navigational schema and the relationship functions. This approach is similar to the philosophy presented in [9].

We are going to illustrate our approach by using the contents graph of a Web site with information about XML and related technologies. In this Web site we will have a general index that allows for the selection of any topic, the indexes about the selected topic, and the contents selected by every topic index. The application also presents some user adaptation capabilities, such as enabling the user to select the level of content detail.

The contents of the Web site are structured according to the contents graph of Fig. 1. Note that throughout this paper we use the graphical representation of the Pipe structures, which are basically equivalent to their mathematical counterparts.

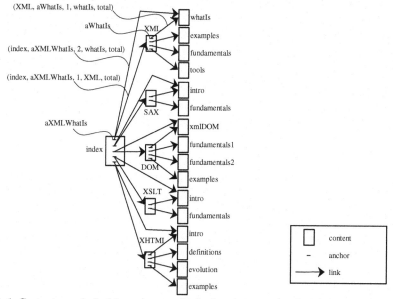

Fig. 1. Contents graph. In this static example the function r can be given by extension

The figure shows an *index* connected to both an *XML* index and *whatIs* content by a binary link. The *index* is connected to *SAX*, *DOM*, *XSLT*, and *XHTML* indexes and contents in the same manner. Finally, these topic indexes are connected with their content. In binary links the same anchor (i.e., *aXMLWhatIs*) originates two links, identified by the link number (*(index, aXMLWhatIs, 1, XML, total)*, *(index, aXMLWhatIs, 2, whatIs, total)*), where the anchor *total* identifies to the whole content. In unary links every anchor (i.e., *aWhatIs*) only originates one link (*(XML, aWhatIs, 1, whatIs, total)*). This numbering is used by the browsing semantics. Note that in this graph there is no information about user adaptation capabilities. This is because it is a presentational characteristic independent of the graph structure. Indeed, in the final application (Fig. 8(b)) it is implemented by a folding list, independent of any hyperlink structure.

Although this contents graph was manually generated, the intended idea is to use the CASE support that we are developing, *PlumbingMatic*, to generate it, together with the other Pipe structures. All this information will be used in the prototyping phase, and reused in the design and development stages.

2.2   Navigational Schema (NS)

The *Navigational Schema (NS)*, represents the user interface of the application (i.e., screens, panes, buttons) and the navigational paths established among and by the elements of the user interface. It is a tuple $<N, A>$ in which:
  – N is the set of *Nodes* of the application.
  – A is the set of *Arcs* of the application.
The nodes of the application represent the elements of the navigational schema. There are *nexus nodes* (N_x) that represent the "windows" of the applications. They work as glue for the *container nodes* (N_c). These nodes represent the "panes" (concrete or virtual in the *context* sense of the Amsterdam model [10]) inside "windows", and they act as the content holders (i.e., text, images, audio, etc.) of the application. Finally, there are *nexus activator nodes* (N_a) that represent "buttons" inside "windows" that activate (by user selection) other "windows".

The arcs of the application represent the structural and timing connections between the elements of the navigational schema (i.e., the nodes). Therefore,

$$A \subseteq (N \times N \times Y) \cup (N \times N \times Y_s \times R) \qquad \qquad (4)$$

being $Y = \{connection, link\}$ types of arcs among nodes, $Y_s = \{sConnection, sLink\}$, types of synchronization arcs among nodes, and R the set of *Real Numbers*. *connection*s represent structural relationships between nexus and container nodes; *link*s represents navigational paths between the elements of the navigational schema; *sConnection*s and *sLink*s represent *connection*s and *link*s which are time activated, and R characterizes the time information attached to both. In addition, restrictions in the relationships that can be established among the nodes appear. There is also a graphic notation to represent these sets (this graphic representation will be used in our case study), but both issues are beyond the scope of this paper [17]. Finally, these sets can be understood as a typed graph that we designate as *extended graph*.

The set of navigational *link*s between container nodes is called *Pipes*, P,

$$P = \{ (c_i, c_j, link) \in A \mid c_i \in N_c, c_j \in N_c \} \qquad \qquad (5)$$

We call them *pipes* because they are going to be responsible for *canalizing* (*interpreting*) the links between contents (i.e., the elements of set L at the contents graph level) to the navigational level (i.e., in terms of set A).

Regarding synchronization, Pipe´s approach is similar to the one presented in [23], where the basic structural and linking information is decorated with timing information (hence, the presence of *sConnection*s and *sLink*s). Moreover, there are several functions that allow for the synchronization of the elements of the set N, based on other elements of the set. Again, we are going to obviate a description of these functions, but their expressive power allows for complex timing relationships such as those presented in [11].

For example, if we want to describe a navigational schema composed by a window (*x1*) with three panes (*c1*, *c2*, and *c3*) such as the first one (*c1*) which has navigational paths (or *pipes*) with the other two, and the second (*c2*) which has another navigational path with the last one (*c3*), we should provide a navigational scheme such as the one shown in the Fig. 2. As in the contents graph, this navigational schema was manually constructed. The PlumbingMatic tool will support the development of such schemas.

Fig. 2. Navigational schema. The square represents to the nexus node (*x1*). The circumferences represent to the container nodes (*c1*, *c2*, *c3*). The lines represent to the *connection*s. The arrows represent to the *link*s (*pipes*)

2.3   Canalization Functions (CF)

The *Canalization Functions*, relate the navigational schema to the contents graph assigned to it. It is a tuple $<d, l, p>$, in which:

- *d* is the *content-assignation function*.
- *l* is the *canalization function*.
- *p* is the *presentation function*.

Function *d* is defined,

$$d: N_c \rightarrow (C \cup \{null\}) \times \wp(C) \tag{6}$$

This function assigns a default content to every container node (it is assigned a value of *null* if there is no default content), and the set of contents that is going to appear inside this node (the set $\wp(X)$ denotes the *powerset of X*). This is done in the same manner that in [23].

Function *l* is defined,

$$l: P \rightarrow \wp(L) \tag{7}$$

This function assigns the set of content-links that are going to be mapped (or canalized) in that way to every navigational path (or *pipe*) in the navigational schema. Several restrictions appear in the definition of function *l*, but are beyond the scope of this paper [17].

Finally, function *p* serves to assign presentation specifications to nodes and contents, allowing for the definition of the presentation semantics.

Using the previous example, the navigational schema is going to be composed by one window (*x1*) with three panes (*c1*, *c2*, and *c3*). In the first one (*c1*) the general index will appear. In the second one (*c2*) the index of the topic selected in the general index will appear (hence the pipe between *c1* and *c2*). In the third one the information selected by default in the general index (hence the pipe between *c1* and *c3*), and the information selected by the index of the theme (hence the pipe between *c2* and *c3*) will appear. The relationships between navigational schema and contents graph are graphically shown in Fig. 3. Again, this figure was manually developed, but PlumbingMatic tool will be able to construct and relate the contents graph and navigational schema.

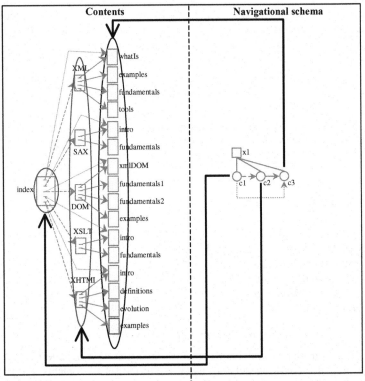

Fig. 3. Relationships between the navigational schema and the contents graph. The bold arrows represent the assignation of contents to navigational nodes (function *d*). Dotted links among contents are canalized by dotted pipe (function *l*). Dashed links among content are canalized by dashed pipe (function *l*). Solid links among contents are canalized by solid pipe (function *l*)

2.4   Browsing Semantics (BS) and Presentation Semantics (PS)

The *Browsing Semantics (BS)*, represents the dynamic appearance of the application according to the interaction with the user. It is a tuple $<a, f>$, in which:

- *a* is the *activation function*.
- *f* is the *link-activation function*.

Before defining these functions we must introduce the sets:

- *Actives* $\subseteq V = N \cup (N \times R)$. Represents the set of active nodes, with their associated timing information.

– *Show* $\subseteq S = (N_c \times C) \cup (N_c \times C \times R)$. Represents the contents that every container node shows (or plays), with their associated timing information.

Function *a* is defined,

$$a: N_x \rightarrow \wp\,(V) \times \wp\,(S) \tag{8}$$

where $a(x_i) = (Actives, Show)$. This function indicates what happens after a nexus node is activated. Basically, by default, every container node shows its content according to the timing information.

Function *f* is defined,

$$f: ((C \times H) \cup \{\perp\}) \times N \times \wp\,(V) \times \wp\,(S) \rightarrow \wp\,(V) \times \wp\,(S) \tag{9}$$

where $f((s, h), c_j, Actives_n, Show_n) = (Actives_{n+1}, Show_{n+1})$. This function (symbol $\perp$ represents nexus-activator and time-activated links) indicates what happens after an anchor (*h*) source of *n* content-link $((s, h, 1, r(s, h, 1)), ..., (s, h, n, r(s, h, n)))$ is activated in a content (*s*) assigned to a container node (c_j). Basically, the destination of every content-link ($r(s, h, 1), ..., r(s, h, n)$) is shown in the container node that holds it. It is necessary for every content-link to be canalized by (assigned to) a pipe that connects the container nodes. Function *f* presents several distinctions according to the content-link and the pipe that canalizes it. The complete description can be found in [17].

The *Presentation Semantics(PS)*, is similar to the browsing semantics, but functions *a* and *f* include presentational information via function *p*.

Note that the presence of PlumbingMatic tool will provide early prototypes *without* any real content. The information provided in Fig. 3 and the Pipe browsing semantics allows for the presentation of the contents graph according to the navigational schema using symbolic names instead of the real contents.

3   Plumbing Process Model

In this section we are going to present the Plumbing process model, evolution of the Fraternali/Ginige-Lowe [6], [8] process model depicted in Fig. 4.

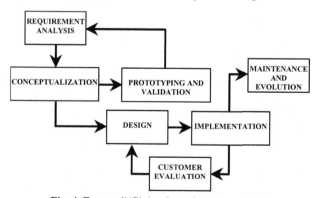

Fig. 4. Fraternali/Ginige-Lowe´s process model

In *requirement analysis,* the mission of the software application is established by identifying prospective users and defining the nature of its information base. In *conceptualization,* the application is represented through a set of abstract models (Pipe in Plumbing) that convey the main components of the envisioned solution. In *prototyping and validation,* simplified versions of the applications are deployed to users for early feedback. In *design,* conceptual schemas are transformed into a lower-level representation, closer to the needs of implementation. In *implementation,* the final application is built. In *customer evaluation*, the user evaluates the final version. Previous iterations in conceptualization/prototyping stages permit a minor number of loops in design/implementation phases that are more costly in development resources. Finally, in *evolution and maintenance* the application continues its lifecycle.

Our goal is to provide a specific description of the conceptualization and prototyping phases using the Pipe model. Therefore, the initial step at the conceptualization stage in *Plumbing* is to provide a Pipe-based representation of the main components of the application (with or without CASE support). The final purpose is to provide the sets and functions *C, H, L, N, A, d, l, p*, or equivalently a graphical representation (as in Fig. 3). Fig. 5 illustrates this Plumbing process model.

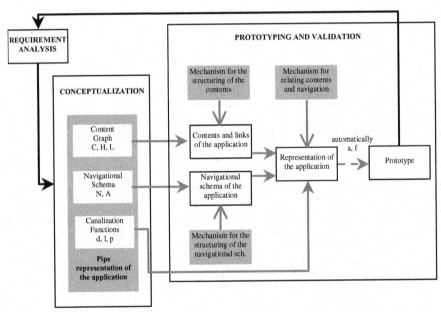

Fig. 5. Conceptualization and prototyping in *Plumbing* process model

At the prototyping phase, mechanisms for the structuring of the contents and navigational schema must be provided, along with one to connect them. The mechanism for the structuring of the contents must be powerful enough to represent the structure of the contents graph, or equivalently the sets *C, H,* and *L* (e.g., a XML DTD with ID/IDREF attributes, or an entity-relationship diagram). The mechanism for the structuring of the navigational schema must also be powerful enough to represent the structure of the extended graph (e.g. a XML DTD or access primitives as those provided by RMDM [12]), or equivalently the sets N and A. Using these structuring mechanisms, the contents of the application and their navigational schema are provided (i.e., the instances of the selected formalisms, or in other terms, the sets C, H, L, N, A). With the help of this data, we can build a Pipe representation of the canalization functions, that is, functions d, l, and p of the Pipe model can be coded. These functions can be used as the input of the automatic generator of prototypes that is guided by the Pipe browsing semantics.

The construction of the navigational schema and its relationships with the contents (according to Pipe structures) can be done manually, or via some CASE tool (as PlumbingMatic) using Pipe structures to produce the specific data, input of the automatic generator of prototypes.

Customers evaluate the prototype developed in this process in the following phase. Finally, the Pipe representation of the application, the prototypes built, and the ad hoc representation of the application are used in design and development phases.

At the prototyping stage, the Plumbing process model does not determine any specific technique in the construction of the representation that codifies Pipe, and consequently, it does not imply any technology in the automatic generation of prototypes. Both techniques must be provided by the developers according to their specific needs. The next process model provides these specific techniques.

4   PlumbingXJ Process Model

PlumbingXJ is a particular example of a Plumbing process model where XML and Java are used to build a prototype of the application. PlumbingXJ is still a process model instead of a development technique because it does not provide specific development techniques, in the same manner that the use of specific techniques for requirements specification does not invalidate the nature of a process model [21]. Fig. 6 depicts PlumbingXJ.

In this model two XML DTDs are the structuring mechanisms applied to content elements and to the navigational schema. The first, *content DTD*, is used to organize all the content elements in the application according to Pipe contents graph. The second, *application DTD*, is used to represent the navigational schema of the application according Pipe navigational schema. Content DTD is specific for each application, due to the specific nature of the contents that it is composed of. The structure provided by this type of DTD is double: a basic tree structure provided by XML elements and its content model (i.e., chapters, sections, etc.), and a super-imposed graph structure provided by attributes (rendering the contents graph of the model). An instance of this DTD represents the actual contents of the application. We denominate it the *content document* and it codifies the sets C, H and L of the Pipe model. In the case of dynamically generated contents and links, set L must be characterized by intension, that is, in terms of the relationship function, r.

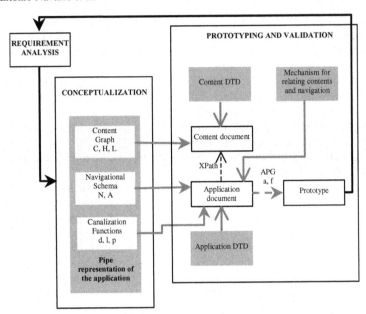

Fig. 6. Conceptualization and prototyping in PlumbingXJ process model

Application DTD is unique and provides a formal vehicle for coding the navigational schema of the application. This DTD does not use Pipe vocabulary (i.e., nexus node, container node, etc.), using instead a more human-readable terminology (i.e., window, pane, etc.) to codify the Pipe model. The instance of this DTD is the navigational schema of the application, that is, it represents sets N and A of the Pipe model. According to the Plumbing process model, we should now specify how to relate both instances, or equivalently functions d, l, p. Although in the former model this was an independent step to obtain a greater generality, in PlumbingXJ it is accomplished at the same time that the navigational schema is provided (compare Fig. 5 and Fig. 6). Therefore, when building the instance of application DTD we are not only defining the set of windows and panes of the applications (sets N, A), but also the contents assigned to them as well as the way they are connected (functions d, l). The question is how to do it.

The answer is called *overmarkup*. The key idea behind this technique is quite simple. The actual contents of the elements of this instance of the application DTD are XPath [28] references to the content document. These references select the contents that must appear in every pane (i.e., in every container node). Information about how to canalize the content links by the *pipes* (navigational links) must be also included. The "overmarked" document (the instance of the application DTD) is named *application document*. If existing contents or a content document need to be adapted, XSLT transformations [29] can be used instead of XPath references to obtain the actual contents from a previous one.

Using the application document as the input for the *Automatic Prototypes Generator* (*APG*) simplified versions of the full application are built prior to its design allowing for early feedback. APG is a Java application that uses the DOM representation [25] of an application document to generate a hypermedia application that works as a simplified representation of the final application. We generate a Java application instead of HTML pages directly because PlumbingXJ is not specific for Web applications, and because it permits a clearer separation between contents and navigation.

As we have stated in Plumbing, this application document can be built manually according to Pipe representation, or it can be built using PlumbingMatic CASE tool. With independence of the concrete construction technique of this document, the application document, or equivalently the Pipe representation of the application, and the prototypes generated are valuable tools in the design and development of hypermedia applications. Although there is no a concrete implementation technique tied to PlumbingXJ, the approach presented in [20] can be a *natural* implementation technique. Moreover, the use of XML in the structuring of the documents offers an easy transition to HTML or another format using XSLT transformations. This approach is preferable to the direct use of HTML for prototyping due to the structuring power provided by XML [22].

5   PlumbingXJ Example

Requirement Analysis and Conceptualization
The information provided through the paper covers this two phases. The Fig. 3 shows the principal outcome of the conceptualization phase.

Prototyping
Fig. 3 is a graphical representation of the Pipe description of the application. In Plumbing this representation has to be translated into a specific description used in the automatic generation of prototypes. In PlumbingXJ this description is provided by using XML. Fig. 7 depicts the application document for the Pipe representation of Fig. 3.

```xml
<?xml version="1.0" encoding="ISO-8859-1"?>
<!DOCTYPE aplication SYSTEM "aplication.dtd">
<aplication id="xmlTutorials">
   <window id= "w1">
      <name>window 1</name>
      <pane id= "p1.1" size=" 140, 320">
         <paneContent>
          <defaultContent>/contents/index</defaultContent>
         </paneContent>
         <linksDestination pane="p1.2"/>
      </pane>
      <pane id= "p1.2" size="320, 200">
         <paneContent>
          <groupContent>/contents/topics</groupContent>
         </paneContent>
         <linksDestination pane="p1.3"/>
      </pane>
      <pane id= "p1.3" size="400, 500">
         <paneContent>
          <groupContent>/contents/information</groupContent>
         </paneContent>
      </pane>
   </window>
</aplication>
```

Fig. 7. Application document. Bold text implement overmarkup technique

When PlumbingMatic tool is available, the generation of Pipe structures depicted in Fig. 3 and its translation to application document in Fig. 7 will be automatic, but in this case it was manual. This document is the input of APG that generates the prototype shown in Fig. 8(a). The explicit separation among navigational schema and contents allows for the change in one aspect without affecting the other, easing the prototyping phase.

At present the *APG* does not support Pipe n-ary links. Therefore, when the user selects a content in the main index, the default content does not appear in the third pane. We are working on a solution to this problem, which is inherently tied to APG implementation technologies (i.e., Java and HTML pages generated from XML data).

The cycle among these three phases is iterated until the customer decides that the structure of the contents and the navigational schema are mature enough to begin the design and development stages of the final application.

Design and Implementation

The final application was built making an extensive use of XML technologies. The XML-marked documents were the basis for the generation of the HTML pages through the use of XSLT transformations. The adaptation capabilities were obtained using JavaScript to manipulate XML documents using DOM. The final result can be found in *http://www.simba.vsf.es/FrameDoc.htm*. Fig. 8(b) shows the final application corresponding to the prototype automatically generated in Fig. 8(a).

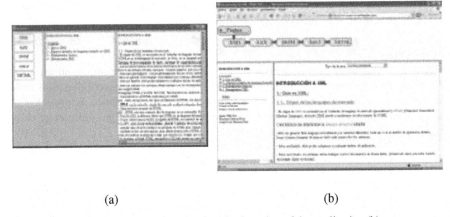

(a)   (b)

Fig. 8. Prototype generated (a) and final version of the application (b)

The availability of the representation of the application in Pipe notation, and the previously generated prototypes eased the development of the application as it was foreseen in the Fraternali/Ginige-Lowe process model. Of course, there were final adjustments, like the inclusion of a folding content index for each topic instead of the index originally conceived, but the main hypermedia structure remained unchanged.

6   Conclusions and Ongoing Work

The specific nature of hypermedia applications demands to pay more attention to the conceptualization and prototyping stages of the development process of this type of software [6], [8]. Classic hypermedia representation systems fail to solve these requirements due to their original conception as design tools, and/or to the lack of specific CASE support [1]. In this paper we have presented the Pipe hypermedia model, designed to represent key information about high-quality hypermedia applications, and specifically conceived as a conceptualization tool. This specificity simplifies its integration in a well-known process model [6], [8] and results in the Plumbing process model. Using markup technologies Plumbing is instantiated in PlumbingXJ, which permits the automatic generation of prototypes using the formalized default browsing semantics provided by Pipe. Moreover, the utilization of the application DTD makes easier the generation of prototypes and, up to the availability of CASE support, the use of XML based descriptive languages improves communication between customers and developers which allows faster changes in the prototyping phase. Finally, the existence of a Pipe based formal representation of the application, with total independence of a specific design, permits several re-implementations of the same application in different environments (e.g., CD-ROM and Web deployment), using a common informational framework.

Ongoing research includes the extension of APG´s capabilities in order to support all Pipe expressive power, the use of alternative development techniques in Plumbing (giving processes similar to PlumbingXJ) and the use of Plumbing and PlumbingXJ in several applications under development. The next step in the project is the construction of the PlumbingMatic CASE tool. As future work, we are considering the possible evolution of PlumbingXJ into a specific development methodology.

Acknowledgments

The Spanish Committee of Science and Technology (TIC2000-0737-C03-01 and TIC2001-1462) has supported this work. We would also like to thank the anonymous reviewers for their useful comments.

References

1. Barry, C., Lang, M.: A Survey of Multimedia and Web Development Techniques and Methodology Usage. IEEE Multimedia 8 (3) (2001) 52-60
2. Bodner, R., Chignell, M.: Dynamic Hypertext: Querying and Linking. ACM Computing Surveys 31 (4) (1999)
3. Bryan, M.: *Guidelines for using XML for Electronic Data Interchange.* http://www.xmledi-group.rog/xmledigroup/guide.htm (1998)
4. Campbell B., Goodman J.M.: HAM: A general purpose hypertext abstract machine. Communications of the ACM 31 (7) (1998) 856-861
5. Diaz P., Aedo I., Panetsos F.: Labyrinth, an abstract model for hypermedia applications. Description of its static components. Information Systems 19 (4) (1994) 33-45

6. Fraternali, P.: Tools and Approaches for Developing Data-Intensive Web Applications: A Survey. ACM Computing Surveys 31 (3) (1999) 227-263
7. Garzotto F., Paolini P., Schwabe D.: HDM: A model-based approach to hypertext application design. ACM Transactions on Information Systems 11 (1) (1993) 1-26
8. Ginige, A., Lowe, D.: Hypermedia Engineering: Process for developing large hypermedia systems. Tutorial at the Eighth ACM Conference on Hypertext. Southampton, UK, (1997)
9. Halasz F., Schwartz M.: The Dexter Hypertext Reference Model. Communications of the ACM 37 (2) (1994) 30-39
10. Hardman L., Bulterman D.C.A., van Rossum G.: The Amsterdam Hypermedia Model: Adding Time and Context to the Dexter Model. CACM 37(2) (1994) 50-62
11. Hardman, L., van Ossenbruggen, J., Rutledge, L., Bulterman D.C.A.: Hypermedia: The Link with Time. ACM Computing Surveys 31 (4) (1999)
12. Isakowitz T., Stohr E.A., Balasubramanian P.: RMM: a methodology for structured hypermedia design. Communications of the ACM 38 (8) (1995) 34-43
13. Millard, D. E., Moreau, L., Davis, H. C., Reich S.: FOHM: A Fundamental Open Hypertext Model for Investigating Interoperability between Hypertext Domains. In Proceedings of Hypertext 2000, San Antonio, Texas, (2000) 93-102
14. Muchaluat-Saade, D.C, Gomes, L.F.: Hypermedia Spatio-Temporal synchronization relations also deserve first-class status. In Proceedings of MMM 2001, Amsterdam, (2001)
15. Nanard, J., Nanard, M.: An architecture model for the hypermedia engineering process. Proceedings IFIF EHCI'98 (Engineering of Human Computer Interaction), Creta, (1998)
16. Navarro, A, Fernandez-Valmayor, A., Fernandez-Manjon, B., Sierra, J.L: Using Analysis, Design and Development of Hypermedia Applications in Educational Domain. Computer and Education, Kluwer Academic Publishers, Dordrecht, The Netherlands (2001)
17. Navarro, A.: The Pipe Hypermedia Model. Software Engineering and Artificial Intelligence Group Universidad Complutense de Madrid Tech. Report ISIA-TR-2001-02.
18. Peat B, Webber, D.: Introducing XML/EDI. http://www.xmledi-group.org/xmledigroup/start.html (1997)
19. Schwabe D., Rossi G., Barbosa S.D.J.: Systematic Hypermedia Application Design with OOHDM. In proceedings of Hypertext 96, Washington D.C. (1996)
20. Sierra, J.L., Fernandez-Valmayor, A., Fernandez-Manjon, B., Navarro, A.: Operationalizing Application Descriptions in DTC: Building Applications with Generalized Markup Technologies. In proceedings of SEKE 2001, Buenos Aires (2001)
21. Sommerville, I.: Software Engineering. 6th Edition. Addison-Wesley (2001)
22. Sperberg-McQueen, M.C., Goldstein, R.F.: HTML to the Max. A Manifesto for Adding SGML Intelligence to the WWW. Second World Wide Conference '94, Chicago (1994)
23. Stotts, P.D., Furuta, R.: Petri-Net-Based Hypertext: Document Structure with Browsing Semantics. ACM Transactions on Office Information Systems 7 (1) (1989) 3-29
24. Tompa F.: A Data Model for Flexible Hypertext Database Systems. ACM Transactions on Information Systems 7 (1) (1989) 85-100
25. World Wide Web Consortium, W3C Document Object Model (DOM). Level 1 Specification. http://www.w3.org/TR/1998/REC-DOM-Level-1-19981001/ (1998)
26. World Wide Web Consortium, W3C Synchronized Multimedia Integration Language (SMIL 2.0), http://www.w3.org/TR/smil20/ (2001)
27. World Wide Web Consortium, W3C Extensible Markup Language XML Specification DTD, http://www.w3.org/XML/1998/06/xmlspec-report-19980910.htm (1998)
28. World Wide Web Consortium, W3C XML Path Language (XPath), Version 1.0, http://www.w3.org/TR/xpath (1999)
29. [W3C XSLT] World Wide Web Consortium, W3C XSL Transformations (XSLT), Version 1.0, http://www.w3.org/TR/xslt (1999)

The Coordination Development Environment

João Gouveia[1], Georgios Koutsoukos[1], Michel Wermelinger[2,3],
Luís Andrade[1,3], and José Luiz Fiadeiro[3,4]

[1] Oblog Software SA
Alameda António Sérgio 7, 1A, 2795-023 Linda-a-Velha, Portugal
{jgouveia,gkoutsoukos}@oblog.pt
[2] Dep. de Informática, Fac. de Ciências e Tecnologia, Univ. Nova de Lisboa
2829-516 Caparica, Portugal
http://ctp.di.fct.unl.pt/~mw
[3] ATX Software SA
Alameda António Sérgio 7, 1C, 2795-023 Linda-a-Velha, Portugal
landrade@atxsoftware.com
http://www.atxsoftware.com
[4] Dep. de Informática, Fac. de Ciências, Univ. de Lisboa
Campo Grande, 1700 Lisboa, Portugal
http://www.fiadeiro.org/jose

1 The Concept

Coordination contracts [1,2] are a modelling primitive, based on methodological and mathematical principles [8,3], that facilitates the evolution of software systems. The use of coordination contracts encourages the separation of computation from coordination aspects, and the analysis of which are the "stable" and "unstable" entities of the system regarding evolution. Coordination contracts encapsulate the coordination aspects, i.e., the way components interact, and as such may capture the business rules [7] or the protocols [6] that govern interactions within the application and between the application and its environment.

System evolution consists in adding and removing contracts (i.e., changing the business rules) between given components (the participants of the contract). As a result of an addition, the interactions specified by the contract are superposed on the functionalities provided by the participants without having to modify the computations that implement them. In fact, the components are completely unaware they are being coordinated. The contracts specify a set of rules, each with a triggering condition (e.g., a call to a method of one participant), and a rule body stating what to do in that case. Contracts are also unaware of the existence of other contracts. This facilitates enormously incremental system evolution, because explicit dependencies between the different parts of the system are kept to a minimum, and new contracts can be defined and added to the system at any time (even run-time), thus coping with changes that were not predicted at system design time.

Consider the banking domain, in which ATX Software has several years of experience. Usually, there is an object class account with an attribute balance and a method withdrawal with parameter amount. In a typical implementation

R.-D. Kutsche and H. Weber (Eds.): FASE 2002, LNCS 2306, pp. 323–326, 2002.

one can assign the guard balance$\geq$amount restricting this method to occur in states in which the amount to be withdrawn can be covered by the balance. However, as explained in [2], assigning this guard to withdrawal can be seen as part of the specification of a business requirement and not necessarily of the functionality of a basic business entity like account. Indeed, the circumstances under which a withdrawal will be accepted can change from customer to customer and, even for the same customer, from one account to another depending on its type.

Inheritance is not a good way of changing the guard in order to model these different situations. Firstly, inheritance views objects as white boxes in the sense that adaptations like changes to guards are performed on the internal structure of the objects, which from the evolution point of view of is not desirable. Secondly, from the business point of view, the adaptations that make sense may be required on classes other than the ones in which the restrictions were implemented. In our example, this is the case when it is the type of client, and not the type of account, that determines the nature of the guard that applies to withdrawals. The reason the guard will end up applied to withdrawal, and the specialization to Account, is that, in the traditional clientship mode of interaction, the code is placed on the supplier class.

Therefore, it makes more sense for business requirements of this sort to be modeled explicitly outside the classes that model the basic business entities, because they represent aspects of the domain that are subject to frequent changes (evolution). Our proposal is that guards like the one discussed above should be modeled as coordination contracts that can be established between clients and accounts.

```
contract class standard-withdrawal
participants x : Account; y : Customer;
constraints ?owns(x,y)=TRUE;
coordination
sw : when y.calls(x.withdrawal(z))
     with x.Balance() >= z;
     do x.withdrawal(z)
end contract
```

The constraint means that instances of this contract can only be applied to instances of Customer that own the corresponding instance of Account. The coordination rule is only triggered when the participating Customer calls the withdrawal operation of the participating Account. The rule superposes the guard (after the with keyword) that restricts withdrawals to states in which the balance is greater than the requested amount. If the guard is false, the rule fails, i.e., the withdrawal operation is not executed.

Having externalized the "business rule" that determines the conditions under which withdrawals can be made, we can support its evolution by defining and superposing new contracts. For instance, consider a contract that a customer may subscribe to instead of standard-withdrawal: whenever the balance is less than the amount, instead of occurring a failure, the whole balance would be withdrawn.

```
contract class limited-withdrawal
participants x : Account; y : Customer;
constraints ?owns(x,y)=TRUE;
coordination
lw: when y.calls(x.withdrawal(z))
    do x.withdrawal(min(z, x.Balance()))
end contract
```

Besides operation calls, triggers may be changes in state. Consider the following scenario, based on a real financial product offered by a Portuguese bank: whenever the balance of the customer's checking account goes below some threshold, money is transferred *from* the savings account; whenever it goes above some upper limit, money is transferred *to* the savings account to earn better interest.

```
contract class automatic-transfer
participants chk, sav : Account;
attributes low, high, amount: Integer;
constraints ?owns(x,y)=TRUE;
coordination
s2c: when chk.Balance() < low
     do amount := min(sav.Balance(), low - chk.Balance());
        sav.withdrawal(amount);
        chk.deposit(amount);
c2s: when chk.Balance() > high
     do amount := chk.Balance() - high;
        chk.withdrawal(amount);
        sav.deposit(amount);
end contract
```

2   The Tool

For this approach to be usable in real applications, it requires a tool to support system development and evolution using coordination contracts. Capitalising on the expertise of Oblog Software in building development tools, the Coordination Development Environment (CDE) we envisage [5] allows the following activities:

Registration: component types (developed separately) are registered to the tool as candidates for coordination.

Edition: contract types are defined, with participants taken from the available component types.

Deployment: the code necessary to implement the coordinated components and the contract semantics is generated. This code is then compiled and linked (ouside of CDE) with the non-coordinated components to produce the complete application.

Configuration: contracts (i.e., instances of contract types) are created or re-moved between given components (i.e., instances of component types) at run-time and the values of the attributes can be changed.

Animation: the run-time behaviour of contracts and their participants can be observed, to allow testing of the application.

The current version of CDE helps programmers to develop Java applications using coordination contracts. More precisely, it allows to write contracts (in a concrete syntax different from the modelling syntax of the previous section), to translate them into Java, and to register Java classes (components) for co-ordination. The code for adapting those components and for implementing the contract semantics is generated based on a micro-architecture we developed [5] that is based on the Proxy and Chain of Responsibility design patterns. The CDE also includes an animation tool, with some reconfiguration capabilities, in which the run-time behaviour of contracts and their participants can be observed us-ing sequence diagrams, thus allowing testing of the deployed application. Future work will include the implementation of coordination contexts [4], a modelling primitive to specify reconfiguration actions.

CDE is written in Java and requires JDK 1.2. Its first public release is freely available for download from the ATX website (`http://www.atxsoftware.com`).

References

1. L. Andrade and J. L. Fiadeiro. Interconnecting objects via contracts. In *UML'99 -Beyond the Standard*, LNCS 1723, pp. 566–583. Springer-Verlag, 1999.
2. L. Andrade and J. L. Fiadeiro. Coordination technologies for managing information system evolution. In *Proc. CAiSE'01*, LNCS 2068, pp. 374–387. Springer-Verlag, 2001.
3. L. Andrade and J. L. Fiadeiro. Coordination: the evolutionary dimension. In *Proc. TOOLS 38*, pp. 136–147. IEEE Computer Society Press, 2001.
4. L. Andrade, J. L. Fiadeiro, and M. Wermelinger. Enforcing business policies through automated reconfiguration. In *Proc. of the 16th IEEE Intl. Conf. on Au-tomated Software Engineering*, pp. 426–429. IEEE Computer Society Press, 2001.
5. J. Gouveia, G. Koutsoukos, L. Andrade, and J. L. Fiadeiro. Tool support for coordination-based software evolution. In *Proc. TOOLS 38*, pp. 184–196. IEEE Computer Society Press, 2001.
6. G. Koutsoukos, J. Gouveia, L. Andrade, and J. L. Fiadeiro. Managing evolution in telecommunication systems. In *New Developments in Distributed Applications and Interoperable Systems*, pp. 133–139. Kluwer, 2001.
7. G. Koutsoukos, T. Kotridis, L. Andrade, J. L. Fiadeiro, J. Gouveia, and M. Wer-melinger. Coordination technologies for business strategy support: a case study in stock trading. In *Proc. of the ECOOP Workshop on Object Oriented Business Solutions*, pp. 41–52, 2001. Invited paper.
8. A. Lopes and J. L. Fiadeiro. Using explicit state to describe architectures. In *Proc. of Fundamental Approaches to Software Engineering*, LNCS 1577, pp. 144–160. Springer-Verlag, 1999.

The KeY System:
Integrating Object-Oriented Design and Formal Methods[*]

Wolfgang Ahrendt[2], Thomas Baar[1], Bernhard Beckert[1], Martin Giese[1],
Elmar Habermalz[1], Reiner Hähnle[2], Wolfram Menzel[1],
Wojciech Mostowski[2], and Peter H. Schmitt[1]

[1] Universität Karlsruhe, Germany
[2] Chalmers Universit of Technology, Göteborg, Sweden

Abstract. This paper gives a brief description of the KeY system, a tool
written as part of the ongoing KeY project[1], which is aimed at bridging the gap between (a) OO software engineering methods and tools
and (b) deductive verification. The KeY system consists of a commercial CASE tool enhanced with functionality for formal specification and
deductive verification.

1 Introduction

The goal of the ongoing KeY project is to make the application of *formal methods*
possible and effective in a *real-world* software development setting. The incen-
tive for this project is the fact that formal methods for software development –
i.e. formal software specification and verification – are hardly used in practical,
industrial software development [5]. As the analysis in [1] shows, the reason is
not a lack of maturity or capacity of existing methods. Our work in the KeY
project is based on the assumption that the primary reasons are as follows:

- The application of formal methods is not integrated into the iterative and
  incremental software development processes employed in real-world projects.
- The tools for formal software specification and verification are not integrated
  into the CASE tools used to support these processes. Indeed, the target
  language of verification tools, in which the programs to be verified have to
  be written, is hardly ever a 'real' programming language used in industrial
  software development.
- Users of verification tools are expected to know syntax and semantics of one
  or more complex formal languages. Typically, at least a tactical programming
  language and a logical language are involved. Even worse, to make serious
  use of many tools, intimate knowledge of employed logic calculi and proof
  search strategies is necessary.

---

[*] The KeY project is supported by the Deutsche Forschungsgemeinschaft (grant
no. Ha 2617/2-1).

[1] URL: http://i12www.ira.uka.de/~key/.

R.-D. Kutsche and H. Weber (Eds.): FASE 2002, LNCS 2306, pp. 327–330, 2002.

Accordingly, a main part of the KeY project is the design and implementation of a software development tool, the KeY system, that strives to improve upon previous tools for formal software development in these respects.

In the principal use case of the KeY system there are actors who want to implement a software system that complies with given requirements and formally verify its correctness. In this scenario, the KeY system is responsible for adding formal detail to the analysis model, for creating conditions that ensure the correctness of refinement steps (called proof obligations), for finding proofs showing that these conditions are satisfied by the model, and for generating counter examples if they are not. Special features of KeY are:

- We concentrate on object-oriented analysis and design methods (OOAD) – because of their key role in today's software development practice –, and on JAVA as the target language. In particular, we use the Unified Modeling Language (UML) [7] for visual modeling of designs and specifications and the Object Constraint Language (OCL) for adding further restrictions. This choice is supported by the fact, that the UML (which contains OCL) is not only an OMG standard, but has been adopted by all major OOAD software vendors and is featured in recent OOAD textbooks.
- We use a commercial CASE tool as starting point and enhance it by additional functionality for formal specification and verification. The tool of our choice is TOGETHERCC (Together Control Center).[2]
- Formal verification is based on an axiomatic semantics of JAVA. More precisely, we confine ourselves to the subset of JAVA known as JAVA CARD.
- Through direct contacts with software companies we check the soundness of our approach for real world applications.

2   The KeY System

The overall structure of the KeY system is illustrated in Fig. 2. We extend the UML/JAVA-based CASE tool TOGETHERCC by adding features to support the annotation of UML diagrams with OCL constraints. A Verification Component is responsible for generating formulae in dynamic logic [3] that express properties of the specification or the relation between specification and implementation. Finally, the Deduction Component can be used to prove or disprove these formulae.

2.1   Specification Services

Support for authoring formal specifications is an important part of the KeY project, not only because it is the basis for any ensuing verification, but also because many problems in software development can be avoided with a precise specification, even without doing a formal verification. The KeY system supports the annotation of UML diagrams by constraints written in the OCL language.

---

[2] http://www.togethersoft.com/.

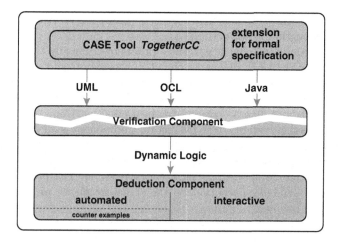

Fig. 1. Structure of the KeY system

These can be used to express pre- and postconditions of methods as well as invariants of classes. The specification of OCL constraints is fully integrated into the TOGETHERCC user interface.

As certain types of constraints tend to recur in many applications, we implemented a mechanism, based on TOGETHERCC's pattern instantiation, to automatically generate OCL constraints for common situations. For instance, an OCL expression stating that a method adds its argument to a set of associated objects may be generated automatically. Another example would be a non-cyclicity constraint added to a composite pattern when it is instantiated.

On demand, the system gathers OCL constraints, parses them[3] and performs type checking with respect to the UML diagram. It is typical of the KeY approach that syntactic correctness of constraints is not necessarily enforced, permitting the user to start with semi-formal specifications and refining them when needed.

Future development will include scanning OCL constraints for certain common mistakes, implausibilities and inconsistencies [2]. We are also planning to support an authoring tool for formal and informal specification in OCL and natural language [6].

2.2 Deduction Services

After OCL constraints have been checked syntactically, the user can trigger the generation of proof obligations. These either capture relationships between the OCL constraints of the diagram, e.g. that the invariant of some class is implied by the invariant of one of its subclasses, or they assert relationships between the OCL constraints and the implementation, e.g. that a method makes its postcondition true. Again, note that the generation of proof obligations is only done

---

[3] We use the OCL parser from http://dresden-ocl.sourceforge.net/.

on demand to let the user benefit from the specification services of the system even when verification is not desired.

The Verification Component generates proof conditions by transforming the information from the UML diagrams, the OCL constraints and the implementation provided by the user[4] into formulae of JavaDL, a dynamic logic for Java [3]. Details of the transformation are covered in [4].

The JavaDL formulae are passed to the Deduction Component to permit the user to show their validity. The Deduction Component is an integrated automated and interactive theorem prover for JavaDL. It features a graphical user interface and is tailored to make the discharging of proof obligations generated by the Verification Component as intuitive as possible. The proof rules follow the principle of symbolic execution, so the structure of the proofs follows the structure of the involved programs.

As verification is intended to be a tool to discover errors in a specification or implementation, it will often be the case that the generated proof obligations are not provable. We are currently integrating a component for counter-example search that will make it easier to identify errors from failed proof attempts.

We are also planning to include a sophisticated proof management system in the Verification Component that allows users to keep track of which aspects of their development have been formalized or verified to which extent.

References

[1] W. Ahrendt, T. Baar, B. Beckert, M. Giese, E. Habermalz, R. Hähnle, W. Menzel, and P. H. Schmitt. The KeY approach: Integrating object oriented design and formal verification. In M. Ojeda-Aciego, I. P. de Guzmán, G. Brewka, and L. M. Pereira, editors, *Proc. 8th European Workshop on Logics in AI (JELIA), Malaga, Spain*, volume 1919 of *LNCS*, pages 21–36. Springer-Verlag, Oct. 2000.

[2] T. Baar. Experiences with the UML/OCL-approach to precise software modeling: A report from practice. In *Proc. Net.ObjectDays, Erfurt, Germany*, 2000. http://i12www.ira.uka.de/~key/doc/2000/baar00.pdf.gz.

[3] B. Beckert. A dynamic logic for the formal verification of Java Card programs. In I. Attali and T. Jensen, editors, *Java on Smart Cards: Programming and Security. Revised Papers, Java Card 2000, International Workshop, Cannes, France*, LNCS 2041, pages 6–24. Springer-Verlag, 2001.

[4] B. Beckert, U. Keller, and P. H. Schmitt. Translating the object constraint language into first-order predicate logic. Submitted to FASE 2002, available from http://i12www.ira.uka.de/~projekt/publicat.htm.

[5] D. L. Dill and J. Rushby. Acceptance of formal methods: Lessons from hardware design. *IEEE Computer*, 29(4):23–24, Apr. 1996.

[6] R. Hähnle and A. Ranta. Connecting OCL with the rest of the world. In J. Whittle, editor, *Workshop on Transformations in UML at ETAPS, Genova, Italy*, Apr. 2001.

[7] Object Modeling Group. *Unified Modelling Language Specification, v1.4*, Sept. 2001.

---

[4] We use RECODER for Java processing, see http://recoder.sourceforge.net/.

ObjectCheck: A Model Checking Tool for Executable Object-Oriented Software System Designs

Fei Xie[1], Vladimir Levin[2], and James C. Browne[1]

[1] Dept. of Computer Sciences, Univ. of Texas at Austin, Austin, TX 78712, USA
{feixie,browne}@cs.utexas.edu
[2] Bell Laboratories, Lucent Technologies, Murray Hill, NJ 07974, USA
levin@research.bell-labs.com

1 Introduction

Specifying software system designs with executable object-oriented modeling languages such as xUML [1][2], an executable dialect of UML, opens the possibility of verifying these system designs by model checking. However, state-of-the-art model checkers are not directly applicable to executable object-oriented software system designs due to the semantic and syntactic gaps between executable object-oriented modeling languages and input languages of these model checkers and also due to the large state spaces of these system designs.

This paper presents ObjectCheck, a new tool that supports an approach [3] to model checking executable object-oriented software system designs modeled in xUML. The approach can be summarized as follows:

- A software system design is specified in xUML as an executable model according to Shlaer-Mellor Method [4].
- A property to be checked on the design is specified in an xUML level logic.
- The xUML model may be abstracted, decomposed, or transformed to reduce the state space that must be explored for checking the property.
- The xUML model and the property are automatically translated to a model and a query in the S/R [5] automaton language. Prior to the translation, the xUML model is reduced with respect to the property as proposed in [6].
- The S/R query is checked on the S/R model by COSPAN [5] model checker.
- If the query fails, an error track is generated by COSPAN and is automatically translated into an error report in the name space of the xUML model.

ObjectCheck provides comprehensive automation for the approach by supporting xUML level property specification, xUML-to-S/R translation and optimization, error report generation, and error visualization. ObjectCheck also provides preliminary automation for the integrated state space reduction proposed in [7].

The most closely related work to ObjectCheck are a toolset for supporting UML model checking based on Abstract State Machines [8], and the vUML

R.-D. Kutsche and H. Weber (Eds.): FASE 2002, LNCS 2306, pp. 331–335, 2002.
© Springer-Verlag Berlin Heidelberg 2002

tool [9]. Both tools translate and verify UML models based on ad hoc execution semantics that do not include action semantics while action semantics of xUML follows a proposal for Action Semantics for UML [10], which has been finalized by OMG. ObjectCheck combines commercially supported software design environments [1][2] and model checkers with research tools to provide a comprehensive capability for model checking xUML models.

2   xUML Semantics

In xUML, a system is composed of instances of classes, which are either active, having dynamic behaviors, or passive, having no dynamic behaviors and being used to store data. There can be association and generalization relationships defined among classes. A large system can be recursively partitioned into packages, which are groups of classes closely coupled by associations and generalizations.

The execution behavior of a class instance is specified by an extended Moore state model where each state has an associated action that is executed in a run-to-completion mode upon entry to the state. State transitions are invoked by messages. State actions can be categorized as follows:

- Read or write actions that read or write attributes of class instances, or dynamically create or delete class instances;
- Computation actions that perform various mathematical calculations;
- Messaging actions that send messages to active class instances;
- Composite actions that are control structures and recursive structures that permit complex actions to be composed from simpler actions;
- Collection actions that apply other actions to collections of elements, avoiding explicit indexing and extracting of elements from these collections.

The execution behavior of an xUML model is an asynchronous interleaving of the executions of the state models of active class instances in the model.

3   Overview of ObjectCheck

To provide comprehensive automation support for model checking xUML models, ObjectCheck is structured as shown in Figure 1. Under the architecture, we selected industrial toolsets such as Bridgepoint [2] or Objectbench [11], as the xUML visual editors and COSPAN as the model checking engine. We incorporated the optimization module of SDLCheck [12] that implements Static Partial Order Reduction (SPOR) and other software specific model checking optimizations. Furthermore, we implemented the following components of ObjectCheck:

Property Specification Interface. The property specification interface enables formulation of properties to be checked on xUML models in an xUML level logic. The logic defines a set of temporal templates such as `Always` and `Eventually`. A property formulated on an xUML model consists of instantiations of these templates with propositional logic expressions over the semantic constructs of the xUML model.

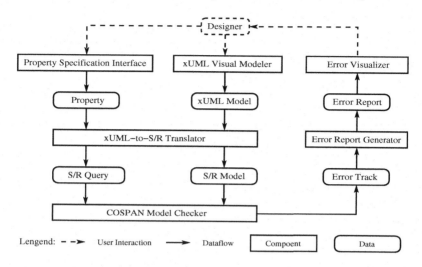

Fig. 1. Architecture of ObjectCheck

xUML-to-S/R Translator. The translator inputs an xUML model and a property to be checked on the model and outputs an S/R model and a query to be checked on the S/R model. Details of the translation can be found in [3].

Error Report Generator. When an S/R query fails on an S/R model, COSPAN generates an error track specifying an execution trace inconsistent with the query. The error report generator compiles an error report in xUML notations from the error track. The error report consists of an execution trace of the corresponding xUML model, which violates the corresponding xUML level property.

Error Visualizer. To facilitate debugging an error found by COSPAN in an xUML model, an error visualizer is provided, which generates a test case from the error report and reproduces the error by executing the xUML model with the test case in a simulator included in the xUML visual editor.

State Space Reduction. ObjectCheck supports powerful state space reduction algorithms. Localization Reduction [5] and Symbolic Model Checking (SMC) are performed by COSPAN. The xUML-to-S/R translator makes use of the optimization module of SDLCheck, which has been modified to reflect xUML semantics. The module transforms an xUML model to reduce the model checking complexity of the resulting S/R model and, in particular, it implements SPOR that reduces the set of possible interleavings of executions of state models (which, otherwise, all should be explored in the model checking phase) by eliminating the interleavings irrelevant to the property to be checked. Currently, a state space reduction manager is being developed, which, together with other components of ObjectCheck, implements the integrated state space reduction proposed in [7].

4   Applications

ObjectCheck has been successfully applied in model checking the xUML models of a number of interesting examples such as a robot controller system, which is previously reported in [13], and an online ticket sale system. An illustration of applying ObjectCheck to the online ticket sale system follows.

The xUML model of the online ticket sale system is composed of instances of three classes: Dispatcher, Agent, and Ticket Server. The system processes concurrent ticketing requests submitted by customers. A liveness property to be checked on the model is that after an agent is assigned to a customer, eventually the agent will be released.

The xUML model is translated into two S/R models: one with SPOR off and the other with SPOR on. The S/R query corresponding to the liveness property was checked on the two S/R models by COSPAN with two different state space searching algorithms: Explicit State Enumeration and SMC. The computational complexities of the four model checking runs are compared in Table 1. Both

Table 1. Comparison of Model Checking Complexities

SPOR	SMC	Memory Usage	Time Usage
Off	Off	Out of Memory	–
Off	On	113.73M	44736.5S
On	Off	17.3M	6668.3S
On	On	74.0M	1450.3S

SPOR and SMC lead to significant reduction on the model checking complexity. The combination of SPOR and SMC leads to less running time, but requires more memory than applying SPOR only. It can be observed that no single reduction algorithm alone can achieve an overwhelming advantage over other reduction algorithms. Therefore, various combinations of state space reduction algorithms on various types of xUML models have to be studied for better combinations.

5   Conclusions

ObjectCheck has facilitated effective model checking of non-trivial software system designs represented as xUML models. Ongoing research in state space reduction at the xUML model level shows significant promise for enabling model checking of substantial software system designs specified as xUML models.

Acknowledgement

We gratefully acknowledge Robert P. Kurshan, Natasha Sharygina, and Husnu Yenigün. This work was partially supported by TARP grant 003658-0508-1999.

References

1. Kennedy Carter: `http://www.kc.com/html/xuml.html`. Kennedy Carter (2001)
2. Project Tech.: `http://www.projtech.com/pubs/xuml.html`. Project Tech. (2001)
3. Xie, F., Levin, V., Browne, J.C.: Model Checking for an Executable Subset of UML. Proc. of 16th IEEE International Conf. on Automated Software Engineering (2001)
4. Shlaer, S., Mellor, S.J.: Object Lifecycles: Modeling the World in States. Prentice-Hall, Inc (1992)
5. Hardin, R.H., Har'El, Z., Kurshan, R.P.: COSPAN. Proc. of 8th International Conf. on Computer Aided Verification (1996)
6. Kurshan, R.P., Levin, V., Minea, M., Peled, D., Yenigün, H.: Static Partial Order Reduction. Proc. of 4th International Conf. on Tools and Algorithms for the Construction and Analysis of Systems (1998)
7. Xie, F., Browne, J.C.: Integrated State Space Reduction for Model Checking Executable Object-oriented Software System Designs. Proc. of FASE 2002 (2002)
8. Compton, K., Gurevich, Y., Huggins, J.K., Shen, W.: An Automatic Verification Tool for UML. Univ. of Michigan, EECS Tech. Report CSE-TR-423-00 (2000)
9. Lilius, J., Porres, I.: vUML: a Tool for Verifying UML Models. Proc. of the Automatic Software Engineering Conf. (1999)
10. OMG: Action Semantics for the UML. OMG (2000)
11. SES: Objectbench User Manual. SES (1996)
12. Levin, V., Yenigün, H.: SDLCheck: A Model Checking Tool. Proc. of 13th International Conf. on Computer Aided Verification (2001)
13. Sharygina, N., Kurshan, R.P., Browne, J.C.: A Formal Object-oriented Analysis for Software Reliability. Proc. of 4th International Conf. on FASE (2001)

Demonstration of an Operational Procedure for the Model-Based Testing of CTI Systems

Andreas Hagerer[1], Hardi Hungar[1], Tiziana Margaria[1], Oliver Niese[2],
Bernhard Steffen[2], and Hans-Dieter Ide[3]

[1] METAFrame Technologies GmbH, Dortmund, Germany
{AHagerer,HHungar,TMargaria}@METAFrame.de
[2] Chair of Programming Systems, University of Dortmund, Germany
{Oliver.Niese,Steffen}@cs.uni-dortmund.de
[3] Siemens AG, Witten, Germany
Hans-Dieter.Ide@wit.siemens.de

Abstract. In this demonstration we illustrate how *a posteriori* modeling of complex, heterogeneous, and distributed systems is practically performed within an automated integrated testing environment (ITE) to give improved support to the testing process of steadily evolving systems. The conceptual background of the modeling technique, called *moderated regular extrapolation* is described in a companion paper [3].

1 Moderated Regular Extrapolation

Moderated **regular extrapolation** aims at providing *a posteriori* descriptions of complex, typically evolving systems or system aspects in a largely automatic way. These descriptions come in the form of extended finite automata tailored for automatically producing system tests, grading test suites and monitoring running systems. Regular extrapolation builds models from observations via techniques from machine learning and finite automata theory. These automatic steps are steered by application experts who observe the interaction between the model and the running system. This way, structural design decision are imposed on the model in response to the diagnostic information provided by the model generation tool in cases where the current version of the model and the system are in conflict.

Moderated regular extrapolation is particularly suited for *change management*, i.e. in cases where the considered system is steadily evolving, which requires continuous update of the systems specification as well.

We will illustrate our method using a regression testing scenario for system level Computer Telephony Integration (*CTI*)(cf. [3, Sec. 4.2], this volume): Here, previous versions of the system serve as reference for the validation of future releases. A new release is required to support any unchanged feature and to enhance it with new or modified features. The iterative process of moderated regular extrapolation (Sec. 2) supports this system evolution, by incrementally building a model comprising the current spectrum of functionality on the basis of concise diagnostic feedback highlighting locations and sources of system/model mismatches.

R.-D. Kutsche and H. Weber (Eds.): FASE 2002, LNCS 2306, pp. 336–339, 2002.

2   Regular Extrapolation in Practice

In this section we sketch the demonstration content, which will successively address the five steps of the model generation by regular extrapolation process by one simple example each.

Trace Collection. To build a model, the system is stimulated by means of test cases and the effects are traced and collected to form an initial model. The example of [3, Fig. 6](left, this volume) shows a simple test case as it is specified in the ITE by a test engineer. Here, three users pick up and hang up the handset of their telephones in arbitrary order. Test case executions are automatically protocoled in form of traces by the ITE's tracer (cf. [3, Fig. 6](right)). In a trace, both states and transitions are labeled with rich labels that describe portions of the system state and protocol messages respectively.

Abstraction. Here, we generalize observed traces to sequential behavioral patterns. The demo will illustrate the effect of abstracting from concrete components to *actors* playing specific roles. An observed trace (actor-set trace) coming from the execution of the test case where this abstraction has taken place is shown in [3, Fig. 6].

Folding. Folding a trace to a trace automaton allows a further powerful generalization of all possible interleaved combinations of actor-set traces. In the folding step, stable states that are considered equivalent are identified and can then be merged. For example, typically all observed devices are classified according to the status of display messages and LEDs. In this step *extrapolation* takes place: the behavior of the system observed so far is extrapolated to an automaton, which typically, due to cycle introduction, has infinite behavior.

The model shown in Fig. 2(left) has been generated via folding from a set of independent traces. It represents the behavior of two users picking-up and hanging-up handsets independently.

Refinement. With new observations, we can refine the model by adding further trace automata to a model. Again, each refinement step is based on the identification of behaviorally equivalent states. In Fig. 1 we show how the trace of [3, Fig. 6](right), is added to the previous model on the left and leads to the model of Fig. 2(left) with four stable system states. Here, a system state is extremely abstract: it is characterized by the number of phones currently picked up. As a comparison, the observations on the original executable test cases were fully instantiated (e.g. they referred to single concrete device names).

Validation. Temporal properties of the models, reflecting expert knowledge, can be checked at any stage by means of standard model checking algorithms. This establishes an independent control instance: vital application-specific frame conditions, like safety criteria guaranteeing that nothing bad happens, or liveness properties guaranteeing a certain progress can automatically checked on the model. In case of failure, diagnostic information in terms of error traces reveals

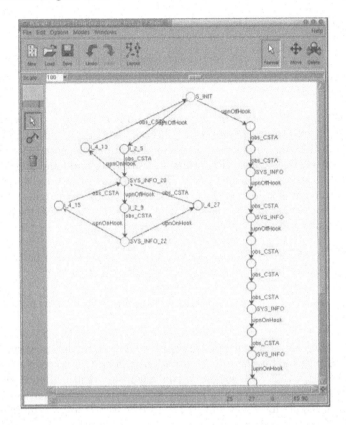

Fig. 1. Adding a new trace to the model

the source of trouble on the model level. An application expert then has to examine whether the revealed problem is just due to the inaccuracies of the model obtained so far, or whether there must be a problem in the underlying system as well.

Validation typically initiates the next iteration of the extrapolation process, which may now also involve technically more updating steps, like, e.g., model reduction, in cases where the model contained too many paths. Our system provides a number of automata theoretic operations and temporal synthesis procedures for the various updating steps. Moreover, it comprises algorithms for fighting the state explosion problem. This is very important, as already comparatively small sets of traces lead to quite big automata. E.g. Fig. 2(right) shows part of a model describing two very simple independent calls. For each call the model describes the correct interplay of the following actions: caller pick-ups handset, dials number, callee pick-ups handset, caller and callee hang-up their handsets. Already this simple scenario leads to a model with 369 states and 441 transitions. Our current research therefore focuses on the investigation of appropriate abstraction methods.

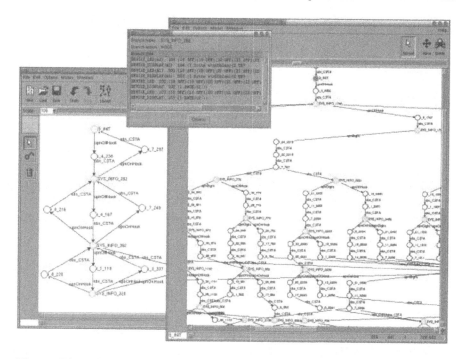

Fig. 2. The refined optimized model (left), example of a larger POTS model (right)

References

1. European Computer Manufactures Association (ECMA). Services for computer supported telecommunications applications (CSTA) phase II, 1994.
2. European Computer Manufactures Association (ECMA). Services for computer supported telecommunications applications (CSTA) phase III, 1998.
3. A. Hagerer, H. Hungar, O. Niese, and B. Steffen: Model Generation by Moderated Regular Extrapolation. In *Proc. of the 5th Int. Conf. on Fundamental Approaches to Software Engineering (FASE 2002)*, this Volume.
4. O. Niese, T. Margaria, A. Hagerer, M. Nagelmann, B. Steffen, G. Brune, and H. Ide. An automated testing environment for CTI systems using concepts for specification and verification of workflows. *Annual Review of Communication*, Int. Engineering Consortium Chicago (USA), Vol. 54, pp. 927-936, IEC, 2001.
5. O. Niese, B. Steffen, T. Margaria, A. Hagerer, G. Brune, and H. Ide. Library-based design and consistency checks of system-level industrial test cases. In H. Hußmann, editor, *Proc. FASE 2001*, LNCS 2029, pages 233–248. Springer Verlag, 2001.

Author Index

Lecture Notes in Computer Science

For information about Vols. 1–2221
please contact your bookseller or Springer-Verlag